"With both dramatic flair and detached fairness, Jacobs eloquently reveals the soul of a charismatic and courageous character. Had Gordon's career taken place on the screen instead of behind it, he would have been the Christopher Reeve of his day."
—**Carol Haggas,** *Foreword*

"A witty, clear-eyed account of a charming and utterly impossible man whose ferocious willpower transformed his personal nightmare into a lifelong Technicolor hallucination."
—**A. J. Langguth**, bestselling author of *Patriots* and *Our Vietnam*

"FDR's body and Sammy Glick's brain? No, but close—and better. Chip Jacobs' Mon Oncle d'Hollywood…is at least as good a story as anything he helped to put on film: welfare case to Oscar-caliber movies, costarring Ed Wood and Pope John XXIII, with snappy dialogue and auto crack-ups, lions and tiger rugs and TV bears."
—**Patt Morrison**, award-winning
Los Angeles Times columnist and author

"Though not about a celebrity or newsmaker, this life being told by Chip Jacobs is an extraordinary one in the history of Hollywood. The raw courage and almost unbelievable stamina of Gordon Zahler—abetted by both love and luck—turns this irresistible biography into a page turner."
—**William Robert Faith**, author of *Bob Hope: A Life In Comedy*

Praise for *The People's Republic of Chemicals*

"An outstanding job of showing the causes and effects of the interdependency American consumers and Chinese manufacturers."
—*Foreword*

"The narrative's power is as much due to its style as substance. The prose is sharp, vivid, and direct…a tonic to those seeking a straightforward take on this urgent subject while also making for a suprisingly enjoyable read."
Booklist

D0018307

Praise for *The Ascension of Jerry*

"Not just another Hollywood whodunit. In the end we find it is really about one man's search and struggle to find his own personal truths and redemption. Well-written an highly recommended."
　　　　—**Steve Hodel**, bestselling author of *Black Dahlia Avenger*

"A seductive tour of an LA rife with murder-for-hire plots, political corruption, and sociopathic schemes...A terrific book—I couldn't put it down."
　　　　—**Stephen Jay Schwartz**, bestselling author of *Boulevard*

"An enticing true tale of getting one's life back in the midst of... skullduggery, highly recommended."
　　　　—*Midwest Book Review*

Praise for *Smogtown*

"[A] remarkably entertaining and informative chronicle of the birth and—so far—inexorable evolution of smog...This book is just amazing, a gripping story well told, with the requisite plucky scientists, hapless politicians, and a nebulous biochemical villain who just will not be stopped."
　　　　—*Booklist* (starred review)

"Style delivers substance in true Hollywood fashion, with character-driven plots draped in glamour and sensation...the history of smog has never been so sexy."
　　　　—*Los Angeles Times*

THE LIFE OF GORDON ZAHLER

is simply so miraculous that it might as well be science fiction. Born into an entertainment family in suburban Los Angeles in the mid twenties, Zahler was a lovable prankster and class clown, exasperating his parents with his endless teenage feats of derring-do. He ran with a similar crowd of teenage boys that called themselves "The Tarzans," and got into trouble everywhere, whether that was leaping off a catwalk into a domed swimming pool or anonymously ordering a case of bourbon to the doorstep of Sierra Madre's teetotaling minister.

But Gordon Zahler's promising career as a public miscreant went pear-shaped one day in 1940 when he and his buddies where fooling around in their high school gym with a spring board. An unsteady jump on the board vaulted Gordon on a deadly trajectory that landed him squarely on his neck, severing his spine. He was fourteen years old. That's when the miracles began.

Strange As It Seems, the journey of former nobody who defied odds and biases racked up against him to frolic in Hollywood, is vividly retold by his nephew, writer-journalist Chip Jacobs. More than just a biography, Jacobs' portrait evokes an early *Day of the Locust* Hollywood where art and fortunes were made by a colorful set of foreigners, weirdos, obsessives, and freaks. During the fifties and sixties, Gordon Zahler became a kingpin in this milieu, as his music/sound effects post-production house scored films for low budget sci-fi films, genre movies like Sam Fuller's *Shock Corridor*, *Popeye* and *Bozo the Clown* cartoons, and hundreds of other projects. Gordon, best known for his clever soundtrack on Ed Wood Jr's infamous *Plan 9 From Outer Space*, was always a better story than the scripts he accentuated.

After Gordon's freak accident, the Zahler family plunged deeply into debt caring for their beloved wild-child numb below the shoulders and suddenly in need of round-the-clock care. His sister (Chip Jacobs' mother, Muriel) was a young single woman in her twenties who found her dreams of college dashed. Gordon's father, Lee, was a moderately successful and extremely prolific Hollywood composer but his paycheck never stretched as far as the medical bills. Gordon's mother, Rose, recognized that the young quadriplegic would need to live a life beyond all expectations in order for the family to survive and thrive.

And Gordon did not let them down.

Using his father's music catalog from the hundreds of films he scored, Gordon assembled a music library that he offered to early TV and film producers desperate to score their work on the cheap. Propped up in a wheelchair, unable to dial a phone, eat on his own, or do much physically, he metamorphosed into a salesman using his outsized charm, wit, and self-confidence to impress his clients.

After cutting his teeth developing scores for a string of low budget sci-fi films featuring space vampires, miniaturized beings, man-eating hedges, and nuked Venutians—many overseen by the likes of Wood, Arthur C. Pierce, and Roger Corman—Gordon was determined to broaden his firm, the General Music Company, into a robust entertainment conglomerate. His relentless networking paid off. Soon, he was furnishing music scores and special effects for big budget films, primetime network TV shows, and more. Eventually wealthy, with a house off the Sunset Strip, a devoted blonde trophy wife, and raucous, star-filled parties, Gordon—ninety-five-pound dynamo—built an existence from scratch that mere able-bodied mortals could only dream about. How many of them could say Lucille Ball loved them, or they were partners with Walter Lantz, Woody Woodpecker's cartoonist and producer, or Ivan Tors, the brains behind Flipper, Gentle Ben, and the nature-drama field still red hot today?

Only the Hollywood recession and oil shocks of the early seventies could slow Gordon's magic. As Tinseltown dried up, Gordon looked abroad for his blockbuster, seeing limitless opportunities in bringing television to South Africa, the last industrial nation not to have it. Bored confining himself to one area, he tried developing futuristic concepts, from audible books to talking gas-station pumps. Unfortunately, the gears moved slowly and his ticking time bomb of a body ran out of miracles. In the end, someone not expected to live two weeks with his injury lived an event-filled thirty-five years. But he lived them on his own terms. Eager never to be defined by his disability or be a poster boy for it, Gordon refused to allow a little condition like quadriplegia prevent him from continuing high jinks. So, he kept a powerboat for boozy excursions, traveled from Beirut to Thailand, was thrown out of moving cars, nearly died after being blessed by the pope, and had a Forest Gump-ian knack for being in dangerous places, including revolutionary Cuba and leopard-prowled wildlands, at the wrong time. Mostly, he refused to be cheated from sucking the marrow from his limited time on earth.

As a boy, Jacobs was not overly fond of a voluble relation with a spidery physique and witchy arms. As an adult hungry to understand his family's past, Jacobs' trepidation gave way to awe and curiosity. *Strange As It Seems* is the culmination of one man's quest to live a life that was almost denied him, and another's to bring that untold legend out of history's shadows.

STRANGE AS IT SEEMS

THIS IS A GENUINE VIREO BOOK

A Vireo Book | Rare Bird Books
453 South Spring Street, Suite 302
Los Angeles, CA 90013
rarebirdbooks.com

Copyright © 2016 by Chip Jacobs

FIRST TRADE PAPERBACK ORIGINAL EDITION

All rights reserved, including the right to reproduce this book or portions thereof
in any form whatsoever, including but not limited to print, audio, and electronic.
For more information, address: A Vireo Book | Rare Bird Books Subsidiary Rights
Department, 453 South Spring Street, Suite 302, Los Angeles, CA 90013.

Previously published in a much different forms as *Wheeler-Dealer* and
Wheeling the Deal, respectively.

Set in Minion
Printed in the United States

10 9 8 7 6 5 4 3 2 1

Publisher's Cataloging-in-Publication data

Names: Jacobs, Chip, author.
Title: Strange as it seems : the impossible life of Gordon Zahler / by Chip Jacobs.
Description: A Vireo Book | Los Angeles [California] ; New York [New York]
: Rare Bird Books , 2016 | First Trade Paperback Original Edition. | Includes
bibliographical references and index.
Identifiers: ISBN 978-1-942600-24-4.
Subjects: LCSH Zahler, Gordon. | Quadriplegics—Biography. | Composers—
Biography. | Film composers—Biography. | BISAC BIOGRAPHY &
AUTOBIOGRAPHY / Entertainment & Performing Arts | PERFORMING
ARTS / Film & Video / General.
Classification: LCC RC406.Q33 J33 2015 | DDC 362.43092—dc23.

STRANGE AS IT SEEMS

THE IMPOSSIBLE LIFE OF GORDON ZAHLER

CHIP JACOBS

CONTENTS

PART II—ROLL

PART III—REDEEM

NOTE TO READERS

A LTHOUGH YEARS OF RESEARCH and dozens of interviews made this book possible, I wasn't able to reconstruct every detail of a story that winds back to the late 1800s. Hence, I approximated most of the dialogue based on the knowable facts. Similarly, I extrapolated and compressed the flavor and sequence of events where I believed necessary. When in doubt about what had occurred, I erred on the side of caution with artistic license, for Gordon's existence was colorful enough. You should also know that the chapter names were cherry-picked from among the hundreds of feature films on which my grandfather, Lee Zahler, served as musical director or composer. In the spirit of these dramas, you'll find relatively short chapters divided episodically. A final word about what you'll read: After they've been introduced, characters are referred to by their first names unless they're considered public figures. To learn more about, well, everything, please visit my website.

Since I'm not including a formal bibliography or endnotes, I want to name the books, publications and media that most assisted my research. My thanks to: *A Hard Day's Write,* Ancestry.com, the *Biscayne Times, Daily Mail, Daily Variety, The Dissolve, Film Score Monthly,* Grave Robbers from Outer Space Wordpress, *KCET,* the *Internet Movie Database,* the *Los Angeles Times, Mimosa Films, Network Awesome, The New York Times, Salon, Site of the Dead, TV Guide, Toonopedia,* the Surfing Heritage and Culture Center, and *Western Clippings.*

"The movement you need is on your shoulder."
—John Lennon and Paul McCartney

PART I—REEL

PROLOGUE: THE FLAMING SIGNAL

ON A HAZY DAY long ago, my mother clenched her jaw to remind me there'd be no escaping the little man behind the door. When the inimitable Gordon Zahler expected someone, excuses were pointless.

"And you'll kiss him hello if *you* know what's good for you," she hissed softly as a pair of nurses walked by.

Dazed, I did what came naturally. I squeezed off a zinger befitting a fourteen-year-old wiseass. "What's good for me doesn't involve being at this stinking place. That's for sure."

The same woman who'd freeze me out for a week after we argued was unwilling to take any guff silently this day. She pinned me against the wall in that ammonia-scrubbed hallway close enough to see her bloodshot eyes, the result of crying and chain-smoking on the drive to Santa Monica.

"I mean it, mister. You be nice to him. Someday *you* may be in his shoes."

Of all the awful fates I ever pictured for myself, nothing compared to that. Me? In her brother's freak anatomy? Just vaporize me.

My uncle's room at Saint John's Hospital hovered in the same mortifying territory as my least favorite spot on Earth. The last time, in fact, my mom keelhauled me here, I held my breath to avoid the stench and wound up so dizzy I banged into an electronic heart-monitoring gizmo, damn near toppling the thing from its steely cart. Frowns shot my way, but a boy has to fend for himself. And anything was better than whiffing that cloying, nauseating smell of decomposition. Every time I was here, I gagged for fresh air a safe distance from his undoing, wishing I were on my Schwinn ten-speed flying downhill. But I couldn't get either, not with my mom's hand clamped on my elbow like alligator teeth. She was doing anything, I guess, to stay upright. The man who'd sunk the family thirty years earlier, her in particular, lay on the other side of the wall with much of the havoc he wrought, unreconciled toxicity between them.

Still, she swung open the yellow hospital door and spoke as if things couldn't be any peachier. "Hey, Gordy!" *Boom*. Two steps in and dread knifed through me. His fifth-floor room didn't seem to be for humans. It was harshly over-lit, as if the patient was a lab specimen awaiting dissection, with a bed pushed dead center and disconnected machinery, cables dangling off to the side. Its one redeeming feature, a view of the sun-glistened beach blocks away, taunted me with visions of Frisbee-slinging at water's edge to impress any cute girls around. But it was way too late for that. Mom kissed her forty-nine-year-old kid brother on the forehead and lowered herself into a green-vinyl chair next to his spotlight bed. "You're looking pretty good," she fibbed. Then her chartreuse eyes tractor-beamed toward me—my turn. For a second, I imagined myself breaking for the stairwell at a trot to the beach, only to sense my captors reading my mind.

I plodded over to the left side of the bed opposite Gordon's IV stand, wishing this weren't happening. His head flopped my way and his breath was gamy, something pre-death and rancid you never wanted to smell again. I already knew better than to peer down at his arachnoid-ish hands. *Don't forget to hold your breath, too.* Leaning forward, I brushed his cheek with a glancing kiss and backpedaled. Just not fast enough. He stopped me before I could get away. "Hold it there, kiddo," he said. "You haven't told me about school. Or what you thought about the Ali fight."

Crap, he was trying to be decent. I lacked a game plan for his charms. So, I stammered out a few curt responses. "School's fine," (it was and it wasn't) and, "Ali really clobbered that guy," (since USC football was my sport, I forgot who received the clobbering). All I wanted was to achieve separation from this oddball by producing a minimum of words. Every time the drill was the same. First, I'd resist being near him and then I'd find a corner in which to recover.

Where, I wondered, was the justice in spending any of my Christmas vacation in this place? Hanging out in Pasadena with my pal Todd was where I should've been. Over the phone the night before, we'd penciled in a day of Deep Purple on my stereo, submarine sandwiches at the corner deli, and video Pong as aperitifs. Time permitting, the hell-raisers in us would chuck purply olives that collected on my folks' driveway at passing cars. Gordon, as I was learning, though, was masterful at reshuffling schedules, a black hole of need whether it was tightroping life or acquiescing to the grave.

While he and his sister conferred bedside about God and money, I relaxed in my patented manner. I peered out the window and fantasized about double-beef patties. After each trip here, we headed straight to the local Coco's so I could order a gooey bacon-cheeseburger combo plate. Mom phrased it my "treat," though both of us recognized the comfort food as bribery for witnessing Gordon's disintegration one icky visit at a time. Did I ever crave it! Juicier than the first tangy bite, better than the icy blast of chocolate shake washing it down, was its magic in making me forget where I'd just been.

Fact was, I disliked him long before his putrid illness. Droll around celebrities ("Burt Lancaster, you old dog"), comfortable with foreign muckety-mucks ("Any questions, mister prime minister?"), Gordon wasn't particularly fond of little kids gamboling around him, carefree. Once, during a visit to his fabled house above the Sunset Strip when I was about eleven, he barked at me to stop skidding over his wood parquet floor in my tube socks. "Get over here for a little talk," he said. *Yikes.* I went over in that dead-kid-walking sort of way, praying he wouldn't make me hop up on his bed for the upcoming questioning. Dance around one of his penetrating questions and he sliced through it. Even as an adolescent with a flippant tongue, I shape-shifted into an insecure little boy dissolved by his blunt observations. "Pigeon-chested," he described me. "Cowardly," he'd tabbed my wimpy reaction to a bully who'd pummeled my arms black. "Fight back," I vaguely recall him saying. The bunch that admired him as a wondrous dreamer surfing the velvety Hollywood life never zoomed in on the spidery-looking grouch I periodically saw.

The last thing he said to me interrupted my burger trance that afternoon. He was ribbing my mother about an embarrassing episode from their childhood—a notorious bike accident or something—when he sought my endorsement. "Isn't that right, kiddo?" he roared, as if we shared a special code forged over decoder rings and laughs. "Oh, definitely, Uncle Gordon," I answered. "Definitely." The thought of that cheeseburger dulled me good.

*　　*　　*

CONSIDERING THOSE BLISTERED MEMORIES, how do I explain dedicating years retracing every breadcrumb of a life some people still find hard to believe was possible, a life outrageous from boyhood to death? Answering that means arcing back to a natural disaster that, while decimating for most, gave me far more than it took.

Eighteen years after Gordon slipped away, I survived a brushfire that, by all sound logic, should've cooked the flesh off my bones. I have witnesses. I just don't have explanations. The defining day of my own existence began when someone I never met—a vagrant living in the stone canyon adjacent to my parent's Eaton Canyon home in east Pasadena—got sloppy. He lit a campfire, either to stay warm or cook. But he couldn't contain what he ignited, and after flames spread to the bone-dry hills, my childhood neighborhood paid, losing one in three houses to costs that no insurance reimbursement would ever make right. An atomic-looking mushroom cloud that caught my eye as I drove sleepy-headed to work was my first inkling that something sinister was afoot. Yep, that's when all this began. The swaying mass towering over the fire was stupefying, almost unnatural in how it shadowed the landscape. The plume had an enormous, brawny center with black and pewter edges that spun like vapory pinwheels. One look and you knew it was trouble. Between it and the gusting Santa Ana winds, smoky carnage was inevitable. And it wasn't just Pasadena aflame, either. Full blocks in Malibu and Laguna Beach were roasting away in what struck me as apocalypse by subdivision.

For three hours, my big brother, Paul, and I believed we could save our old house by playing amateur firefighters in the evacuated foothills of Kinneloa Mesa. But was it belief or macho delusion? There were no rescuers around or hose water to tap. Our escape road was barely open. Even so, we hacked and rubbed eyes while the gorge we once played in was partially deforested. We filled discarded Sparklett's jugs with pool water to douse flare-ups where we could. The only sound you heard was the *pop-pop* echo of canyon homes imploding from the scorching temperatures, and that God-awful hiss of fire on the ridgeline.

Deciding it was too hairy to stay much longer in the acrid whiteout, we set out to take a final loop around the property. We should've just gone home. At the concrete embankment where the pool water heater sat, Paul, my folks' longtime housekeeper (who had no idea what she was getting herself into), and I shuffled to a comedic stop. Orange whips of flame were melting our neighbor's vintage cars across the gulch, and it was hard not to rubberneck. Sparks buzzed and danced around us, meanwhile, searching for fuel. A millisecond later, a row of weeds smoldered, and that's when the Santa Anas kicked up again. *Whoosh!* The ravine fire barreled up the hill at us like a ground-hovering tornado. The yellow-orange drape was fifteen feet wide and, seemingly, six hundred degrees of flambé. So rapidly did it barrage that all I could do to shield myself was turn sideways and cower. My imagination rewarded me with a cinematic short—me running with my clothes aflame before I burned to death twenty yards from where I once built my childhood forts and read *Playboys*.

The fireball curled over us, closing in for the kill, and then, miraculously, fluky intercession saved us. As quickly as it jetted upslope, that scalding drape retreated downhill. I cracked my eyes and peered at my brother. He couldn't believe it either. We were alive! Our shrill chuckling might've originated from a pair of delirious hyenas. The concrete was our firebreak. Or so I assumed. When I felt my shirt, sweat glued it to my rib cage and my pounding heart was about to pop the buttons.

At dusk, with the sky a burnt tangerine, we broke the good news to our septuagenarian parents staying at my house a few miles away.

The sole casualty was the "boathouse," a wood-slatted, salmon-colored structure at the bottom of a forlorn hill where we dry-docked our old ski boat and exiled passé furniture and heirlooms. If something had to burn, Paul and I nodded, it was best that. Definitely that. My father, a Caltech-schooled engineer cozier around equations than humans, smiled thinly, scarcely expressing an "Attaboy." Whatever idiotic valiance we displayed, he considered it our obligation.

Far more dumbfounding was the slack reaction of my mom in learning she would be bunking in her own room that night, not some Holiday Inn. "That's good," she said, before retreating back into quiet. Something was wrong, this being the same mercurial woman prone to grand expressions and stubborn opinions. In her mind, Ronald Reagan would forever be a political god and John Lennon a "druggie loudmouth." For her to be so indifferent now, after hearing how fortunate she was compared to her neighbors, blew anger through me. Maybe still in shock from my near-death experience on that ledge, I trapped her near my kitchen sink, where she stared vacantly out the window. Did I need to take the day's events from the top? "No," she said.

Her drooping face worried me that she was on the cusp of a stroke. I asked her if she needed a doctor, and she asked me to back away. I wouldn't. Was she having fire flashbacks, I pressed, more bitter dissension with my dad? "Stop guessing," she chided me, as if I were that insolent fourteen-year-old again at Saint John's.

"Then spit it out," I hounded her. At last she did, begrudgingly. Inside the boathouse was her father's antique organ, a relic from the thirties, and hearing it was now ash seemed to chop a foot off her height.

"Let me get this straight. After everything that's happened, you're upset about that beat-up, old thing?"

"Yes. Yes, I am."

"Why? It probably didn't even work anymore."

"That's not the point," she shot back, inhaling a quarter-inch off her Benson & Hedges.

"Then what is?"

"My dad wrote all his music on that organ. For years and years and years."

"And?"

"And that music rescued Mama Rose and Gordon after your grandfather died. That organ was...everything." Mama Rose was my maternal grandmother. "Gordon wouldn't have soared without it. He might not have even lived."

"I didn't know," I responded meekly.

She was no longer listening, instead returning to her morbid thousand-yard stare.

Observing this jogged childhood memories, very specific ones. When I was eleven or so, she decided it was time to reveal my Hollywood ancestors, gushing about their fame and delighting in their starry chums. She practically lilted the names—Carl Laemmle, Mickey Rooney, John Wayne, Gene Autry, Irving Thalberg, Nat King Cole, Pancho Villa, Lucille Ball, Sidney Sheldon, Jerry Lewis, Chuck Connors. "You know," she added, "you're connected to Universal Pictures." I later prodded her to elaborate, but she either repeated herself or offered descriptions of relations no deeper than cardboard cutouts. Once, after she tired of my questions, she let slip that her grandfather was killed and a son of his, as well. My eyes widened. "You mean there were two murders?"

"Quit," she snapped. "I'm not saying another word." And she wouldn't.

That evening, with the hot spots extinguished by regrouping firefighters, I returned to the Mesa. The former boathouse was nothing more than a blackened heap destined for a landfill. Seeing its incinerated skeleton hurt knowing my mother's grief. Using a tree branch, I tried identifying a few globs baked into the gravel. For an instant, my heart somersaulted at what appeared to be an ivory key near a wedge of mangled rebar. Alas, it was only a sliver of melted steel. How shamefully I had treated my grandfather's pride-and-joy back in the days when the boathouse was our makeshift rehearsal studio. When I blew the fingering on a song my teenage rock band was practicing, I thought nothing of giving the thing a swift kick. Other times it served as our Coors beer coaster, joint holder, or coat rack. That something so cherished was banished to the boathouse was a crime against family.

In the weeks after the fire, my lungs recovered but my soul felt breached. I couldn't stop thinking about why I survived those charging flames or the odyssey of that liquefied piano. The two events were connected. I just knew it. Four years later, still fixated by the mystery, I quit a fantastic reporting job at the *Los Angeles Daily News* to unearth a past evidently waiting for me to dig up. My whole life a cast of characters had sat under my own nose: pompous Broadway stars and studio prodigies, Tin Pan Alley musicians, and black sheep executed mafia-style. Most passed from this world before old age, accomplished yet shipwrecked from bigger dreams and dying without their stories plumbed. None burned as bright as the uncle I once disliked and now perpetually worship. From Hollywood to Johannesburg, Ed Wood Jr. to Golden Globe-winning projects, he conquered worlds by the seat of his pants, and did it with brio and a defiant smirk.

Gordon today lives mainly in the bandwidth of the *TV Land* network and as sci-fi trivia answers on the web. But I see him all the time in the sky above.

CHAPTER ONE: THE LOCAL BAD BOY

THE BOY PERCHED FORTY-ODD feet in the rafters aimed to leap into history, a junior cannonball hell-bent to fly. Ten minutes earlier, while the lifeguards were distracted by a commotion in the deep end, he scampered into the curved, steel girders over an enormous indoor pool and hid behind a column. Only a monkey could've made it up there faster. Squatting on his heels, the brown-haired lad with radar-dish ears grinned in the shadows, thrilled with his altitude. Per custom, he was exactly where he shouldn't have been, in this case on a narrow beam not far from the "Danger—Keep Out!" signs he'd ignored shimmying up the four-story maintenance ladder at the Venice Plunge.

Below him on that sunbaked, August day was a patchwork of bobbing heads, most of them middle aged women yammering nonstop as they floated in their goofy bathing caps like so many bottle tops. Gordon's intent all along was to surprise everybody, especially that chatty bunch, by his impression of a human projectile. For days he plotted a spectacular, high-velocity dive—fifty mph if the physics allowed it. His accomplishment would have to best somebody's record. When his knees juddered high on the beam, his bravado knew how to still them. Think glory!

Since none of his rule-busting chums had reached this forbidden plateau before him, he planned to grandstand before launching himself. His warm-up act necessitated leaping from one span to the next until he covered the length of the pool, east to west. Slip? He wouldn't slip. From the spans he would tiptoe to the center catwalk, bow mockingly to the spectators squinting up at him, and then execute a whistling, headfirst maneuver reminiscent of an Acapulco cliff diver. Everyone would be jawing about it for days to come. Gordon the infamous, Gordon the intrepid—it was all the same to him in 1939 Los Angeles. Back home, his friends would mob him, taking stock of his deed. And yes, he appreciated the peril. One misstep would send him hurtling into the waters—or the concrete deck—on a lethal trajectory. Daredevils scoff at safety nets.

There was just one snag, and it was below the belt. A lifeguard who spotted him lurking amid the joists betrayed him by ratting him out to his mother.

Rose Zahler had already lectured her youngest child about acceptable behavior before she allowed him into the domed building. "Just for once," she might've said before parting, "see if you can stay out of trouble for a few hours." Probably doubting it was possible, she headed off anyway for relaxing beach sun with a novel under her arm. Lee, her husband, was too preoccupied to play hooky alongside her, let alone reinforce her message about comportment. He was where you'd normally find him most days and some nights: inside his fleabag mid-city office writing film music under studio deadlines, which kept a fist over his free time. The slapping surf and bronzed shoreline would have to wait for him to dip his toes in until the directors he slavishly worked for called it a wrap.

The Venice Plunge was one of a handful of Coney Island-style attractions that Southern California's seaside towns lured for the tax revenues they drew and the jubilation they advertised. But the Plunge was the grand dame of them of all, erected in 1907 atop a pier overlooking the indigo seas of Santa Monica Beach. Abbot Kinney, a tobacco man turned developer, had created a kind of playground sanctuary, where saltwater was pumped into the pool through a warming fountain and everything was designed for a family-friendly atmosphere. People readily paid to swim at his concourse when the ocean waters grew too chilly or the outdoor heat became unbearable. Parents could watch their kids from bleacher-like "indoor balconies" knowing towels were furnished and lifeguards were on station. Around the Plunge were roller coasters, bathhouses, a Pacific Electric Railway terminus, and a theater. It was an age of five-cent hot dogs and Coppertone suntan lotion. Furthermore, a beach stroll here meant the chance for pedestrians to ogle movie stars during daylight. One day it might be Paul Stader, the stunt double from the *Tarzan* movies, taking a dip, the next Buster Crabbe, the former Olympian popularized by *Flash Gordon* and *Buck Rogers*. Comedic lead Bob Hope was as entranced by the Santa Monica shoreline as much as the other A-listers signing autographs and then hitting the waves.

Unluckily for Gordon, the honchos who managed the Plunge could visualize the incriminating publicity and subsequent drop at the turnstile if he wound up splattering himself bloody on their property. After they located Rose at the shore, they escorted her inside to pressure him to give up. They wanted "the boy out of their ceiling, good riddance to him." He wasn't welcome there anymore. Let him take his juvenile death wish to Redondo Beach or another complex. And Rose, not all that surprised some adult or another was angry with her son, wanted him to listen. On the deck, stories below him, she squinted up at the latticework bracketing the curved roof. A massive, plate glass window to the side magnified everything. "Come down right this instant!" she yelled. "Do you hear me? *This* instant."

Gordon at first pretended that he couldn't hear her, the oldest trick in the book, if not the lamest in a dome with echo chamber acoustics. Anybody with ears heard Rose's furious wail. Many of the bathers afterwards pointed stiff fingers at the diminutive face nuzzled against the ceiling. This wasn't just some kid busted for running on wet tile. *There. See him. No, to the right. Behind the truss. If he were mine, I'd give him a whooping for the ages.* Outed by half the pool, Gordon still refused to budge. Every time his mother hollered for him to relent, he at least hollered back a defiant "Noooo." The impasse lasted for about ten minutes, until she resorted to more incendiary phrasing.

"I want you in the pool, where it's safe," she said, her voice downshifting from anger to torment. "For Lord's sake, Gordon. For Lord's sake. Get out of there."

Brighter than most of the teachers prone to flunk him, the boy understood the gravity of Rose's L-word invocation. He'd obey his devout mother, yet, as pre-wired, he'd comply on his own terms. From the rafters, he crouched on his wiry legs and sprang. Sprang fiercely. A hundred saltwater bathers and spectators watched as he just missed clipping a beam on his parabolic flight pattern. When he splashed home into twelve-foot-deep waters, it produced a collective "Oooh" from the crowd and a frothy splash that doused anyone nearby. Rose gave him a purple-faced tongue lashing in front of the crowd after he toweled off. What didn't he understand about "staying out of trouble?" Had he been honest about his thrill-seeking motor, he would've answered, "Everything."

* * *

PUNISHMENTS FOR SIMILAR SHENANIGANS came and went. Mostly they dissolved into the halo of good times that Lee had arrayed for his family writing and composing music for grainy westerns, action-adventure serials, and similar genres in demand by the weary masses looking for some popcorn escapism. Lee, as breadwinner and artist, made this possible with the insane hours he logged in Hollywood as an independent musician. Every film he was hired onto kept his wife and two children housed in a charming, four-bedroom Craftsman across from a citrus grove in Sierra Madre, a tidy, postage stamp-sized foothill hamlet about twenty miles northeast of downtown Los Angeles. That the Zahlers lived there, or could enjoy a peaceful Saturday sleeping in and eating waffles, was a luxurious existence, pained backgrounds considered.

Those ditties Lee conceived and scored were the family GDP. They put floral dresses on his girls, a deluxe bike under Gordon, a Filipino cook in the kitchen, and a riding horse named Dixie in a converted barn. Sunday nights the Zahlers enjoyed leisurely suppers at the Seafood Tavern, a local mom-and-pop. For special occasions, Lee would cart everybody to Hollywood Boulevard for dinner at the Musso and Frank Grill, a brass-appointed, bourbon and steak celebrity hangout where my mom would skip down the aisles for customer laughs. In Lee's estimation, the sum total of these delights, the future he was building for his offspring, was more than enough to tolerate the showbiz libertines and scoundrels hovering off camera. His own slavish workweek was worth it, too. While America stood in soup lines at the tail end of the Great Depression, his family could cherish full meals without scrimping on their next.

Moviemaking was their patron saint, their meal ticket to this better life, even if Brooklyn-born Lee had to grind where others basked in overnight success. Lee made his showbiz debut in Los Angeles sitting down. During the twenties, he was the piano-playing bandleader for the Western Association of Motion Picture Advertisers (WAMPAS), a clubby, press-agent fraternity able to score annual publicity by handpicking thirteen luscious, young beauties for studio screen tests. Hanging around future head-turners like Ginger Rogers was a nifty perk, but it was the connections Lee made and the fat cats he impressed that were career fairy dust. Pretty soon, he was in a starched black tuxedo, throwing off hambone smiles, leading orchestras of fluctuating size as they performed before audiences gathered to watch silent movies.

Later in the decade, Lee's self-reinvention from obscure Tin Pan Alley songwriter to pianist-for-hire to musical director/composer for the studios was complete. Out early, home late, he penned countless songs under his own name, as well as under the mysterious pseudonyms Nico Grigor and J.H. Wood. In 1929, when Gordon was three, Lee registered one of his first, official movie credits scoring *King of the Congo* for small Mascot Pictures. Regular jobs cascaded afterward through outfits like Invincible Pictures and Producer's Releasing Corporation. These were second-tier independents that made surprisingly good B-movies despite frenetic production schedules that rolled out new features every month. Catching wind of him next were the big boys—Columbia, Universal, RKO. They hired him to compose music for serials that ran atop double bills. Popular flicks of the era—*Rin-Tin-Tin, Ellery Queen*—had Lee harmonies all over them.

His first intersection with the Hollywood star machine he owed to the chief of indie Darmour Studios. Larry Darmour, in the early thirties, asked him to mold a song-and-dance man out of a talented little boy whose mother colored his hair with black shoe polish. Mickey Rooney, a sassy, male answer to the ever-adorable Shirley Temple, was being groomed to be the irrepressible Mickey McGuire in a series revolving around his capers. Lee's tutorials obviously succeeded, even if Lee's daughter, Muriel, once bloodied Rooney's nose in a tiff over a sandlot baseball game at Darmour. Audiences went bananas for the all-American boy that the studio bosses later had trouble keeping from front-page womanizing and boozing. Having proved himself with a box office winner, Lee's market value skyrocketed. Directors sweating production timelines had, in him, someone who could write melodies across the genres and on the fly.

His one, nonnegotiable stance was that his fingers only create on his own keyboard. Some generic house piano with chipped ivories and slushy pedals had nothing on his sidekick, likely a portable Hammond organ. Up-and-comers like Gene Autry, "the singing cowboy," practiced with it. The scuffed, boxy device was there when Lee scored *The Three Musketeers* with a young John Wayne, and *The Galloping Ghost* with former football icon Red Grange. Train robbery scenes in the desert, musical numbers in a tilt-up Parisian quarter off Hollywood Boulevard: that Hammond could tell some war stories. Professionally speaking, it was all Lee needed. Rose, whose older brother had torn it up as a Universal Picture's director, tight with Carl Laemmle and Irving Thalberg, appreciated the blessings of this celluloid life just by inventorying all the smiles it fostered.

Sierra Madre, the Zahler's adopted hometown, provided day-to-day tranquility. Add a cigar factory and train tracks, deep six the Starbucks and BMWs, and the leafy village of then remains the same quirky boondocks today. Less was intentionally more here; no traffic stoplight, lush parks where there could've been bland stores. Willowy Kirsten Court, half the size of a tennis court, was its Times Square. The knuckled San Gabriel Mountains behind the town loomed as kind of topographical guardians, offering cool shadows, water, and a connection to all manner of critters big city folks had only eyed in books. Santa Anita Racetrack, where Seabiscuit would win the Handicap in 1940 (and where Japanese-Americans soon would be interred by the thousands) rested only a few blocks south in Arcadia. Pasadena, with its much bigger population to the west and distinguished landmarks, was the area's crown jewel. Among its riches were the Tournament of Roses Parade, the country's best college football bowl game, a symphony, and a technical college known as Caltech. Sierra Madre's gems were a wisteria vine festival and a cluster of tuberculosis sanitariums, and the relative invisibility suited the locals just fine.

After all, they resided on capacious plots originally swiped from the Indians, cleared by the Franciscans, and deeded over by the Mexican government. No one in this bucolic setting had to live cheek by jowl in a rat-infested tenement or by a slaughterhouse as Chicogoans and New Yorkers often did. In the 1880s, much of the civic land was snapped up and subdivided, mainly by rancher Elijah "Lucky" Baldwin and the Southern Pacific Railroad. Property sales boomed in the ensuing years. Rows of quaint Victorians and three-bedroom clapboards sprouted along magnolia-lined streets that took time adding modern gas lamps. Above their rooflines sat enormous stone canyons and the piney outer stubble of the Angeles National Forest. Living on nature's front porch never got stale. People could take what they needed from nature—land, recreation—without succumbing to its extremes. A Massachusetts native gifted at hucksterism in recruiting newcomers from the East had chartered something utopian. "It contains almost everything that mortal man would desire," Nathaniel Carter wrote of his discovery in a pamphlet. Roses, heliotrope, hiking, climate, serenity, commerce: all here and only a trolley ride from a rising West Coast metropolis. Intrigued by Carter's words, the curious arrived in droves—New Englanders pasty from the snow months, Midwesterners enchanted to discover a familiar aesthetic in the fertile, California loam.

Director D.W. Griffith, himself, was so infatuated with Sierra Madre that he established his first California production office there. When he later relocated to Hollywood to be closer to the action, the citizenry shrugged. They'd take privacy over glitz and notoriety any day. The Zahlers never wanted to leave this honeysuckle spot under the San Gabriels.

Of course, the real blessings had faces. Muriel Bernice, Rose and Lee's firstborn, delivered parental bliss through her steadiness and grace. By 1940, my mother had blossomed from a gangly child doted on by her folks into a curvy, nineteen-year-old hit on by aspiring doctors, dentists, pilots, and soldiers. As a teenager, she earned good grades, submitted to church, took up smoking, and was named "Miss Catalina" in a hokey island beauty pageant. Curfews for her were mandates, not negotiations. Her displeasure was usually reserved for Gordon's infuriating incursions into her room. Whatever rebelliousness coursed through her was limited to a brief flirtation with the family business. Without her father's permission, she signed up for a screen test at Universal Pictures—one that yielded no contract. Muriel accepted the verdict that there'd be no klieg lights for her without much anguish. Save for her ability to shed tears to get her way as a daddy's girl, she'd always known she wasn't much of an actress. But that didn't mean she wasn't creative. When she was accepted at a prestigious liberal arts college east of Los Angeles, to study music no less, Lee was incandescent with pride. In this field, there was no question his daughter had organic ability.

While Muriel accumulated brownie points at home, Gordon stockpiled demerits faster than a movie-screen gunslinger fired bullets. About a year before his dive at the Venice Plunge got him banned for life, he'd pounced on another dare. This time he jumped twenty feet off the Redondo Beach Pier, landing in the turbulent waters around the pilings. Some months later, he persuaded Muriel to sit in the crook of his handlebars on a hair-tousling ride down a local street. Near the bottom, the bike jackknifed, sending his sister flying—first onto the pebbly street, then the emergency room, where her bloodied knee was stitched closed. Guilt-smacked, he'd never co-opt Muriel again.

Outside the family, Gordon was already gaining a reputation as one of the area's most prolific scalawags. He was nothing if not versatile in his mischief, which tended to be of the clever "gotcha" brand that most adults couldn't seethe about for too long. At his mother's church in Arcadia, he and others bored with the sermons turned minor profits selling "fresh-squeezed tomato juice" they concocted by mixing ketchup and water. In the garish movie houses along Pasadena's Colorado Boulevard, he and his chums often used the balconies to pepper spitballs at old ladies until the ushers chased them away. But it was in Sierra Madre—folksy, prudish, Mayberry-esque Sierra Madre—where some authorities and residents that Gordon targeted daydreamed about wringing his hooligan neck. They witnessed his handiwork, be it newspaper shreds on the hedges of curmudgeonly retirees, Halloween pumpkin launching, or doorbell surprises, probably involving lit bags of dog shit.

The Zahler boy need only spy the Red Car trolley to inspire flashier, public high jinks. Either by luck or intention, blasting caps designed to trigger detonations at major construction jobs wended their way into his possession. Gordon and his grade school friends quickly designated a special purpose for them. They affixed them to the rail tracks carved along Baldwin Avenue. By scoping out the terrain, they knew exactly what shrubs to crouch in to watch the commotion unfold without some righteous elder grabbing them from behind. When the steel train wheels ground over the caps, causing them to explode in firecracker-ish *puh-puh-puh-pup*, the show had only just begun, too. The older passengers on board jumped out of their seats as if they had cacti in their trousers. The conductor, apoplectic at the frequency at which the micro-grenades were going off, sometimes halted the train to rip through the nearby bushes. "I'm gonna find you smug punks! One of these days I will, and then you're in for it."

Aside from the ulcer he gave the Red Car engineer, Gordon's proudest lark involved Sierra Madre's Congregational minister, a self-described teetotaler and rather insufferable morality cop. Why Gordon, then about twelve, placed him on his hit list, no one knows, though the preacher's attitude toward rambunctious kids on the Zahler's block might've provoked it. Representing himself as the man's aide, Gordon one weekend phoned in an order for a case of bourbon from Robert's Market. Deliver it to his home, no questions asked, the boy with a faux-husky voice instructed. He'll pay his tab later. Being a tightknit community, alcohol on the doorstep of a community leader avowed to abstinence titillated more than the gossipmongers. Everyone heard about it. The first Sunday afterward, he had to tell his flock that the liquor was someone's idea of a gag—a gag he regarded as intensely unfunny.

Gordon, shrewd about concealing his rascally fingerprints, typically went un-apprehended. Those occasions he was caught, Lee dragged him into the living room to mete out corporal punishment by swat. *Thwap*—Gordon would be vigorously spanked with the back of a hairbrush, the number of swats calculated by his crime. Muriel, ordinarily tickled to see him get his lumps, bawled sympathy tears during the sternest lashings. The buildup could be intense. But the accused was determined not to weep. Gordon acted stoic about his thrashing, believing it strengthened his reputation and toughened his hide. Whatever scolding was dished up to teach him, he wanted his peers to know he shook it off as his miscreant badge of honor. Once, he received a hairbrush whipping for fabricating a story at a crowded dinner party attended by a big-wheel producer. "Hey, Daddy," Gordon chirped, "remember that time you were in jail and I came to visit you?" An uncomfortable silence hovered until somebody who appreciated the boy's ruse giggled.

Though neither parent could control Gordon outdoors, they could be zealots about house organization. Rose ironed the curtains maniacally, sometimes at night, and if guests were expected, she'd be on the floor, arms under sofas, on search-and-destroy missions for dust bunnies. Lee, meantime, was a despot about how his children's days commenced. Rooms "immaculate" before school, he insisted. Shoes buffed so thoroughly you could comb your hair in their leathery reflection. Fiercely protective of my mom, especially with her suitors, Lee must've revisited his approach to his son when traditional punishments failed to curb him. Only the long view must've had merit: that Gordon's recklessness would peter out before any lasting damage was wreaked. Boys being boys, it was the adrenaline he craved, and that would die down when girls hypnotized him more.

Lee's wishful thinking, as it were, detonated like one of Gordon's blasting caps one fateful afternoon in 1940. St. Rita's Elementary School, deciding it could take the boy no more, expelled him from its grounds. Obviously on the Zahler end, this required more than a scolding and the hairbrush. Gordon, it should be noted, was the reason the family had moved to these sticks from mid-city Los Angeles. After his asthma progressed from a small health concern to wheezing and coughing that wouldn't stop, where he could barely catch his breath, his physician recommended they make a geographical change. Drifting marine layer that sometimes enshrouded their old place in Carthay Circle seemed to instigate his attacks, so the doctor pointed them toward Sierra Madre, where the foothill air was almost never foggy, just dry, clean, and, if you believed the chamber of commerce, indisputably therapeutic. Lee had acquiesced to the change of address, despite the hour-long commute it meant for him into Hollywood. Ten years later, he found himself puzzled over what discipline, if any, would shake sense into his son. Ground him for summer? Threaten boarding school? Where Lee fumed over the situation, Rose prayed for whole afternoons. Gordon's wild streak had to be tamed, so she beseeched God to convert this black mark into a blessing they'd see later.

Strides, Rose knew, had been made at the school an easy walk from their home. Prior to his dismissal, Gordon had improved from a C- average in sixth grade to a C+/B- pupil in Sister Mulbuss' seventh grade. It was his misbehavior toward the nuns, whom he nicknamed "grumpy penguins," that earned him the label as the class problem child. In April 1940, a teacher in her habit turned to write on the blackboard, and Gordon did that thing he did. Skulking away from his desk, he ambled over to an open dormer window and crawled out of it, celebrating his freedom with a victory jig on the sidewalk for the benefit of his awed classmates. St. Rita's principal, who'd talked herself blue warning him about such tomfoolery, bounced him with little outward regret. It wasn't just the gags and lack of academic focus that consigned him to a two-month head start on summer vacation. According to his St. Rita's transcripts, it was Gordon's "general conduct."

CHAPTER TWO: THE LASH

A SURPRISE RAINSTORM BARRELING out of the north soaked Pasadena the day Gordon tumbled. At sunup, the sky was the pastel blue of a forgettable autumn morning. By the time the first school bell warbled at John Marshall Junior High, it was as if night had never relinquished. Ominous dark clouds nobody had expected lopped the peaks off the San Gabriels. An hour later, drenching rain painted the city streets a lustrous black sheen.

One gander at the soggy grounds was all Marshall's principal needed, and the school loudspeakers broadcast his decision: no outdoor sports today, lunch inside. Many of the students groaned in unison at the announcement; being cooped up for eight hours in the musty confines with the grown-ups made the clocks tick slower. But for Gordon and his gang, the rain was kismet, a reason to whoop. Staying indoors meant forty-five minutes to play *Tarzan: Lord of the Jungle*. Sailing through the gymnasium air imitating their hero, Johnny Weissmuller, snickering about the loincloth liberties they imagined he was taking with Jane, was terrific entertainment. The storm could last all week as far as Marshall's own Tarzans were concerned.

Hormones aside, ninth-grade gym class still operated under the authoritarian regime of Coach Harold S. Turner. His boys had five minutes to undress, don their school PE clothes, and assemble in position in the gym or on the field. Any horseplay had to be done slyly because Coach was a stickler about locker-room protocol. Irritate him, and you'd be doing calisthenics until the bell rang. Admire him and take a number. Turner's tough-love approach had elevated him to one of Marshall's most beloved instructors, particularly among the bigger kids out to learn every play he could teach. Just the reverence in which the boys spoke of his football smarts deified him as a sort of local Knute Rockne. On this particular Tuesday, though, Turner cared more about the kids' cracking soles than double wing formations. Fungus had invaded the boys' locker room, and he was determined to inspect every toe of every student in his 10:00 a.m. class for athlete's foot. Should peeling be detected, powder and hygiene lectures would be dispensed. Afterward, the boys were freed onto the gym floor while the rest of the students were examined.

Marshall's Tarzans—Gordon, Don Berg, Wally Gilmore, Benny Gouin, and Rob Bowman—interpreted their passing muster first as more swell fortune. Once they'd tugged their socks back on, they sprinted out onto the hardwood floor yipping and yapping about all manners of things. Swiveling their heads, another fact struck them about being unsupervised. The jumping maneuver Turner had specifically forbid weeks earlier, a maneuver most Olympians would've declined, was ripe for their taking. One of them must've said, let's milk their chance.

The equipment was set up with giddy delirium, the boys mindful of the villainous clock. Realistically, the Great Athlete's Foot plague would only distract Turner for so long, and in his absence their object was simple. They'd fly indoors and then fly some more. A thirty-yard sprint down a line was their tarmac. From a dead run, each would take turns bounding off a springboard to vault over a "mountain" they'd stacked themselves. Metaphorically speaking, their Tarzan "mountain" was more animal than topography as a wooden-legged pommel horse central to gymnastics competitions. Since there was little challenge in endlessly leaping over the same height, the boys committed to raising their obstacle inch by inch. Now and before, prickly, mackinaw-like gym mats were draped over the pommel horse like some overtaxed mule. By launching themselves off the springboard positioned in front of the apparatus, they could gain just enough altitude to grip a set of hanging gymnastic rings behind it.

Some of them celebrated their milestone jumps by imitating the classic yell of the man who lived with apes, *AAAAH-AHAHAAAAH*. After dangling for a bit, the boys would let go of the rings for a cushioned dismount on the pads below. The nuttiest of the group attempted flips on the way down. Nobody dwelt on margin of error, of what could go kablooey. At thirteen and fourteen, they were freckled gods.

By rushing, Coach Turner's boys needed about ten minutes to spring over the mountain layered with one, two, and then three mats. Several near crashes transpired, but the brinkmanship in everybody's sweat glands kept the pace brisk. Anyone likely to hesitate had a reason not to: they were chasing a world record, or theirs anyway. Four mats! Even Marshall's top jocks, with their nickel-plated trophies and letterman's jackets, couldn't surmount this peak.

Out of respect, Gordon was awarded the first crack at the obstacle that Turner had admonished them to forget. His chest, I imagine, puffed out as he loped to the head of the line, confident of his skills that'd awed so many. In his six weeks here, classmates learned he was funny and charming, a natural around the opposite sex or bumming cigarettes from the seniors. Athletics further distinguished him from the customarily shy new kid. Teachers, Turner in particular, realized that Gordon had a virtuoso athleticism that set him apart. His darting, jitterbug speed made him elusive to tackle on the gridiron and almost impossible to throw out on the baseball diamond. Toss a ball to him and he gunned it back with pinpoint precision. To suggest he would be on the varsity squad ahead of his peers was forecasting the obvious.

If Gordon was slippery on grass and clay, he was doubly that with the misbehavior that gave him so much satisfaction. One morning, he and friend Rob Bowman snuck out of science class, fished matches from their jeans, and lit a pair of long fuses they'd hand-rolled. Cherry-bomb firecrackers erupted in a hallway trashcan minutes later, rattling the walls and prompting the high-strung kids to yelp, "Earthquake!" At the lunch tables that day, the garbage-can fireball was the talk of the campus. Yet, the sweater-wearing Napoleons who ran Marshall like a fiefdom never unearthed evidence implicating Gordon. They must not have believed a lad at his second-chance school would engage in such a risky stunt.

Under the gym's fluorescent lights, Gordon rocked sole to heel, calibrating his leap. Boys released by Turner after the clubby jumping game had begun now stood watching the others take flight. Several of Gordon's friends hung with him at the front of the runway, waiting their turn. A few dallied around the landing zone, hands on hips, squawking for the rest to move double-time. "What are you waiting for?" somebody hollered. "An invitation? Go!" As the pressure accreted for him to rush, Gordon tried his best to drown it out. Even his try-anything spirit recognized that he'd need an enormous amount of air under him. He would be flinging himself higher than he or his band of rowdies had ever attempted.

Had Coach Turner emerged from his locker room fungus quest just then, the generation that produced me might have surged out of the 1940s unpunished. Yet free will is forever, and Gordon-the-Tarzan galloped toward the pommel horse immersed in his present. He blew down that runway in a whirl of pumping elbows and knees impressive to onlookers and too fast for control. *Crack.* His aerial maneuver was gummed up from the second he made contact with the springboard. As his right foot hit it, the device with coils on the underside canted sharply to the right, slicing his acceleration and angling him off course. The board didn't so much catapult him as ragdoll him sideways. With too little air under him, his left foot snagged on the outermost mat and further reduced his momentum. The gymnastic rings that he'd been able to seize every time before might as well have been on Jupiter.

Up seven feet in the air, with gravity tapping its watch, Gordon may have tried to tuck into a ball for a last-second bailout. It was too late, fatefully so. The effect of his stumble brought him twisting downward, headfirst, crashing into the pads with a sickening thump. On impact, his neck torqued to the right, which compressed his cervical spine like a Slinky toy lobbed from a roof. Underneath him, a pool of dark, sticky blood from a half-severed calf blotted the hardwood.

Pounding their sneakers to reach him, the boys who weren't there when Gordon took his swan dive saw that he'd knocked himself out cold. More gruesomely, he was on his back and his flank simultaneously. Indeed, his *head* seemed to have been dislocated, ratcheted so abominably to one side that his mop-top brown hair brushed his shoulder blade. From above, he resembled a misshapen "S."

An icy panic sliced through his friends, who tried futilely to wake him. "Gordy, you okay? Gordy, can you hear us?" They jostled his shoulder. No response. They shook his knees. Same result. The longer he was unconscious, the more broken he seemed. He wasn't springing up hooting, "I fooled you, suckers!" as he had after other gut-clenching spills. But how could he be playing possum now with his neck skewed at that unnatural angle? Once this sank in, that Gordon might die, one of the Tarzans ran into the locker room frantic for "Coach, anybody!"

Turner, dressed in a gray sweatshirt, came right out, shooing everyone away. "Snap out of it, Zahler," he said. "C'mon. Wake up." Marshall's beloved coach was in a catcher's stance, eliciting nothing. "Zahler, can you hear me? Gordon, don't do this. Open your eyes!" Crickets. Turner massaged his crinkled forehead and then stuffed the whistle dangling from his neck into his sweatshirt. By now the entire PE class had lined the perimeter of the cramped, white-walled gym. The Tarzans were the only ones with gall to inch closer for a better peek before Coach yapped at them to move back. Minutes passed. "Zahler!" Coach repeated, no longer looking his authoritative self. "Zahler. I know you're in there. Move, kid. Do something!" He didn't, so Turner had someone throw him a towel to wrap Gordon's bleeding leg as a tourniquet.

Outside the hard rain became deluge. Small, filthy rivers sped down curbs. Umbrellas clicked open. Lee, at the time, was chockablock in sheet music, arranging the soundtracks for four movies. Among them were two serials for Columbia Pictures: the western *Deadwood Dick* and *The Shadow*, based on the pulp magazine character. Rose was probably at home, Muriel at Pasadena Junior College taking general-education courses needed to transfer to a four-year university. Everybody was doing what they were supposed to, feet on the ground, when Gordon flopped to earth.

Suddenly, he too was awake, whispering into the coach's bent-down ear, still splayed in the zigzag where he'd landed. A minute later, his limp body was on the move. "What the hell is Coach doing?" one of the numbed boys asked another. This was what: Turner had gingerly locked his arms under Gordon's armpits from behind, almost as if he were trying to squeeze him into a wrester's half nelson, and drawn him upward. With that leverage, Turner hefted Gordon into a standing position. He must've wanted to get the kid's blood circulating, revive him on his feet. But Gordon could no longer be vertical. Lifted up, his chin slumped into his breastbone and his legs bore no weight; Edgar Bergen's puppets had better body control than him. Turner had no choice except to carefully set Gordon down on the floor, away from the pooled blood. Visible on his cheeks was now a dusting of the athlete's foot powder. Turner, in his first seconds over him, had tapped Gordon's face. That'd been when the coach reckoned he could shake his pupil out of it.

Never before had Turner grappled with what lay crumpled before him: a gravely wounded kid. "Coach," Gordon mumbled in his supine position. "I can't move. My arms. My legs. I can't feel them anymore. Are they still there? What's happening?"

An ambulance was summoned, arriving before anyone could give Gordon a straight answer. Two husky men in alabaster suits materialized at the gym's double doors, solemn and efficient. They wheeled their gurney over the hardwood, and its rusty squeak would live in memories for years. One Tarzan asked another if Gordon was going to die. "Of course not," he was told with manufactured assurance. Some in his circle cried, others masked their faces, waiting to sob at home. Such confusion roiled his group: relief it wasn't them, guilt about their game. Twenty minutes ago, it had all been laughs.

At the pads, the attendants lifted Gordon from the floor, strapped him into the noisy gurney, and rolled him off the school premises from which he'd never return. Through the rain he went, straight into a Schaefer Co. ambulance en route to the nearest hospital. Eyewitnesses said the indentation his body left on the gym pads remained for hours.

*　　*　　*

HE LAY FROZEN—JUST HIM, his thoughts, and those metal rods that surgeons had drilled into his skull. Christ, he wanted his bearings back. Was that too much to ask after he'd been chloroformed? It had been days since he'd been whisked from Marshall to St. Luke's Hospital on Pasadena's eastern border, not far from his Sierra Madre bedroom. His drug-addled brain processed that nebula of memory, at least. Rushed in from the ambulance, he'd heard a deep voice express alarm to the doctor in charge. Something about a cervical fracture and a nicked leg artery.

As best as he could recall, he'd just been at St. Luke's a short time. The X-rays taken there had bred a commotion that'd put him back into the same Schaefer ambulance, siren blaring, presumably en route to where he was now. Time had skittered ahead after that, if he could trust time anymore. It had been Tuesday morning that he'd been fretting about the algebra quiz he was supposed to take—when not daydreaming about showboating for a girl he liked. Now, as consciousness reintroduced itself, he fumbled for a more accurate mosaic of how he'd gone from that springboard to this bed. If his memory reboot had succeeded, he'd have known that he was in intensive care at Los Angeles County General Hospital with dire medical jargon scribbled on his chart.

His awakening startled Rose, there in a chair mashed up against Gordon's chrome bed frame. She'd been there for days in a vigil after the hurried operation to stabilize his fractured neck. She had been praying nonstop, begging God with predictable desperation to allow her to switch places with the boy, and then modifying it to simply keep him alive. She'd been stroking his face, close to the red incisions where surgeons had drilled pins into his skull, when he pried his eyes open. Her euphoria lasted a nanosecond. Gordon's expression was of such terrific confusion, of such primal fear, that she hurriedly leaned over him to peck his forehead. She wanted him to see her before he saw anything else.

"Where am I? What's happened? Where's Dad? Where are my arms? What's pinching my head? Why can't I move? Am I going to die? I don't wanna die. Mom, Mommy, help me!"

Rose grew hysterical, welling up despite an inability to decipher a garbled syllable from her son's chapped lips. Gordon's shattered back had compromised his breathing, so a ventilator had been inserted down his throat. His terror just hadn't focused on that part yet. Sensing this in his *mm-u-nm-mm* babbling, Rose lied beautifully about his condition. "Stay still," she said. "You're going to be fine. Just fine. There's a machine helping you to breathe—that's why you can't speak. It's just for precaution. Hear that? Nothing to worry about. It'll be out soon. The Lord is taking care of you. Now breathe easy and rest, sweetheart."

Squeezing his eyelids shut, listening to the respirator's mechanical wheeze, Gordon couldn't let it rest. That wasn't him. He exhaled hard through the ventilator, and worked to transport himself back to his arrival. Eventually, his brain organized a chronology as the sedatives wore off. From St. Luke's he had been hustled into County General's emergency room half-conscious and three-quarters gone. Under blinding lights there had been a flurry of gloves and instruments around him. Somebody with scissors snipped the Marshall T-shirt off him, and he felt colder than he'd ever been. The two doctors over him spoke in a clinical, coffee-breathed prattle of Latin-rooted words. One asked him whether he felt the pinpricks on his feet. Groggily, he'd responded, "What pinpricks?" Ether—he smelled so much ether, too, when one of the sawbones clamped a mask over his mouth. The cloying gas made the room spin until a chemical sleep ferried him into the galaxies of his mind. That's how his recall ended—raggedly. Three lost days later, he was gagging on his respirator while his mother invoked the saints. Soon enough, he'd learn that the traction pins drilled over his ears were bastards. They immobilized the remaining part of him still capable of movement.

To a one, the doctors assumed Gordon was destined for the mortuary. By 11:00 p.m. the day of the accident, they'd almost lost him several times. A few days later, County General's chief of neurology shepherded my grandparents into his office for a well-analyzed prognosis. Gordon, he said, had almost no chance. Few patients with a smashed vertebra so high up the spinal column had lived more than a few months, much less recovered. Cervical paralysis had too many fatal complications to overcome: respiratory arrest, pneumonia, kidney failure, bacterial infection, heart failure, pulmonary embolism, as well as other side effects that one could scarcely pronounce. The

X-rays that the neurologist gave Lee and Rose to inspect corroborated this view. The boy's neck was so acutely cracked that the force of his impact had almost decapitated him. Hence, the doctor's primary advice was more logistical than medical. He recommended that my grandparents keep the family minister available, because in all likelihood they'd need him for a service.

Careening between grief and shock as they were, Gordon's folks refused to accept their son was doomed. In those first weeks at County General, they were there constantly, sometimes sixteen hours a day. Gordon heard them exalt that he was improving, that a return to his old life was probable. After they exited his room was when their conflicting philosophies emerged. Lee browbeat and stamped through the ward scavenging for hope. His son was lying there, and he wouldn't tolerate poppycock runarounds from the hospital personnel as he tried to glean what he might about future surgeries, second opinions, realistic odds, and such. Medicine held Lee's trust, science was the answer.

Rose, by comparison, was kindlier to the physicians and nurses and more accepting of their "we're doing everything we can" proclamations. This tolerance originated from a reserved, albeit opinionated, nature saturated by God All Mighty. Rose believed that the Creator, whatever the turmoil in his lap, could instantaneously cure any of His children of any affliction. It was simply a matter of the devout and the needy asking Him with a sincere heart. Back in Sierra Madre, worshipers from the quirky Christian church she belonged to chanted for God to work his magic on the youngest Zahler. For Rose, this was no spiritual long shot. It was a proven survival technique.

The forty-year-old wife and mother had reached middle age by burrowing into the day-to-day, doing good work as her rampart against the memories of her father's murder near the US-Mexican border. Rose had told little about it to Muriel and Gordon, figuring they'd learn for themselves how sadistic the planet could be. Even so, the timing of this latest incident challenged her belief system. Gordon had wilted forty-eight hours before his favorite night for merriment, Halloween. He'd been injured two months into his fresh start at Marshall. Most glumly, he'd been consigned to his deathbed on the eleventh anniversary of the 1929 stock market crash that sunk America into the Great Depression. She and Lee used to remind each other how good they'd had it until October 29, 1940 ended the aura of exemption with its own free fall. Nothing, Rose knew now, was more merciless than the calendar.

CHAPTER THREE: THE LATE CORPSE

O UTSIDE HIS HOSPITAL ROOM, the two girls steeled themselves, creeped out as much by what lay inside as who it was. Normalouise and Mary Georgine had waited a seeming eternity for permission to visit their stricken friend when, by calendar-count, it'd only been weeks since the ambulance screeched away from Marshall. Now in the corridor of the biggest hospital in California, in a ward lined with the brain-damaged and neurologically mangled, the two hoopskirt-clad eleventh-graders were unsure whether to press on out of loyalty or high-tail it home. LA County General could be a mortifying cube for the healthy. *Stay or go, go or stay?* Before they nudged open his door, they took deep breaths and swallowed hard.

The Gordy they cherished swiped ice cream cups at church socials for them. He enticed them into the scariest seat on the beach roller coaster, the lead one, and bent over howling afterwards at their white-knuckle yips. When his allowance dried up, he wasn't below shoplifting a Hershey bar or performing a small street con for pocket money. How he committed these acts almost said as much about him as the wrongs. Nabbed by an adult, Gordon wouldn't disclose the names of his co-conspirators. Never. Instead, he'd act remorseful, parrot the grown-ups' homilies about distinguishing right from wrong: "It'll never happen again, sir. My mother raised me better than this." Twenty minutes later he'd be making faces in windows, doing as he wished with roguish liberty.

In the months before his accident, Mary Georgine and Normalouise had noticed changes in him, nonetheless. The opposite sex had begun taking note of him, and his friends thought it cute how the butterflies made the sometime-terror of Sierra Madre blush. The tomboyish girls two grades older than him were his unofficial big sisters, advising him on how to win over crushes and setting him up on a date with a Monrovia cheerleader. Being precocious sure opened doors for Gordon. Normalouise, blue-eyed and bold, and Mary Georgine, a creamy-skinned beauty from early age, thought him a pip from their first meeting in grade school. They used to wrap a chain around Gordon's leg so he would playfully drop on all fours and pant like their boy schnauzer. As the years went by, they ditched inside gags like that to hike to waterfalls. They cooked beans on open campfires. They talked adult matters under magnificent skies, speculating on the people they'd be once they shook Sierra Madre's dust from their feet.

The companion they discovered at County General, though, wasn't going anywhere. He was cadaver-ish, bound this way and that. Thick, leather bands strapped his arms and legs down. Mysterious tubes rising from the floor disappeared under a sheet, presumably headed for his privates. A ventilator rested along the wall, a morphine drip sat near his bed and, next to all that, were comic books out of reach on a table. Just registering all the weight he'd shed from a previously beanpole body was wincing enough.

Prior to arriving, they were cautioned to brace themselves for the macabre. The newspaper stories, while devoid of the mortifying particulars, previewed just what dire shape he was in. What had occurred at Marshall had ballooned from small-town catastrophe into a major news story competing for front-page space with articles about Nazi conquests and school bond measures. "Boy, 14, Critically Hurt in Leap Over Gym Horse," said *The Pasadena Post*. "Gym Accident May Cause Boy's Death," shouted the *Sierra Madre News*.

But nobody had forewarned them about his head, his shish kebab head. Metal pins a quarter-inch in diameter had been harpooned into shaved squares just above his ears. Surgeons had drilled them there to preempt any movement from the neck up, as a twitch could be fatal. Those spooky intrusions, "tongs" in medical anodyne, were also reference markers for his guests. A few months earlier, after catching his reflection in a cigar shop window, Gordon had nattered about having his protruding ears surgically pinned back once he turned eighteen. You couldn't lead the high-stepping life he'd planned if he resembled "Bambi's cousin." Taping them back didn't work—he'd tried; cartilage, like him, was resistant. County General's skull pins were a savage contrast, as if inspired by a medieval torture rack. They were attached to wires fed through a pulley counterweighted by miniature sandbags. How, exactly, all this traction gadgetry worked was flummoxing, but it didn't seem to either of the girls that a human being—especially one they'd regarded as their neighborhood Huck Finn—should be latched up in the middle. His brown almond-shaped eyes and messy bangs were his only recognizable features.

"So, there's nothing we can bring you? Just a milkshake from Burt's?" asked Normalouise. "Not a cheeseburger, double pickles?"

"Just the shake. I can't have any solids yet, remember?"

"Oops, I forgot."

"Do me a favor? Lean over the bed so I can see you." The two moved closer, skittishly.

"If it isn't Mary Georgine. Hi-de-ho. I've missed seeing you guys."

"Oh, Gordy, I don't know what to say."

"Sure you do."

"No, I don't. I feel awful about what's happened. I still can't believe it—you're just fourteen." She started to lose it, breaking her hallway pledge to Normalouise to be strong. "Guess it doesn't help nobody can stop talking about you."

"Let 'em, Mary. We'll hear what they say when..." The words stopped cold by a ten-second coughing jag.

"See," said Normalouise, coming to the rescue. "I told you he'd be the same old Gordy." She pinched a tissue from the wall dispenser and handed it to Mary with bugged-out eyes. "Those doctors must be fixing you up swell."

"Depends," said Gordon.

"On what?"

"On which doctors you're talking about."

"You got more than one?"

"Do I. Hey, can you give me some water from that glass next to me?"

Normalouise held a straw to lips that Rose salved at night with Vaseline.

"That enough?"

"Yeah. Thanks."

"Now, what about your doctors?"

"You really want to hear this junk?"

"Ding dong. Of course we do."

"But what about Halloween? Anything killer diller?"

"You have a one-track mind, you know that."

"Just tell me you blew up one pumpkin, Mr. Long's? For me."

"Without you, never. Now what gives?"

"Since you're the first friendly faces I've seen, I'll tell you. But you have to swear not a word to anybody. Okay? That goes double for my parents. Sometimes I think they're doing worse than me."

"Promise."

"You too, Mary?"

"I won't tell," she sniffled.

"All right. When I got here, what a month ago or something, the doctors said I was in pretty lousy shape."

"They said that?" Normalouise asked rat-tat-tat.

"Not to my face, but I could tell from how everyone acted." Gordon's voice cracked on the word "face," so he closed his eyes and swallowed. "My dad, you know how he gets. He didn't trust what they were telling him. This one chrome-dome thought he knew everything. So my uncle Sonny flew out these doctors from New York to examine me. Guess one of his Hollywood buddies suggested them. Supposed to be hotshot specialists."

"What'd they say?"

"Nothing. Nothing new."

"What do you mean?"

"One night they came into my room and talked to the side when the nurses weren't around. They thought I was asleep. But I tricked 'em. I heard every word."

"And?"

"And they didn't think my body could handle it. They gave me a two percent."

"Two percent? Of what?"

"Of living, dope. Ain't you listening?"

"Jesus," Normalouise said, louder than she intended. "What happened next?"

"Beats me. I never saw them again. They must've gone back to New York. Wasn't much they could do."

"So that's it. You lie around all day with these, uh, things in your head?"

"Yeah, but once I can I'm gonna make the doctors eat their words. Been thinking about this for a while. Pretty soon, I'm gonna get out of this stupid bed. Then I'm gonna walk right down the middle of Sierra Madre Boulevard and start directing traffic. Next Halloween we'll paint the whole town."

"But what about what they said? I'd be crying my eyes out if they told me I was going to die." Normalouise looked up at the traction pulleys, then down. "Damn, Gordy. That didn't come out right."

"That's okay. I've decided something."

"Yeah."

"I don't believe in death. I mean, the idea of it. This can't be all there is, can it? And if you don't believe in it, it can't hurt ya."

"Geez, I never thought of it that way."

"Me neither. Not until now. Some of the Bible stuff my mom made me sit through must've gotten through. Bet you never thought you'd hear *me* say that."

"No kidding. You were always more interested in the ice cream afterwards."

"I know. Can I tell ya another secret?"

"Not if it's as big as the last one," Normalouise said with a puckered smile.

"I do cry. Lots. I just do it at night. That way nobody sees."

The girls stayed another half an hour, hoping each minute there that Gordon was better off than his pin-drilled head. Out in the hallway, however, the delusion ended. Surveying where they were, despair socked them, and both wept until a nurse walked over to comfort them with tissues and available shoulders.

*   *   *

WEEKS AFTER THE NINTH-GRADER in gym shoes arrived, the doctors of East Los Angeles were stumped by the anomaly in their midst. Intrigued, some might've flirted with drafting a story for a medical journal. Small wagers might've been shook on, professional arguments unleashed on the ward. Gordon, inexplicably, was still alive. As in refusing to die. None of the physicians who'd examined him and nothing in the technical literature they'd consulted had a good explanation for how he could possibly still be there. A battered spinal column garbles the brain's instructions to muscles and organs the body needs not just to move limbs, but also to draw oxygen, metabolize food, circulate blood, and manifold electro-chemical tasks in between. Spinal nerves are equivalent to the body's master switchboard. The higher up the damage, as in Gordon's case, the more likely the circuitry below it is blown out.

Then again, laws of probabilities beg to be flouted, and so far Gordon's constitution had flouted a potent adversary. His resolve to lie there staring at the ceiling, grinding his teeth to gut it out through another County General night was the area that the doctors with all their bloodless, statistical references could never forecast. He'd ridden out seizures and infections, and grunted through the periodic stabbing pain in limbs no longer in his control. No wuss in that room.

Near Thanksgiving, though, just around Rose's birthday, the patient almost made the standard thinking crowd look prophetic. Inside his spinal canal, bone fragments bobbed in fluid. Wary as they were about dragging him back to the operating room table, the doctors were more anxious about removing the chips. They had to keep precarious swelling down. On the day of the surgery a nurse disconnected the traction tongs from his skull. Painful as that was, it felt wonderful having that metal out of his head; just two more steps to go. Before they extracted the fragments, the doctors needed a new set of X-rays to isolate where to scalpel him. A milquetoast orderly with slicked-back red hair was assigned to transport him to the imaging area. He'd tended to Gordon before and, liking him, made small talk about one of the cranky, head nurses with a signature phrase to patients: *"I'm telling, not asking."* When the elevator closed, it was just he, Gordon in his bed-on-wheels, and the laws of averages.

Halfway down to the imaging area, those averages took over. Gordon's chest began heaving, as with violent hiccups. His breathing turned shallow. Every time he clenched his jaw to inhale, you could see he got no more air than you would from a busted straw. Blue lips, shrill gasps: his respiratory system, such as it was, had picked this hermetical location to conk out. When the cab doors parted, the orderly shrieked, "Help!" And here he thought his job with the quick-smiling kid was easy as pie.

Gordon would've asphyxiated in the depths of County General had dumb luck not been there to rescue him. Providence here was stocky, balding, Iowa-born, and, for no valid reason, loitering in front of the elevator when it shuddered open. Joe Risser, orthopedic surgeon, maintained his composure facing the unresponsive patient whose name he didn't know. He had seconds to hunt down a ventilator or consider cracking the boy's chest to get his breathing going. As Risser racked his mind, his eyes prowled the floor. That's when a third option sang out to him. White lab coat fluffing behind him, he charged toward an iron lung that someone, serendipitously, had left down the hall. And plugged in, too. "Let's get him in there," he told the attendant. Into the polished metal cylinder Gordon went, where pressure changes restarted his breathing. The contraption, the dimensions of a barbecue smoker, was a lifesaver—well, it, the attendant, and Risser's extemporized thinking.

The traumatizing hangover from it, if not the prospect of more setbacks around the bend, were less easily reversed. The tungsten-strong spirit that had amazed the nurses and tore at his parents' heartstrings recoiled into hiding after his elevator scare. Back on the respirator again, the tongs reinserted, Gordon now appreciated how far that springboard had flung him from everyday existence. Ornery, withdrawn, dark: his outlook plunged. He'd been ripped from the lush, tactile world to one where dependence on others was both absolute and unceasing. The similarly disabled had all experienced their own psychological bloodletting. Their injuries had shackled them in dungeons of fear, denial, rage, and gloom. Suicidal leanings inconceivable to them in their walking days no longer seemed an absurd or shameful exit. After sticking his tongue out at his long-shot odds, Gordon must've contemplated requesting the next friend to visit for assistance. Would they mind stuffing a pillow over his face? He'd off himself but he was unable to use his arms.

Paraplegics, at least, enjoyed some functional control over their hands—control that afforded them a dollop of self-sufficiency. Unlike them, without a working finger, he'd never be able scratch his own nose. His parents, jittery about his mental tailspin, strove to convince him the respiratory arrest was a one-time event, an aberration to forget. Try as they did, the hurt rising out of his words and expressions let them know he didn't give a rat's ass.

Around County General, the graveyard shift was the worst time to be wallowing in a funk. Prolonged screams and code blues resonated across the ward, and the nurses were always interrupting your sleep to check some inconsequential vital sign or another. It was on one of these night shifts that Joe Risser slipped into Gordon's room and plopped down into a chair. He directed the nurse stationed there as part of the boy's round-the-clock care to stretch her legs, have a smoke. The bones specialist was not Gordon's primary doctor when he invited himself in. The two had probably yet to speak, since Gordon was unconscious entering the iron lung and on the breathing machine for days afterward. In the half-darkness, Risser clicked on his pocket flashlight and reviewed the thick chart; moonbeams splashing the window enabled him to trace the X-rays. An hour later, he had all the information he needed to know.

The practitioner of science was about to practice some magic. Risser cupped his right hand onto Gordon's forehead, resting it there as if it belonged. From his fingertips, the patient reported later, a cleansing heat flowed through an anatomy that had been numb below the collarbone. Where needles, washrags, and bandages failed, the Midwesterner's touch connected. He made the boy feel, be it by intuition, fluke, or the otherworldly. "Gordon," he said firmly, "listen to me. It doesn't matter what anyone else here tells you. It's all hooey. You *are* going to make it. I'm positive of it."

After he'd stopped breathing in the elevator, Gordon had no reason to believe him. He just did.

CHAPTER FOUR: MEN WITH STEEL FACES

T EAR DUCTS RUN DRY, Lee and Rose had another crisis at their
doorstep: how to finance calamity. Months after his fall, Gordon was still trapped inside an anaesthetized body. None of
the doctors, even Risser, could estimate how long he would remain
strung up in "Chinese Water Torture," Gordon's sarcastic moniker for
his traction contraption. Most days his room felt like a disinfected
battleground, other times a portico for the funeral parlor. The one
reliable constant was the math. Everything at County General cost
triple its street price.

Lee's wages at first offset the bills clogging his mailbox, and why
doubt that shouldn't continue? After all, the floor of his dingy office
on Santa Monica Boulevard was stacked two-feet high in places with
the scores and accompaniments that studios had assigned him over
the years. Since his debut as a "tunesmith," hundreds of songs had
migrated from his right hemisphere, through the recording-booth
glass, and into the theaters. Deposit slips were testimonial. He cared
little that classically trained musicians, the ones writing Broadway
musicals and plays, regarded their Hollywood counterparts as sellout
hacks. Knocking out ditties was how independent composers like him
thrived, and if he was anonymous compared to Warner Bros' famous
Max Steiner, he managed. Lee was doing what he was born to do in
showbiz's new mecca.

Often, inspiration struck while he was in his Ford puttering back and forth from Sierra Madre. Long stoplights gave him time to tap out beats and rhythms, his steering wheel a desk to jot down the notes. Just because he worked out of a dumpy section of western Hollywood ridiculed as "Poverty Row" for its concentration of second-rate production outfits was no indictment of his talent. Lee's take-home allowed him to be philosophical about the industry hierarchy he inherently mistrusted. From 1937 to 1939 alone, he'd earned seventy-five hundred dollars (one hundred twenty-eight thousand today), a handsome sum for the era, plus cash under the table. Toted up, it had been enough for him to fantasize about buying the house they leased, a decent retirement, heck, even an around-the-world cruise for he and Rose before their arthritis set in.

Gordon's ten-second aerial misstep threatened to annihilate every one of those dreams. The hospital bills fanned across Lee's roll-top desk were already poking holes in the nest egg he'd been feathering with each movie wrap. Back then, there were no HMOs or Obamacare, and Rose's loaded relatives in San Francisco couldn't be bothered for compassion. Every day Gordon lied in acute care in the neurosurgery ward scraped four dollars and sixty-one cents off the Zahler's net worth. Two surgeries and mini-casts fitted around his torso exacted further damage. So did those six X-rays at thirteen dollars a pop. The double nursing shifts cost an additional six bucks per day. While Rose's youngest brother, former Universal Pictures director, Nat "Sonny" Ross, had picked up the tab for the New York specialists, Gordon's two local doctors (Rudolph Marx and W.W. Worster) were sticklers about invoice collection. Where it once was a joke, Poverty Row was sounding more accurate by the minute.

Lee before long informed Rose of what he knew would tear her up inside, however inclined she'd be to downplay it as a minor sacrifice. They'd have to vacate their Mountain Trail Avenue home, and forget about making any purchase offer. What they'd once chanted was within reach was now out of the question. The rent by itself was too exorbitant if they wanted to conserve every nickel before the bill collectors snatched it. The A-frame house with its wraparound porch and fragrant breezes would have to be somebody else's foothill

Shangri-la. Accessories to the good life there were soon junked with it. Barnaby, the live-in cook who baked scrumptious lemon pies, was let go. Sunday-night dinners out were shelved. Rose, deferring to her accepting nature, submitted to the harsh economizing without complaint. The way she saw it, her affection for the house or anything material—jewelry, calfskin books—were expendable wishes not worth mourning. As long as they had decent shelter and Gordon was alive, she was just fine. In a way, she was glad for the diversion. Their new place on East Laurel Avenue, a two-story Cape Cod with a latticework arch and decent charm, was uncomfortably smaller than where they'd come. Still, its low rent was prudent budgeting after the one thousand dollars they'd sent County General from their rainy day fund. Rose could do that subtraction.

It's just that Lee's bad days were unrelenting—humiliating days of soliciting charity and forsaking pride. One Wednesday after work, he had had no choice but to steer his green, swayback car toward the Motion Picture Relief Fund a few miles away. The Fund's doors had been opened in 1921 as a sort of public relations gimmick to soften Hollywood's wanton reputation among Washington lawmakers and Bible Belt types. Donations initially were collected from a single coin box. Mary Pickford, Charlie Chaplin, Douglas Fairbanks, and other big names bulked it up in the succeeding years. Great Depression or not, having colleagues living cold, sick, and hungry on the margins of a glitzy business, they knew, was shameful. By the time Lee entered the building, the nonprofit had sprouted into a well-run, private welfare agency catering to down-on-their-luck showbiz families. A tithing system for movie people making more than two hundred dollars per week and a popular, CBS radio program, *The Screen Guild Show*, were cash flows.

Lee submitted his application, written out on in his elegant cursive print, on December third. "Excuse me, miss, I think I have this filled out right. Do you know how long a decision will take?" The executive action committee understood the restrained desperation. It approved Lee's request the very next day. That settled that—Gordon could afford his nurses. And his forty-seven-year-old father accepted the generosity by slapping a binding condition on it. It would be a loan, he assured Fund executives, a temporary advance, for he considered public handouts for vagrants.

* * *

THE ZAHLER HOUSE PHONE on Laurel almost shorted out its wiring, the ringing was that manic. Kin, neighbors, church-mates, pump jockeys, studio acquaintances—the condolences were dialed in and delivered. Between the jangling and the persistent newspaper coverage of Gordon's condition, a rueful miasma shadowed Gordon's parents. It was there when Lee and Rose motored down Sierra Madre Boulevard and when they grabbed the morning paper. Everywhere they went, plaintive smiles and wincing nods greeted them, where relaxed grins for a family uninterrupted once had.

One call from downtown Los Angeles' commercial core stood out from the avalanche of "I'm sorry." Maurice Rose, though my grandmother's cousin, would normally never bother contacting them to voice his sorrow. The hard-charging attorney had met Lee at a family picnic some time back near Griffith Park, where the musician had given him an earful about his contempt for the legal profession. To him, they were in the same snake-in-the-grass genus as traveling con men and carpetbagging politicians. Actually, everyone in Lee's orbit had heard of his loathing of "shysters" because he'd expressed it so often after dealing with them at work. Disdain was simpler, of course, when he hadn't needed practical representation, or had a son all the experts said was terminal. Consequently, after the man from Spring Street phoned to extend his sympathies and whatnot to Rose, Lee kept him on the horn for a lot longer.

When they'd first contemplated how to avoid going broke, shouldering the entire burden themselves had been the end of the thinking. Their child, their tragedy, their dime. Not that the Zahlers had forgiven Coach Turner. His decision-making that rainy morning had been inexcusable. On his watch, he'd permitted a bevy of adventurous, junior-high boys to police themselves around the gymnastics equipment while he'd crusaded against athlete's feet. *Foot fungus!* The upshot was lying there near death in the neurology ward.

As much as Lee must've wanted to chug over to North Allen Avenue to thump Turner in the nose, he had reasons to refrain. At the top of the list was a more elemental truth. This outcome was primarily Gordon's doing. Anybody conversant with his past knew the odds would snare him eventually. Turner himself had wagged his finger at Gordon about attempting that vault, but Gordon had rolled his eyes.

Lee and Rose, no doubt, felt guilt-pocked that they had fueled his abandon—that they'd given him too much liberty tromping through early adolescence. St. Rita's nuns, for example, had reported his IQ test score at ninety-one, nine points below average. His parents knew that was folly. He'd either tanked the exam on purpose or approached it foolishly. Behind Gordon's puckishness were smarts he rarely applied at school. Others recognized it. Muriel took piano lessons. Gordon took apart radios to time how fast he could reassemble them. She enrolled in tap dancing. He chauffeured an elderly neighborhood couple on a long drive from Sierra Madre to Lake Elsinore out in Riverside at thirteen with his parents' approval. In the crush of regret, that was a mistake. They bred overconfidence in him. People blowing their stack at him railed at someone inoculated to believe he was indestructible. Given a time machine, they should've reprimanded him so memorably for his St. Rita's expulsion that just being near a footstool would give him pause.

Knitting these strands together, the Zahlers tried to be levelheaded about blame. By disregarding Turner's admonitions, Gordon had boxed them in. Their child, their tragedy, their dime. As the days went by, so did some of that naïveté. Perhaps by quizzing one of the Tarzans there when Gordon got hurt, perhaps by a whisper from another source, Lee grew suspicious about Marshall's culpability. School administrators heretofore had portrayed the accident as a ghastly mishap committed by a ninth-grader who should've known better. They were all heartsick about it, wished him the best. They had delivered bouquets to his hospital room so he'd know they would forever be thinking of him. After a spell, Lee no longer accepted this narrative as the entire truth. Anything but. That's why, moral heartburn and all, he retained Maurice Rose.

The deep pockets of the Pasadena Board of Education were their target. Reconstructing the state of the gym the morning Gordon plunged was how they aimed to dig into them. For days, Maurice Rose and his subordinates dredged Marshall's white, Spanish-stucco campus for evidence. They examined the springboard and the vaulting horse, and scoured maintenance logs by the carton. They cased the accident spot. They recorded Turner's deposition and his boss'. They interviewed doctors Marx and Worster and a few of the Tarzans. Gordon recounted what he could from his hospital bed. Evidence accumulated and chests were thumped. The school district's lawyer requested the judge toss the complaint in pretrial motions, but the plaintiff's attorney and his self-described "elaborate" brief squelched any chance of summary dismissal.

For Rose, the proceedings were less about institutional accountability and more about survival means. How, she wondered, could anyone assert integrity when legal statute compelled a ninth-grader to hear the specifics of his abbreviated future? From his brass-appointed suite a few blocks from ziggurat Los Angeles' City Hall, their lawyer tried explaining the logic behind the system. She cut him off. It wasn't Gordon sanctioning the action on his behalf that so alarmed her; she knew they were seeking a small Fort Knox in reparations. No, it was exposing him to his dire prognosis that tormented her. Ever since he'd been at County General, she'd censored the vocabulary used in his presence. Doctors, nurses, and visitors had all received her zero-tolerance, finger-wagging hallway briefings. Certain nomenclature—quadriplegia, cripple—were *never* to be uttered, double that for the starkest word of them all, "permanent."

Thanks to this suit, the jargon was freed from the embargo list. California law mandated that Gordon hear the damages before the court endorsed the filing, and those damages all skewed toward fatalistic and unknowable conclusions. Pretty deplorable, rubbing it in the face of someone so impressionable, if you wanted a maternal assessment on the matter. So, when Rose revealed to him what the law said she had to do, she parsed it her way. Never forget, she said, that lawyers hyper-exaggerate for a living. Qualifiers aside, Gordon learned real substance from the civil complaint, just as she expected.

Learned he had no bladder or bowel control and never would. Learned that his limbs were useless appendages, whatever the phantom feelings that galvanized secret hopes. Learned he was a quadriplegic who'd mashed two cervical vertebrae high up on his cord. Then the curtain really dropped. As a "permanent cripple," there was no point in him resuming school and no way he would *ever* be fit for gainful employment. Rose couldn't wait for the legal recitation to be over. The wording was hope annihilating. In her appraisal, their two-hundred-thousand-dollar claim ($3.4 million today) might buy them a ration of peace. But it was toothless in returning anything more.

The Zahler's case against Marshall went to the court clerk two days after a nominal Christmas. In previous years, Rose cooked a sumptuous Christmas Eve feast trimmed with exotic, European side dishes. Lee, bolting early from Hollywood, tinkled holiday standards on his home Baldwin piano. Before bed, he tantalized Muriel and Gordon per custom by having them add an extra layer of wrapping to their *own* presents. Just to inflate the excitement, they'd wait until that night to decorate the tree. While agnostic Lee was skeptical of Jesus, he cheerily participated in holiday bashes for the three believers under his roof. But this Christmas Day 1940 was an anti-event. Most of it was spent in the acute-care ward at County General, where the gift exchange was as flat as everyone's complexion. At their downsized rental, Lee's piano was silent.

Where the Zahlers made noise were in the filings accusing the Pasadena school district of imperiling their child. Indicting a community institution responsible for educating half the town was a polarizing act. Old-timers might've grumbled the suit was unseemly, avaricious, and even myopic considering Gordon's track record. The family only had a puncher's chance, too. School lawyers then routinely blocked negligence suits by waiving the immunity statutes that Congress and state legislatures had granted them. The premise was that "the king can do no wrong," the king being any government agency integral to the common good. In challenging the status quo, the underdog Zahlers had pitted themselves against a steel-clad opponent. "Big Damages Asked for Injured Boy," one newspaper summarized.

Damages indeed. The charges sounded grave just as Maurice Rose designed. Marshall, he contended, had endangered Gordon by giving someone of his "tender age" access to a dangerous apparatus without supervision. Kids, he added, never should've been leaping from a timeworn springboard better suited for the garbage dumpster. Despite supposed repairs, it lacked side supports after the original ones split wide from overuse. Gordon had catapulted off course for a provable reason. The same lethal disregard applied to school employees. They'd positioned a sharp, metal turnbuckle anchoring the high-bar to the floor too close to the landing area. Thrown askew, Gordon had slashed a calf artery on it. These blunders set the stage for the evidentiary bombshell. A Marshall staff member had raised the height of the pommel horse by ten full inches without notifying anyone first. Did they feel good about themselves?

Louis Vincenti of Hahn & Hahn, the blueblood Pasadena law firm representing the school district, contested every allegation Maurice leveled. In formal responses starting in early 1941, the owlish-looking, Stanford-educated Vincenti said questions about the springboard and the rest of the gym equipment should be disregarded. They'd all been operable that day. Coach Turner, he argued, should be held harmless, too. His class hadn't officially commenced when Gordon embarked on his aerial lunacy. Furthermore, the district had immunity against most employee mistakes. "The king can do no wrong," remember? For every cause of action Maurice Rose blustered about, Vincenti had a grenade-loaded rejoinder. Gordon's "negligence and carelessness" were to blame.

CHAPTER FIVE: THE GREAT SWINDLE

JANUARY 1941 ALMOST FINISHED off what the Marshall gym started. Gordon's previous asthma attacks, in which he'd gasp for oxygen in his County General bed, were trifles compared with the bang-bang succession of complications mauling him now. The round robin of infectious bugs with unencumbered access to his bladder and kidneys drilled him with no letup. With his fevers, weakness, and vomiting, it was remarkable that his biology hadn't just collapsed under the onslaught. Doctors who'd minimized his chances from the get-go had harped on the killing power of squiggly bacteria perceptible only under a microscope. Feasting on the vulnerable was all they knew.

It wasn't a fair fight, and sometimes barely a contest, either. When it came to treating paralysis, Depression-era medicine was not so much barbaric as primitive in countering one of the more grievous disruptions to one's biology. People back then surviving the first years after an acute spinal cord trauma represented the rare exceptions, the miracle cases. Statistically, they'd beaten the same odds as those outlasting advanced leukemia. Other than sedating folks with morphine, sending them for X-rays, wiring them into traction, or mummifying them in casts, hospitals were starved for remedies that didn't involve extended waiting and hoping. Technologically and curatively, the inner workings of the central nervous system were beyond their capacity to unlock it with precision. Consequently, some eighty to ninety percent of the seriously paralyzed died within weeks of their trauma. Those who survived that critical period could look forward to a life expectancy of two to three years max, mostly in brittle health inside institutions.

Judged against modern medical firepower, quadriplegia was mostly a death sentence in the FDR era. Antibiotics that today's victims typically get prescribed to defeat bugs festering in internal organs or bedsores had yet to be developed. Operations to ease pressure on the spinal cord were impossible, as well, because surgeons were unable to cauterize potentially lethal hemorrhages that they can staunch in a jiffy today. *Superman* actor Christopher Reeve, the world's most celebrated quadriplegic, survived his 1995 horse-riding accident for one reason: the science was primed for him. In the forties, ER doctors couldn't have injected Reeve with anti-inflammatory steroids that can spell the difference between breathing and asphyxiation. Nor could they drain his lungs of pneumonia-induced fluids without risking losing him on the table.

As if Rose bought any of that scientific helplessness. Whatever internal doubts she muffled about Gordon's longevity, she was adamant the infections had no chance against her tenacious son. Joe Risser must've believed that as well with his unshakeable belief in recovery ahead. Then again, Rose was at County General so much she could've talked herself into anything. Most nights she'd be in his room, dishing out the comfort and performing small tasks, until the late nursing shift came on. Around 9:30 p.m., she'd throw her stuff into a duffel bag, speed-walk down the corridor in her sensible shoes, and catch the final outbound Red Car trolley east. This late, the train was her last way home. (She'd decided against obtaining a driver's license after plowing Lee's Ford into a telephone poll during her maiden lesson.) It wasn't until she disembarked from the Sierra Madre station around 11:00 that she'd ponder her own leftovers dinner.

Leaving Gordon behind every night was the most anxiety-knotting part of her day. County General was America's second largest hospital, a facility stocked with wise doctors and pallets of the latest equipment, and mocked all the same as the undisputed white elephant of American public health facilities. Though erected mainly for the impoverished, it charged more than private competitors. Investigators, too, were always faulting its overcrowded wards, billing excesses, woeful training, and graft. Conditions had only marginally improved when Gordon took up residency. Some days, Rose was beside herself that this was the best they could afford. She didn't trust a couple of head nurses, or how well the rooms were disinfected. A frightening polio outbreak that spread from a supposedly quarantined ward had infected three hundred people, hospital workers among them. New reasons for her to worry about what was happening to Gordon cocooned inside that white monolith were never distant.

* * *

THE PHONE PROBABLY RANG sometime after midnight on February 25, 1941, minutes after Rose's head sunk into her pillow. Never must she have so badly wanted it to be a misdial. If it was the hospital calling a few hours after she had left, then they really might need that minister. Had a fatal blood clot traveled to Gordon's brain? A runaway fever not even prayers and aspirin could derail? Whatever the can't-wait rationale for such a late night jarring, the news on the other end was bound to be painful.

Rose's sister-in-law, Audrene Brier, was probably the one calling to lower the boom. If not the woman about to cry herself a Nile River of tears or another relation, then perhaps a Los Angeles Police Department officer accustomed to communicating devastating news to perfect strangers. Sonny, Rose's older brother, was dead. That's what the call was about. A boozing psychopath, jealous over his estranged wife, had ambushed him in cold blood a little after 10:00 p.m. at the textile factory that he co-owned at Seventeenth Street and Broadway. No one on Laurel dozed a wink after hearing that.

The days ahead were a numbed blur of information gathering and funeral arrangements. In between was *déjà vu* to a period in Rose's life that she had labored to forget—the period when she'd been yanked into the vulgarly publicized Texas trial of the man who'd slayed her father. Just as then, Rose needed to be careful picking up any of the big newspapers if she hoped to remain steady on her feet. Coverage of Sonny's killing unleashed a media feeding frenzy in a tabloid-ish reporting culture in which blood made for good reading and sold papers by the news rack. For rival city editors duking it out for scoops, this drama had everything: sex, jealousy, gore, Hollywood, stalking, the gas chamber. The *Los Angeles Times*: "Ex-Producer of Films Slain by Employee." The *Los Angeles Herald Express*: "Love Slayer of Film Man Defiant, Says He 'Would Do it Again.'" It was agony by the paragraph. The suspect's given name was the same as Rose's father's— Maurice. But this Maurice, with the swashbuckling features of a young Errol Flynn or Justin Timberlake, was more viper than man, bragging about what his shotgun had achieved and soaking up its limelight.

Losing Sonny was another unreal whacking to the group system, and Rose knew the drumbeat coverage meant that Muriel would be exposed to its most lurid details. Gordon's isolation shifted that burden to her, and she couldn't blame either of them for lashing out. Their favorite uncle had been taken out four-and-a-half miles southwest of the County General with no parting words or last embrace. Sonny had been the family's happy-go-lucky, though he'd often had justification for feeling neither. His breezy personality and trusting nature was ingrained into who he was. In carefree times, he'd kidnap Gordon for a day of rollicking laughs at Universal, followed by dinner at a jumping restaurant. He'd doted on Muriel equally, sending her leather-bound, first edition books and swag from his wanderlust travels. Two shotgun blasts later, one of the most selfless guys around rested on a metal table at the county morgue while the lowlife who put him there smiled for the cameras.

Gordon must've sensed horror, even in his insensate bones. Must've known someone had died from the moment Rose's lightless eyes slipped over his bed to tell him. Hearing that a beloved East Coast relative had passed would've stung. Finding out that Sonny, his kindred, fun-loving Sonny, had been killed a short car ride from where he lay, scraped the bottom of the psychic barrel. Some Tarzan he was: lord of nothing. He couldn't even hug his mother with every reason to fear the phone.

* * *

MURIEL HAD BETTER OPTIONS for movement after Sonny was interred in the private mausoleum of the studio founder who'd wooed him to Los Angeles: his mentor and possible uncle, Carl Laemmle. By March 1941, she, too, was living outside Sierra Madre. But she wasn't a Red Car away as Gordon was. She'd put almost four hundred miles between her and home as a guest of the enigmatic Rosenberg's. Her parents had plunked down the train fare to San Francisco and given her spending money from the little they still had. "Don't worry, darling," they told her. "Have yourself some fun up there." Normally, Muriel never would have been granted such freedom, but nothing about the last six months even masqueraded as ordinary. How often she'd been alone at the house—or out for the sake of it—as her folks wore grooves into County General's floors. They knew she deserved attention from their dwindling reserves, just as they appreciated another city could be an expedient getaway.

My mother, social butterfly, had her own reasons for going, and double those for not returning as scheduled. Neon San Francisco was jubilee for any footloose twenty-year-old. In Southern California, her luminous smile, cheekbones, and mousy brunette hair (clipped to fashion-magazine dictates) had a rotisserie of boys asking her out. No reason, she saw, Bay Area fun couldn't match Los Angeles. There was tea dancing at the Mark Hopkins hotel, drinks at the Fairmont, cable car rides in the fog, acrobatic rides in biplanes. Plus, she could drag herself in at one o'clock in the morning assured her dad wouldn't be waiting for her at the door, eyebrows in attack mode, simmering over a blown curfew.

Independence aside, every trip to Gordon's hospital room had reaffirmed his canceled childhood. She knew, miracle notwithstanding, they'd have to box up his marble collection and models, sell his bike. Never, either, would the two of them chase each other around the house in sibling warfare screaming holy hell, Gordon exasperated over Muriel's bathroom hogging, she accusing him of cadging her fancy fountain pen or other cherished possessions. Their last tiff not long before his fall glowed in her memory. Gordon had caught her and a boyfriend necking in his Chrysler down the block and threatened to "spill the beans to Dad" unless she bought his silence with a quarter. *Blackmailer*, Muriel called him. *Fink*. While she had craved revenge then, a girl could get sentimental over the juvenile when it dissolved forever.

Wasn't she, Muriel asked herself, entitled to some grand times on account of what he had cost her *now*? Damn straight she was. The crossing out of dreams warranted a certain ration of self-indulgence. Before she'd departed from Union Station, her father had sat her down to express "how terribly sorry I am about this, Muggs," his pet name for her. "It's the last thing your mother and I wanted. The last confounded thing." Lee's remorse derived from a broken promise. He'd just reviewed their bank accounts again, and there wasn't enough to fund her tuition at Pomona College, the school where she and a knot of girlfriends had been accepted as juniors for fall semester 1941. They might've been able to scratch out a semester's worth, but college was about continuity. Hard as he'd labored to protect their savings, Lee confessed that Gordon's hospital bills were merciless drains. If she still wanted higher education, she'd have to think smaller. It would have to be two lousy years at Pasadena Junior College, where she already was, or nothing.

At Nob Hill's ritzy Stanford Court Apartments, where the Rosenberg clan occupied a whole floor, my mom unpacked her things, unaware she was at the epicenter of a betrayal still festering thirty-five years after the fact. Rose had been vague about the sordid history, thinking it best to let the bitterness fade, and Muriel rarely asked. Weird, how it worked out. Muriel now whittled some of her Bay Area time playing canasta with the patriarch responsible for much of the heartache: her great grandfather. Robert Solomon Rosenberg had once been a feted industrialist, known from city hall to factory row. Now, in 1941, he was a doddering old man in his eighties without his wife of fifty-eight years and few teeth in his gums. Nevertheless, corncob pipe in mouth, he regaled Muriel every morning on the veranda with the same yarn about how the grade-A leather army boots his company had manufactured "saved American regulars in World War I," and every day she would sigh, "You told me already."

Robert, bearded and ambitious, had immigrated by steamship to the West Coast from Eastern Europe in 1876, determined to manufacture his own wealth. It wasn't empty talk. Using wiles and grunt labor, he'd become a prominent area businessman holding interests in steel and textile plants. Robert's sons, once they were grown, diversified the portfolio into restaurants and ownership of second-rate apartment houses. The profits ensconced everybody into black-tie wealth that inspired one offspring to reportedly shriek, "Look at us. We own San Francisco!"

Muriel herself witnessed this money-bought haughtiness on Friday nights, when Robert's offspring gathered for fancy-pants suppers at Nob Hill. Here, highballs sloshed and deception ruled. Across the ornate dinner table, Robert would occasionally stutter questions about how an absent son was doing. None of his high-society kids made rich by him, though, had the backbone to remind him that their sibling had died years earlier. Intimate thievery came easier to them. After the servants bused the meals, some of them were in the habit of pilfering their father's curios—candelabras, figurines—piece by expensive piece. Questioned about this practice by outsiders, they'd justify it as self-serve bequest, not larceny. Dad, they murmured, was too senile to appreciate the flourishes anymore. Naturally, with a new face like Muriel present, the legal difficulties that'd embroiled two of Robert's sons, Joseph and Isador, were steered off the conversation list; grand juries that'd subpoenaed them on fraud charges related to their textile business in the thirties dealt in unpleasantness tricky to explain. Rose's willingness to ship her daughter off for safekeeping to this branch of the family—one complicit in hornswoggling taxpayers, among lesser sins—was a blunt-force reminder of how lousy the Zahler's options were.

Muriel logged hours around them engaging in pleasantries and withstanding the tedium of snobberies as her Bay Area price of admission. Being up there let her reconnect with Al Altfield, a sharp kid from an affluent family stationed at Fort Ord Army base in nearby Monterey. Between that boyfriend and a local cousin clued in to the best bars, there were oodles to entertain her.

Any notions she kindled about staying here forever were torpedoed by the mail—specifically Sierra Madre mail arriving twice weekly. In letters executed with flawless grammar, Rose updated her daughter with sanitized personal news, followed by the dos-and-don'ts of her hiatus. *Write Gordon. Help your relatives. No wastrel spending. Beware of strange men. Avoid sunburns. No weeknight dates. Stay as long as you wish. Read your scriptures. Write your brother more often (just not via special delivery; the sixteen cents was extortion). Take a math class. Beware of your relatives. Start planning your return.*

The savvy of Rose's correspondence was their careful omissions. While she acknowledged that Lee was still moping over Gordon and being on industry welfare, the money spats she was having with him were blanked out. But hey, he had the new *Ellery Queen* serial about to premiere, and wasn't that great? Nothing much, either, was conveyed about the family's legal impasse with Marshall or the showboating ravings of Sonny's murderer, Maurice Briggs. None of these upsetting details reached Muriel through the mail because Rose was convinced the girl had already gotten a snootful of them. Rather, frivolous distractions suffused with unusual importance—what San Francisco stores sold the best monkey-fur coats, the cake-and-punch wedding of a local girl—were accented for Muriel to associate with home.

Whether her brother was improving or in actuality still fighting for his life was the most bewildering for her to interpret from Rose's letters. Some days, she wrote, Gordon's stomach had "revolted" and his bladder stopped functioning. Post enemas, he was too frail to eat anything, even his mother's addictive oatmeal-raisin cookies. Other days, his ravenous appetite for goodies that he washed down with homemade apple cider reemerged. Despite this yo-yoing metabolism, Rose portrayed him as nicer to everybody and more like his mischievous, sweetheart old self.

But Muriel also recognized Rose's hushed panic from the little "favors" she sought, usually outlined in the bottom half of the letters in an oddly casual air. Her mother, the Christian dogmatist forever saying "what ought to be is," was searching for cosmic reassurance by way of tarot cards, crystal balls, mystic tea leaves, and other insights not endorsed by the New Testament. Since her daughter was up north, Rose figured Muriel should visit a celebrated Bay Area fortune-teller that Rose hoped could better peer into Gordon's future than his dour-mouthed physicians. Down home, Rose used to pay a few dollars to a two-hundred-fifty-pound clairvoyant whose popularity sprang less from her mystical prowess than the fact that her cousin was czarist sage Grigory Rasputin. Rose, Holy Roller that she was, told everyone that psychics like these were "pure entertainment," a lark. Obviously, there was more to the contradiction where a son in traction was concerned.

On June 21, 1941, Muriel received this dispatch: "*Darlin...Gordy is looking better each day and continues to retain whatever he eats, for which we are on our knees in gratitude. I didn't write you what Dr. Feder had to say, because his personal opinion was not encouraging. At the time Gordon was looking very bad and vomiting, but from that day on he is decidedly on a new way... Someday everybody will see. I'm just waiting to hear what the fortune-teller told you about Gordon. You know we only believe the (spiritual) truth, so if the prophecy doesn't correspond, we know what it's worth.*"

Muriel was riveted by Feder's prognosis, maybe more than any other, as she'd been dating him when Gordon was raced into County General in his body-numbed stupor. Connecting the two now made her want to scream. Communicating to Rose what the San Francisco psychic had foretold was another landmine. Weren't there enough specialists, nurses, lawyers, administrators, and charlatans concluding that her brother's future had a headstone attached to it?

By July 1941, when the land-grabbing Nazis were still chiefly Europe's headache, my mother's priority was devising ways to avoid a return train trip to Los Angeles. She and the "Fogtown" clicked. Like her, it was mercurial and a bit naughty, sophisticated and original. Already her planned two-week stay had swelled into four months. Had she been able to support herself it would've extended into residency, because her parents couldn't tolerate her living off the greasy Rosenbergs forever. Toward that end, she interviewed with the downtown department stores. Rejected there, Muriel applied to the five-and-dimes. An uncle from United Textile Co. next wrote up a letterhead recommendation guaranteeing prospective companies what a bang-up job she would do. When none were willing to take a chance on such a greenhorn, she abdicated to the return date that her folks badgered her to accept. Pasadena Junior College, here she came (back). It was all such a gyp.

CHAPTER SIX: HAPPINESS C.O.D.

THE NURSES HAD HEARD the cussing before from the men with dead legs. How they were a bunch of "motherfucking Nurse Nightingales." Into which of their own orifices they could shove the glass thermometers they brandished night and day. The veteran white-hats reminded their young colleagues that vicious language was an occupational hazard. Whether it was a boozy 3:00 a.m. car wreck or a miscalculated pool dive, ludicrous misfortune had banged its gavel. Never again would ward patients stand on their own. Never again would they be as free as they'd been. After a few months at County General biting down on that truth, many of them decayed into the sullenest of people.

Like theirs, Gordon's body remained a hothouse for infections. Several of them cooked him in fevers registering over one hundred five degrees. But that's where the comparison ended. He was no longer that ward misanthrope liable to berate hospital staff for doing what they'd been trained. No sooner had they checked his pulse after he had weathered some foul bacterium or another then he was asking with an impish grin how to get a hot-fudge sundae smuggled into the joint. He had shed the brooding fatalism that had enveloped him after he was rushed into that iron lung with no breath. That sort of accomplishment was exceptional around here.

Pretty soon, his personal effects were bundled into a container, and not because he was "hopeless" anymore. Gordon had done it.

County General discharged him nine months after he'd checked in. Though still paralyzed below the shoulders, he was frisky for the homecoming that every physician besides Risser had squawked was unthinkable. Showing up the MDs as sort of group thinking, negative nancies was his winnable war.

Attendants strapped Gordon into another Schaeffer ambulance amidst the planetary topsy-turvy of July 1941. New York Yankees outfielder Lou Gehrig was dead, German troops had massed on the Soviet border, and Gordon would be going home on the highway of the future—the just-christened Arroyo Seco Parkway linking Los Angeles with Pasadena. After the rear doors shut, they beeped the horn for the nurses waving in the hospital driveway and pressed the accelerator. Eastward they went, transporting the boy to a modest rented house on Laurel that was new to him.

Everybody waiting inside knew that his Marshall nosedive had consigned his family here. No matter. The euphoria of the movement provided temporary amnesia and an excuse to party. Hearty applause burst out as his gurney was carted up the steps of the baby blue house. Lining the entry were friends and relatives crammed into the living room for the sweaty homecoming. "Welcome back, kid!" they gushed. "See how prayer works?" Or, "You hot dog, we knew you'd fight your way out." Most of the table space was occupied by gifts. The rest Rose piled with plates of steaming roast beef, Gordon's favorite, and other snacks. The guest of honor barely had time for six bites, what with all the well-wishers mussing his hair and beaming like pirates. Alive. He felt so fucking alive.

Just as his accident upended the family, his presence back in Sierra Madre precipitated a rearrangement of its quarters. Rose and Lee's first act had been to convert the airy, first floor living room into an infirmary that they euphemistically tabbed "Gordon's room." What the guests that day saw, necessity had compelled. The boy was still too delicate for Lee to carry to the second-story bedroom, and they lacked space up there for him, anyway. Downstairs, conversely, was wide open. Around him were the provisions of his home care to keep him alive. Glass cabinets were stuffed with cotton balls, gauze, hypodermic needles, catheters, and pills. Near them were oxygen tanks, carbon dioxide canisters, and the sponge-rubber mattress for a special adjustable bed, much of it inscribed with brand names like Owl Drugs and Western Surgical Supply Company. To Lee's ongoing disgust, the Motion Picture Relief Fund had subsidized this MASH unit, and he'd vowed to work even harder to reimburse it. Once the area was organized, he and Rose adorned it with their own conceptions of earthly protection. She hung a ceramic Virgin Mary and a portrait of a winged baby Jesus on the wall behind her son's bed. Lee opted for a militaristic motif, hanging an imitation Winchester rifle off the curtain rack and a model warplane painted with shark teeth from the ceiling.

The most discernible result of Gordon's release, though, was Rose's desertion of her marital bed. Not that she'd wanted to. But she'd grown jittery that Gordon might suffer a convulsion or another emergency during the night while they were upstairs, oblivious. What if they didn't hear him wheezing? From his first day home, Rose insisted that she be within arm's reach of him when the lights went out. A cot in a small alcove about five feet wide was now where she sacked out. Her gauzy dab of privacy was a makeshift curtain tugged across the nook. This nocturnal shift gutted pillow talk and relations with Lee. Still, it was a sacrifice they both made. Each understood there are no single-victim accidents.

Gordon's pals had their own visions for re-acclimation, and fluffy pampering was not going to cut it. Within a month of his homecoming, they showed up at the Zahler house with liquor, cigarettes, yearbooks, and swing records. They aimed to rattle its foundation, suspecting Gordon wanted action, not misty-eyed congratulation, and they knew their boy. As the weekend parties flowered into larger, rowdier affairs, the kids became bolder about doing for Gordon what he couldn't do for himself. Which was just about everything. They lit his Lucky Strikes. They adjusted his neck brace settings. Gordon's perkiness, his parents observed, was reignited every time the gang knocked. Quickly, too, they caught on that he wanted them upstairs out of the way when they did. The firewater sloshed then—Harper's with lemon wedges, Canadian Club, Tanqueray gin, and fizzy seventy-two-ounce beers. Clouds of smoke twirled overhead every time. Some of the guests paired off to French kiss on vacant chairs, others for clopping dance steps. Only able to rotate his head slightly at first, Gordon had to pick his spots in the mayhem. Usually that meant him retelling a limerick, daring a cutie there to dive under his bedcovers, or having one of them put a straw to his lips to get him drunker.

The hangouts were merry and boisterous, themed with ribald jokes and beer-money collections, but they were never carefree or without stunned glances. Gordon's troop, which included the ex-Marshall Tarzans and other former classmates, was dumbfounded by how much his accident had enfeebled him. His head, gingerly propped up on a pillow, was the most noticeable difference. It loomed grotesquely over a body that appeared to have gone on a hunger strike. His whippet-like torso, in fact, cast such a passive ruffle under the sheets that you weren't sure if his lower extremities made it out of County General with him. His plumbing was shot to hell, as well—an indwelling catheter and shiny bedpan where he did his business. Apart from his colorful mouth, nothing functioned on its own accord. From his clavicle down, he was mere bone and gristle. Limbs in perpetual motion before October 29 rested listlessly on the mattress. Hands that had dragged Gordon into all manner of trouble before had also begun their own evolution, bony fingers curving inward into peculiar claws. Girls shaken by them might've seen them again in night terrors.

When the chance presented itself, his parents tried calming the teenagers spooked by the before-and-after comparisons. In doing so, they never expressed their own internal trepidation: that Gordon's party-mob would eventually forget about him as able-bodied pursuits—camping trips, school sports, backseat hanky-panky—enticed them away. County General had cautioned them about this phenomenon of reconnection and forsaking. Best, they said, that Gordon befriend other crippled kids if he desired lasting companionship.

Again, Gordon's individualism made mincemeat of standard expectations. The-ring-around-the-bed festivities became the equivalent of a neighborhood clubhouse assembled for a higher purpose. His folks ignored the adolescent drinking and grab-ass, and his outgoing chums never stopped showing up. Something uncanny about him—his irrepressible wit, that livewire fearlessness, his refusal to mope—

kept him as popular as ever with the old crowd. The apple-cheeked boys in their souped-up cars peeled rubber when they left for the evening, but they always came back (often with contraband tucked in their waistband). Gordon was a convalescing partner-in-crime only a jackass would ditch. With buddies around, he lost interest in the grown-ups' conversations about him on the periphery. Head at forty-five degrees, he jabbered about adventures past and planned as if his legs were asleep. As far as Rose and Lee were concerned, the carousing was aromatic therapy so long as Gordon remained the focus. When he sassed them for throwing his friends out at midnight, they'd wink at each other. Hope budded from the strangest soil.

* * *

SILVER LININGS LIKE THESE would've surpassed their utility as touching distraction had the Zahlers been able to melt the silver down into coinage to pay off their medical bills. Those never took a day off. Now that they were at legal crossroads, they had decisions to make. They could instruct their lawyer, Maurice Rose, to terminate the settlement discussions with the Pasadena school district and prepare for trial. Or, they could take the district's insulting offer and be done with the school and *him*. He'd hit one bull's-eye with Marshall's negligent gym program and had been weasel-like ever since. You couldn't choke an honest answer out of him. Rose hoped to fire him after Normalouise's father, a Spring Street insurance executive, advised her that their smooth-talking representative was the wrong guy to stake their claim. His forte was defending corporations, not litigating personal injury cases. Rose broached the topic of a replacement with Lee, but he snarled in opposition. Flip-flopping attorneys midstream, he said, was a recipe for defeat. They'd stick with their choice, even if they had to hold their noses. More and more, the two bickered behind closed doors over conquering dilemmas like this, and more and more a thick silence raw in meaning hung afterward.

In their first meetings, Maurice had been cocksure about their odds to rope in the whole two hundred thousand dollars despite the immunity statutes. Between Marshall's dilapidated springboard and its slack oversight, proving the school's liability would be a snap. The damages sought were so colossal, the hospital invoices so steep that the Zahlers had agreed to the fat commission Maurice negotiated for himself if they prevailed. A pretrial settlement would net him twenty-five percent of the award, a successful jury verdict thirty percent. The attorney said this was his standard rate. No family discounts existed. His office had overhead to bankroll just like Lee's studio employers.

After Gordon was released from County General, Maurice Rose's certainty receded into a less strident enthusiasm. Lee rebuked him to stop playing coy, so their representative backpedaled. He was no longer sure he could sway a jury with the facts. Evidence of the school's disregard for its charges was not as damning as he'd believed. Clouding matters further, doctors whose professional opinions the court depended on were staunch that Gordon would die. If not now, soon. That consensus stiffened the district's resolve. It was too shrewd to approve one deal only to face a wrongful death suit afterward if the physicians were right. Maurice's advice: settle.

With that, Lee and Rose realized they'd been hosed and maybe hustled. They'd been outmaneuvered by the school district's attorney and misled by their own. Later it would surface that Maurice Rose was cronies with lawyers from the school board's underwriter, the Traveler's Insurance Company. Had he played the sides off against each other so *he* couldn't lose? Either way, the options were bleak. The Zahlers could accept the district's take-it-or-leave it offer of fifteen thousand dollars or gamble on Maurice in a trial he was ambivalent that he could win. They mulled their choices until instinct and logic dovetailed. In September 1941, they opted for guaranteed money that provided temporary relief without any justice.

Minus their litigator's three-thousand-seven-hundreds-and-fifty-dollar share, they deposited eleven thousand, two hundred, and nineteen dollars into their savings account. The district threw my grandfather a supplemental two thousand, five hundred dollars as Gordon's guardian, but most of that was predesignated for County General. All told, the Zahlers walked away with eight cents for every dollar Maurice Rose's brilliance was supposed to lasso. Lee's slimeball opinion of attorneys remained unbent.

And so it went. There would be progress in one area, and just as hopes bobbed, a destructive event punctured it. It was as if an undertow was determined to drown them. For a spell, fortunes burned brighter. With Gordon home, Christmas 1941, while fuzzed by Pearl Harbor and the smoldering of world war, was better than the Christmas before it. Lee's surprise present to him was one he never imagined giving. He arranged a slow-speed ride around downtown Sierra Madre in a leased ambulance. This way, Gordon could get a good look at town and its landmarks without the town returning the favor. Having his own buddies gape at him was excruciating by itself, he'd told his dad. He didn't need the old ladies, who'd pick up the phone over a noisy squirrel, blabbering about him, too.

There were already enough novelties around, one of them named Jenny. The austere, big-boned nurse from Sweden had taken a leave of absence at County General to care for Gordon on weekdays. Someone with his proclivities, she'd said, required professionals. With her ashen hair tied up in a severe bun, Jenny had a stony demeanor about doing tasks her way. "Gor-dun," she would say, sponge bathing him or prepping an injection, a little Greta Garbo in her enunciation, *"I van you to vurk with me."* A riotously funny Scottish woman whom Gordon dug even more substituted when Jenny had other obligations.

Rose's fatty home cooking helped Gordon pack on a few needed pounds. Breads, roasts, goulashes, tapiocas, soups: her culinary dexterity had been crowd-pleasers since she was in New York cooking for her little brothers; some posited she could make grass clippings tasty. Fluky neurological bounce-back also permitted Gordon to regain small, if twitchy, movement in his left arm by contracting his shoulder muscles. His neck was responding, too. He could now crane his head in both directions. Once in a while, if something provoked him and his legs spasmed, his mouth showed it had caught up. It'd blurt what nobody realistic thought was possible. "I'm *going* to get up, someday. Ain't planning on being here my whole life."

Yet when America marched to war, paralysis still glued Gordon in bed. There was no sweeping aside his blankets so he could take a quaking step toward what he'd been. On the contrary, conflict abroad edged him into a second mental grounding. Friends visiting the Zahler house a few months after FDR's "there's nothing to fear" speech no longer donned V-neck sweaters and pleated cotton trousers. Drafted or enlisted, they'd exchanged them for Army khaki and Navy black, the girls smitten with the uniforms. Visually, they appeared to be teenagers posing as soldiers, but they were shipping overseas to fight the Germans and Japanese as some of their fathers had done in the smoky foxholes during World War I. Gordon, wearing his best fake smile, wished them well knowing he could contribute zilch as they trained to shoot rifles, load cannons, and parachute from airplanes. He could do nothing except be rotated in and out of fresh pajamas, flannel usually.

Everywhere there were reminders, from Muriel's narration of the preparations she'd seen to blackouts in case Japanese bombers decided to firebomb a pipsqueak township. Sierra Madre was doing its share for Old Glory; Gordon could hear the background racket of hammers and bulldozers constructing barracks at parks, schools, and empty land. Most every boy around was part of the Allied war machine by 1942. Those too young to join often just fibbed about their age. Ladies eager for patriotic tasks got jobs at defense plants. "Imagine," my mother wrote Steve, a boyfriend with the Navy's twenty-first Pursuit Squadron, "women working amidst mass production!"

Muriel, who had assumed she would be in college rather than home scribbling letters, was adrift in despondency herself. Trying to stay active, she'd found work at J.W. Robinson's department store at Seventh and Grand in downtown Los Angeles, singing for customers. After hours, she made conversation with the soldiers her parents invited home for dinner and attended USO dances. In her letter to Steve, she confessed her blues in a life that had "utterly changed." *Gordon's predicament and lots of other things have really broken my heart. The doctors still have no hope for him—even though I do believe in miracles—and it hurts. The other day Gordon remarked that the minute he gets up he is going to join the Navy. And knowing Gordy, he would... By the way, he was sixteen on the tenth of this month.*

Steve never read a word of the dispatch. Not even the last part where she disparaged the notion of being a "war bride" so she could be "a little original," perhaps for him. The post office returned her note marked "service suspended," Army lingo for a member killed in action. Muriel remembered that parlance when it rematerialized soon on a letter she'd sent to Al, the beau she'd last seen in San Francisco. Japanese bombers attacking his weapons depot in the tropics had arrived there ahead of the West Coast mailbag.

CHAPTER SEVEN: DARK SKIES

THE CAR, AS WITH everything in Rose's world, was not as durable as it appeared. The sedan that T-boned it in downtown Pasadena crumpled the passenger door of the whaleback vehicle as if it were a flimsy can of tuna. Rose's upper body absorbed the brunt force the car's chassis could not, which knocked her sideways and practically unconscious. Bleeding from the head, she was whisked to St. Luke's Hospital, where Gordon had been, with two primary injuries: an ugly gash across her scalp and a wrenched neck. An X-ray showed why Rose's pain almost caused her to faint: she'd suffered a hairline crack in one of her upper vertebrae. Wasn't March 1942 swell?

The doctors treated her the best they could, wrapping her neck in a small cast before sending her home with heavy-duty painkillers and recommendations. Given the severity of her fracture, she'd need to recuperate in bed for a month to six weeks. Rose, never much for cussing, must've wanted to holler right there on the examining table, "No fucking way. I can't be out for two days. I have a crippled son." Then find someone to help, the doctors said. A split vertebra needs time and rest to mend. The irony must've burned as much as the throbbing.

Lee, professional musician, had to moonlight as a caretaker to two homebound patients, though Gordon's part-time nurse carried some of the load. Directors impatient for his scores and cue sheets would have to hold their water. Lee couldn't be their music man in between busing food trays, dispensing pills, changing pillowcases, and emptying bedpans. The Motion Picture Relief Fund once more footed the hospital bill in his stead. The undertow had, once again, made landfall.

∗   ∗   ∗

NOB HILL, SAN FRANCISCO, turn of the century: the narcotics escorting Rose into REM sleep hauled her back to where murder and despair that had lasted a generation seemed to be now recurring.

Rose was a tyke of four-and-a-half when the San Andreas Fault ruptured with Old Testament intensity. The "Great" Quake of 1906 was a subsurface Leviathan that killed thousands, reducing much of the grand city to fire and rubble. So ferocious were the tectonics that morning that Rose's father, Maurice, had to leap from the stoop of his Oakland home with Rose's little brother, Sonny, in his arms. It was that or risk being devoured under the buckling roof. Everyone survived it, but there would be no rebuild from disaster for one simple reason: the Rosenbergs, led by Joseph, refused to supply any meaningful assistance. Sympathetic as they might've been that Maurice's family of five was now homeless, principle—or, rather, hideous vanity of the upwardly ambitious—blocked them from reversing their earlier decision to disown him. Maurice's willful decision to wed Sarah "Sonya" Carr—a pretty, vivacious, and full-figured Russian émigré (by way of Canada)—had been too humiliating a stain on their reputation. And the stain hadn't faded. Maurice, in their view, had polluted the family gene pool with his selfishness. He'd picked love over kin, so they'd picked money over him. Natural disasters, it turns out, can sway crystal chandeliers, just not the heads of the nouveau riche.

Maurice, with just the clothes on his back, vamped the best he could. He brought the wife that the Rosenbergs disdained as a hoi polloi peasant and their three youngsters to a jury-rigged tent encampment at Golden Gate Park, where thousands of other traumatized city dwellers with no place to sleep had gone as a last resort. They'd resided there for a miserable year in the damp and cold, surrounded by infectious illnesses and grubby neighbors, miles from where his brothers and sisters gorged themselves on caviar and profits. When a cousin he admired described the opportunities of El Paso, Texas, Maurice said, why not? A clean slate far away from here sounded like the answer to his dreams.

It was: he and the American Southwest fit like hand in glove. Before long, Maurice had reinvented himself from family black sheep to prosperous merchant. The general store he owned trafficked in basic goods and commodities that he was continually replenishing. El Paso was a dusty, low-slung border town with a freewheeling ethos and interesting characters. As the gunfire echoes made clear, battles from the Mexican revolution were just across the way. Nobody would confuse this sagebrush town for San Francisco, but it wasn't tent city, either. Maurice's jingling pockets financed good times. His family had a house, a chauffeur, and a future shorn of betrayal. Sociable, deal-minded Maurice also knew how to make friends. Sometimes, when he wasn't eluding the American military or leading raids in towns named Tierra Blanca and Chihuahua, rebel legend Pancho Villa stopped by Maurice's place on Montana Street for drinks and laughs.

The ink on Maurice's storybook redemption was almost dry when February, 1915 smeared it. R.E. "Red" Mullen was a dark-eyed, red-haired stranger who strolled into Maurice's store eager to do business with him. *Nice to make your acquaintance, Mister Rosenberg. Fine shop you have here.* The industrious newcomer full of blandishments had a proposition. He needed a buyer for the assortment of high quality animal hides that had come into his possession. If Maurice wanted to inspect them for himself, all he had to do was let Mullen drive him to the wooded clearing nearby where he'd stashed them for safekeeping. Fishy story and all, Maurice knew a bargain when he heard one. Taking his coat, he left. When he failed to return and his family got worried, Villa reportedly formed a search party to find him. Four days later, trench diggers shoveling dirt along the Rio Grande River noticed boot tips protruding from the silt. Beneath them was Maurice's mutilated, bullet-riddled corpse. The good-natured "junk merchant" had been a dead man from the moment he clasped hands with the stranger.

Mullen was as crafty a fugitive as he'd been a killer, evading police dragnets and fleeing to a boarding house in Juarez, Mexico, about ten miles away. Nabbed by Mexican police, the twenty-something was turned over to El Paso authorities. They'd initially assumed a robbery-gone-bad was the motive. Evidence showed that Mullen had stolen some of Maurice's baubles, including a gold-encrusted watch. But, suspiciously, he'd left other valuable jewelry untouched. Why he'd stooped to such a petty crime mystified detectives. Mullen spent most of his time as a shady arms dealer selling munitions to both sides of the Mexican conflict. Facts and intent clashed.

El Paso's newspapers sensationalized the murder trial as one of the most complex and demented in local annals. In saloons and barbershops, everyone was chattering about it. Once the proceedings began, townsfolk elbowed one another for courtroom seats to hear the wicked details in person. How Maurice was forced to shovel his own grave, how he had been savaged almost beyond recognition. Mullen amped up the intrigue himself, acting nonchalant, chewing gum, and smoking his briar pipe as if he were contesting a jaywalking charge instead of homicide.

El Paso's district attorney had kept a secret weapon to wipe the smirk from Mullen's insolent, young face. A pair of eyewitnesses in Maurice's store when Mullen had tricked him was prepared to testify against the "coldblooded killer." Of the two, the most convincing was a fifteen-year-old schoolgirl. She whimpered on the stand when she glimpsed Mullen at the defendant's table, cavalier in his blue serge suit. No one could forget what she said. "He left with that man (over there) and I did not see him again until his body was found." After she spoke, the quivering witness was such a basket case that she had to be sent to another city to regain her sanity.

That girl was Rose Zahler.

Another overflow crowd was on hand for the jury's decision. When it returned a guilty verdict, Mullen whipped his leg over a chair for melodramatic effect. On April 1, 1915, he was sentenced to a maximum of thirty-five years in prison. Quizzed if he planned to appeal, Mullen was his usual cryptic self, proclaiming himself satisfied with the outcome. "What do you think I am?" he told the court. "A fool?"

Thanks to him, Sonya had three fatherless children to support on a dead-husband's savings. What was she to do after that money was gone? Her rich California in-laws would do nothing, so San Francisco was out. Relocating east to New York, where her older brother lived, was the sole destination that'd have them.

Alexander Carr was a peripatetic kid committed to being a somebody someday. His family, previously known as the Karchefsky's, had immigrated from Rumni, Russia to Winnipeg, Canada, but the boy wasn't done moving. Carr ran away at twelve to pursue his calling on any stage willing to pay him. His meandering path found him dancing in Tennessee, crooning in St. Paul, and, according to *Ancestry. com*, even "working the back half of an elephant in [a] vaudeville" act. After he settled in New York, Carr channeled his experiences and ability into a burlesque sketch that critics applauded. Next he composed a revue titled *Wine, Women and Song*, which, incidentally, described his after-hour hobbies. In 1913, Carr crushed it again playing Mawruss Perlmutter in the *Potash and Perlmutter* comedy routine on Broadway.

Offstage, Carr projected the same foghorn voice and ostentatious style as he did on it. Bigheaded as he could be, he was too much of a stand-up guy to let his star-crossed sister and her brood go under. He paid their rent for a Brooklyn apartment and other expenses, and then showed them the sights of Manhattan, his luxury Fifth Avenue apartment top of the list. But he could only do so much. Sonya, despondent about Maurice's killing, sank into widowhood growing fat, lazy, and loopy. She didn't know how to be a breadwinner. Her children handled the scenery change better. Harold, her youngest, attended public school dutifully. Sonny, his thirteen-year-old brother, did as well. One day, though, he told his mother he was ending his formal education. Just like that, he'd persuaded Lewis Selznick of World Pictures, a feature-film production and distribution outfit, to hire him as his reception clerk. Any objections that Sonya might've registered were silenced by the precious dollars Sonny would bring home. Rose, her oldest, meantime, excelled in the classroom; tearing through every book she could check out at the corner library. When not there, she was in the apartment doing most of the cooking and cleaning, acting as a mother-by-default.

Brooklyn then could be dog-eat-dog, where people in brick tenements coexisted cheek by jowl while trying not to freeze in the bone-aching winters. Rose wouldn't have lived anyplace else! It was there she met a charismatic musician nuts for cigars, George Gershwin (his professional idol), and the Dodgers of Ebbets Field. Leo Arthur Zahler, or Lee for short, wasn't your average East Coast loudmouth talking game he didn't have. When Rose met him, he'd already completed a rough-and-tumble apprenticeship as a ragtime pianist in the city's Nickelodeons. Dancing images of cowboys and sheiks projected onto the walls foreshadowed the rise of America's cinema-industrial complex. Dazzled crowds asked: *what will they think of next?* Lee was animated and opinionated, squat and no-nonsense, with long fingers that flew effortlessly across the ivories. The Nickelodeons thick with cockroaches, drunks, cheap instruments, and tightwad owners were his basic training. Skills honed, he wasn't in there long. Music publishers along New York's Tin Pan Alley, in need of catchy movie tunes they could sell as sheet music, hired him and other young talents to compose at a factory-like clip.

Against Brooklyn's clanking streets, the musician and the bookworm, different as could be, swooned for each other. Lee, seven years older, looked to be closing in on middle age in his late twenties. He dyed his premature white hair blond, slicking it back with a part down the middle. He had an oval head, a five-foot-eight fire-hydrant frame, and a black trench coat he wore everywhere. Even around goofball friends on Coney Island, Lee seldom smiled with unrestrained glee. Rose kept tight rein of her emotions, as well. She'd inherited her mother's fleshy limbs, not her glamorous, high cheekbones or once-effervescent personality. Instead, she was a reedy, studious girl whose wide nose and pronounced brow suggested she was still growing into her face. Skittish eyes and the dowdy, woolen dresses she favored gave her a wallflower's silhouette. Her grace and inner-grit, though, were more than sufficient to put Lee on bended knee.

In marrying her in 1920, Lee wed a young woman fleeing her Jewish bloodline. The borough where her family resided boiled in anti-immigrant hostility. Older Jews were taunted as "Christ-killers." Younger ones lived wary of random beatings and rainstorms of spittle. Sonya's clan, never devout in the first place, felt embattled enough. So, they all dropped "berg" from their last name and *voila*, Rosenberg became Ross. Rose afterward reshuffled her spirituality further. She renounced the inherited faith that she didn't practice and immersed herself into then New Age Christian Science. Lee's denominational history was more linear. He was born of Jewish extraction in Budapest, Hungary, and lived as a steadfast agnostic in America.

Rose delivered a tubby-cheeked baby girl, Muriel Bernice, a year after their lakeside honeymoon. The year after that, Lee sold his Model-T and booked his family onto a sleeper train to Los Angeles. Tin Pan Alley composers were leaving in droves for "Hollywoodland" to perform and write music as accompaniments to silent movies, all the rage across a prospering country. Boosters claimed it was seventy degrees year-round out there—a mountains-to-beach oasis whose unsullied air was a cure-all for alcoholics, the tuberculosis stricken, and the disconsolate.

They moved into a comfortable, stucco house in mid-city's Carthay Circle, which was later subsumed into the Miracle Mile district near ritzy Hancock Park. Much earlier, in the Flapper Age, there was little mind-blowing about the flatland dotted with citrus orchards and gurgling oil derricks except its proximity to filmmaking. Just after suppertime on February 10, 1926, Rose gave birth to a son at Hollywood's Benedict Maternity Hospital. With his first gulp of air, the Zahlers had the configuration they'd craved: a girl and a baby boy growing up in a metropolis high on sunny possibility. Gordon Robert, in a wink, morphed from a curly-haired toddler with his arms around a pet collie into a pixie-eared little kid into everything he shouldn't be. At eleven, he'd already closed the height gap on his big sister. Lee, spiffy in an argyle vest and white knickers de rigueur in the movie world, boasted about him to his studio colleagues. The kid with the squinting, jack-o-lantern grin was developing a ballplayer's physique. "Yep," he'd say, "those legs are going to take Gordon far."

Lee's parents, Joseph and Anna, soon joined them in Los Angeles, tired of the East. They colonized their son's backyard guesthouse, Anna cooking to pass the time and her husband, bald as an eraser, arguing with Lee that Hungary, the Zahlers' ancestral seat, was nobler than pushy America. Both died before World War II.

Joseph wasn't supposed to have wound up like this. He was supposed to have fulfilled his role in Budapest as one of the genius boys of the last century. Lee's father had descended from a long line of gentlemen farmers with acreage in what is now probably the Slovak Republic. Theater was also in the family DNA. Among its most notable performers was Magda Zahler, one of Europe's marquis stage dancers, renowned for her elegant pirouettes and saucy photographs posed on divans and in giant fingers. But Joseph towered above them all, a child prodigy who spoke and wrote five languages before he reached twenty. At the University of Budapest medical school, the thin-lipped, prematurely balding student finished top of his class. Educated sorts were sure he'd be the most revered doctor ever to practice along the Danube River. After he wed a comely actress, Joseph's superior life was bankable destiny.

The Austro-Hungarian military, in need of fresh recruits to draft, ran its tasseled saber through that eventuality. Joseph, a pacifist devoted to healing people, refused to join the army as a conscientious objector. He wasn't bayoneting anybody. His parents, uncertain what to do, could only think to ship him, his wife, Anna, and their kids—one-year-old Lee among them—to America "on vacation." The Hungarian military wasn't amused upon his return, and threw him in prison. This, it said, was what happened when anybody—including a scion of a wealthy family—shirked their patriotic duty. The Zahlers, dignified people deep into arts and education, had to pander to baser instincts. They bribed a pair of jailhouse officials to spring him. Afterwards, in 1884, they hustled Joseph and his family onto a second steamship to New York City. The superior European life they had mapped for him had gone poof.

Joseph still hoped to be a doctor worthy of his prodigal roots. It wasn't to be. Soon after he landed, an officious bureaucrat near Ellis Island informed him that his Hungarian degree failed to qualify him to practice stateside. America's academic standards, the clerk said, were more exacting than Europe's. Joseph's only recourse was repeating medical school. Fuming, maybe even shouting across the counter, Joseph declared he'd never bow down to such arrogance. Mindless labor was better that having to relearn what he already knew. Instead of curing the ill, he'd spend his life—often bitterly and homesick—cutting patterns in dressmaking and working in insurance.

For their first twenty years in California, Lee and Rose severed the carry-over pain from their folks' pain and blood, enjoying freedom from baggage in a place where umbrellas were ornamental. Los Angeles, it was clear, definitely agreed with Rose. Now a wife and mother, she appeared a different woman than her Brooklyn self. She'd shed a good twenty-five pounds, cut her wavy hair short, and smiled confidently in pictures, a wallflower no more. Moving east, to the foothills of Sierra Madre, further enhanced the newfound sparkle about her. Oh, the times they had and the people they met. Half their block, it seemed, always found excuses to come by to kowtow to her uncle, Alexander Carr, when he popped in to hold court about his life under the lights. He'd relocated to Hollywood himself now. Some days Rose must've wanted to pinch herself.

But then Gordon got hurt, the hospital bills gashed their savings, and her brother Sonny, everybody's crutch, was shot stone dead. The obliteration of his Cinderella life just went to show that lighting can strike twice, no matter the state, regardless of open wounds.

*   *   *

CHARACTERS TROTTED THROUGH HIS dreams. He edited scenes on packed trains. Imagined dialogue burned in his ears as he noshed hot dogs from street vendors. The longer Sonny apprenticed in the film business, the surer he was. He wanted a life in film. He'd die with that conviction.

After an entry-level job clerking for World Pictures, theater-chain owner Stanley Mastbaum hired the kid to sit in the audience. His assignment: chart people's reactions to what they saw on screen. Before his voice had dropped, Manhattan's Mark Strand Theatre at

Forty-Seventh Street and Broadway scooped him up as an assistant manager for its luxurious, three-thousand-seat movie palace. Universal Pictures, headhunting young talent itself, cut in line for him. Before long he was in California, just beating his sister, Rose, and her new musician husband. The eager beaver with piercing blue eyes, diminutive height, and a head of tight, black curls was sixteen. His job? Only personal assistant to studio founder, Carl Laemmle. Staffers called their paternalistic boss "Uncle Carl," but in this instance Laemmle may have been Sonny's relation. Laemmle wanted him locked down as a keeper for his growing operation. His nephew had smarts, ambition, and character worthy of an executive position. The same went for Sonny's roommate and chum, Irving Thalberg. Ultimately, Thalberg chose a studio-management gig that would make him a name brand in Hollywood while Sonny received what he craved most: the opportunity to direct.

During the Roaring Twenties, he oversaw fifty Universal movies— romantic comedies, madcap sports sendups, serious westerns—in the Cahuenga Pass. He enjoyed hits and suffered bombs. He adapted a Sinclair Lewis novella, helped discover the "It Girl" (the hyper-sexualized Clara Bow), and perfected his craft as a zealous auteur. *April Fool, College Love,* and *The Leather Pushers* confirmed Laemmle an excellent judge of ability.

Sonny's thirties, conversely, were fraught with personal sinkholes. He filed for bankruptcy. Then he had to recover from a frightful accident in which he was thrown from a filming tower by spooked horses in, honest to god, "Killer Canyon." Meanwhile, Universal's emphasis on quality productions—*Phantom of the Opera, All Quiet on the Western Front, Dracula*—and other factors sunk the company into the red. Laemmle was ousted in 1936, his landmark studio sold to cost-cutting Standard Capital Company; three years later he suffered a fatal heart attack. Sonny, though without his mentor, regained his footing. He wed Audrene Brier, an actress-dancer with golden tresses and chipmunk cheeks whom he'd once cast for a part. Newly married, he expanded into producing and talent management. Later in the decade, he and Audrene relocated to Europe, where Sonny produced films for MGM and Columbia. Once Hitler threatened to light the entire continent aflame, they returned home to Van Nuys.

Instead of the directorial chair, Sonny ensconced himself on the southern fringe of downtown Los Angeles on a parcel that's now a Jack in the Box franchise. He needed a break from moviemaking, so Laemmle's wunderkind became co-owner of a rag-making textile plant. It was on Cotton Products Inc.'s factory floor, a few months shy of Gordon's accident, that Sonny's future murderer introduced himself. Maurice Briggs was a twenty-six-year-old smart aleck with a mysterious past and a hunky jaw. He wanted a job, and Sonny had an opening.

At first blush, he was a helluva find. Briggs' output within months won his promotion from worker-bee to "foreman of the washing machines." A lusty sort, he also turned the head of an attractive, pouty-lipped colleague named Susan. Before you could hum *Only Fools Rush In*, they wed and she was pregnant. But domestic bliss never achieved lift. During a quarrel, Briggs cold-cocked her and shredded off her clothes. Susan threw him out, but the wife-beater, now bunked in a flophouse, was resolute about getting her back. He miscalculated. Susan enlisted a divorce attorney, tried faking a miscarriage, and pretended that she was in love with another man. Briggs believed none of it. He began stalking her, pleading for forgiveness, and attributing his temper to work stress. Again, Susan told him to vamoose.

The crazy in him refused. He drank harder, stewing over an abysmal life in which his happiness never lasted longer than a jar of mayonnaise. The abandoned orphan, onetime bank-robber, and violent drifter had blown his chance. He'd neither be proud father nor redeemed husband. Briggs knew who was at fault, and it wasn't staring back at him in the mirror. It was Sonny Ross, who'd just fired him for showing up to work pie-eyed; the same Sonny who later sympathetically rehired him, only to terminate him a second time. In Brigg's depraved logic, the Hollywood big man must've stolen Susan for himself.

"You're not going to be around much longer," he warned Sonny in early 1941, a pocketknife on him. Nobody took the lout's threat as a time bomb, despite the LAPD later arresting him on a minor charge after shooing him off the property. That harassment accelerated his plot. On February 25, 1941, Briggs cashed his unemployment check at a Main Street pawnshop. With it, he purchased a .25–.35-caliber Winchester rifle and strode back to where he'd met Susan. At Cotton Products, he stashed the weapon and ammo behind a side door. Hours dripped by, black rage percolated. At 10:00 p.m. he rapped on the side entrance. Politely, he asked for a moment with you-know-who. "What does he want now?" Sonny muttered to a group of workers. "I'll be back, girls."

Actually, he wouldn't. Briggs grabbed the rifle he had lying in wait and squeezed off a point-blank bullet into his imagined enemy's thorax. Sonny screamed at a macabre octave, staggering backward. Without blinking, Briggs reportedly let off a second round into a man probably already dead before he hit the cold factory floor. Two dozen employees, Susan among them, witnessed the muzzle-flash butchery. Some darted for cover into the bathroom. Others shrieked or fainted. "Oh, I just killed a guy. Better call the cops," Briggs remarked to a passerby minutes later as he casually walked away in a sport coat and black shirt. In the back pocket of the deceased, LAPD detectives soon tugged out the document that drove the knife deeper. It was a movie production contract. Sonny had planned to return to his professional love, until Briggs' rage stole everything.

Los Angeles had just been handed a scandalous murder drama that Briggs perpetuated as his own press agent. "Am I sorry I did it?" he roared. "Yeah, I'm sorry I *can't* do it again. I'm ready for the gas or whatever they give you in California." Briggs, cigarette in teeth, pencil moustache under nose, had adapted a tough guy veneer. He admitted to police that he intended to murder Sonny ten days earlier, until second thoughts about using his hands delayed it. His Winchester took care of that. Sonny's widow, Audrene, under a doctor's care and preparing to leave for Europe to insulate herself from the media circus, denounced Briggs' suggestion that her husband had been an adulterer. Exploitative hogwash from a madman, she cried. "He was the kindest man I knew, a man who…said there was good in everyone if you brought it out."

Briggs might've been the exception. He refused to testify at the coroner's inquest, after which he was charged with murder aforethought. Story after story ran from late February 1941 into March. After once sneering he wanted "no mercy," he said he wasn't guilty. By July, he reversed course, pleading insanity to avoid the gas chamber that he'd jeered before. At trial, he reached for heartstrings. When he'd learned about his divorcing wife's abortion (an "illegal operation" in those days), he said he'd purchased the firearm to kill himself. In his suicidal gloom, for reasons he was unable to clarify, he decided to mow down the one person who'd given him a break. The jury saw through his bogus contrition. They voted for his state execution.

California Governor Culbert Olson, a New Deal Democrat, granted Briggs a thirty-day reprieve so Briggs could exhaust his legal remedies for executive clemency. He had. On August seventh, the doors at San Quentin opened. Briggs glanced around at the eyewitnesses present for his extermination. Unrepentant to the end, he mock-saluted them with an arm the prison guards had neglected to strap down. Minutes later, oversight corrected, Briggs' goodbye became his final act.

Rose wasn't anywhere near there to forgive or remember. Nor does it appear she attended any of the court proceedings, or followed what was the city's most scintillating Hollywood-connected murder. There was just shock, void, and repression. The horror of it was too much with a chronically ill teenager at home. The less spoken about it the better she told Muriel. Pray for all, hate no one, and know that "death" was mankind's confusion about transition into a velvet hereafter. "Trust the Lord," she'd say.

The cosmic tumblers knew how to spin, even with grim happenstance. Maurice Rosenberg and Sonny, his eldest son, were the first casualties of the undertow, or whatever pox was on their family. They were murdered at the same age (thirty-six), on nearly the same February day of the year, in an eerily similar manner: bullets discharged by killers capitalizing on their gullibility. Had the Nob Hill Rosenbergs not spurned them after the quake, the pair might've made it to their white-hair years with a twinkle in their eyes rather than pennies over them.

Again, Rose knew the score kept by this calendar. Males in the family had a running tendency to shine brilliantly before a gory death or slow kneel-down in the grave. If it wasn't her father, it was her son, and if it wasn't him, it was her brother. Alexander Carr was now a member of this thinning herd, too. His Hollywood film career never harnessed the same buzz as his Broadway heyday, and his personal affairs were messier. During the later half of the thirties, he'd spent much of his time searching for a wife who didn't want to be found. In 1938, Helen, a Ziegfeld Follies girl, gassed herself to death in a New York apartment, first making sure her bedroom door was sealed to protect her twelve-year-old daughter and dog. What the stage had given Carr it had now stolen, and he'd never recover. He'd be gone soon.

* * *

TAKING ALL THIS IN, flat on her back recovering from that cracked vertebrae, Rose knew *her* own challenge had crystallized. Gordon's survival was everything. Upon his puny shoulders rested a legacy more gothic than ascendant. He had to live beyond expectations, even if she had to die trying, because the undertow had sucked everyone else down.

CHAPTER EIGHT: SILLY ODDITIES

THE CASTS WERE FLYING at the house on Laurel. Just as Rose's was being sawed off, a lengthy immobilization was being arranged for Gordon. A full-body, Plaster of Paris wrap was slated for him after an operation at St. Luke's, where the Zahlers should've received a frequent-customer discount. Gordon's glass jaw of a spine still required fusing. Without the procedure, Dr. Risser predicted, a significant jarring could re-break his neck, this time lethally. Risser, supposedly, asked Gordon how he preferred to be soldered: in a V-like sitting position—awkward for sleep but better for action—or laid flat. Gordon voted for the "V." Without this reinforcement, there would be nothing keeping him upright. He'd slump forward like a jellyfish, if he ever made it to a chair.

Gordon's kidneys had their own agenda. They stopped functioning twelve days after the fusion operation, ratcheting his temperature up and spurring Lee to phone for an ambulance. Gordon was rushed back to St. Luke's, a cupola-tipped building inspiring thoughts of ancient Rome if you ignored the dirt-clod fields around it. Up in surgery, the doctors sawed off the cast and jump-started his kidneys. He recovered ahead of predictions. Two weeks later he was mummified in a neck-to-pelvis cast. There it would remain on him, scratchy and hot, for three *years* and ten months.

Back in Sierra Madre, the boy was still on the invisible margins of the bomb bursts and machine gun fire that had put his buddies into harm's way overseas. Listening to updates from the Motorola radio on his nightstand was as close as he got to World War II. Lee saw how glum this indoor imprisonment made him, this forced passivity. So he tacked up, on the wall opposite Gordon's bed, a large Rand McNally map of Europe. Any night he was home for dinner, Lee would sit with him while *CBS Radio* broadcasted updates from London, the Solomon Islands, and elsewhere. Based on the combat reports, Lee stuck black pins into the areas where the Axis was advancing, red ones for the Allies' position, all to stimulate debate about General Patton's master strategy. Understanding more than he said, Gordon pretended to be interested in the path of the attacks after the novelty was gone. From his father's voice, he knew the amateur battle diagram was his macho way of keeping his son's head in the world. Better to be distracted than sulk.

Strangely, Gordon owed his life to Adolph Hitler and Emperor Hirohito. Without their fascist aspirations, the infections that pecked at his organs probably would have finished him off before his cast was jettisoned. World conflict, in this respect, was his savior. Legions of wounded and maimed soldiers now depended on Western scientists to trail-blaze medicines for bacterial infections sustained on the battlefield. Penicillin, the world's first antibiotic, was their answer. Before its rollout, the paralyzed like Gordon were susceptibility on the half shell. Pathways created by bedsores, catheters, and fouled-up intestines permitted invaders free entry. Once inside, they did much of their destructive work incognito, since spinal-cord victims typically lose pain-sensitivity below their neurological dent. Mass-produced penicillin changed all that, dropping the mortality rate within years for them and injured GIs alike. Gordon, hence, was indebted to the drug, though maybe more to the Axis for necessitating it.

∗   ∗   ∗

His body, all the same, remained an unyielding need machine, and Rose insisted she be its lead mechanic. Whatever her own achy neck and other woes, she was the force in his room. Indeed, she might've aced a nursing exam, she was that fleet with a catheter, injections, and medicines. She'd already lopped in half the near hour it once took to prep Gordon for bed. Every night, weekend, and holiday, she was there, or ready to assist the nurses when one pair of hands in the reek of body fluids and teenage back talk wouldn't do. Tending to a son who'd never be healthy in any meaningful sense was what she was about. To know her history was to be positive of that.

Rebuilding Gordon's psyche was Part-1A in her vision for him. More than anything, she knew he needed to be reinserted into society. The four walls at the Laurel house, where he'd been bedridden for more than a year, was a shabby reflection of the planet outside. Rose, amiably as ever, suggested he try a reclining wheelchair they'd leased from Abbey Rents. "You could get some sun that way, darling, or a hamburger out with your friends. Benny could set it up."

Nope, he'd say. Not yet. Thus he stayed in bed, through lavender spring days and a sweltering Fourth of July, through bashes he might have attended and matinees he might've chuckled at if his fear of public humiliation, a fear ten feet tall, would have relented. Give him credit, nonetheless. His blarney about needing "just a little more time" or "not feeling up to it" was garlanded with persuasive lament.

At wit's end, Rose resorted to the clandestine. One evening in September, 1942, about a month after Maurice Briggs was executed at San Quentin, she spoke with her hand cupped over the phone. A surprise face was at their screen door the next morning. Gordon recognized him from his "y'alls" and "whatchas." There weren't too many Southerners in Sierra Madre, and definitely none like Father Eustace of Little Rock, Arkansas. At six-feet-seven, pretty-boy handsome, and literate to go with it, he had townsfolk sending him dueling dinner invitations. Exactly how he got tangled up in Gordon's mess no one can say. Somehow it must have been tied to his job at the Mater Dolorosa ("Mother of Sorrow") Monastery, where Sierra Madre's hilltop runs smack into the San Gabriels.

Inside the house, the sandbagging of Gordon commenced. He wanted to know why Father Eustace was there, and Eustace answered that Gordon must have heard about the big football game at Arcadia High School that day. "Yeah, so?" Gordon said. "So, let's git you up, cuz I'm taking *you* there with me. No hemming about it. Got to be back at the monastery for afternoon prayers." Gordon, tilted up in bed and writhing with his ego, said no thanks. Eustace didn't blink. "How about a rain check for next week's game, Father?" Eustace kept staring. "Oh, oh, I got a better idea!" Gordon said with a nervous titter. "We'll go see their grudge game, you know against Monrovia High. How's that strike ya?" Another misfire.

Eustace, there in gray civies, stood off while Gordon's parents hefted him out of his near-permanent pajamas. They then bundled him in a pair of baggy pants and a sweatshirt large enough to fit over the body cast. (Rose had furtively handpicked the ensemble that morning.) As she began combing his hair, Gordon woofed that he didn't care how he looked. He berated her and Lee as traitors for ambushing him like this, spitting out curse words he reserved for bantering friends. "Holy shit, you think this is fair, pulling a goddamn surprise?" His voice pitched with teary rage as he was cradled into a wheelchair, rolled down the driveway, and buckled into the front seat of Eustace's rusty, black Ford truck.

Before Gordon could fabricate another reason to exempt him, the truck was chugging south on Grandview Avenue, backfiring, just him and the monk. His folks had assumed they'd go along, too, but Eustace had convinced them that Gordon would be better off without them mollycoddling him with a sweater or hot cocoa in the view of the bleachers. Rose knew he was right, however it made her choke up. Watching her son going off without her, in fact, might have sent her into her preferred defense mechanism: vacuuming and cleaning the house with obsessive-compulsive disorder ferocity.

The particulars of the football outing have been lost to the years. What everybody recalls is that a change broke over Gordon in the weeks afterward. His paranoia of being singled out began sloughing away. A few jaunts later, he disciplined himself to look beyond the double takes trailing him. Some of his wild-child spirit slinked back, too. He now smiled wherever he went, be it on a mountain drive or at a brass band concert at Memorial Park. Letting scenery rub up against his skin bred a ticklish excitement in him, a new philosophy, as well. *Everything* was gravy compared with County General. If he could outlast pins drilled into his cranium, he could outlast the looky-loos.

By V-J Day, Gordon was outside regularly, whatever his fickle biology and a standing order to be steered wide of Marshall Jr. High. The sunshine was intoxicating. Hoping to make it more accessible, the Zahlers had Muriel's new boyfriend and one of his buddies build him a screened-in sun porch next to his room so he could inhale fresh air in view of Mount Wilson. That mountain meant a lot, both as grandeur and memory, and Gordon lounged deck-side still enamored with it. Father Eustace, sadly, probably never spent more than an afternoon there. Not long after dragging Gordon to that game, he was reassigned by the monks to the deep South. There he died abruptly, as if he'd completed his mission.

Part Two of Rose's reconstruction project involved schooling. Never much of a pupil to begin with, Gordon had been absent from the classroom for two and a half years when the calendar flopped over to 1943. It wasn't just him lagging behind academically. He'd been lapped. Peers too young for the draft were now in the second half of their junior year in high school. Gordon had all of six weeks as a ninth-grader! Allow the gap to widen and he'd enter adulthood as educated as a backcountry illiterate. Rose sprinkled into conversations with him why he "had" to resume his studies. In sit-down chats, her eyes shone belief that he could achieve anything. Thomas Edison, she knew, had gone deaf, John Milton blind when he wrote *Paradise Lost*. When FDR's polio was revealed after his death, she referenced that too, though she detested his politics. America tended to warehouse its handicapped where they couldn't be seen then, and Rose's stomach knotted when she envisioned Gordon being dumped there.

As hard as she campaigned for him to ease back into textbooks, her words pinged off him. "Not interested." Come on. He preferred fraternizing to algebra, beer-swilling to the European Renaissance. What was he supposed to do with a diploma anyway, he asked? "Use it as serving tray?" No one, he believed, was going to hire him, not for a real job anyway, so why squander everybody's time in a charade? Not long after this rebuttal, Rose played her ace. Gordon either accepted homeschooling a few days a week or he'd enjoy a lot less time around his pals.

Flora M. Strong, who taught in the school district the Zahlers sued years earlier, bade hello around Gordon's seventeenth birthday. Both instructor and student tried to make their sessions worthwhile. Flora presented lectures while Gordon fended off his daydreaming. She quizzed him about the periodic table and Hamlet's motivations, and he answered from memory. From February 1943 to June 1944, she was a fixture by his medicine cabinet of a nightstand. Every week lessons were outlined, schedules kept, Rose tolerating nothing less.

For all the effort, the results were hit and miss. Turns out the ability to write, erase, and redo with pencil in hand oils the brain's hydraulics in a way nothing else can, especially in the fundamental sciences. Gordon's inability to clutch an implement was the stumbling block, no matter his fascination with mechanical gadgets. Accordingly, biology, chemistry, and geometry were de-emphasized, economics too. English and social studies, reading-driven and orally testable, hardened into his core subjects. By the end of her stint, Flora judged Gordon a B student. Tenth-grade coursework behind him, he'd finished his formal education. If Flora shared notes on him with a teacher-friend, she might have remarked that when Gordon concentrated, he could summon material with a semi-photographic memory. Another tutor showed up later, but not like her.

*   *   *

THE PAST YEARS' TURMOIL had driven the three other people in the house deeper into their own fields of interest. Muriel hunkered down on classwork at Pasadena Junior College, learning music theory and notation. When not on campus, she evaluated any number of young men with hopes of slipping a ring onto her finger; a USC dental student and a Caltech engineering grad were the lead candidates. West of downtown, Lee fine-tuned his material to appeal to the popular, wartime aesthetic. Westerns and pot-boiling whodunits were no longer as chic as fare about Nazi spy rings pursuing dangerous chemicals (*The Dawn Express*), or a woman running a dance resort on a remote island attacked by Hirohito (*Prisoner of Japan*).

Rose's intellectual penchants were higher and closer. For years she'd been a fervent acolyte of a hybrid-Christian philosophy called "The Instruction." The faith borrowed liberally from Catholicism, some from Christian Science (of which she was no longer a member), while jilting their most extreme doctrines. The Instruction's small flock, which probably numbered in the hundreds like many of Southern California's offshoot religions then, held Sunday services on folding chairs with punch served afterward. Rose devoured every word that George Edwin Burnell, the Instruction's founding minister, wrote about his creed in the blue-backed reports he cranked out at a Herculean volume. When darkness fell over her life, be it illness, gunshots, or emptied savings, she reflexively cited his prose the way some quoted their favorite English poet. Gordon's busted neck further addicted her to the teachings of the snowy-haired, stern-faced man of God from Minnesota. Every time her teenager was on the ropes, it was a good bet where his mother would be later that evening: on the phone with her spiritual professor at his Arcadia home, imploring him to send forth special prayers known as "treatments."

Rose's faith in Burnell's evanescent theme—that our time here is a whitewater ride before the glassy afterlife—was her oxytocin during rough patches. His explanations made sense. Shouting from the pulpit, the septuagenarian exhorted his followers to brush off tragedy and confusion filtered out by heaven. In The Instruction's map of what was, saints were ubiquitous and hell was nonexistent. Consciousness was God's personal gift, Burnell told everyone, so remember St. Thomas Aquinas. "The end of man is not death but happiness." Mortal life in this tautology was akin to a movie whose most vicious scenes never lasted.

Rose's dogged adherence to this crystalline belief system was hard for outsiders to fathom. Whole Sundays could be consumed reading and debating the reverend's words with other parishioners. Harold Ross, Rose's kid brother, was in the congregation for a bit. Lee, having little to offer in the faith department, occasionally felt uncomfortable and even snubbed when the Gospels and Instruction reports took over the house. But he adored the wife who practiced her faith, so he gave wide berth to her mystical toehold. After Gordon's accident,

Rose's fidelity to it might have worried him as an obsessive hunt for the irreversible. During certain weeks, she'd be on the horn daily with Burnell for extended conversations. At night in her alcove, she fell asleep reading the "Axiom" book he'd authored. His words were her breakwater and Lee knew it.

And it wasn't just Burnell's afterlife doctrine that Rose found tantalizing. It was the possibility that shamanism might triumph where conventional medicine could not. The Instruction offered the incapacitated hope not advertised during the laborious sermons that younger Gordon had difficulty staying awake through (as I would). Burnell, simply put, dabbled in faith healing; the sort found then inside sweaty, lamp-lit tents crammed with palsied believers on crutches and repentant itinerants sworn off the bottle. Please, Rose implored Burnell. See if laying of hands can jolt Gordon's deadened body. Burnell answered he would give it a whirl.

In doing so, he'd be imitating a technique to which he owed so much. A faith healer had vanquished a childhood illness that'd nearly killed him. His wife, Mary, subscribed to its power after knowing about the funeral it had averted. As a tot, their daughter—Gordon's sometimes-partner-in-crime, Mary Georgine—had toppled from the window of a three-story building in a drop few adults could've withstood. Mary Burnell, reciting the magic prayers her husband had taught her, rushed downstairs. When she lifted the girl from the hard ground, it was as if her touch brought her daughter back to life unscathed. In subsequent years, the reverend privately shared stories like this—of eyes suddenly sighted and hunchbacks straightened, all by human contact.

Rose, having heard the anecdotes and soured on fortune-tellers, couldn't wait to try it on her son. After all, she was positive the Burnell prayer circle had saved Gordon when he'd laid in critical condition at County General. After Burnell went through with the procedure and nothing twitched, he may have interpreted it as a sign from above. Perhaps, he said, it wasn't holy will for Gordon to stand again for reasons that would dawn later. Consider the pitiful odds he'd beaten. Rose probably nodded her head and wiped a tear. She'd be reading a Burnell report that night.

CHAPTER NINE: SCENES AROUND HOLLYWOOD

THE GANGLY ENGINEER THAT stole Muriel's heart may have been a Lockheed Corporation draftsman, but his analytical skill was no preparation for the odd mechanics of the blue house on Laurel. Center stage of it was an effusive, older teenager whose limp torso was shuttled between bed, bathroom, and wheelchair. Often floating nearby—or hunched over him—was his cheery, graying mother. Rose's servitude was willingly offered and continually tested. A fresh bedpan, a different radio station, an unopened letter, permission for beer-time with his pals: Jesus, Gordon disliked waiting. "Mom, it's been twenty minutes." Muriel's fiancé could've written about the physics of mother-son action-reaction just watching the impatience ricochet off Rose's floral dress. And he hadn't even gotten to Lee, an inscrutable paternal equation if there ever was one.

From his outsider vantage, Muriel's father was your typical entertainer, fun loving and hot-tempered, spontaneous and self-absorbed. Though not physically imposing, his personality compensated with energy that filled rooms with a baritone laugh and snap opinions. A stogie, puffed on the stoop looking toward Mount Wilson, was his antidote to a fatiguing day scribbling music and addressing domestic crises; other times he'd curl up with an anatomy textbook. Lee never grinned more than when his kids and their friends sweet-talked him to play an era sing-along, like the sarcastic "Der Fuehrer's Face," on his home piano while everybody riotously joined in. Yet he sure scowled when the engineer, Millard Jacobs, was there.

And, to Lee's consternation, Millard was there a lot. Muriel was over the moon for his wavy, dark hair, wide-arched nose, and quiet gravitas different than the other fellas. Natural smarts and a fanatical work ethic had earned him a 1940 civil engineering degree from Caltech, where physicist Albert Einstein had once pondered his unified field theory. Millard might have stuttered when nervous and lacked any observable magnetism, but Muriel spotted a decency in him to be a future provider. Her romantic choices certainly weren't what they used to be. Most of her old flames had either died in the war or moved away. And *this* was love. Muriel rooted him on as a bench-warming guard for the atrocious Caltech basketball team, and whinnied for her parents to warm up to the six-feet-one introvert. You know, the guy with the slide rule in his shirt pocket.

They'd met on a set-up date in late 1942 that, by all accounts, should've ended there as a personality mismatch. Muriel, gabby and cigarette puffing, was a small-town socialite who acted big city. Millard, three years older, tilted to the opposite polarity—gawky, light drinking, and impenetrable. In public, Rose blessed the relationship and in private voiced her wish that it had been another boy. Lee made little effort to contain his hostility and disappointment. This was whom his little girl picked? The religious divide was another of his grievances. Millard was a non-practicing Jew, whereas Muriel and Rose were impassioned Christians. They'd fantasized about Burnell officiating Muriel's wedding since Muriel was in pigtails. Lee's dislike of him was such that he may have retained a private detective to snoop. Millard, though, was just grateful if Lee called him by name instead of a variation of "hey you." During the engagement, he lunged at his chances to express what he thought about Muriel's selection. If the lovebirds nuzzled at the dinner table, he'd rap Millard's fingers with a butter knife. "Cut that out," he'd snipe. "You're embarrassing me."

Getting to the altar almost did them in. Millard insisted hardheadedly that a rabbi conduct the honors. Lee and Rose pushed for an affair festooned with lace and ribbons in Burnell's garden. Seeking compromise, the pair tried arranging for a two-denominational affair.

No takers there. When the big day arrived—Valentine's Day 1943—more dreams died than were born. Millard had won the first power struggle. Muriel stood in a white dress listening to a rabbi's unfamiliar pronouncements of man and wife with not a mention of Christ. Lee stood nearby trying not to explode. Gordon observed the service a few feet from his bed, aware that Muriel's willingness to marry in such a low-budget, chilly atmosphere—after she'd pledged not to be a "war bride"—was traceable to him. *Congratulations!*

Millard, nonetheless, worked to soften up a father-in-law whose animosity toward him remained unthawed. Lee concessions to him were small. He'd sometimes invite his son-in-law to watch the local, semi-pro baseball team, the Rosabell Plumbers, play in Monrovia. Still, if Millard wasn't on the street, ready to be picked up the second Lee's Ford arrived, Lee wouldn't honk. He'd just leave. Those times they made it to the bleachers, Type-A Lee rained down catcalls against the visiting team. Millard might've thought better them than him. On his commute home from the studios, Lee habitually stopped by their Hollywood rental on Beachwood Drive, a property owned by actress Bette Davis's mother. The open secret? He was checking to ensure that Muriel, a wastrel shopper and novice cook, was getting the princess treatment she deserved.

*   *   *

THAT, OF COURSE, WAS when Lee was present. Because he was a musician attached to the Hollywood production treadmill, ten-to-twelve-hour workdays were often his customary shift. Nobody in the family traversed such dissimilar worlds: studio hubbub by day, mountain breezes at night. Gordon's crippling accentuated the divide. He and Rose would steady themselves when a complication sent Gordon back into an ambulance, and often exchanged verbal gunfire later over how to pay the tab. If Gordon's liquor brigade were over, they could relax upstairs. Other than that, there was a whole lot of drab, smelly routine caring for the boy, most of which Rose handled.

Lee and Gordon's interactions also blew hot and cold now that Gordon was stronger. Days ran together when they were peas in a pod, jawing about sports, tracking the war, and downplaying paralysis. Then prideful tempers interrupted, and raised voices could rattle the screen door. After a tiff, Gordon was known to grumble into his bed sheets as his dad sent cigar clouds into the skies.

Both babysat remorse. Before that day at Marshall, Lee had nurtured ideas about molding the kid. Someday, Gordon's pranks would lose their allure and he'd steer his boy's ambitions through college. The flip side? Gordon itched to show his father what he could do. A pilot, à la Charles Lindbergh, would serve that cause. With those dreams fried, he couldn't knock anybody's socks off. Lee appreciated this just as much as Gordon wallowed in it, so they made do. Certain mornings before work, Lee sat on Gordon's bed, ripping through the morning paper for the pennant race standings. *The Brooklyn Dodgers were how many games out of first?* Next, he'd turn to the horseracing results from Santa Anita to evaluate the imaginary bets they'd placed. Sometimes they needled each other about ten thousand dollar payoffs and rigged races. Everything considered, those rituals were their only sure-fire camaraderie.

A few months after Muriel's wedding—a ceremony that generated not *one* preserved photograph—the undertow splashed again. Doctors noticed a suspicious mass within the tissue of Rose's right breast. As was her nature, she downplayed it, assuring people that she'd be fine (because she needed to be fine for everybody else). In September she underwent surgery to remove the benign tumor. The month after that, Lee reimbursed the Motion Picture Relief Fund one thousand one hundred dollars for the medical expenses. While he could've used the dough, he reviled taking charity almost as much as the snakebit times.

*   *   *

MURIEL FELT CIRCUMSTANCE TUG the rug out from underneath her by way of a splintering marriage. The department store bills she racked up exceeded what Millard's Lockheed paychecks could bear. Between discord over her shopping and fissuring doubts about their general compatibility, the couple did the obvious. They separated.

Muriel slumped back to her parent's house to weigh her future. By the time she'd opted to give her nuptials a second try, there was no place to live, not with returning GIs flooding the housing market. Millard had to move into her upstairs bedroom on Laurel—a room separated by a thin wall from where her disapproving father slept. The arrangement was the ugly baby syndrome: no one wanted it, but they all had to accept it.

Midway through 1946, another relationship unraveled. Lee made this official to Rose in a wrenching confession. He wanted out. Their relationship wasn't worth fighting for anymore. Not with her chained to Gordon's bedpost and him on the emotional skids. Believing they could reignite their flame was as far-fetched as thinking they could rebuild any savings. What Lee said he needed were suitcases, for he was relocating to a nondescript apartment close to his Santa Monica Boulevard office. At some point, he acknowledged to his wife of twenty-five years that he wouldn't be alone there. He'd be cohabiting with another woman with whom he'd been having an affair.

Lee's revelation was at turns appalling and predictable, wounding and random. Nobody had suspected his interest in the actresses and dancers around him, sometimes in risqué costumes that could make a eunuch randy, was anything but vocational. On the other hand, everyone knew how his disgust for off-camera Hollywood conflicted with the moral code embedded in his Budapest genes. The sausage making of films nauseated him; that hypocrisy of do-gooder story lines juxtaposed with casting-couch sex. Payoffs, vice cover-ups, blackballing: "showbiz integrity" to him was an oxymoron. He was so jaded, in fact, about the industry most Americans glamorized that he'd made Muriel and Gordon forswear any interest in it. Don't let the cesspool trick you, he'd say.

Once he'd vacated Sierra Madre, Lee's high-minded ideals must have sounded like an infuriating double standard. But one man's infidelity was another's desperation. Chest pains thumped him regularly now, not just during anguishing times. Whoever had dropped a barbell on his sternum was welcomed to remove it. Being the son of a genius medical student, he tried diagnosing the compressions himself. He ascribed the tightness to heartburn caused by financial strain and ingestion of greasy, commissary fare. After another symptom clutched him—shortness of breath walking upstairs—he visited his internist. The doctor ran tests and diagnosed him with moderate-advanced coronary heart disease. Lee kept the depressing news under his hat for a while.

A life bookended by freebies from the Motion Picture Relief Fund and domestic warfare was not his conception of middle age comfort. At fifty-four, laboring to start over while his calcified arteries permitted it, he hoped a different woman would refill the air in his tanks. To this day, no one has cracked the chickadee's identity, though she may have been a Sam Goldwyn dancer or contract actress. If Rose was squashed by this, the fences she put up to keep the focus on others obstructed it. If she knew in advance about the concubine, she mentioned not a breath of it to Gordon and Muriel. Later she'd concede that she was less furious than resigned at the breakdown of her marriage. It was a balloon payment on six years of bad luck, narrowed choices, and collateral damage. When at last Muriel was told about the split-up, she covered her ears. As for Gordon, who knows?

The estrangement that propelled Lee and Rose into confusing new beginnings stretched for months. They managed a poignant hug the September day Muriel gave birth to my oldest brother, Paul, at St. Luke's. Afterward, they departed in separate cars going opposite directions. Fate being the traffic cop that it is, Lee's driving days were numbered. One afternoon in December 1946, perhaps on the set for *Queens of the Amazon*, the heart attack you could've seen building from space clubbed him. He blacked out, and off *he* went, probably in an ambulance. Hours later he was at Cedars of Lebanon Hospital in Los Angeles (Cedars-Sinai Medical Center today) with an oxygen mask over his face. Asked by the nurses what they could do for him, Lee didn't hesitate. "Call my wife," he rasped. "Call her now!"

The Zahlers had their Tracy and Hepburn moment with Lee flat on his back. After apologies were whispered and contrition voiced, they banned all future discussion of destitution and adultery. Lee gripped Rose's hand from his hospital bed and made his case. What did the doctors know? Remember how Gordon had defied them? "Yesiree," he promised, he'd recover. Once he had, they'd rustle up the money for the two of them to go on a long-overdue trip to Paris, let the bubbly flow. They'd borrow the whole amount if they had to. Rose kissed him when he said that.

For a few weeks anyway, the reconciliation was Lee's battery charger. With Cedar's nurses holding his elbow, he walked the corridor to regain strength. When he felt spunky, he tried inveigling them to let him enjoy a quick cigar on the sun deck. His coronary vessels refused to cooperate after that. There would be no more strolls or smoking. The plaque clogging his arteries was a bottleneck preventing oxygen and nutrients from circulating right. Instant remedies via stent, blood-thinning medication, or bypass surgery were decades away. Lee's high blood pressure and a bum kidney shaded his prognosis from gray to black. Never mind all that hooey, he said. Keep his favorite chair at home warm. Now that he had his devoted wife and family around again, what else did a man need? (Not the woman he'd been living with; he'd already phoned her to tell her to find someone else.)

Gordon made the trek to West Los Angeles to see his father. The hard-bitten nurses, I imagine, must have fought to see that—a quadriplegic visiting somebody sicker than him. Rose was there constantly, Muriel occasionally. The two prayed with passages from Reverend Burnell that Lee's heart would reverse its wear and tear to beat normally again. They encouraged him to view his atherosclerosis as an illusion, a lie. His body, though, was noncompliant, shutting down like a ramshackle factory. Going back and forth to the can sucked the wind out of him. The most he could do was stick on a brave face around company. All he'd ever wanted was to go where his talents would take him in the entertainment gold rush while featherbedding a comfortable existence for his family. For almost thirty years that formula had sustained him. Bedridden at Cedars, it was pancaking to know that formula had lapsed.

As the holidays came, Lee realized nothing shy of witchcraft could bust him out of Cedars. When his son-in-law, Millard (previously "Hey you"), turned up on Christmas Eve, Lee nicely ordered him to sit down and take dictation. It was imperative, he said, that Gordon receive his message by nightfall. The opening was a satire of one of Lee's studio contracts:

My dear Gordon: In consideration of the sum of $1 and other good and valuable considerations, in good old American dollars that I was going to spend on you in goodwill for your happiness, I wish you good cheer for a Merry Christmas that was unfortunately interrupted due to power beyond my own control.

With God's help in the near future I will pick up Christmas with you where I have left off. Just call it a short interruption.

Dad, Xmas '46.

This cheer was relayed, just as desired. You never knew what miracle Santa or the Burnell prayer circle might bring.

CHAPTER TEN: ROARING TIMBER

C AN YOU SEE THEM in their funeral black? Sure you can. Rose and Gordon are in the living room of their Laurel Avenue house, rubber-faced as the sun droops behind the foothills. Shadows bisect the floor into a maze of trapezoidal patterns, every one razor-like. A neighbor has dropped them home from Forest Lawn cemetery in nearby Glendale, and made his goodbyes. Someone else has left a mystery soufflé next to the forest of condolence flowers. Rose refuses to slouch in her chair for too long, as it reminds her of why she loathes February, the most lethal month of the year. Tea: she needs tea. She rocks onto her feet, moving toward the kettle. Gordon, reclined in bed, staring at the wall where the World War II combat map had been pinned, could've been a mannequin. He's just turned twenty-one.

It's then, for no good reason, that unexpected hilarity inflates inside Rose, and she's defenseless to stifle it. At first she chuckles, tea cup in hand, but this is about absurdity not subtlety, so it expands into a snort, then a procession of them, before its manifestation as a gusty hoot. Tears stream down her cheeks. Gordon asks what could be funny on this shitstorm of a day, but Rose just shakes her head. It was as if she had solved the punch line to a joke told long ago. In reality, she is crying from laughing and laughing instead of screaming, "What's next? Locusts? A case of the piles?"

Almost. Bargain-basement existence would be their new standard of living. Even with the Motion Picture Relief Fund bankrolling the medical bills and a seventy-five-dollar-a-week "maintenance" subsidy, Rose had only a few hundred dollars to her name. They were belly up. No bankruptcy filing was needed to formalize it when they slept every night in this dumpy apartment hard up against a flood control channel. As Rose confessed in a letter to a Fund social worker, everywhere she went she discovered necessities she wavered whether they could afford. Hunting for a cheaper place left her "a little jittery." Price and value were "out of whack" for Sierra Madre's newest widow.

Another heart attack had polished Lee off just after breakfast on February 21, 1947. Rose, recognizing the end was near, had been inches from him when he'd expired. If there had been any solace for her, it had been that he'd explicitly mentioned God by name in the months before he went up to meet Him. Muriel had been at home stirring baby formula for Paul when a member of Reverend Burnell's church, as a favor to Rose, broke the news. Once she'd gone, Muriel had bawled tears into the pan.

Since he'd been ill for months, Lee's death shook the family more like a debilitating cramp than a puncture wound. Just the same, inside Gordon knew they were dog meat. Outside, he pretended the misery would fix itself, as if it ever had, and salivated to be out romping with friends. What else did he have to latch onto? His homeschooling was done. And the want ads for menial labor assumed a prospect had functioning hands.

Nihilistic thinking like this dizzied him in the months after Lee died. His response: feed his cravings and deflect the guilt. He had connections. Pals like Don Berg and Benny Gouin had returned from war without forgetting him. Some of them were enrolled at Pasadena Junior College, where they'd pledged the "Catawabas," a renegade fraternity that initiated Gordon as an honorary member. He had a humorous deal for them to take seriously: he'd divulge the names of the loosest girls in town *if* they took him clubbing. Staying cooped up with his mother, he'd gripe, was only a step up from sleeping. In the months to come, they'd party at Tom Breneman's and Billy Berg's, both on Vine Street. They became repeat customers at the Café

Trocadero, a former booze warehouse on Sunset decorated with a Parisian mural and a glass wall. (Louis B. Mayer reputedly discovered Judy Garland here in the thirties; mobsters like Bugsy Siegel later took a shine to it.) Classy, neon-lit places like this—with headlining crooners, potent drinks, wide dance floors, and star-sightings—were the adrenalized diversion he needed. "That handsome guy in the wheelchair over there needs a prime booth," his posse would tell club managers, sliding a few bucks in their hands. How many, they'd ask? The common answer: "five couples *plus him.*"

Getting a table was one thing, resisting the temptation to cower underneath it another. Public settings were pins and needles for anyone unable to walk in on their own. The clubs could be frantic, spinning rooms. None offered normalcy for somebody told he'd never be vertical again. When the other guys' dates in their fluffy dresses poured alcohol into him, he sometimes felt like their mascot. After the patrons pointed at him and his combat-vet pals grumbled about folks "who'd never seen dick," he sensed he was deadweight better left home. Maybe the strangers could detect the real him behind the *ain't-this-grand* aura he tried to radiate.

The hole in his calculation was his underestimation of self. Fact was, he was rarely excluded from the clubbing. No one sized him up as a portable sob-story they were obligated to amuse. They just viewed him as one of theirs—an action junkie who needed a little assistance. Sitting at Billy Berg's in a bow tie with a plaid blanket over his lap, Gordon was reminded about the stretchiness of loyalty. Developing psychology for the newcomers he met was a skill in progress. Over time, he condensed it to one word—attitude. *Be clever. Flirt with the cigarette girl. Laugh about my jug ears. Just downplay the wheelchair. Never let them confuse "it" with him. Attitude cubed!*

Gordon's theory of preemptive charm was road-tested at the Trocadero that spring. His favorite singer, given the heads up by Benny, sat down at his booth between sets to chat and snap pictures. The singer stayed longer than he had planned because the birthday boy was a lot more than met the eye. As soon as Nat King Cole and his musicians climbed back on stage, they performed a number for "that smilin' cat in booth number six." Gordon saw this swagger thing had promise.

In Sierra Madre, however, the pity was trickier to manage. Pound for pound, the Zahlers were the heavyweight champs of hardship. Lee's passing, Gordon's snapped neck, Sonny's murder, Rose's tumor: small towns cradle heartbreak that metropolises can't. Tragedy had mauled the house on Laurel but good. Rose was loathe to discuss the last seven years with strangers, these being "private matters" to her. What, however, was she to do when badly needed assistance was extended? Tell them they had the wrong address? The city's all-volunteer fire department had circled them for benevolence long ago. These were compassionate souls brave enough to tame mountain brushfires and agile enough to rescue the needy. As the city's charitable arm, they had another job. They hand-delivered happiness.

In late December, 1947, maybe on Christmas Eve, a group of uniformed firemen with seasonally wrapped goody baskets in their arms arrived at the Zahler's drab, little Camillo Street apartment that they'd relocated to after Lee's burial. There, Rose offered them cinnamon-spiced coffee before they extended a hearty Merry Christmas and Happy New Year to Gordon. Apparently, he'd been expecting friends, not surprises, when the firemen in black boots clomped into his field of vision. Gordon assumed it as a gag prearranged by Benny, who'd probably be sauntering in any time. But after he noticed what his visitors were holding, he knew he'd confused a practical joke with something much worse. When one of the younger firemen clumsily asked if turkey was on the Christmas-Day menu, Gordon astounded even himself by the salvo from his scrawny throat.

"Sorry to say this, but you can take your measly gifts and scram. Now."

"Come again?" the pump-man said.

"We don't want it, okay? What do we look like, bums or something? Go!"

"Just one second, son," the assistant chief said. "All we brought was some fruit and candy and a few trinkets. You can at least say thanks. Thanks like everybody else."

"Fine. Thanks. Now get your stuff and leave. I mean it. *Moth-er.*"

Rose heard the hullabaloo and jogged in. Gordon told her he wanted to be left alone, so she escorted the baffled firemen with their unopened baskets out the door.

"You have my sincere apology for that scene," Rose said at the curb. Around her, neighbors had their wreaths and Holiday decorations up. "I haven't seen him that agitated since, well, since he was in the hospital."

"Tell me, Mrs. Zahler, what does he have against a little goodwill?" the assistant chief asked.

"I don't know," she said. "Maybe he's more like his father than I'd gathered."

*   *   *

Biological envy; Gordon was jealous of people who could be blithe about their health. Just because he never pouted about it didn't soften the yearning. The organs he'd lost sensation with lived under the threat that a pesky bug was readying for invasion. How he'd never been blitzed by one during his nights out he wasn't sure. This he did know in March 1948: his bladder was on the fritz. His urine either had bloody clouds in it or he couldn't pee at all. Rapid fevers sometimes accompanied it. One evening, Rose pressed his stomach, asking, "Does this hurt?" and his head throbbed.

"Yeah," he said. Sometimes he felt downright breakable. When the pain continued, Rose got him to West Pasadena's Huntington Memorial Hospital. He was on the operating room table in two shakes.

The surgeons who carved Gordon open understood why his waste stream was obstructed. His bladder was pebbled with calcium stones, miniature fragments of salts and minerals that had clumped together first in his kidneys. They removed the debris field and, believing him cured, shipped him to recovery. The nurses hardly got his name. Hemorrhaging internally, Gordon was rushed back into surgery, where the doctors cut the sutures they'd just sewn. In examining his innards more carefully, they spotted the ominous root of his discomfort. The mouth of his bladder was so swollen that his urine in effect had been corked. He would poison himself to death with his own toxic waste—otherwise known as sepsis—unless something drastic was attempted. Problem was, nobody knew quite what to try. Nobody but the doctor who suggested that an experimental treatment developed by the Veterans Administration might be Gordon's last shot. Hoping that the blockage would vanish by itself was suicidal.

The doctors explained it to Rose while she sat in the waiting room longing for something to clean. How, they asked, did she want them to proceed? She had no idea. Until now, Lee had been Gordon's medical shot-caller. What would he do now? *Lord, what?* "Operate," she answered. "Do something!" What they did was inject alcohol through a hypodermic needle into the tail (or lumbar) section of his fused spine. The alcohol worked like a good masseuse on an uncooperative muscle, except in this case it was a nerve that relaxed. Pressure and gravity once again streamed urine from Gordon's bladder into the collection bag tubed from his catheter. By dodging sepsis, his anatomy had weathered another attack on itself. The crapshoot procedure worked.

In the following weeks, Gordon tried forgetting about his return to another arctic surgical table. Tried forgetting that nothing was going right. But forced amnesia was not his only reason for still being in bed on a Monday afternoon with an extended hangover bongo-drumming his head. No, the US Postal Service was the instigator of that. Two days earlier, Rose had told him what they both knew was coming. In the mailbox had been a letter from the Motion Picture Relief Fund letter alerting them that they'd exhausted their benefits. "What'd you expect, Mom?" Gordon had said as Rose brooded into dusk. "They weren't going to keep sending checks forever." He went out that night with the guys, boozing it up in Hollywood as if the earth was about to end. They drank themselves pie-eyed, spending so much on liquor they'd had to sneak out without leaving a tip. They weaved home on the serpentine Arroyo Seco Parkway, pulling in around 2:00 a.m. A friend we'll call Stan Lufton had parked the car in his family's garage, and the occupants had stumbled into the house.

Early the next morning, Stan's mother walked past the snoring revelers conked out on her custom living room set. Angrily, she went off to inspect the car, knowing whiskey and dings went together. *What's that in the back seat?* she asked herself in the dark. She inched closer. *No, it couldn't be.* Gordon was slumped over. Back in the living room she appeared, except this time she was hollering. "Get an ambulance! And call Rose Zahler. Tell her to come over. I think Gordon's dead."

By 7:00 a.m., her cotton-mouthed son and friends had been startled awake. Brain-fogged, they jogged toward the garage. The forgotten one was in there, sentient. Numskull mistake, they explained. They'd just been so "pooped" after their night out. "That's right, Mrs. Lufton," Gordon added once he'd been laid on the sofa, hair askew. "And I'm fine." He said he'd come to around what he guessed was four a.m. Since nobody had heard him call out, he'd wiggled himself into a half-sleeping position with his face squished into the vinyl seat.

"But you weren't breathing. I felt your chest. I..." Mrs. Lufton said.

"Aw, don't feel bad," Gordon interrupted. Other people had mistaken him for dead when he slept.

Forty-eight hours later, Rose hoped that Gordon's bender had taught him a lesson. Too bad they were out of aspirin. Didn't he appreciate how close they were to genuine indigence? How she'd thrown herself at the mercy of the Relief Fund administrators? She'd cried to them over the phone and in person, and her sniffles hadn't budged them. "Just send fifty dollars a week for another year," she'd begged; it had already been pared back from seventy-five dollars per week. "We'll never ask for another cent after that. You have my word."

But the Relief Fund's pat answer by late 1948 was an echo of their answer from earlier in the year: "Sorry, Mrs. Zahler, we can't." County welfare would have to be their safety net keeping them off the streets. The Fund's finances were under such duress it had been forced to enact tighter guidelines. Families seeking aid had to have somebody "actively employed" in the Industry to be eligible. Rose poked around for exceptions. Fund officials bit their lip responding. In the years since Gordon's accident, the organization had forked over twenty two thousand dollars (about five hundred thousand today) to them. Bottom line: the last check had been written.

The social worker from Los Angeles County's Bureau of Public Assistance was there that Monday with Gordon's head still throbbing at the faintest sound. The bureaucrat posed the usual questions about their situation and scanned the financials documenting it. She looked around the front room that Rose-the-neat-freak had purposely let get dusty for effect. Once she'd checked off a few more boxes, she gave them a sympathetic smile. Don't fret, she said. They were a cinch for welfare.

Something, though, about how she enunciated the word "welfare," or the helping-the-helpless gestalt in the room zapped Gordon, who'd said little during the visit. The Fire Department's pity baskets would've been a thousand times better than living off the dole. Borrowing ten dollars from friends or eating four-day-old meatloaf was, too. Welfare lowered them into the same sad-sack column as rummies, deadbeats, ne'er-do-wells, and the chronically unemployed. His father, who'd gone to the next world ashamed of taking Relief Fund handouts, would have rejected it from the get-go. He'd have taught piano scales to every bratty little girl in a five-mile radius rather than sponge off the government. Gordon lambasted himself next. Lying on his bony ass all day, eating ice chips as a substitute for the electric fan they couldn't afford, was no way to be the man of the house. It was surrender.

For the next two weeks, Gordon chased an idea, a moneymaking idea that had been pickling inside him for a while. Cartons brimming with Lee's sheet music and reels, which Rose had stuffed willy-nilly into a closet, had jarred his curiosity. A few of his chums then filled in the blanks by making calls and researching the feasibility of the conception. Rose was slicing carrots for a cheap stew when he sprang it on her.

"Mom, can I talk to you about something?"

"Not if it's about permission for another night at the Trocadero." She sat down on his bed.

"No, it's nothing to do with that."

"Good, because you just about gave Mrs. Lufton a heart attack, the poor thing."

"I know. I know. Look, I want you to phone that welfare lady."

"You mean Mrs. Harrington?"

"Yep, her."

"Okay, I'll play along. Why am I phoning her?"

"To tell her we won't be taking her checks very long. A year tops. After that you let her know we'll be paying the county back. Every cent."

"My goodness, the spunk that's gotten into you."

"Forget that. I think I've figured out a way for us to make a living. On our own."

Rose swept the bangs off his forehead, assessing him for a few seconds.

"I love your chivalry, sweetheart, but let's be realistic. Unless there's money buried someplace, I don't see how. I haven't held a job since I was waiting tables in New York. And the Fund. You know about that, already."

"All that's in the past."

"Oh really?"

"Mom, will you please let me finish?"

"You're right. Go on."

He gulped air. "I think we should try and resell Dad's old music. All those songs he wrote could be worth a ton. There's a market for them. The studios—they're hot for anything they can get."

"A-ha! That's why you've been so secretive lately. I knew something was afoot. It's those boxes from Daddy's office, aren't they?"

"*Mo-om.* Stop, okay?" He paused. "We own the rights. I had one of the fellas check with the union. What's in that closet could be our answer."

"All fine and good, dear, but why are you assuming the studios are buying? They have their own orchestras. Who do you think performed all of Daddy's scores?"

"That's right—for movies! But the networks—the TV networks—need music for all these new shows they're planning. They're dozens of them. It'd cost them a fortune to record it themselves right now."

"And?"

"And. It was all over the radio. I asked Benny to buy me a *Daily Variety*, and guess what? There was a front-page story all about it. It's in my bottom drawer. I've been saving it for you."

Rose digested the article inches from her nearsighted eyes while Gordon tracked their movements. "Well," she said with a developing smirk. "You're right about the music. It says here there might even be a strike over it."

"Let's hope so. They'd really be eating out of our hands. You know better than anyone how many songs Dad wrote. When did he start, nineteen twenty-nine?"

"About then."

"Everything we need to get started are in those boxes."

"Gordon, I can see you're excited about this, and I think that's marvelous. But there's one piece you left out. Who's going to organize this little enterprise? I don't have the time. Or the first notion to how to go about it."

"You're talking to him."

CHAPTER ELEVEN: THE BIG BLUFF

HE KICKED OFF WITH a sales pitch bolder than any of his batty stunts—leaping off piers too close to their pilings, sim-
ulating (thanks to his double jointed hips) self-copulation
under the Marshall bleachers on a two-dollar dare. As he told the
buddies he'd assembled into the apartment that evening, his scheme
to launch a Hollywood music company was going nowhere without
them. Whatever he owed them for their camaraderie, for motivation
not to wither away, he'd never sought anything this profound. He'd
had his mother dress him up executive-like, in Lee's tweed coat, to illustrate *this* Gordon was different. Getting off "goddamn welfare" had
assigned him purpose. Between it and his zeal to continue making
fools out of those insistent he had little time left, he was a self-winding
motivation machine. *Giddy-up.*

The catch was that he had nothing to pay them beyond gratuitous
thanks. What he needed would have to be either a freebie or an IOU.
"Fellas, think of it as the last time you let me bug you. In a couple
of years, after I've hit the jackpot, you can hit me up for as much as
you need. Deal?" A few of them cackled, but the snickers tapered
off when his green eyes lasered on them. Gordon had measured the
dimensions of the favor he was seeking from his volunteer brigade.
In his name, they'd have to pester the studios for authentic copies
of Lee's music and rent equipment, no money down. They'd have to
scour libraries for answers, fill out union forms, run and splice audio

tapes, convert them to new media, indexing every verse. Over and over and over again.

"What kind of time are we talking about?" someone asked.

"Every free weekend you can spare for a year, if you want to hear it straight," he answered.

There was a chorus of sighs. A few from the peanut gallery wanted to know what he'd be focusing on during the launch. His answer: supervising them and hunting for contracts when he wasn't. Rose, at that moment eavesdropping from the kitchen, would manage some of the paperwork. Every amenable family friend would be co-opted. The boys were almost afraid to say "no" listening to Gordon's showbiz entry-plan.

The actual workload, as they learned, put them at the frayed edges of the red carpet. About the closest they got to the flashbulb culture was when they'd drive in from Sierra Madre, pass through a studio arch, and speak with a mid-level executive. On good days, they'd return to Camillo Street with armfuls of tapes from Lee's film-music career that he hadn't brought home. Any buzz they registered when a knockout actress swished by dissipated in the tedium of the apartment. Each tape had to be transferred from old-fashioned optical format to standard, one-quarter-inch. Every tune had to be categorized by the movie it appeared in, its defining genre (honky-tonk, classical, etc.), length, studio origin, and other taxonomies. Next, all that had to be typed up onto crinkly onion paper as a primitive database. Columns were added. All told, Lee had scored hundreds of films and serials with fingers trained in Tin Pan Alley and overworked by the studios.

Attrition within the contingent of former Marshall Tarzans, World War II veterans, and others hurt the cause. Some members shaved their hours or quit outright after hearing about the marathon ahead. The defections slowed the reformatting and documentation just as much as the equipment screw-ups. The eight or so who stayed on, each of them full-time college students or newly married men with full-time jobs, had to divvy up the extra workload. Still, nobody bitched outwardly about it at the onset. When the eventual jokes surfaced in month three about slave-driving Gordon, Rose motioned to speak with the boys one-on-one in the entryway. If they needed to bolt for *any* reason, she wanted them to know they'd be going with her eternal appreciation. She knew there was no logical reason they kept showing up every Saturday, before 11:00 a.m., asking what "the count" was. They shouldn't have been sitting cross-legged on the ground, feet from Rose's church-mates, with papers and musty tapes strewn around while Lee's lead-ins and crescendos echoed, Gordon in the center of the frenzy swiveling his jumbo-size head to stay apace. With all the humanity they'd bestowed they should have been out in the sunshine thinking of themselves for a change.

But here they were, every weekend of every month. Fifty tapes to go, forty-nine, forty-eight... Gordon's fanaticism with the tracking—he bet someone he could memorize the full library—colored their strategy. They'd finish his catalog, however long it took, get him drunk for posterity, and then make him Hollywood's problem. Once they had, they'd own their weekends again. Gordon, worshipping his pals as he did, sometimes feared this was all a masquerade. Recovering from a fractured neck took grit. This required courage *and* smarts.

*   *   *

THE FORTIES SAW JACKBOOT fascism repelled in black and white. The whiz-bang fifties, by contrast, were a Technicolor spectacle. Chairman Mao and the bomb shelter made affordable, Pork Chop Hill and TV dinners. There were Rosa Parks and Jack Kerouac, stainless-steel counters and the sock hop. And here was Gordon on the cusp of a profession sixteen months after that light-bulb flash. Smack dab in the business Lee made him swear he'd avoid, his mission was ironic: he'd sell his father's creations to end the handouts and explore the unforeseen.

His first office was a twelve-hundred-square-foot bungalow on eastern Sunset Boulevard with chipped acoustical tiles, a claustrophobic layout, and all the pizazz of a scuffed, white napkin. Los Angeles glamour crowd stayed west of here, closer to Scandia restaurant, the Chateau Marmont building, the Sunset Strip, and Beverly Hills. This expanse, next to the future, smog-doming Hollywood 101 Freeway, clustered the rest in dubbing houses, postproduction shops, and fly-by-night distributors grinding anonymously away. The real estate brokers Gordon negotiated with sugarcoated their listing as "grade-A back-office space." Gordon was unfazed. The piddling rent was his deal-sealer.

Near the front door was a reception area leading to a regulation-size office (his) and four smaller rooms—basically glorified closets just big enough for an editor and his machines. Gordon's "desk" was a leased, adjustable bed accented by a bumble-bee-colored throw-blanket. The décor was a connect-the-dot clown watercolor he'd painted as a kid and blank walls. The bungalow's place in celluloid history was its niftiest quality. It rested on the "service side" of a stately Colonial building studded by graceful, fluted columns. Warner Brothers had started here. Indeed, the first movie with synchronized sound (*Don Juan*—1926) was cut on this land. When the studio later bugged out to Burbank, it sold the property to rival Paramount Pictures, which housed its subsidiary, *KTLA*, the first commercially licensed TV station in the Western US there. But a section of the property went recreational, converted into the largest bowling alley in the US. Had Gordon preserved a responsive tendon in an arm, he could've almost rolled one of those balls into the lobby of Lee's former building a few blocks south. He couldn't, so he played down the sentimentalism.

The locale, overall, was suitable. The weakness was the Zahler Music Library was more hope than ongoing concern. Gordon and his executive assistant Rose still needed to bum rides into Hollywood. Their only employees then were a couple of part-time music editors for whom they had almost zero work. The catalog tapes they'd meticulously stored on a set of industrial shelves—the tapes that Sierra Madre villagers made possible—had no takers. The black phone slept in its cradle all day.

Feeling anxious one Monday, Gordon tried reaching out to one of Lee's old Columbia Pictures associates. He'd retired. Downers and disappointments like this could have been his theme song. Had it not been for a sympathetic Paramount executive who steered three or four commercials to him, who knew if he could last much longer? Something had to change. The question was what? He pledged to beat the bushes harder, and that meant Rose wheeling him around the Paramount offices to try to overhear conversations about shows needing soundtracks. Word remained that the networks producers were as hungry as ever for the music that Gordon had ready to go, but he was so outside the loop he might as well been on Venus.

Judging his approach still too passive, still too amateur hour, he pivoted to cold-calling producers and underlings. His pitch: a robust variety of prerecorded music at competitive prices was theirs for the taking. "Give it a listen," he'd say. "You'll be surprised." Omitted in these get-to-know-you conversations was any mention of his physical ruin. When producers expressed interest in hearing a sample, Gordon had excuses ready-made about why they'd be better served letting him messenger one over to them. Ten years into paralysis, he'd had a lifetime of experience with new acquaintances frightened into statues gazing upon him. (And that was with his hands tucked under the lap blanket.) Because of this, his salesmanship had to be bait-and-hook. He'd keep prospective customers at a ripe distance until the music had sold itself. This way, their delight over a consummated transaction would exceed the horror of taking in his grizzled corpus after a meeting could no longer be delayed. Observing a human being with a large, marionette-type head strapped into a chair at harsh right angles wasn't confidence inspiring. It harkened memories of a carnival freak show.

But there were ways around that, technological ways that undoubtedly lit the backfires of Gordon's imagination. Through the phone company, he acquired a microphone headset—a gadget their operators might have worn—to give himself a measure of independence. A receiver went over one ear. A small, boom microphone looped in front of his mouth. With a controlled flail of his left arm, he could swipe a padded lever clipped to his bed frame to connect and terminate calls. Though he needed Rose or someone else to dial the number, being able to pick up a call or drop one on his own, admittedly herky-jerky, felt like progress.

Continued lack of activity brought him back to the carnival analogy. The idea that he could break into a word-of-mouth industry was as illusory as a hall of mirrors. Folks just weren't interested in his exclusive proprietorship. In another round of self-interrogation, he tensed thinking that someone had bad-mouthed him—that the crippled son of a dead composer was too untested for network pressure. Maybe they'd pegged him as so desperate that he'd try to splice tape with his own teeth. If not that, perhaps his catalog was fine but his partner was wrong. A mother-son combo like his must have telegraphed they were bush league. Those mornings at 3:00 a.m., when he'd slept all he needed to and would have killed for a cigarette, Gordon replayed the occasions when there had been in-person meetings. It had been Rose who'd pushed him into the offices, after struggling to get his chair in the elevator, and shook hands in his name. She'd been the one who'd played the demo tape while he'd narrated and exaggerated Lee's career. That time he'd had a sneezing fit at NBC, she'd retrieved his handkerchief and wiped his nose. *Crap, he thought. I'm doing half of this for her, more than half.*

Still, this was his time to pounce. Steady upheaval around the musicians' union had, theoretically, made his father's music even more valuable. James Caesar Petrillo, the imperious labor boss of the American Federation of Musicians (AFM), was the provocateur. Most Americans—rapt over congressional witch-hunts for Hollywood communists and starry movie premieres—had barely heard of him, but Gordon had. Petrillo, a balding germaphobe and former trumpeter, reckoned that Big Labor had the leverage to strong-arm the corporate world. Tens of thousands of stage musicians had lost their jobs as sound movies, the record industry, and canned-music slashed demand for live performances. Only fair, Petrillo said, their working colleagues share the wealth with their hard-luck peers. Under his orders, the AFM taxed the record labels and deposited the money into accounts earmarked for unemployment subsidies. As the studios emptied their film vaults to sell vintage movies to TV, Petrillo next demanded they pay twenty-five dollars to *every* musician who played on the original score. Gordon, aspiring entrepreneur, would have been rolling in as much as fifty thousand dollars in seed money if Petrillo's redistribution scheme went unchallenged.

The labor boss, though, was his own worst enemy by sowing the perception that his egalitarianism was a self-serving racket. Seeing his clout grow, Petrillo reversed course on the twenty-five dollar fee. Instead of going to slighted musicians, he channeled the money into an account that he managed. Next, he slapped a five percent tax on *all* filmed TV production. From the industry backlash, you'd have thought the earth had belched out Satan with a pro-union button. The big studios decried the levy as extortion and refused to pay it. Federal lawmakers threatened action, too. When it was divulged that most of the AFM rank-and-file in need were middle class breadwinners, Petrillo was fingered for operating a multimillion-dollar slush fund. A strike that had been hovering for years loomed.

TV producers, by then, had already devised ways out of the impasse. One popular remedy was a harbinger of today's globalized economy. They'd outsource soundtracks to Europe. They shouldn't have to pay one thousand one hundred dollars to American musicians—plus one thousand four hundred dollars in union fees— when they could snag a half-hour of material from Germany, Belgium, Italy, Austria, and England at a fraction of the cost.

∗ ∗ ∗

JACK PERRY, CERTIFIED PUBLIC accountant, lobbed the question, as did Nat Winecoff, promoter. After pleasantries with their newest client, Gordon's advisers fast-forwarded the conversation. Its essence: what the fuck was he doing? His little start-up should have been ringing up thousands of dollars a month in sales by now. Never before had such a seller's market for tracked music existed. If he wasn't phoning executives like mad, or wearing out his wheelchair treads meeting producers frantic for clips to dramatize and lighten their shows, then he was screwing up epically. Gordon, referred over to these men by a studio contact, responded he was doing all that and more. Which circled Jack and Nat back to their original query: "What the hell's going on at your office?" Fine, Gordon conceded. He needed a teensy bit of direction.

Actually, he was lost. Twenty-six episodes supplying and overseeing the music for 1952's *Craig Kennedy: Criminologist*, a syndicated—and short-lived—*CSI*-ish, mystery series about a science-hewing detective, brought the slimmest of paychecks. Orchestrating the opening and closing numbers on a limited trial basis for *The Adventures of Wild Bill Hickok*, a syndicated western that CBS picked up, was but a nominal lift. Music from one of Lee's B-movie serials introduced the show. (In it, Guy Madison portrayed the womanizing, longhaired gunslinger that shot his way to frontier fame; character actor Andy Devine played his sidekick, "Jingles.") *Craig Kennedy, Hickok*, and a couple of two-bit jungle movies *were* Gordon's resume.

Winecoff, well connected and taken with the "kid," diagnosed one of his flubs right there. Gordon had to learn empathy. Instead of thinking myopically about what he needed from clients, he should be contorting himself to make them look better. "Like it's that easy," Gordon said, waving a snowman arm. Winecoff elaborated. Given the heat the networks were under to keep costs down, Gordon should better package his merchandise to sway them with a bargain. After he'd low-balled them and impressed them as reliable, he could raise his prices. "Make them need you!" Winecoff said. "Not the other way around. Understand?" A mousy, nondescript man in demand, he couldn't have known that Gordon had misplaced his swagger.

On Winecoff's counsel, Gordon steeled his ego and now invited executives to pop by his office to kick the tires on the catalog. There, Rose handed them price sheets while Gordon hyped the economics. "You're not going to find a better catalog in town at this price." Of course, Capitol Records and another indie, postproduction firm like his were the only competition for soundtracking jobs the studios bid off the lot. "Give us a shot," he'd say, remembering Winecoff's words. "You can't afford not to with all this union horseshit." With bonhomie and firm salesmanship, Gordon tried distracting attention from his body in one of the earth's vainest towns. He puffed off cigarettes his mother lit, sometimes querying customers if they'd want a drag as an icebreaker. This reformulated shtick had promise. By the second or third meeting, most of those he met no longer faltered or stood back negotiating with the coat-and-tie curiosity.

A little bravado suited the newbie well. The producers for *Private Secretary*, a network sitcom about a brassy, busty Girl Friday, signed on with him. New commercials dribbled in. Either from inexperience or corner cutting, Gordon sometimes failed to secure the proper legal rights for the music he offered, including for a group of his dad's old acetates. Obscure British composers, whose songs he sliced and spliced into desirable cues, weren't always compensated, as they should've been. Whatever shortcuts he took, the copyright police never surfaced at his office bungalow, as paychecks that weren't there a year ago started appearing.

Winecoff, realizing Gordon had just scraped his potential, not only planned to stick around as a rainmaker, but to invest an envelope of his own money with him. At last, the Zahlers had tail winds. Gordon's first business partner was a futuristic thinker with an aptitude for promotion and services that plenty of headliners wanted on their team. Spike Jones, the clowning bandleader, had turned to him. So would cartoonist Walt Disney for financing angles at the fairy-dust flatland he was scoping out in Orange County. Before the future, gazillion-dollar Magic Kingdom employed him, Winecoff was Gordon's inaugural partner.

They made quite the impression, tooling around the studios in Winecoff's whale-shaped Chevy convertible hunting for deals, Gordon in the front passenger seat wearing a cocksure grin and classic Wayfarer sunglasses. When need be, Gordon's five-feet-seven confidante hefted him in and out of the sedan. The physical labor was worth any backache. Gordon was a fire hose of ideas, though many were harebrained twists of existing programs. Winecoff fleshed the best of them out and flew with his ninety-five-pound friend to New York City to shop it to television syndicators. Back East, Winecoff handled the diapering, dressing, and whatnot that Gordon required to be presentable. (In doing so, Rose enjoyed her first true break from him in *fourteen* consecutive years, worried sick as she was about him in her absence.) When they returned to California, having bagged a rinky-dink production contact, Gordon emitted more composure. Winecoff buttonholed Gordon in his office soon afterward. How adamant was he about making it in Hollywood, he asked? Really making it? Gordon said he was all in. Fantastic, Winecoff replied. But there was the catch. If Gordon hoped to scale the next rung, he needed to wade into taboo waters by opening up on a touchy subject: doing business in a ticking time bomb of a body for which few were prepared.

On July 8, 1954, *United Press International* reporter Aline Mosby interviewed the twenty-eight year old for a feature story half the planet seemed to read. For the first time in eons, the family had a headline to celebrate rather than covering their eyes in disbelief. "Genius Who Can't Use Limbs Scores TV Coup." The lead-in: "Next fall television will offer a new program that teaches you how to sew, but the real story behind the show rivals most of the dramas on TV. Gordon Zahler… who successfully filmed and sold the interesting series, was not rich and had no experience. He is a hopeless cripple who cannot use his hands or walk. Yet, lying on a couch in his office with scripts clipped to a board near his eyes and a telephone headset over his ears, Zahler has produced thirteen color (episodes) on sewing. They already have been sold in seven major cities to begin in September."

Incredible. Impossible. Weird. Sierra Madre's former jokester would be responsible for placing a show dedicated to binding buttonholes and managing hems onto the airwaves. Elizabeth Chapin, a couturier who'd taught sewing lessons at department stores, would be the one-woman star, instructing on needle and thread behind a counter. "Being able to sit back and observe TV a lot, I noticed every station has two or three cooking programs, but none on sewing," Gordon explained to the era's wire service version of *CNN*. "There's a tremendous amount of home sewing in the United States—30,000,000 women do their own sewing. I decided it would be a saleable show." Gordon conceded the X-factor in his pitch was visual; whether network fat cats in New York would deem *him* as saleable was the enigma. "It was difficult getting around," he admitted. "When I'd phone for appointments, I wouldn't tell people I was in a wheelchair. I was afraid they wouldn't see me. So I would just arrive. It was a shock to some people. I worked with the hope my ability and being able to deliver a good program would overcome their feelings. I didn't work on the basis of their feeling sorry for me."

The executives must have dug what he was selling, because Gordon flew home having lined up two additional fall programs. He could even show off photos of himself at a taping in a light gray suit between the director and a boom mike. The phone, as Winecoff forecast, went bananas after *UPI's* piece ran. His hometown friends called first to congratulate and parody him. "Bravo, Mr. Genius," they said. "Can you teach us a French hem? What about an embroidery stitch?" *Hardy har har.* But *The Wild Bill* people reached out next to nail down Gordon's services for the upcoming season. In subsequent months, he finalized soundtrack deals with the *The Ford Television Theatre* and *Fireside Theatre*, both network anthology programs, and scored additional commercials. *The Red Skelton Show*, a high-ratings variety program, bought cues, too. The flattering photograph of Gordon accompanying the story even showcased his dimples, sprinkles on a sundae that he hadn't been sure was makeable.

Those victories notwithstanding, the "company" was still a ragtag operation. Gordon was a born salesman, but he managed impulsively or not at all. Rose, the untrained administrator, tackled the monotonous: answering phones, typing correspondence, stubbing Gordon's cigarettes, emptying his urine bag, and heating his tea. The temp sound editors supervised themselves; it wasn't as if their boss was an expert in the craft.

Jack asserted himself into this mix of inexperience and potential via soft-sell offensive. Let him let manage the financials—budget, taxes, insurance, payroll—since Gordon knew even less about money management than pinprick music editing. Concentrate on wooing clients, Jack urged him. Learn the nuances of the job. After watching inertia transform into momentum through Winecoff, Gordon astutely said yes.

They'd become fast friends, he and Jack, with more in common than Hollywood. Entering a restaurant, looky-loos must've compared them to hobbled veterans of foreign wars in a steamy Fourth of July parade. Winecoff had to push Gordon's chair because Jack was occupied shuttling forward on a set of canes. His legs weren't with him anymore. They'd been shredded by a land mine buried by the Nazis on the Belgium side of the Ardennes Forest in preparation for what would be the Battle of the Bulge. The GI separated from his unit should have bled out. But he'd hung on—and hung on even after the

Germans rained artillery shells at the field hospital that finished off Jack's legs for good.

Jack survived it all, first in US military hospitals and then through college at a time when there was no handicapped parking or other accommodations for the disabled. After college, he put out a shingle with a fellow accountant near seedy La Brea and Pico Boulevards. As his showbiz clientele proved, Jack's shrewd guidance and quiet integrity more than compensated for missing parts. Nobody cared that he was two-thirds whole and he never begged for pity. He limped his way into an expensive suite close to West Los Angeles' "Golden Triangle" and business came to him.

The final member of Gordon's wise-man troika was one of Jack's recommendations. Abraham "Abe" Marcus was a swarthy Beverly Hills music lawyer by way of New York's Columbia Law School. Abe was short, like most of Gordon's advisers, and walked with a ramrod bearing that got him mistaken around the golf course for a sitting superior court judge. Away from the links, Abe defended Hollywood's musical underdogs: composers long exploited by the studios over copyright and royalty payments. Many were irascible Europeans— guys named Dmitri and Miklos—convinced they'd been dragooned by an unjust system until their pinstriped representative stepped in. Abe wasn't afraid of decorum; he'd once had an accordionist perform in court to prove that a client had been cheated. As for Gordon, he valued one quality above all else: though raw, he was a lightning fast learner.

During the mid fifties, these men encouraged Gordon to chase more film work, however spotty the plot. They wanted him to sock cash away for when his TV shows went on hiatus. Paychecks shoved through his mail slot were a seasonal thing. On their recommendation, Gordon hustled a few movie projects, ludicrous as they were. He then dictated the letter he'd been champing to send. The addressee was the county welfare department. The message: stop sending vouchers. From now on, he and his mother didn't need them.

CHAPTER TWELVE: HERE COMES FLASH

E DWARD D. WOOD JR. had a plan—a plan to boggle minds with a tale of science fiction necromancy sure to punch his directorial ticket. Bela Lugosi, America's onetime *Dracula* of film and stage, was his star, and just because he was a seventy-year-old has-been strung out on morphine was no reason to bypass him. In Wood's cinematic judgment, Lugosi, a poor man's Boris Karloff, could still terrify audiences onto the edge of their seats, even if the broke, recently divorced actor had just been discharged from a mental hospital. The other elements for Wood's horror classic were similarly unorthodox. A fundamentalist church from Beverly Hills had agreed to be the movie's banker—provided the title was renamed something less sacrilegious and that it baptize the whole crew. (Which it did at a swimming pool owned by someone Jewish.) A bald, four-hundred-pound Swedish wrestler, who spoke unintelligible English, and a willful "Vampira," who rode the bus to the soundstage costumed in her slutty undead outfit, were his side characters. Special effects were in the bag, courtesy of scale model flying saucers that some later swore were hubcaps or pie tins.

Filming for *Plan 9 From Outer Space*, previously known as *Grave Robbers From Outer Space*, began in 1956 at Quality Studios on Santa Monica Boulevard near Western Avenue. Wood, a decorated World War II Marine who claimed to have charged into battle in bra and panties beneath his combat greens, had written the script in two weeks.

Unfortunately for the mustachioed auteur, the plot he intended to be groundbreaking and *avant-garde* for its cosmic politics was not just ridiculous. It was incomprehensible. In it, aliens hatch their invasion by raising the Earth's dead and enslaving them as their zombie army. Lugosi, who played an old geezer mourning his wife, did Wood no favors, either, when he died in real life, days after the shoestring production commenced. Instead of rethinking his storyline, since he had just five minutes of usable film of Lugosi, Wood went another way. He hired a local chiropractor as a body double and had him hold a cape over his face. No one was fooled.

Under Wood's command, night and day mixed in the same scene, fake headstones got knocked over, "UFO" wires were visible, and a shower-curtain imitated a cockpit barricade. Wood, who'd fancied himself the next Orson Welles, was over his cinephile head at thirty-two. His passion for filmmaking greatly surpassed his talent, leaving critics to savage him "an oddball hack." But he was so determined that you wanted to root for him. So *Plan 9* wasn't *The Bridge On the River Kwai* or even *Creature From the Black Lagoon*. All Wood's leaden-talking extraterrestrials desired were for man to abolish atomic weapons and live in intergalactic peace.

BRAVE AIR FORCE COLONEL: Why is it so important that you want to contact the governments of our Earth?
TESTY HEAD ALIEN: Because of death. Because all you of Earth are idiots.
AIR FORCE OFFICER NO. 2: Now you hold on, Buster.
ALIEN: No, you hold on!

What would gain cult fame decades later as one of the worst movies of all time —a kitschy, Golden Turkey-Rotten Tomato love child that Tim Burton seized on for his 1994 Wood biopic—just needed music for completion. How Wood discovered Gordon, already known for his fast turnaround time and low prices, is cloudier than Wood's action sequences. Still, the Zahler Music Library went under contract to soundtrack the score, probably for less than three hundred and fifty dollars, after filming had wrapped. Gordon, according to one music journalist, selected material by English songwriters Trevor

Duncan and Gilbert Winter from the Video Moods and Impress libraries; Emil Ascher Inc. was their American distributor. The horror songs, pastorals, and other ditties they'd composed for other projects were transferred from rented discs onto magnetic tape, from which Gordon's editors shaped them for *Plan 9*. Naysayers viewed my uncle as a "bottom rung music packager" who would snatch foreign music and rename them. True or not, Gordon's soundtrack artistry may have been Wood's saving grace. "Surprisingly effective" as an interplanetary-themed underscore, one critic contended; music that "greatly" enhanced the ham-handed spookiness, added another. But it only disguised so much. *Plan 9*, after premiering at Los Angeles' Carlton Theatre in March 1957, was so critically panned no one else would screen it.

Gordon by then had a more sobering problem: trying to avoid his own rendezvous with the grave. All the telltale signs had reared of another bladder obstruction—the headaches, the sweating, the hard belly. X-rays revealed calcium stones in his left kidney and a few in his bladder and urethra. Dr. Risser said they needed removal pronto at Huntington Memorial. Gordon, contemptuous of most doctors, saw the bespectacled, freethinking orthopedic as a soothsayer. If Joe Risser believed he needed to be cut open, he welcomed the incision. But paying for the three-hundred-dollar surgery was another matter. Wood was stiffing him for the *Plan 9* soundtrack, and Gordon wasn't swimming in one-hundred-dollar bills. Headset secured, ego on ice, he dialed the Motion Picture Relief Fund. Now that he was in the industry, would they pay for his surgery? Fund administrators, impressed by his achievements, typed up a check.

By all rights, this should've been his last mortal request. As the surgeon fileted open his inflamed kidney, Gordon's blood pressure fell precipitously. In a couple of minutes, the needle was at zero. His breathing stopped, then his heartbeat. Technically, he was dead. Forgetting the kidney, the doctor grabbed his scalpel. He sawed a hole a few inches wide through Gordon's sternum, wiggling two fingers into the cavity and poked around. There was the heart, limp as a rag. The surgeon started massaging it, prodding the chambers to thump, this being the age before defibrillators. "Beat!" he said. "Beat, goddamn it." It wouldn't. He squeezed it harder. If he failed to get the heart pumping soon, Gordon's oxygen-deprived brain would be so scrambled it wouldn't be worth the resuscitation. After a minute, he withdrew his fingers, having done what he could.

Everybody in the operating room stopped breathing, watching for cardiac movement. Seconds passed. Black thoughts ricocheted. Then *boom-boom, boom-boom.* The heart twitched. Before long a normal rhythm was there. Breathing restarted, and Gordon's blood pressure surged. It was if he'd been plugged back into a socket. Two weeks later he was well enough to have those meddlesome stones excised. But this wasn't only about what they took out of him. Far from leaving Gordon sulky, this latest biological melodrama produced a stronger, opposite reaction. Inside of him eddied the realization that he could outlast practically anything except borrowed time. The zipper scar sewn across his breastbone was evidence. He was a shade unkillable. The "Amazing Criswell," the hokey psychic who introduced Ed Wood's movies, should've narrated that story.

*   *   *

Rose, when she wasn't at the office or praying for Gordon, was fitting herself in her own armor around this juncture. Don't let the black granny glasses and saggy eyes deceive you. However much she preached benevolence to defeat malice, she was willing to challenge some very influential industry men. Her flashpoint was one that still resonates today. Where do the rights of an artist end and a corporation begin? Rose made this a three-hundred-thousand-dollar question in the lawsuit she filed against Columbia Pictures. She wouldn't be a brick in their wall.

Of all the studios she could have foreseen picking a fight with, Columbia was about the last. Rose had long been sentimental about the home of Frank Capra, Rita Hayworth, and the Cohn Brothers. It'd been the first major outfit to hire Lee as he climbed the Hollywood totem pole. *The first!* Perhaps, Abe suggested to her, a different culture presided there now. Throughout the fifties, the Old Guard studios continued to clean out their film vaults for the TV networks, which broadcast them by the bushels to fill dead airtime. In doing so, however, they turned intellectual property into an incendiary device. Should songwriters or other artists be compensated when their material resurfaces on new media that hadn't existed when the original agreement was signed? That was the question. After Columbia's *Crime Takes A Holiday* aired on local television, Abe's typewriter clattered. Where, he wrote Columbia, was Lee's money for his compositions on the legal thriller? No return letter arrived. As other films Lee scored trickled onto late-night TV, Abe sought a meeting. Again, Columbia blew him off, so he threatened injunctions. A suit, perhaps, would get executives talking.

Lee, as was customary in his era, used to bang out a *pro forma* license granting his studio employers the right to play his music in conjunction with their movies. For legal symbolism, he'd charged them one dollar per synchronization license. Nothing had been in the paperwork about TV. How could it be? The revolution of beamed electrons didn't exist commercially until after he'd died. Columbia, in releasing dozens of films with Lee's music on them, assumed that one agreement was a catchall. And that nobody would raise a commotion. Rose and Gordon, while ticked off at the injustice, also appreciated that relative nobodies like them were at a lopsided disadvantage against a beloved corporation with no shortage of legal muscle. Abe concurred; at best, he said, they had a puncher's chance. After *Daily Variety* wrote about the case, they knew all the studios would close ranks around Columbia to discourage others from stepping forward. Rose needed to buckle up. With the three hundred thousand dollars she was seeking, her enemies would have no misgivings depicting her as a gold digger. If she laughed, you can understand. She'd dealt with a lot worse than a slander job in her fifty-odd years.

The standoff between the studios and the musicians' union was another fiscal cliffhanger. Should a new labor pact be forged to protect Hollywood orchestras by abolishing sound-tracked music, the Zahlers would be in possession of a catalog that no producers could legally use—not *Wild Bill Hickok*, not Ed Wood. They'd have to close up shop and reapply for county welfare. Mercifully, Big Labor had overestimated its clout again. When the mainstream studios ignored the levies the union tried imposing, James Petrillo attempted smoking them out. He ordered a nationwide musicians' strike, assuming he'd grind movie production to a halt. Paramount and Twentieth Century were ready. Let 'em picket, they said. They'd jack up their use of cheaper European and Mexican players; all the studios were already on an economizing kick with TV competition eating into their profits. Los Angeles film musicians jittery about their future reacted, too. They voted to abandon the American Federation of Musicians and join a new, more democratic organization. With that move, the strike was over, as was Petrillo's reign.

The architecture of showbiz music was resolidified in follow-on agreements. From here on, TV shows were not required to use newly recorded music from beginning to end, just parts of them. Studios that had employed their own orchestras since the Golden Age of film would disband them in exchange for musician pay raises. Their movies would be scored on an *ad hoc* basis or with soundtracks. The Zahler Music Catalog could earn its tomorrow.

Nobody, certainly, was willing to give them anything free. On January 20, 1959, the day before director Cecil B. DeMille died, Rose's bid for a gigantic payday from Columbia Pictures was snubbed. Los Angeles County Superior Court Judge Kurt Kauffman was unswayed by Abe's argument that the studio had infringed on Lee's copyrights. Abe had recited Lee's own contractual wording to bolster their case. "This license shall apply only for public reproduction and performance in theatres or other places of public entertainment…" Columbia's lawyers were more persuasive. They argued that Lee was a contractor already paid for his work and that TV was irrelevant. Gavel down. Between this ruling and the settlement with the Pasadena Unified school district over the accident, the Zahlers were 0-2 against the powers-that-be.

✷　✷　✷

FOR ROSE, JUST BEING Gordon's office assistant nine to five, then his home attendant every night, could be punitive enough. She was ancient in her mid fifties, her hair a tangle of wiry, gray locks, jowls flopping prematurely into a turkey neck. When she wasn't on her feet, either parked in front of the stove or cantilevered over Gordon's bed, she typed letters for him hunt-and-peck style. The svelte legs that Lee used to rave about now swelled up, painfully stiff with elephantiasis. Every week of every month she had but a few hours to lavish on herself, typically late at night when Gordon was snoring. A long bath or reading was her temporary battery recharge. This caretaker existence was devouring her.

Nobody could have faulted her for throwing a hissy fit those times Gordon unloaded on her for taking too long to complete a task. The more successful he became, the more his impatience dictated his mood. "Hurry up, Mom," he'd yelp from the other room. "I don't have all day to go through the mail, you know." How she must have wanted to slam down her spatula and fling herself onto a tropical island for a week. *That's it. I can't do this anymore! Have one of your friends look after you*, she could have yelled, suntan lotion in bag. Could have but wouldn't. Rose absorbed his exasperating ways with the docility of a Buddhist monk. In her mind, this wasn't her son playing the tyrant. It was the conflict between the dependence he loathed and the aspirations he was sharpening. A kid that Hollywood had laughed off as a chump was now a red-blooded capitalist going places. Rose saluted the change, lauded him for it, whatever it exacted from her. When irritated or dog-tired, she'd try being philosophical or slathering niceness on the closest person. A thousand meals standing up, friendships lost, arthritis gained, holidays on bedpan detail. It could make a person sick if they weren't careful.

One day, about ready to drop, she could withhold it no more. She needed a breather in the short term, and regular days off after that. What if they advertised for a part-time attendant? Someone dependable? Someone right here in the Yellow Pages. She pointed to employment agencies. "What could it hurt to make a few calls?" Gordon knew there was the gasp of burnout in her low-volume words. Her inflamed ankles told the story by themselves. If they'd won the suit against Columbia, he responded, she could have retired. Could have as much time away as she pleased. But they hadn't. "I'm sorry, Mom. The business is taking everything. You know I don't want you getting worn down." Two hundred bucks was too much for a part-time caretaker. "Hell," he added, "a hundred was." Sighing, Rose went back to the typewriter. She looked out of it.

And Gordon returned to being Ed Wood's music man. His tonal flourishes were there in *Final Curtain*, Wood's twenty-minute-long TV-series pilot about a vampire roaming a theater after its last horror-show performance. (Tabbed his "lost project," the 1957 production was unseen until 2013, when a film festival aired it.) In 1959, the waxy-skinned director with the mannerisms of a cheap magician and the Sierra Madran who'd really died twice collaborated on *Plan 9's* "sequel." *Night of the Ghouls* followed a story line not dissimilar to Patrick Swayze's *Ghost*, except the latter supernatural tearjerker held together in the end. Wood's involved a doctor tricking people that he could contact the deceased. It was his third consecutive flop. Wood couldn't get any commercial traction, though he was sure adroit at eluding postproduction invoices. Gordon pushed on, ticked that Wood had stiffed him and yet confident that the company would be venturing back to outer space with directors who knew what they were doing.

*   *   *

GERTRUDE DUCREST, GORDON'S FIRST secretary not named Rose, called out that, "A Mister Fields was on the line."

"A Mr. Who?" Gordon bellowed from his office.

"A Mister Fields," she yelled back.

He swiped the lever and spoke into his headset. Twenty minutes later he told Gertrude to have his mom drop everything and come in. The Howdy Doody grin he wore for that *UPI* story had reappeared.

"What is it?"

"Mom, take a load off. Relax." She eased into a chair with a frown. "Remember how we were talking about finding new work? You know, now that *Wild Bill* and *Ford Theater* are going off the air?"

"Yes, I do. You said *The Ann Sothern Show* might pick us up." (It was the spin-off from *Private Secretary*.)

"Forget that now. It's small change compared to the appointment we have in Culver City next week."

"Culver City? What's in Culver City?"

"Oh, I don't know. How about a little company called MGM?"

"Gordon, I'm in no mood for any guessing games. Just say whatever it is you have to say so I can go back to my typing."

"Maybe this will brighten your day. Our appointment is with Joseph Fields. Apparently, he's producing the next big Doris Day movie. And he wants us—us, Mom—to score most of it from the catalog!"

"I don't believe it. You're pulling my leg."

"No, I'm not. Not when it's MGM were talking about. We have to cover about forty minutes, give or take."

"Why us?"

"I don't know. Maybe we're getting a reputation. We'll find out from Mr. Fields. He's treating us to lunch to sign the papers."

"To sign? You mean you already agreed to what he was offering?"

"Uh, yeah. It was quadruple what we'd normally ask."

"This sounds too good to be true. Especially with our luck."

"Tell me about it."

"Did he say who else is going to be in the movie?"

"Richard Widmark. Gene Kelly, the actor, is directing. His debut, I think."

"Do they have a title?"

"*Tunnel of Love.* It's based on a play. Some romantic mush. As long as it doesn't have Ed Wood anywhere within a mile of the lot, I'm gung ho."

"Gordon, I'm speechless. This is the best news we've had in, gosh, I don't know how long."

"It's better than that. With the four-thou we stand to make, we should be able to put down a deposit on a house around here. According to Jack, anyway. No more back and forth every day. It'll be sayonara, Sierra Madre. Farewell peasants."

"Don't speak ill of Sierra Madre. It's been wonderful to us."

"Loosen up, Mom. I'm only saying that since we work in Hollywood, we should live in Hollywood. Hey, are you listening?"

"Sorry. I was just daydreaming. Doris Day. Maybe I'll get to meet her. Heavens, I love her movies."

"Well, you may love the check more."

PART II—ROLL

CHAPTER THIRTEEN: THE LITTLE BIG TOP

MIDWAY THROUGH THE CELEBRATION, Gordon whistled. "Hey, Stan, a little help here?" A minute later, he and his curved spine sat in a wicker chair, the type of chair doctors expressly warned him to avoid in a new kitchen. "Get the camera," he said. "Let's save the moment." Stan, the same Stan from Sierra Madre who had once forgotten to bring Gordon in from his garage after a boozy night clubbing, clicked the shutter button.

"Should I come get you now?" Stan wondered.

"Absolutely not," Gordon harrumphed with a giggle. "Just make sure to get a picture of me if I fall off. And refill my drink!"

Earlier that morning, Rose wept. Gordon hummed. Moving day was their screw-you to the undertow. The money from sound-tracking MGM's *The Tunnel of Love*, a comedic romp about a New England couple bumbling their way through conception, pre–sexual revolution, became their down payment on this house. Just as Gordon had predicted! After five rentals, each one scuzzier than the last, the Zahler name was duly recorded on a deed. Hectic as it was amid the newspaper-wrapped glassware and tottering stacks of cartons, their first night at 8979 Shoreham Drive in Hollywood was an enchanted one. Rose cooked roast beef with Yorkshire pudding for everyone who helped with the relocation, and the flowing alcohol could've outpoured the closest bar.

The cream-colored residence was in a blue-collar neighborhood in the hills overlooking Sunset Boulevard, just west of Laurel Canyon. Properties around here were so squished together you could almost hear your neighbor cooking, but the overall geography more than offset for the lousy setbacks. The TV detective show *77 Sunset Strip* was set down the road as its own cool meter of Los Angeles life. Inside were a small kitchen, two back bedrooms, a vanity nook, a brick fireplace, and a bottom-level garage. Floor-length mirrors gave the living room, where Gordon's bed laid, a deceptively bigger footprint than the sum of the square footage. Shoreham owed its bright aura to a cheery palette—beige carpeting, a lavender parlor couch, and a bay window that beckoned golden sunbeams inward. The hillside elevation offered a telephoto view of western Hollywood, particularly the skin joints and garish nightclubs blinking neon down the road. The house cost twenty-two thousand seven-hundred dollars. What the bank didn't own, mother and son split fifty-fifty.

Under the existing pecking order—Gordon the boss, Rose the bossed around—not much else was divvied up. Where Gordon had once been content to run the office, he now asserted control at home, as well. Details he'd never cared much about—how the furniture was arranged, mortgage rates, nursing bills, custom-tailored suits—mattered. In his early thirties, he wanted to rule everything. Rose, often too winded to contest him, allowed the maturation to take wing. It wasn't like she could keep him corked up, anyway. Not anymore. She'd been there when industry folks had scoffed at his ideas, and ridden back to the office with a son whose determined jaw Sonny Liston couldn't have dislocated.

Gordon should have sent every doubter he'd faced since County General a silver-engraved thank you. Nihilistic critiques of what he could do in that laugher of a body was his motivational springboard to accomplish the extraordinary with a smirk and a wink. His vision for a clever and flagrantly illegal elevator at Shoreham Drive was an exclamation point of that spirit. A contrarian needs to hear "no" on the same wavelength the insecure need to be reminded they're safe. Besides, this was no supplemental challenge. It was their key to remaining here.

From their first glimpse of the interior, the stairs leading from the garage jumped out as a deal-killer. Rose couldn't haul him and his chair up those bumpy steps a single time, let alone multiple times daily. The sole remedy, Gordon knew instinctively, was a mechanical lift. Before they'd settled in, he'd discussed its practicality with some engineers. Okay, they were Hollywood *sound* and *recording* engineers he'd met at dubbing sessions, plus Nat Winecoff, but they were a resourceful bunch, if totally unqualified for construction. When Gordon demanded to pay them, their universal chorus was "stuff it." Free beer, sandwiches, and repartee were compensation. Rose was eager for the personal elevator to work, but the improvisational approach unnerved her. What if they misjudged the cab's weight and the cables snapped? Gordon's brother-in-law, Millard, was another project cynic. Attempting something this complex absent blueprints and load-bearing calculations would be a fiasco, he believed. Perhaps even a risk to life and limb. He suggested they install a ramp. "Guess time will tell if my way's better," Gordon answered at a get-together, looking poised between spoon-fed bites.

Over the next few weeks, he almost had to eat his words, too, as he visited stores and waited on hold while merchants searched their spare parts inventory. On top of his treasure hunt for a motor and gears, Gordon also had to keep city inspectors in the dark. One whiff of his back-of-the-envelope diagrams would have gotten the project yellow-tagged into a code-compliance circle jerk. They pushed onward nonetheless. Soon, a crudely mined shaft appeared where a stairwell used to be. Gordon "managed" the job as he had the conversion of Lee's music from one media to another. He argued with his pals about the electronics, and cheerleaded their refinements and revisions that fanned thick dust onto the furniture with puppy-ish enthusiam. When he wasn't at the con, he rummaged for missing items to cannibalize, finding, among other components, a discount, fighter pilot seat complete with ejection handle at a war-surplus store. *Shazam*: there was his elevator chair.

Trial runs were clammy. Should the secret elevator malfunction or a city bureaucrat come around, the house the Zahlers had scaled an abyss to buy would probably go back on the market. Rose might have begun asking about their options feeling the jackhammer-like vibration the mechanism sent through the walls. But that was just nerves. The two-person contraption the size of a phone booth was a slap-dashed beaut of engineering. For years it ran dependably, requiring almost no maintenance save for lubrication. Gordon needled Millard every chance he could. Perhaps, he said, you didn't need a Caltech diploma to think like you had one.

*   *   *

THE HUSTLE-BUSTLE WAS A victory bell. Show pitching trips to New York and London, adding music to one hundred and ninety five *Crusader Rabbit* cartoons, even a tug from the Old West. Gordon, in the late fifties, was named musical supervisor for ABC's hotly watched *26 Men* series about the Arizona Rangers, early-century lawmen who'd policed the Southwest's anarchic territories. Producing the syndicated program was Russell Hayden, a square-faced, easygoing, former character actor known for playing Lucky on the Hopalong Cassidy western films. Hayden, who'd once starred for Universal and Columbia and been the suit behind the *Judge Roy Bean* series, knew he had something untapped in the man from Shoreham. Sometimes Gordon's prize wasn't just making powerful friends. It was watching secretaries who'd stuttered lies before about why their bosses weren't available brownnose him now. "Good morning, Mr. Zahler," they'd say. "We've been expecting you."

It was all promising, a concrete pour on a sensational future, but he was grinding such long hours that he often broke into pale sweats or felt whipped hours before lunch. Gordon's head whirled in business eighteen hours a day even as his body panted for time out. Worn down herself, Rose pestered him to be careful, and parsed it in terms he understood. "You're going to work yourself back into intensive care if you don't take it easy," she'd say on the drive home. "You don't want to put me in charge at the office, do you?" CPA Jack had a healthy suggestion for the candle-burning-at-both-ends routine. Since the TV-shooting season was over, treat yourself to a vacation.

Well, tell that to the quiver at the nape of Gordon's skull. *Be content you're making money,* the voice chastised him when he got bigheaded. *Stare hard in the mirror if you're antsy for more. The answers are there.* Existing above the neck, Gordon had severed himself from the devil-may-care movement that had defined him. No backslaps or knuckle cracking, no joke playing or food flinging. If he couldn't take a leak on his own, his chance at lifelong romance was infinitesimal. How could it be otherwise when others were in charge of his every wish? By the time they'd done it, the fresh things streaking across his mind were already green with mold.

Too often watching the blood drain out of new acquaintances' cheeks epitomized the theatrical part of his day. Some forgot to blink. Others covered their agape mouths. Many panicked whether to attempt shaking hands with whatever emerged from his lap blanket. To spare them the agony, he'd tell them to pat him on the shoulder and start talking business. Guests still unglued necessitated him to play therapist. He'd learned to act nonchalant about the obvious: his gnarled stick-figure frame. When no icebreaker cut the awkwardness, he'd reminisce about his wild childhood—daring stink-bomb attacks or riding bikes off roofs—with a chuckle. Guests' appreciation that he'd once stood and wasn't embittered over his wheelchair existence helped curb the shock, though it didn't always quell their inner voices that *they* were a hideous fall away from being him.

As if the comforting boosted him much. Twenty years of sponge baths and catheters had decked expectations. In that time there had been two thrill rides and one genuinely interested woman. The drunken nights from his early twenties was adolescent stuff. Now that he was in Hollywood, around soundstage gunfights and peroxide sex kittens, he saw how indescribably frustrating it was to be numb in a touch-me town.

Which is not to suggest he was lying about, pining over his tactile denials. Having a dormant body was no barrier to laughs and spontaneity. My big brother, Paul, was a regular guest at Shoreham, where Rose spoiled him silly and Gordon treated the teen like a pint-size adult. "Hey kiddo, whatcha know?" If Paul acted squirrelly, Gordon faked a sneer and mimicked *The Honeymooners'* Ralph

Kramden. "Do that again and I'll send you to the *mo-on*." Paul ate it up. On trips to the studios, Gordon introduced his nephew to Lucille Ball, Ann Sothern, and cowboy stars. He'd gush about his hope to patent a miniature record-player you wore like a wristwatch. On Friday nights, the two watched the televised boxing matches on Gordon's bed munching takeout Hamburger Hamlet cheeseburgers while screaming for knockouts. Nobody had an uncle like this. You couldn't beat him at gin because he'd memorize the deck. Impress him with your chutzpah and he'd let you drink coffee—or light his smokes.

When Paul grew older, Gordon hired him as an apprentice music cutter for a few summers. It was there he learned what the regular editors already had: the boss was a perfectionist who bird-dogged your work. Be off a hair on a cue for a *Popeye* cartoon and you'd have to re-cut it endlessly. If Gordon judged that a rifle-shot sound effect sounded too much like a fart, plan to be in the desert sun with him the next day firing a real shotgun next to a portable microphone. Gordon's nit-picky ear not only provoked snide comments among his crew, it'd also instigated fisticuffs. As Paul heard, Gordon had once coaxed two actors in *Young Dillinger* to re-dub a fight scene, unhappy with the take they had. "Fellas," Gordon had explained, "I want to hear a *pow*. You there—slap the other guy with an open hand. Lean into it." Somehow, his instruction had been garbled, and one of the actors had walloped his counterpart when he hadn't been ready. Real punches were exchanged, with a live mike between them and Gordon shrieking, "Cut, guys. Cut!" Editors knew they were in for meticulous scrutiny when Gordon had them replay their rough cuts. Merit reward was something else, too. At Zahler Music, demonstrated ability led to promotions to more important shows, not necessarily more money. On payday, everybody grouched and few received raises. Paul himself earned minimum wage.

Gordon, the skinflint, flat disliked the administrative duties of being *the* boss, being as he was a right-brained, creative dude from an extended lineage of them. His irritation with workplace necessities extended to his body's maintenance protocol, as well. Bedsores that had to be sterilized on schedule distracted him from screenplays he was thinking about. "Just leave it," he'd tell Rose if she approached with gauze at an inopportune point. Bladder-infection prevention sliced into contract-review time; he'd have to swallow his pills between appointments later. Once at the office, Paul felt nauseated after spilling urine on his fingers emptying Gordon's "pee bag," a tapered, rubber container tubed to his catheter. "If that's the worst thing you ever get on your hands," he glowered, "consider yourself lucky."

After work, Gordon's motto was to hell with the splicing. It was time to joy ride! One Friday evening around 10:00 p.m., he ordered Paul to load him into the car and take the onramp onto the Hollywood Freeway.

"We're going to Balboa Bay to check out the boats," he said in the garage.

"But," my brother faltered, "I don't have my license. To be honest, I've never driven on the freeway before."

"Who cares?" Gordon said. "You just drive faster. Can you handle it or not?"

"Yeah, I think so," Paul answered, sweat dewing on his fifteen-year-old neck.

"Great. Time to punch it, kiddo!"

Gordon's yearning to cavort was a simmering cauldron. And it went beyond the Hollywood in-crowd within sightline of his bed. It was Los Angeles, the East Coast, the Swiss Alps, the Riviera, Western Africa. Baby steps toward an extraordinary life felt too measured. He needed a shove.

Rose admitted she was baffled by his recreational ennui. Why couldn't he be content with his accomplishments? Everybody was so proud. "Remember the article that called you a genius?" Because, he retorted, that was faded newsprint. Watching Milton Berle on TV after work left his juices cold. Rose reminded him of the merriment from a recent costume party, where a friend had dressed him up as Whistler's Mother and he snatched first prize. "Couldn't you be satisfied going to a party once a month?" Gordon's eyes torched holes in the ceiling. "Mom, you haven't gotten it, have you? We both know how unpredictable my health is. But getting cheated when there's so much to explore? To be honest, I'd rather be dead if this—this—is all there is."

Neither of them plied the subject further. Rose might have lumbered to bed that night replaying the words of the physician who'd given Gordon a checkup a month earlier. She was so disturbed afterward that she'd phoned Dr. Risser at home for a second opinion. Was it true, she said? That he couldn't live five more years, as his respected colleague had just predicted? Depends on him, Risser told her. As it was, he'd never heard of anybody with a cervical injury like Gordon's who'd made it this long. An orthopedic journal had already commissioned an article about his anomalistic survival. Rose tossed and turned through a sleepless night. Yet Gordon was in his living room bed, snoring and dreaming of freedom.

Ultimately, it was Rose's mother—the fat, folksy Sonya Ross— who bestowed on Gordon the adage he needed. The quiet, old woman in the mink coat was the family authority on darkness—murdered husband, slain brother, chronic depression. But she thought she had a secret formula for bliss. The occasion was the party Rose threw for Gordon at Shoreham to celebrate his thirty-third birthday. While most of the guests surrounded the coffee urn in the kitchen, Sonya leaned in close and whispered to him what she sometimes told her neurotic pet dachshund. "Don't strain yourself too much. You're here for pleasure."

∗   ∗   ∗

PLEASURE. EARLY ONE FRIDAY evening, a month after the party, Gordon sat alone in the rear seat of a Chrysler ragtop gunning along Interstate 10, the wind restyling his dark-brown hair. He was being driven to Palm Springs, an affluent, desert playground populated by celebrities, white shoes old people, and thirsty cacti a hundred miles east of Los Angeles. Samuel Bronston, Jr., the son of one of Gordon's producer-pals, was behind the wheel. (The elder Bronston, who'd once been an official Vatican photographer, then was a few years away from his professional apex masterminding big-spectacle films like *El Cid* and *The Fall of the Roman Empire*.) Nuzzled up close to junior that night was his actress-girlfriend. Who'd instigated the trip—Sam Jr., Gordon—was less important than its intent: a relaxing weekend of poolside card games and indulgent, four-drink dinners. They had the radio turned up, and Sam let everyone pull swigs from his silver flask. Anybody mentioning anything business-related would lose their next sip.

As the Chrysler hurtled toward its destination of pastel-colored hotels and smoky cafes, focus became an issue. Sam Jr.'s attention span wandered from conversational etiquette to obdurate lust. The more he allowed himself to steal peeks at his girlfriend's sweater-displacing rack—hey, his father was in business with Sophia Loren—the less he concentrated on the vagaries of the one-lane road. Sam might have even been fantasying about impressing the hottie at his father's movie studio in Madrid when the rut in the asphalt made its appearance. Twenty miles from the hotel, Sam was a prisoner to his reflexes. Hands jumping, he swerved to avoid the ragged pothole the width of a pizza box. Stomachs salivating for a good steak a second earlier were instantaneously up in their throats from his jerking overcorrection. The Chrysler fishtailed toward the highway's right shoulder, slowed only moderately by Sam's frantic braking. The car smashed into the protective berm, showering dirt and lowering the engine pitch from RPM growl to guttural whirr. Sam and his girl rubbed their whiplashed necks. "You all right?" he said. "Too soon to know," she replied. But that wasn't the end of it. News flash: Gordon was missing.

Night was coming. So was the weekend getaway traffic. Sam Jr. flashed ahead to what he might be facing—manslaughter charges, his father's wrath, a skewering in *Daily Variety*. This trip was supposed to be pure kicks. Why does disaster often erupt from that? "Gor-don!" he yelled. "Where are you? Gordon! Where in the name of Christ could you be?"

About a dozen feet up the highway is where. As he'd tell and retell in vivid reconstructions, he'd been catapulted from the backseat in an unexpected demonstration of Newtonian physics. The second Sam yanked the wheel thirty degrees to avoid the furrow in the road, there was nothing restraining Gordon from continuing to move forward—no seat belt (un-standard then) or his ethereal torso. He was jettisoned like flaming ammo during the Crusades, probably a couple feet over the door-lock if he had to wager. Along the way, he blacked out, remembering nothing about being airborne or the landing. His memory revived when a car near where he landed tore by. That was because he saw it from the tires up and assumed he was a goner.

Actually, lying face down on Interstate 10, he was sure he was dead. Gordon wasn't just near the highway. He was inches outside the narrow, white line separating the blazing traffic from the shoulder. Visibility was no solace here. Twilight speckling the desert in amber hues and deceiving shadows were picturesque from afar; they just made for poor lane guidance. Pointed northwest, Gordon could see what was speeding toward him. It was a large set of headlights, probably from a big rig half a mile away. A few seconds later, they illuminated him with supernova intensity.

"Help!" he called out. "Somebody."

"Where are you?" Sam whimpered. "Jesus, man. I killed Gordon. I can't believe it. I fucking killed him."

The truck headlights wound around a little bend, bathing Gordon in white glare like a downed fugitive in a prison yard. The sixteen-wheeler was one hundred and fifty yards away. Closing fast.

"Over here!" Gordon shrieked, his voice cracking on the vowels. "I'm over here. Near the white line. Hurry up. Hurry."

Sam was there in a few seconds, scooping up his passenger and apologizing with near tears in his eyes. "Nice driving, asshole," Gordon said in his arms. "Five more inches over the line and my head would've been a squished grapefruit. Next time give a guy some warning before you crank a turn like that."

The miracle was that Gordon hadn't re-broken his gossamer neck and perished where he'd landed. Incredibly, it'd gone uninjured. His face was intact, as well, if you ignored the purple knot on his left temple. Not until Sam Jr. had laid him back into the car that indestructible Gordon acknowledged he was doing crummy. He was queasy, and it had something to do with his spasm-ing right arm. Sam jumped into the Chrysler and waved at his girlfriend to join Gordon in the back. Hold on, he told them. He straightened the car out and floored it east, but not to any flamingo pink hotel with long happy hours.

At Torney General Hospital near Palm Springs, Gordon calmly said he'd injured his arm when he hit the pavement. The ER doctor, a freckled young man not long out of medical school, was skeptical a quadriplegic could detect limb damage from the type of headache he felt. His counter theory? The voluble patient was delirious after sustaining a concussion. "Just grab my elbow and pull up if you don't believe me," Gordon said. Still ignoring him, the doctor asked the male staffer there to help him remove Gordon's sweater, which kept getting snagged. Once off, they saw the inseam of his shirt was soaked with blood. Some concussion.

People in the room felt their lunch surge up, everybody, that is, but a patient inured to medical theater. This, however, was a new one. The bone in his upper arm had snapped in two with a compound fracture. The jagged end closest to his elbow had broken through the skin as a twig might poke through snow. Inside, viscous, yellow bone marrow oozed through the blood. Out of nowhere came a dull *thunk* behind the examining table. Gordon asked Sam Jr. what happened and Sam Jr. reported the attendant had fainted off in the corner. The doctor apologized for his squeamish helper and shipped Gordon up to surgery to set the arm.

A couple days later at work, wearing a sling over a cast, Gordon informed Nat Winecoff that Palm Springs could wait. He'd zeroed in on something that'd guarantee him real pleasure. A speedboat—that's what he needed.

CHAPTER FOURTEEN: STRANGE AS IT SEEMS

Josef "Joe" von Stroheim was getting recruited, simple as that, and it was up to him to judge whether the headhunting was ego-padding or irksome. His pursuer was relentless, allergic to the word "no." Whenever Gordon spied Joe on the Sam Goldwyn lot, he instructed whoever was pushing him to make a beeline in the direction of the twenty-something sound editor with the polarizing last name. "Joe, hold up!" A better gig than the one he had with *The Roy Rogers Show* was just a "yes" away, Gordon yakked. Huge upside: one hundred fifty dollar a week salary, ground-floor potential, no union hoops. Why the heavy press to fill a technical job as unglamorous as can be? Plenty. Joe had the acronym credentials Gordon revered (MGM, NBC) and the extroverted, smart-alecky personality mirroring his. The sound-effects library that Joe was amassing was extra frosting for a businessman hopeful about packaging them with music. All that incendiary history about his father, the maverick, silent movie director Erich von Stroheim, was incidental. His son was the up-and-comer.

Joe was intrigued by the buttering-up, even if his reservations told him to watch what he did. Jumping ship for a small, postproduction shop quarterbacked by someone like Gordon was nervy. Having been reared in a celebrity family, where Clark Gable gave him lifts to school on his motorbike, Joe knew perception could be a vicious maiden in showbiz. He'd been a lighthearted kid, into surfing, cameras, and girls, but the mesmerizing world his dad showed him gave him the bug. In the late thirties, Joe quit high school his senior year to take a job photographing stars in MGM's publicity department. His career laid ahead of him, his father's was dust. Erich, who'd directed *Greed* and other epics of that age, had so enraged Louis B. Mayer and the other studio honchos with his bold, spare-no-expense approach to moviemaking that they'd blackballed him. His days making big-budget films were done, and so was his lifestyle. Where the von Stroheim's once lived in Beverly Hills, they'd struggled to get by on Erich's lowly screenwriting jobs doled out to him as crumbs. Where they once basked on European trips, the family needed the collection plate passed around by William Powell, Myrna Loy, and others after Joe's mother was injured in a freak beauty parlor accident. If Hollywood had a Siberia, this was it.

Joe left MGM and family misery behind during World War II, joining the Marines as a combat photographer. For the next four years he traveled between the Pacific theater and Europe with a 35-mm in one hand and an M-1 rifle in the other. In between battlefield assignments, he drank hooch, gallivanted with his buddies, dodged mortar fire, and almost got nabbed by the Germans at the Rhine River. (This wouldn't have been good; his father's sadistic portrayal of the black-clad Nazis had placed a bounty on Joe's head.) Near the end of the hostilities, Joe snapped pictures that graced national magazines. He was at a German POW camp, where one thousand eleven hundred people were incinerated, and stood with Japanese war criminals—Tokyo Rose, Little Glass Eye—who mugged for his lens. Delivered home, Joe went straight to his girlfriend's apartment. When she didn't answer, he lifted the mail slot and heard her schtupping his best friend. After all that, landing an editing job was a cinch.

Years later now, Joe found himself on the fence about leaving stable MGM for burgeoning Zahler Music. Watching Gordon lay it on thick with a studio suit increased his apprehension. In those days, Gordon was known to stalk his contacts and then feign surprise when they noticed him. After the chin-wagging was done, he'd bleat his purpose. "Anything new on that show? They need music?" If he smelled a deal, Gordon was a pit bull in a poodle's body. Joe supposed his pursuer was overcompensating, trying not to be felt sorry for, and so far no one had run for cover hearing his voice. Questioned by many whether he had the Wheaties to get the job done, Gordon's answer was his trademark: "You betcha."

Joe could only weigh the pros and cons for so long, what with a family in the suburbs to support. Gordon's offer would fold extra money into his wallet, and the chance for more responsibility was tempting. His remaining doubt was about parachuting out, specifically whether he could secure another studio job if employment with Gordon soured? Deciding he'd still be marketable, Joe—after Gordon's umpteenth pitch—said yes. "Okay, you got me," he said. "Will that shut you up?"

Not really, but they were quite the duo. Joe, with his thick, chestnut hair, sarcastic grin, and exuberant storytelling, could hardly believe he'd agreed to work out of a dumpy office on the wrong end of Sunset. Gordon, his hair now receded into a widow's peak, his arrowhead-shaped face bookmarked by a pair of radar-dish ears, had a hard time believing his good fortune enlisting him. From a passing car, you might have confused Joe for John Cassavetes and Gordon for a malnourished Sinatra. Listen to their banter at a stoplight and you'd know they weren't.

*   *   *

JIMMY GILLARD, THIRTY-FIVE, REQUIRED no charm campaign to enter Gordon's world. He asked to be invited. Out of work, living off unemployment insurance, he had five kids and a wife to think about before any professional pride. Unlike Joe, Jimmy was never a pampered child of Hollywood. His roots were off the bayous near Shreveport, Louisiana—roots he'd severed in the late forties to move to California with tempered aspirations and a supple, handsome face.

Toby Gillard, Jimmy's father, had been one of the few prosperous black farmers in the Jim Crow South. He'd harvested crops from okra to cotton, using his spare time to help maintain the area's shaky racial peace as a Methodist preacher. Jimmy was the fourth oldest in Toby's family of ten, and the freest spirit among his taller brothers.

For him, playing hooky from school to loll, swim, ride horses, or swill moonshine was good-time abandon. But where most of his siblings enrolled in college, Jimmy never did. His talents were mechanical; busted machines always seemed to operate again after he'd tinkered with them. By his mid twenties, Jimmy had heard stories about factory jobs galore in California, a place where a grade-school dropout like him could flourish.

Out West, Jimmy downgraded that blabber to unverified myth with every door slammed in his face. None of the major plants would hire him. Scraping for rent money, he humbled himself changing tires on Greyhound buses. His next greasy, dead-end job was pouring iron and melting pipes at a Compton foundry. Even that was rocky at a company roiled by labor strife and picket lines. Jimmy, grandson of a slave, finally had to lower himself further for the sake of his country-girl wife, Lovella, and their young children. He climbed aboard an LA trash rig as a garbage man and prayed nobody he knew recognized him. When that grind ended, it was back to the metal works and when it went on strike again, it was back to the unemployment line. Ten years in dreamland California and enterprising Jimmy was doing circles.

His round-and-round might've been eternal had Isaac Ross, a mailman-friend whose route included the Sunset Strip, not mentioned a customer looking for a driver. "Here's the number in case you're interested," he said. Jimmy was there by nightfall. Rose spoke with him first, deciding she trusted Jimmy's face before he confessed that he'd never spoken with anybody in a wheelchair before. "Don't be scared," Rose told him. "He won't break easily. Some coffee?"

Introductions made, Gordon was pure business. This job was about doing the things he couldn't, not mere chauffeuring. Another man given a test-trial was too hardheaded about that. Whoever he retained would have to be willing to rotate him in his chair and bed to forestall bedsores, hand-feed him sandwiches, grab tapes from racks, flip document pages during meetings with fussy executives, know when to fade into the scenery, empty his urine bag, and swab him down with hydrogen peroxide at night. Got it? Jimmy said he did. His attendant, Gordon said with less vinegar, also had to master the traffic shortcuts on a steep learning curve. And forget about being home by 7:30 p.m. His day operated on its own clock. "Think you can handle it?" Gordon asked, noticing his prospect was an elfin five-feet-seven. "Absolutely, Mr. Zahler." The negotiations continued. The job paid seventy-five dollars a week to start plus free meals and Sundays off. Probably some travel as a bonus. Jimmy said it all sounded perfect.

"Can you start tomorrow, say at 10:00 a.m.?" Gordon asked. "It's Saturday, you know."

"I can be here at eight thirty if you want."

And so it began, the go-getter who'd juked the grim reaper and his proxy limbs by way of Shreveport. Jimmy wasn't complaining. He was rejoicing. His maiden weeks on the job put him in a dubbing room at Desilu Productions on Cahuenga Boulevard, one of America's best studios, in his single dark suit, feeding Gordon his tea while saying nothing. Thereafter came handshakes with Lucille Ball and Doris Day, both actresses nurturing soft spots for his boss, and other luminaries he'd only seen projected on screens before. In those months, Jimmy made a promise. Someday, he'd understand the secret of what was happening here—how editors chopped up music and sound effects into a crazy heap of cues for reassembly into tracks that could reach millions of ears.

His brothers whooped, often during Sunday afternoon phone calls, hearing him describe his microscopic place in the California limelight. "What's it like?" they'd poke him. "Strange," he'd answer. Gordon was a hoot, but the money was just north of insulting. Driving a powder blue Cadillac convertible was fantastic, too, though Gordon sometimes yelled out lane changes as if his loafer was on the gas pedal. Jimmy tried impersonating Gordon's nasally voice when he wanted him to switch lanes. *It's clear on my side!* Or, if late for meeting, *"Yellow light's coming—step on it!"* Already, Gordon's forehead had rammed into the glove compartment twice on account of his side-seat driving. Jimmy said he'd learned to stick out his right forearm when he'd have to slam the brakes stopping short, and the boss was mighty appreciative. The Gillard boys cackled loud at that.

Jimmy then took his brothers on a tour of another side of Hollywood. On more than a few occasions, he acknowledged, Gordon requested he jump into a smelly, gray dumpster in an alley off the Paramount lot where producers discarded rejected screenplays. Do it nonchalant, Gordon urged him. *Clang*—Jimmy hopped in pinching his nostrils, and worrying about griming his straw hat. Usually, it was empty pickings down there, and most of the manuscripts—stained with cold cuts, sanitary napkins, cigarette butts, coffee grounds, and Lord knows what else—were heaved back without thumbing through to the end. Before long, Gordon nixed Jimmy's dumpster diving, realizing the filthy chore was reaping little gain. Thankfully, Jimmy's next task didn't require him to wash his hands afterward. It required a passport, because he was accompanying Gordon on a recording trip to Stuttgart, Germany. Jimmy, heretofore accustomed to cold bus seats and rebuilt cars, was getting his wings.

All the same, carting his employer up the narrow Pan Am airplane ramp at Los Angeles International Airport was a treacherous start to his first trip overseas. One slip backward onto the tarmac with Gordon in his arms might do both of them in, and if not that, then definitely his new occupation. Jimmy, once buckled into his seat, said he experienced an ecstasy he hadn't known existed. The shimmering whitecaps below, the foreign languages he overheard at twenty-five thousand feet, the smoking-hot stewardesses bearing gourmet meals: the former farm boy was almost hyperventilating. It was once they cleared customs and checked into their German hotel, a drab place with geraniums in window flower boxes, that Europe no longer seemed so emancipating. The concierge surveyed Jimmy as he would a side of beef and in broken English laid down the rules. Blacks weren't allowed as guests there. *Verboten.*

Quick as he booked the reservations, Gordon canceled it. He requested Jimmy push him to the house phone, where an operator connected him with another inn, one with rooms available and a colorblind policy. "I didn't say nothing," Jimmy told his brothers. "Was afraid to." Later, wheeling Gordon around a cobblestone-lined street on a sightseeing trip near a castle, he twisted his head around at the voices trickling behind. A group of German kids in cloth jackets were following them about twenty-five yards back. Every time he stopped, so did their junior fan club. From the children's gestures, Jimmy surmised they'd never seen a black man up close before; maybe they assumed he was a ballplayer. London, with its Beefeaters and towers and more progressive attitudes, helped incubate their camaraderie in the smaller things. Gordon, for instance, observed Jimmy drooling over a bowler hat in a haberdasher's window. By day's end, Jimmy was wearing Gordon's spontaneous gift. Jimmy said he sported it every day the rest of the trip, never wasting another breath on that racist German hotel.

They stopped off in New York City for meetings with the big media outfits on their way back across the Pond. Over Jimmy's bowler were skyscrapers that disappeared into the clouds. At his elbow were landmarks Radio City Music Hall and Tavern on the Green. The swarming sidewalks were electrifying, if precarious while guiding a wheelchair, and he wished they could've stayed longer. After wrapping up business there, they rented a car and drove through upstate New York and into Montreal. It was at that point that Jimmy knew he needed to give Isaac Ross something nicer than a cheap bottle of wine that Christmas.

How many Louisianans could brag about dipping their toes into the subtropical waters of Havana, Cuba? None of his brothers, that's for sure. On another trip, Gordon and he traveled to the Las Vegas Caribbean, a hotbed of delectable beaches, hotel-casinos, exotic women, and starry, tipsy nights. But they weren't there just to play blackjack and drink rum. Russell Hayden had flown them all the way from California to assist him with a prospective series or film set against Cuba's spicy culture. Someone, Hayden said, had to do the legwork rustling up local musicians and scouting postproduction. Gordon was that someone.

Then fires started raging and buildings began to shutter, and it became obvious that a regime change hostile to the West was boiling. Talk of the martial law—and worse—was in the air. Fidel Castro's khakified Marxists were seizing territory and towns, and they didn't care about US Nielsen ratings. Jimmy said they tossed their clothes into suitcase, wrinkles be damned, and took a taxi on a mad dash to the airport. Somehow, they wrangled seats on a flight out, clinking glasses over Florida airspace to commemorate the escape. Thus began

Gordon's Forrest Gumpian knack for being at historically volcanic moments, living as no one dreamed he could. Jimmy saw it all.

Operating Gordon's "sewer line," on the other hand, was the one duty that Jimmy could've skipped. "The movie stars wouldn't want to see that, believe me." If the private nurse that dealt with Gordon's medical issues in the evenings was away, Jimmy had to act as the stand-in. He couldn't merely deposit Gordon at Shoreham and rush home to his family in Compton. Oh, heck no. With Rose supervising, Jimmy pressed the heel of his hand into Gordon's belly. The object was to "wake up Gordon's bowels"—involuntary peristalsis if you will – to goad his lower intestine to poop out its contents, Play-Doh-like.

Yeah, Jimmy relayed to his brothers, "strange" just about covered it.

*   *   *

WITH JIMMY ON SCENE, Rose supposed she was free to plot her own East Coast holiday. "Vacations are for other people," she used to sigh. Now she was one of them. In November 1960, she phoned TWA to book plane reservations to visit Lee's sister in snowy Springfield, Massachusetts. She informed Gordon that night that all the arrangements were in place. The male nurse would stay with him at night for the two weeks she'd be gone. Just in case Gordon tired of his cooking or takeout, she'd left a pallet of casseroles in the freezer.

"You'll be in good hands. Nothing to worry about at all."

"Fine," he said tartly. "Stay as long as you want."

"Oh, Gordon, don't be this way. I'm not made out of iron, you know."

"I can't believe you, Mom. You're jetting off for two weeks and you expect me to be doing cartwheels. You know what the nurse is going to cost me?"

"Us, you mean. What it's going to cost *us*."

"You know what I'm saying."

"But you've taken trips. A long one to Europe and New York, if memory serves. And you managed some fun for yourself."

"Those were mainly business. And I hired Jimmy so you could have your breaks."

"And I thank you. That's why I'm taking this opportunity. Where's your gratitude?"

"Mother, spare me the guilt trip. I'm one hundred percent for you getting a vacation, but two weeks is a little exorbitant, don't you think?"

"You're trying my nerves."

They didn't speak much about the trip until the eve of Rose's departure. She was zipping her Samsonite up on the dining room table when Gordon said he'd reached a decision.

"Let's have it," Rose said, sitting on the arm of the couch. "I know you're still mad."

"I'll make this short. While you're gone, I plan on using every free second to find you someplace else to live. Nothing personal. We've just been roomies too long."

"Roomies. That's what you think I've been doing all these years?"

In Springfield, Rose for once was indulged. She was shown the town sights, stuffed with Maine lobster, caught up on Lee's family, and instructed not to lift a finger around the house in preparation for Thanksgiving gluttony. Later in the week she'd be meeting up with Lee's other siblings, and was promised a first-rate dinner and Broadway show, as well. "Oh Happy Day," Rose wrote Muriel hinting at her depression two days into the excursion. Why, she chided herself, had she planned such an extended stay? Untethering herself from her responsibilities—namely Gordon—already made her antsy. As she was reminded in Massachusetts, she was no more comfortable in relaxation mode than she'd be in a nuclear submarine. Downtime could still be sinister, could still wrap her in a gloomy fog over all she'd lost through murder and other circumstance. Staying occupied doing for others was her technique for keeping those ghosts well buried in her psyche, but when she was idle like this, all bets were off.

So, she paced in her guestroom, fixating on her son three thousand miles away. She'd never commit this mistake again. Frazzled, she pressured her daughter to spy. "Darling," she wrote, "find out what you can if his bladder equipment is being sterilized." Jimmy, she said, wasn't yet proficient at it; Gordon had returned with him from an outing to Phoenix with a rump full of pressure sores that took weeks to heal. "How can I have a free mind if I'm not kept informed? In fact, I don't know if he's alive from day to day. It isn't as if he is a normal, healthy human being... I sleep very little." Fast on its heels was a concessionary follow-up about what she dreaded would be a prickly homecoming. Gordon, she inferred, regarded her as an old prune. "You cannot possibly imagine," Rose bemoaned to Muriel, "how uneasy I feel." When she did walk in from the airport, however, Gordon apologized for blowing his stack and asked about the snowdrifts. Nothing more was uttered about her moving out.

But Rose knew it was a temporary armistice, and that their cohabitation was liable to end poorly. Consciously or not, her son resented her, partly because she was one of the few females on the North American landmass willing to be seen with him in public. Since arriving in Hollywood, Gordon had flirted with any number of eligible women. A few studio secretaries he charmed had almost said yes to a dinner date with him. Almost. In the end, the burden was too much, their vanity about being caught with him at a restaurant or club too suffocating. Doubting voices in them asked what possible future might they have with someone so physically dependent? Put on the spot about a Saturday night, they'd often vamp cellophane lies about having boyfriends or nursing a sick aunt. "Got it," Gordon would tell them. "Understood." A guy petrified of forever bachelorhood had to try.

One gal—a lanky, brunette divorcee—had gone where others wouldn't. Marilyn Seruto was a lighthearted chiropractor that lived next door to Muriel in Pasadena's Hastings Ranch, a leafy, postwar suburb. The doctor acknowledged to girlfriends that she could fall in love with Gordon if she permitted herself; that blowtorch energy, his infectious smirk. They went out for a few months, and then she ended it. However much he captivated her as a potential second husband, she understood that the warmth she felt wasn't worth the duress that his anatomy would impose. *Goodbye, sweetie.*

Excluding her, there was only one other woman designated as Gordon's post-accident "girlfriend." Connie was a pixyish thing from San Marino with shiny, raven hair and a salty tongue. She loitered around him in Sierra Madre as he collected the pieces for the Zahler Music. Connie was affectionate, playful, and a good sport. But one day, with no explanation, her lovey-dovey fondness for Gordon vanished and she became a diminishing presence. Gordon later heard she'd gotten engaged to the scion of the Cornet five-and-dime-store fortune, and he couldn't fault her for picking money over someone unable to unzip a dress.

Still, those relationships were from another era, before he'd learned to stride without standing. At a wrap party on the set of *26 Men*, Gordon's libido was about to burst its britches. Across the checkerboard tablecloth littered with paper cups was a pinup-caliber number. The ravishing brunette in a slinky white dress could've been Sofia Vergara's grandmother. All the men, Martin Landau possibly among them, leered at her with testosterone intent. Gordon, in a starched black suit, out smiled everyone, a frustrated horn dog forever numb in the loins. Jimmy, standing behind him in a ruck of doughy, white faces, had to clamp Gordon's shoulder. "Down, boy." What was a paralyzed bachelor to do? The dish had pursed her mouth suggestively at him and not the others.

Well aware that was probably as good as it would get, Gordon chafed at the lady with whom he resided. How much he relied on his mother and his utter exasperation wishing it wasn't so was the paradox that the universe sicced on him after his tumble at Marshall.

All the same, his sexless existence presented benefits that he was sharp enough to exploit. While his able-bodied rivals navigated stop-and-go traffic, checked off "honey-do" house repairs on the weekends, or chased extramarital ass at the office, Gordon's mind was free to whirl. Among other tricks, he trained himself to recall everything he could in his galaxy of information. His thousand-song music catalog was the first metadata he engrained. For hours a day, he stared at different lists affixed to a stand by his bed. Next, he memorized the hundreds of tapes the songs were recorded on, then their order on the tape, and so forth. When he was through with them he uploaded into his head music-publishing contracts and other documents. By the early sixties, he could recite those same contracts, cue sheets, negotiating memos, and tapes in such phenomenal detail that a few outsiders suspected it was a parlor gag.

Jimmy could assure them it was no hoax. It was about efficiency. Gordon's recall and energy were the symbiotic gears of his cranial hard drive. Within a few moments of listening to a director or producer explain the type of score they needed, he could guide Jimmy to yank out multiple tapes by their file number. The blizzard of numbers, in fact, sometimes moved so rapid-fire that Jimmy had to chicken-scratch them on a pad of paper so he didn't mix them up. Clients from Piccadilly Circus to Melrose Avenue were dumbfounded, and they only witnessed a dollop of what Jimmy did. That so much focus was packed into so small a space seemed to violate the laws of thermodynamics.

Periodically, associates like Nat or Jack quizzed him what he wanted to accomplish with this prowess—excluding wealth? "One great thing," he'd answer. "One great thing no moron can ruin." Clearly, he was thinking blockbuster. According to the incorporation papers he filed with the state, Gordon envisioned himself in the corner suite of a mammoth conglomerate with diversified interests. He'd produce films and theatrical events. He'd publish educational music and books, invent photographic techniques, traffic in patents and licenses, invest in oils, minerals, and hydrocarbons, and maybe sell merchandise on the side. Entertainment being his forte, he'd own movie studios, radio stations, and TV franchises for the big money. At the extreme, Gordon expected to be an upstart tycoon or a rich flake. He listed thirty "primary" purposes. Even the corporate moniker he selected accentuated these humongous aspirations. It rolled off the lips like a Fortune Five Hundred company: General Music Corporation. Big deal if the initial stock capitalization was all of four hundred dollars.

CHAPTER FIFTEEN: THE FINE ART OF KISSING

THE CREW-CUT COLONEL HAD Gordon's attention the second he leaned into his ear. Was General Music capable of editing a hush-hush project for the Air Force? Sure, the specific topic was a yawner—how electronics in Soviet MIG fighters reacted to American radar—but the context was urgent. Two months earlier, a covert, White House-backed plan to topple Fidel Castro had backfired embarrassingly at the Bay of Pigs, and now Havana and Berlin lurked as potential tripwires in a superpower collision. American pilots gearing up for aerial dogfights needed the leg up. Gordon's response to the officer in the cobalt-blue uniform: let's do it. This was the Cold War.

The job was pretty elemental. Gordon's editors would only have to splice sound effects into the pilot-training film. Where the complexities thickened was the military's obsession with secrecy. Any employees involved required security clearances vetted through Washington. They could never reveal what they saw afterward, either, not a single frame. The MIG-cockpit data had been bootlegged from behind the Iron Curtain. Loose lips, the colonel inferred, might imperil US spies. Maybe even provoke the Kremlin to get even. Gordon, then up to his gills with westerns, cartoons, and post-Ed Wood sci-fi movies, was amped. The notion of him aiding his country, when he'd done nothing in World War II, was a red-white-and-blue rush.

Until, that is, he was mired in the reality of defense "contracting." It was sometimes exhausting enough making payroll. Now he had a sneering military guard with a sidearm skulking around his office. After the taped footage arrived from the Marine Corps Air Station Miramar near San Diego, a base mechanic wrapped an industrial-gauge chain around the editing-room door and secured file cabinets with baseball-size locks. Office windows got no reprieve; they were covered sash-to-sash in aluminum foil, with not even a pinhole of light visible in case any KGB agents were snooping about in eastern Hollywood. With each day in this makeshift bunker, the sex appeal of national security became a waiting game for it to end. The one thousand dollars the Air Force agreed to cough up was underwhelming given the hassles it entailed.

But they plodded through it—every cockpit beep, buzzer, and bell—and the colonel was tickled with the final product. "Outstanding work, soldier," he told Gordon. When he drove away, General Music could breathe again. Down came the tin foil and off came those locks. A month later, the colonel phoned Gordon again. This time, though, he was calling about something personal, not classified.

"Son, I was so impressed by the job you did, I was hoping I might steal a few hours of your time for you to talk to the men out at the Van Nuys VA."

"The VA?" Gordon had his headset on over a puzzled expression. "I don't understand. I don't know anything about the service. Or war."

The colonel laughed. "Let me clarify what I'm looking for. I've talked this over with my commanding officer, and we both agreed it'd be a real boost if you could give some of the wounded men a pep talk. Tell them how you overcame your, well, your adversity."

"Gosh, colonel. Not my favorite subject. Let me…"

"Talk to them about the picture business, then," he interrupted. "Explain how you get your people to stamp sounds onto the right spot."

"You mean splice?"

"Exactly. Splice. And back on point, let 'em know how you keep from feeling sorry for yourself when you're not one hundred and ten percent. They could sure use advice in that department."

"Colonel, I'm humbled you're asking me, I really am, but I'm awful busy. I just got a new show and the producer's a buffoon."

"Don't be so coy, Gordon. This can't be the first time someone has asked you for motivation. Just look at what you're doing."

"It is. Sorry."

"I don't have to tell you how devastated the mind can become after a bad injury. These men at the Birmingham center have had a pretty rough go of it. Their heads need recalibration."

"I'm sure they do. I know a few vets myself. But I still feel like you're asking the wrong guy."

"Can I be totally blunt?"

"You mean you haven't been so far?"

"Funny. But, here's my point. If the fellas see all the piss and vinegar in you, their situation won't look so bleak. You'd be doing me a big favor."

Some weeks later, Gordon was parked center stage in the recreation room of the Veterans Administration Hospital in the western San Fernando Valley. The décor was government-issued despair right down to the ratty, gray curtains with the cigarette burns in them. Gordon, having capitulated to the colonel, was delivering his first official speech. *Yippee!* Not sure what to say, his takeaway message was uncharacteristically sappy: the blue skies of possibility for anyone willing to push through breakers of self-doubt. For forty-five minutes, he chronicled how applying that philosophy had ringed him in celebrity associates, movie credits, entrepreneurship, and daredevil travel. "And let me tell you it was *never* easy."

The audience that Gordon's crapshoot journey was designed to inspire—men with amputated limbs and inerasable memories—were nimble to react. They rolled their eyes in formation and brayed loud enough to be heard in the kitchen. One fake-coughed "horseshit" under his breath, which made Gordon's words choppier as he neared the finish. Another, the apparent ringleader named Barney, dreamed up his own custom-made jab, chanting it several times: *"Lights, camera. Inaction!* Hostility and mockery were the standard treatment for civilian sunshine pumpers. Basically, Gordon was staring down a room full of Lieutenant Dans.

Gordon steamed on the way back to the office with Jimmy, his face resembling an allergy patient in a pollen field. "I knew I should have told that goddamn colonel no. Nobody could get through to those people."

"Don't beat yourself up, boss," Jimmy said. "You're done with them."

"You bet I am. I'm calling the colonel today to tell him I ain't doing a second talk there. No chance in hell."

"Want me to take Laurel Canyon to the office? The scenery might do you good."

"I don't care."

"What about Pink's? A chili dog and fries might hit the spot. You haven't eaten for hours."

"Pink's? A hot dog isn't the answer, Jimmy. I don't even know what is. Oh crap, forget it." Five minutes later, Jimmy's passenger spoke in a purposeful, gravely cadence. "What I want is for you to follow one simple rule from here on in."

"Yeah."

"Don't get me within a hundred feet of another cripple, okay? You see another wheelchair, you hightail me out of there. I'm not like *them*."

"What about Jack (Perry)?"

"Jack's cool. You think he'd sulk like the whole world hated him? Still can't believe what that one clown there said?"

"Which one?"

"The one that said I didn't know shit about suffering. What'd he think? I wanted someone dragging my carcass around?"

Gordon reverted to silence the rest of the trip, worrying Jimmy that another eruption was coming. But when they turned into the parking lot, Gordon's signature grin was tucked into his cheek.

"I've been meaning to ask you something," he said. "Nothing to do with the VA."

"All right."

"How would you feel about a little beach time?"

"Does it involve your new boat?"

"Not that I was planning."

"I'm all for it then."

* * *

GORDON'S FRESH DOGMA WAS not all that different from what he'd first sensed at the Trocadero. He'd dazzle the world with his signature hustle and marginalize the horror-show body whence it came.

It'd been Muriel who'd encouraged Jimmy and him to cut out Friday at noon for a weekend at the shoreline festival of WASPy relaxation known as Laguna Beach. She and Millard had rented the bottom floor of a beachside duplex for a quickie vacation, and the extra room there was ideal for him. "C'mon, Gordy," she'd said. "We never see each other now that you're living in Hollywood. It'll be like old times. Please!... I want to hear what Lucy's really like." He'd hesitated before saying yes. Muriel hadn't yet seen the brutalities of quadriplegia in a pair of Bermuda trunks. Count him in, anyway, he told her. Dogma rules.

The beach was a shimmering canvas of umbrellas, rafts, coolers, and other recreational paraphernalia by the time Jimmy killed the Cadillac's engine. Gordon, sheathed in a white, terry-cloth robe and Ray-Bans, sniffed the saltwater air riding the offshore breeze. "Get me down there," he told Jimmy. "We'll find Muriel later." The sandy fresco before him—the gurgle of the waves, that intense heat on his face—had triggered something unexpected in him, a tingly jolt of reacquaintance from days past when nothing else mattered but the water. Giddy. Delirious. Carefree. He was all of them. Even if it was just fleeting sentimentalism, he needed to live exuberantly in his own head and constrain his peripheral vision. Other beachgoers would be guessing about his motivation for being at a place where an ankle-deep water miscue could drown him. Screw 'em all.

Jimmy, as usual, was Gordon's dream-keeper, responsible for whatever enjoyment was attainable. He sweated through his T-shirt, plowing the wheelchair forty yards through that tread-catching, pristine white silt. After they'd picked out a spot, Jimmy's next assignment was lighting Gordon's cigarette against a pesky wind; one successful ignition creamed half his pack of matches. *Terrific. Some leisure day for me.* In two years in Gordon's employ, he'd scarcely had more than a weekend off.

At the shoreline, Gordon shut his eyes as the ocean spray misted his scalp and his ears sucked in competing radios pumping the Everly

Brothers, Little Richard, and others in the pre–British Invasion. On dueling sides of him were a thousand crazy-eyed children romping and splashing harder than they would the rest of their days. It was mind-boggling to fathom he'd once been one of them—the kid whose mother used to drag him across the sands by his ear when he'd stalled getting out of the surf. Harder still was realizing no amount of willpower could reanimate his legs, scientific marvels notwithstanding. Telling himself no regrets, he glanced over at Jimmy. Sweat beaded down his face, serf-like. "Jim," Gordon said. "Go cool off in the waves. That's an order. I'm not going anyplace."

The men split along capabilities. Jimmy waded into the foamy surf, flopping about like a dizzy mackerel, while Gordon tried imagining the soothing cool of those green breakers. It was during this yearning for small pleasures that the cosmos tried atoning for what they had exacted from him—with a fifty-cent plastic beach ball. The bouncy orb in sun-bleached flag colors pinged off the right armrest of his chair, spinning a sand divot at his feet. Gordon glanced at the pumpkin-size plaything, unsure of its origin and not really caring. When he blinked again, a willowy blonde with a cat-like face was bending over to retrieve it. "Sorry about that," the woman said blushingly. She wore a beige one-piece suit that accentuated a lithe frame. "My friend doesn't have much of an arm. She beaned a seagull yesterday."

Gordon was unsure what to do with this opening except not to fumble it, so he launched the first thing off his tongue to corral her from walking away. "Tell me about it. All my friends accuse me of throwing too hard." She giggled, and his cheeks flamed noticing her large eyes matched the ocean. He blathered out his name and heard hers. Judy Wetzel—it fit her as snuggly as her bikini swimwear. She and a girlfriend had driven down from the city, Hollywood to be specific, a few days earlier for respite from the smog and the time clock. Made sense. Judy's fair, damsel skin was tanned a light pink, including a left index finger missing a diamond ring; even Gordon's southern extremities stirred absorbing that. They chatted for a few minutes about their favorite local restaurants and the hair-pulling traffic. He knew he had to act. This pretty thing was teed-up to ask out for next Saturday night. He went inward, auditioning lines. *Should I go the humor route? Mention a celebrity buddy? And where should I take her?* But Mr. Smooth had dithered too long. Five seconds too long.

A tall, featureless brunette in Jackie O sunglasses had walked over, kicking up pockets of sand in every sandaled step. Gail Somethingorother tugged at Judy's elbow, causing Judy to scowl at her to let go. "I'm sunburned," she said. "Can we head in before I become a lobster?" Her eyelids arced artificially when she spoke, as if she were doing Judy a favor extricating her from this weirdo encounter. "All right, all right," Judy said with muffled irritation. She pressed the beach ball into Gail's surprised arms in preparation to leave. Before she walked away, though, she stroked Gordon's insensate hand. "Very nice meeting you, Gordon Zahler," Judy said beguilingly. Within a minute, the two collected their towels and wicker bags and were gone. That was it: another beauty shooed away.

Now he had to relive his slip-up within optical range of it for the next three days. "Very nice meeting you," she'd purred. Yeah, so sugarplum-sweet that she'd fled with her pushy friend. Before he'd met her, he'd contemplated having Jimmy dunk him in the surf, but that sounded asinine now. By 4:30 p.m., as families began shaking off their towels and loading up their station wagons, Gordon felt hollow. "Jim, wheel me in, will ya? I've had it." It wasn't that he'd whiffed. He hadn't swung.

Inside the leased duplex, Muriel was their cheery greeter. "Even better than I described, don't you think? Look at that stunning view." Gordon, trying to mask his dejection, said nothing of the woman from the sands. "Join us on the patio at six for drinks," Muriel added obliviously. She was in a patterned maternity blouse holding a drink and a smoke. (This is where I enter the picture as cargo in her womb.) "Sure, Mur, sure," Gordon exhaled. "Let us get cleaned up first." A double, no, triple whiskey sounded beneficial. He arrived twenty minutes late, punctual for him with the elbow grease required of Jimmy to shower, dress, and prop him in his chair. Rolling in, his flamingo pink forehead presided over a downer face. Realizing there must be a reason, Muriel asked for his drink order. But Gordon never answered for he was stammering under his breath. "Huh. It can't be." No, it could.

Lying on a plastic recliner in a green-and-yellow polka dot sundress—cater-corner to him on the duplex's concrete patio—was the women who got away. "Why, hello there!" Judy pepped up. "You didn't say you were staying here, too. We're on the second floor. What a nice coincidence?" Nice: there was that word again. She came over and gabbed for two hours.

Judy Marie Wetzel was a bubbly, working girl that, by aesthetic measure, should have been married in the suburbs by now. She was thirty-one and lived with her mother and an older lady above a quirky weight-loss clinic on Commonwealth Avenue in southwest Hollywood. She exuded sweetness in her perceptions of things, friendly and warm, but had a noticeable composure about her that showed she was no pushover. Judy did own up to one weakness that just happened to be Gordon's strength. Much as she enjoyed her life, it was dishwater-dull next to anyone in the Hollywood dream-making machine. Gordon never had a better audience for his anecdotes. In that, she was a pushover.

He studied her better in the dusky light, no half-squinting this time, and was more bowled over than he'd been at the beach. Maybe this was his day. Judy's prize feature was a cheek-to-cheek smile, especially becoming when she threw her head backward laughing. Shoulder-length, gossamer blond hair framed a small, delicate nose and alert eyes spread dollishly apart. When the breeze picked up and she strode over to her bag to grab a scarf, her stride was not pedestrian. She kind of floated with a slinky grace that accented her neck, and held her cigarette with the arched wrist of a debutante. Flaxen skin, smallish breasts, endearing laugh: Gordon was lighting up like a power substation and determined not to show it.

Never married, Judy supported herself with a job in the fashion trade. Clothes—she adored clothes. She reveled in fabrics, be it velvet or linen, tweed or wool. Circling dresses in *Vogue* that she couldn't afford on her skimpy pay was a guilty pleasure. Between the designs she could sketch out and an impressive eye for color, it was no surprise that Bullocks Wilshire, one of Los Angeles' premier department stores, employed her as an assistant buyer. Judy described it as a fairy-tale job that freed her to express her own creativity. Let her influence trends. The big negative in the grainy, art-deco tower were the exhausting hours. The best part was her specialty: wedding dresses. And here was the kicker: *she* soon could be a customer for one of the white, lacy gowns on storefront display. Judy said that she was dating a special somebody edging toward commitment. What's his name, Gordon asked, feeling sucker punched. "Fred," she said.

Joke—a guardian angel's demented joke. All this just to learn that she was off the market, to a schlub named Fred, no less? *Guess I have nothing to lose, he bright-sided himself. You never know.* The rest of the afternoon, as everyone drank and smoked and dabbed cream on flame-broiled skin, he played it dispassionately, gleaning what might unfurl from an accidental friendship. After Judy went upstairs, where her friend, Gail, probably chastised her, Gordon did a post mortem on the day's events. If Judy were so in love with Fred, why wasn't he with her in Laguna? And how to explain why she'd been so touchy-feely toward him? His weekend improved markedly on a hunch.

He rolled into Bullocks a week later to say hello, jaunty and decidedly un-desperate. "Being a clotheshorse," he laughed, "I had to come." Muriel, the department store enthusiast, bumped into Judy an indiscriminate period later. Judy hardly knew her, but she made a point of announcing that she and Fred were breaking up. "Know any cute bachelors?" she neighed. She wanted that message delivered to Gordon without doing it directly. But Gordon reacted more cautiously than triumphantly. It struck him as game-playing. She could always reconcile with Fred, or use him as a rebound date, and where would that leave him?

Then out of the nowhere she phoned. "You awfully busy?" If he was, Gordon didn't say. He invited her over to his packed office on Sunset, which she termed "quaint." Now that she was in his wheelhouse, he let slip the network shows he had going. Did she ever watch *Wrangler* on Thursday nights on NBC? He and Loren Ryder of Ryder Sound—*the* Loren Ryder, the former Paramount sound-directing icon, eight-time Oscar winner, innovator of the magnetic tape, etc.—had dubbed the audio together. Copycats were already scrambling to emulate it. *Wrangler* was the first TV program recorded on film and transferred to videotape using VistaVision. The oft-fuzzy picture on Joe Schmo's home set now had a big-screen sensibility. To synchronize everything, editors nearly had to block traffic as they unspooled the film, extending it from the dubbing booth into the street outside its doors. "People were looking at us like we were lunatics," Gordon told her. "But, it was worth it. The critics loved what we did. It was the show's plot they hated."

Judy was speechless, so why stop with TV? Gordon flailed his working arm at the blueprint pinned to the wall across from the desk he sat behind, "Interested?" he asked.

"Oh, yes," Judy blushed.

"Well, me and Nat Winecoff, one of my partners, we're noodling around with doing something pretty unusual."

Gordon explained to his audience of one the themed amusement park they'd sketched as a destination for newlyweds, tourists, and Bible thumpers. Niagara Falls and Yosemite were possible locales. The motif would be Old Testament meets Disneyland, and who better than one of Walt's chief advisers to breathe life into that? A Tut's Tomb ride, a Dead Sea cruise, a Noah's Ark attraction, and other brimstone thrills could tempt millions. "We'll have to do it in stages. But if we get the right investors, it could be a gold mine."

"A name. Do you have a name for it?"

"Bibleland. Or Bible Storyland. Kinda catchy, huh?"

"Definitely."

"I've also been exploring an idea closer to home—a Hollywood museum. You know, an ode to the glory days, memorabilia, booths? We'd wire a cable car to get people up there."

"I don't know what to say," Judy cooed, "other than my goodness. By the way, I've been meaning to ask you if were free for dinner next week? I hope that doesn't sound too forward for a gal to ask."

Recognizing he'd struck the right note, Gordon strummed it. Judy, meantime, had given herself a dilemma. Fred was an upstanding Catholic who worked in stocks and bonds. He wasn't as rich as Gordon would become, or the creative dynamo that Gordon already was. Rather, he was healthy and predictable and indubitably the safer long-term bet. She hadn't completely buried the notion of a future with him. Before she'd met Gordon, they'd played tennis during the day and waltzed at night. He'd insisted on opening doors for her, and she'd flounced through them.

But the longer she spent around Gordon, the less Fred seemed to matter. The more Gordon spit out his ambitions, the less intimidating he became. When Judy observed Gordon press Joe and the other editors to stop dogging it near quitting time, she ascribed it to his atomic drive, not his paralysis. Judy also fixed her eyes above his collar. In her idealization of him, Gordon's chiseled, handsome face was a smidge buccaneer. It took her breath away. Everything else would require acclimation.

Girlfriends listening to her florid reports about his dimples and get-rich schemes acted like Judy was steaming toward a deadly iceberg. "Having a crush is one thing, but a long-term relationship?" they asked. "You might end up just as much a mother as a wife. Doesn't seem like a prescription for happiness." Before she digested the warnings, romance sparked during café dinners and backseat necking while Jimmy waited outside smoking. Pounding hearts meant peering ahead, too. Camelot love this could never be. Ardent, practical affection, with a chance to goop into more, however, was attainable. Each saw the outlines of a possibly fabulous arrangement. Judy could have her security and glamour, Gordon a show-wife/companion and anti-loneliness potent.

But a dozen dates into the courtship, apprehension set in— Gordon's. Judy, he was sure, had half-fabricated her past, tangling up the facts of her own history—the year she'd graduated from college, names of past boyfriends. Who was she? An ingénue with gold-digging tendencies, a single woman going for the cheaper cuts so as not to wake up an old maid, none of the above? Gordon's mind was swampy in doubt when he met Judy's mother, a folksy sparkplug, five feet two in heels. It wasn't afterward. Judy had learned the art of embellishment from her master.

*　*　*

"BILLIE" WILLIE MAE WETZEL, in not so many words, had a plan for her daughter. Judy was to marry upward, preferably to a film-world executive. This, Billie believed, represented Judy's best shot for contentment, if not her own. In that Southern twang of hers, she acknowledged waiting for a son-in-law who could be her financial huckleberry. She'd tired of the dreary, working life. She wanted to be plopped into a classy Westside apartment, alongside other middle age retirees. Billie said she'd grown up in a venerable, Tennessee family that had once controlled a plantation and a battery of Civil War-era slaves, a family that had educated her at the top finishing schools and expected the finer things. Dash bourbon into her milk and she'd proclaim she deserved to be a lady of importance, "don't you know."

Gordon, by listening and learning, concluded he was getting half the picture on the Wetzels. Billie's Southern-belle shtick was buttercups over the pain. Rose leaned on God, Billie on selective memory. Much of Billie's life had been about finding cover from one shit storm after another. Long ago, she'd had a husband and a little girl named Anna Katherine that she loved to pieces. Sometime after World War I, thinning began. Her spouse, a dark-haired man of twenty-five, was killed violently in a California railroad accident. Discombobulated and out of money (sound familiar?) Billie remarried a Gas Co. office manager, a geeky fellow with a Neanderthal forehead and accounting training. Together, they conceived Judy. As the years sped by, Billie knew she'd erred in her quest for stability. Husband No. 2 was a rotten spouse and even worse dad. They divorced when Judy was twelve.

Billie, now a single mother again, had to hawk goods door to door in Long Beach to feed her two daughters. Her ex, the wolf, had left her no choice, dipping into Judy's college fund to pamper his new wife. Some years later, misery galloped from another direction. Anna Katherine, Judy's half-sister, had slipped from a problem drinker into an undeniable alcoholic. Billie wanted her child sober for all the right reasons, but she was also neurotic that the drinking would discredit the Wetzel name. She couldn't have that stigma, not after the others. Consequently, people aware of Anna Katherine's skid into the bottle were instructed by Billie to maintain strict silence about it. For a while, the charade succeeded. Anna Katherine married and presented

Billie with a granddaughter. Motherhood, though, just delayed the inevitable. Anna Katherine's pickled liver caught up with her, and she died at thirty-two.

Hoping a change of address would buffer the grief, Billie and Judy relocated from Long Beach into the upstairs apartment of a Hollywood Victorian. On the building's ground level was an unorthodox fat farm that Billie managed with its owner, an industrious widow named Sadie Cosby. Their secret weight-loss weapon? Vibrating pulleys that customers belted around their flabby waists and cottage-cheese thighs. Actors, some famous, were repeat customers there. Billie enjoyed that aspect, just not the grind.

Gordon let it all sink in, and then it made sense. It was only natural Judy would gloss over—or rearrange—a past that veered from Billie's script. So, she allowed the impression to linger that she'd graduated from UCLA when she'd only taken classes there. She hinted that she was a member of a sorority, but had never been initiated. The stable of college boys supposedly jostling each other to ask her out was another coat of varnish.

Gordon, with his own industry-honed knack for bullshit and hyperbole, could have confronted Judy about the embellishments and still won her hand in marriage. Judy was antsy for a ring from him, no two ways about it. Being stuck on his ass all day, he thought more three dimensionally about his predicament than your average potential groom. In his estimation, Judy's flourishes were pardonable offenses as scaffolding she erected over a barren past. So what if she was trying to snag a man for herself and her mint julep mother? Give them sodium pentothal, and thousands of other California girls would admit the same. Judy had little inkling of Gordon's other doubts. Truth be told, she expected they were about to make the engagement official when he invited her to Nicodell's, a red-meat/libations grill on Melrose Boulevard built into the side of Desilu Productions.

Once seated and cozy with their drinks—cocktails, not iced champagne—Gordon disabused her about them skipping off into the night. It was the antithesis. Gordon said they'd never survive as a couple. It was loony tunes, a delusion, to believe otherwise. Did Judy appreciate what marriage to him would look like? Where a simple bladder infection could be a killer? Where his every birthday was gist for the medical journals?

"I don't care about any of that," Judy keened. "You're stronger than most men I know."

"Come on, Judy. You'll be Jimmy in a dress."

Why was he being this fatalistic? she asked, froggy voiced. Because, Gordon answered, a diamond over her finger would've amounted to an obligation around her neck. Cubing his steak and feeding it to him bite by bite at the Brown Derby would have been as good as it got. Eliminating genuine sexual activity and any hope of children was the truer reflection. Now lop off midnight strolls, spontaneous weekenders, and card games. After that, delete back massages, doubles tennis, opened car doors, filled out tax returns, even adjusting the rabbit ears on the fuzzy TV. Judy was on the cusp of a sterile union—a marriage by conversation. He couldn't do it. She'd be clawing her way out in two years or less, regretting the sure thing she'd tossed overboard with boring Fred, and he'd be more disillusioned than if he'd remained a single man living with his mommy. Go back to him, he urged her. Dance. Bowl. Clip the hedges. Toast normalcy. Gordon assured her she'd thank him in the long run.

Thank him? Judy wanted to brain him. She didn't want to be Mrs. Fred So-and-So, she cried, tears smudging her blue eye shadow. She didn't require conventional. She needed him. *Him.* "Don't you trust me when I say I love you for what's inside? Isn't there another way? Isn't there?" After twenty minutes of beseeching, Gordon said stop. Give him a second. Let him think. *Jesus.* Tortuous seconds passed. Okay, he came back. He'd make her a deal he told her he didn't expect would be consummated. Starting tonight, they'd go their own ways without seeing each other for an entire year. Again, not six months, a full calendar year. If she was still interested, and he was still living, they would know that errant beach ball was destiny.

CHAPTER SIXTEEN: WHAT'S YOUR RACKET?

W HERE PURSUIT OF THE all-mighty buck had once been an exercise in raw survival—get jobs or go back to Sierra Madre—Gordon repurposed it as a distraction from the woman he'd cut adrift. Self-exiled from Judy, he widened inroads with executives across genres, partly on the strength of General Music's credentials with saddle-up westerns of early TV. Come 1961, he'd already supervised the music for dozens of episodes of *Bozo: the World's Most Famous Clown*, a ho-hum cartoon series. The producer, though sometimes lampooned around Gordon's office as a piker and pussyhound, was well worth Gordon's attention as someone who commoditized what others didn't see, in this case franchising for an exploding medium. Larry Harmon had adapted a character that *he'd* once played for kids—a makeup-wearing jokester in a phosphorescent, orange wig made from yak hair—into his own fatted cash cow. Clown-TV was good money. Stations around the country paid him for the right to hire their own Bozos for their own shows. (*KTLA* in Los Angeles had launched it.) *Mister Magoo*, another animated series about a nearsighted, dementia-suffering grouch riffed from the movies, also featured Gordon's licensed songs. Potential investors for his Bibleland theme park heard from him more, too, as did music sellers with material Gordon craved to broaden his library. *Don't obsess over her, he reminded himself at stoplights. Romance deals.*

When his inner monologue got too phony, he leaned on routine as his force field from regret. By 9:30 a.m., Jimmy usually had him natty in dark, cuffed trousers and quality, white or blue button-down Oxfords as the first stage of his workday prep. Next, Jimmy parted Gordon's hair just so with a wetted-down comb, and positioned his tartan lap blanket symmetrically on his lap. Save for him and Rose, no one knew Gordon wore a geriatric diaper in case his inert bowels turned rebellious, or that a chest brace padded with downy sheepskin kept him spry in his chair. For good measure after the Palm Springs incident, a rope sold at boating shops lashed his torso to the car seat as a do-it-yourself, *Beverly-Hillbillies*-esque seat belt.

Jimmy then switched from butler to human people mover, chauffeuring Gordon the four and half miles from Shoreham Drive to the rear bungalow on eastern Sunset Boulevard. Sometime after 10:00 a.m., the rims of the light blue Cadillac convertible would come to a stop there, though Jimmy's muscles remained on the clock. He'd untie the rope seat belt, ladle Gordon out of the front seat like a honeymoon bride, and situate him in the unfolded, collapsible wheelchair he'd extracted from the trunk. When they rolled into the bungalow, Gordon was focused and Jimmy sometimes out of breath. Inside, Gordon worked from bed if no visitors were slated while Jimmy honored protocol. He'd fasten the headset over his boss' ears, stand at attention for cigarette lighting, straw-holding, and nose-scratching, and, naturally, flip the pages of *Daily Variety* so Gordon stayed abreast of entertainment news.

"Tape fifty-four, cue twenty-one. Tape sixteen, cue eighty-seven." Jimmy on hectic weeks might've logged ten kilometers jogging back and forth from the racks. Film and TV clientele happy with the music and sound effects that Gordon preselected for them departed with a copied tape in a canister, a license, and an invoice. Folks disappointed by what he'd picked out created a second round of commands from Gordon to Jimmy, as well as others. And that was before lunch. Should Gordon hear about a new project worth bidding on, they'd speed over to MGM, Desilu, Paramount, or elsewhere trolling and cold-calling. Jimmy might puff a quick smoke or chamois the smog grit off the Cad when Gordon wasn't puppeteering his hands for the thousands of jobs he needed done.

Jimmy had mastered the basics of the job within months. But their appreciation of each other as wingmen, as friends in the pretend world of Hollywood, had quick-dried almost as fast. Now the rapport was brotherly and humorous. On the commute home, they might relive a particularly lame sci-fi scene—think laughable dialogue by characters in Reynolds Wrap spacesuits—an editor had to enliven, or the carousel of eccentric personalities streaming through the door. One Wednesday had begun with Larry Harmon kvetching he couldn't afford Gordon's prices and pestering him for the single publicity photo he'd "given" the staff while leering un-*Bozo*-like at the secretaries' legs. Midday entered Hugo Grimaldi, a dandified, European film importer who feted every woman he met with a suave, "Well, hello there, my dear." A few hours with a mercenary in alligator-skin boots trying to make it in TV and a visit from *Mr. Magoo* himself, actor Jim Backus, rounded out the day. After Gordon and Jimmy discussed such moments, opening up about their own interior lives was organic.

His work-friend circle also widened toward Mr. Grimaldi in the months after he told Judy goodbye. Since Jack was always riding him about always keeping one foot in movie production, Gordon found Hugo good for more than his ornate storytelling. My uncle couldn't get enough of the aristocrat who'd made schmaltzy, low-budget films his business. Here was someone who thought nothing of wearing a smoking jacket and foppish ascot to gas up the car, someone who spoke flawless English tinged with an Italian accent. In true renaissance-man tradition, he'd spend hours high up on a ladder chiseling grape leaves and family crests into the exposed beams of his legendary living room. Hugo had purchased actor John Barrymore's old hilltop spread, the "Windsor Estate" near Miracle Mile, and its history was as intriguing as Barrymore's bad-boy reputation. Gordon wangled as many invitations as he could to the white Mediterranean surrounded by towers, lily ponds, secret passageways, even a rathskeller where Barrymore had stowed his treasures and scribbled booty-call phone numbers. During Hugo's ownership, actress Katharine Hepburn rented one of its chateaus without worry about autograph-seekers peeking through her window. If anyone appreciated the needs of the elite, it was the fifty-ish Hugo. Not only was he the most interesting man in Gordon's sci-fi encounters, but he was also of royal, French Riviera ancestry. The House of Grimaldi had ruled Monaco, a tiny, super-affluent principality bordered by France and the Mediterranean Sea, since after the crusades. Yet the House wasn't completely united. A branch of the Grimaldis living in England and elsewhere contended that its bloodline was the purest, and that several of its males had been wrongfully denied the throne. Hugo was one, his brother another.

Stiffed of his crown, Hugo had immigrated to the US from Italy aspiring to become a top-shelf MGM producer as his solace. When he could gain no traction there, the epicurean with a passing resemblance to Peter Sellers adapted again. He reinvented himself as an expert importing and dubbing cheaply-made European outer-space movies into English. This gave him plenty to do, though Hugo didn't need the money, for he'd married into great wealth. What Hugo required was Gordon's postproduction magic, and Gordon coveted the diversion.

They paired on *Assignment Outer Space*, an Italian-shot feature that American International Pictures released in the US. In it, a journalist writing a piece for *The Interplanetary News* has to—big surprise— drop his notepad to save the earth from bloodthirsty extraterrestrials. Though a critical bomb, lead Rik Van Nutter impressed the James Bond people enough to cast him in *Thunderball* a few years later. *The Phantom Planet* was the same dime-a-dozen ilk—far-fetched, stiffly acted, but sufficiently engaging to keep you searching for a plot payoff that never materializes. Here it's 1980, and the US Air Force isn't worried about Soviet MIGs. It's gobsmacked by the disappearance of another of its Mars-voyaging spacecraft. Two intrepid souls sent to investigate fare little better. One lands in a hokey, galactic *Gulliver's Travels* of six-inch-tall humanoids, including a couple natives frisky for him. In due course he's miniaturized, put on trial, and then needed to save planet Rheton from its trigger-happy enemies. Portraying one of these dastardly "Solarites" was the metal-mouthed giant who'd steal scenes in two 1970-era Bond flicks: Richard Kiel. Neither his cameo, nor Hugo's film editing, nor Gordon's music could de-stink the cheesy waft from the movie.

You might have expected them to quit outer space after two lackluster results, yet Hugo was there again at General Music, sprawled out on Gordon's office bed next to him watching a rough cut of *First Spaceship on Venus*. This storyline wasn't half-bad, beginning with a *2001*-esque discovery in the Gobi Desert. Scientists deduce it's a flight recorder traced to Venus that they must investigate. As in *The Phantom Planet*, everything after the space flight is live-action comic book. The explorers, for instance, wend through a quartz forest, scrap with metallic insects, flee villainous sludge, and puzzle over where all the Venetians had gone. (Spoiler alert: the aliens had inadvertently nuked themselves in preparation for an earth invasion.) The critic who reviled it as "post-dubbed, pseudo-scientific gobbledygook" filled with anti-war rhetoric was on to something. From one slant, *The Phantom Planet* was less art than ideology. East German filmmakers under Moscow's influence had produced it as one of the few sci-fi movies approved for export to the West. Flattering allusions to "cosmonauts" and "Soviet astronomy" were hammer-and-sickle propaganda.

The irony for Gordon was a silver screen hoot. Within a few years into the sixties he'd worked on a Cold War film for the US Air Force and a communist-green-lit project advocating disarmament. But the quality of the latter was so crummy he couldn't trumpet it, and the secrecy of the former prohibited him from speaking of it. Even so, he refused to make his end slop. For him it was about applying a salvage job. It was the same technique he executed with *Plan 9*: the more wretched the screenplay, the more smothering the music. "Mickey Mousing" they tabbed it, and it was remarkable what it could cover up. On *First Spaceship*, Gordon had Walter Greene insert up-tempo horns to accentuate plot surprises and background strings and bass drums to enhance the dialogue. As the crew squabbled about aborting the mission, a wall of violins moaned behind them. Joe went heavy with the sound effects, and the net result lifted the absurdity around it.

In the pre–digital age, success as a music editor or an effects guy meant being an extemporaneous craftsman. The director would sit with you viewing a cut of his denuded product, in which dialogue was the only sound. "Lay something down in this scene, not that one," he'd say, and you'd visualize how it would flow with a stopwatch in your hand by a time-honored process called "spotting." If this were a soundtracked job, you'd scan your music library and flag candidate cues stored on ¼-inch master tapes. It would be trial and error, hours of fast-forwarding and rewinding until your eyes watered. Once the cues were sequenced, you'd transfer them from tape to film at a sound lab like Ryder's or Glen-Glen. Lastly, you'd break down the picture on a cutting bench and synchronize the different elements to the nth degree—that or risk an outburst from the director about a sound effect where there was supposed to be a syrupy ballad. Your butt was on the line to create a flawless strip of effects and music that would be embossed next to the dialogue on the finished sound reel and run with the movie. If you were in this for the girls and glory, reconsider. Your credit wouldn't appear on screen until most of the audience had left or the TV station had been changed. When it did flicker, it was somewhere after the picture editor, who made more than you, and the ending Technicolor logo.

Gordon, wheeled into editor cubbyholes to either approve the work or direct it, became expert at calling out cuts himself. He'd spent hundreds of hours observing editors make music waltz with on-screen action. Remembering their tricks, he could watch a segment on the Moviola, a clunky, metallic device with knobs and viewfinder used by editors to review film to splice, and in a few minutes unscramble what had given others fits. His ability to polish campy escapism quickly and effectively was a feather in his cap that brought him more of it. On one project about man-eating shrubbery attacking a Navy air base, the producer was reputed to have uttered into Gordon's ear: "Save this turkey with your music."

*   *   *

JIMMY, WATCHING THESE DUDS from the corner of stuffy editing rooms, was probably kept awake dreaming of weekend nights at the clubs. Saturday in daylight was just another shift to log, though increasingly he logged it at Newport Beach. It was here that Gordon docked the eggshell-white boat that Jimmy fretted would be the death of both of them. The twenty-four-foot-long Chris-Craft Overnighter owed its pickup to a feisty, Chrysler inboard engine and its name from the soundstage: *The Take One*; any confusion about the reference was solved by the motion-picture clapperboard painted over the stern. Gordon and Joe had gone in halves on the one thousand five hundred dollar, fiberglass vessel able to sleep a couple in the galley. Travel was just one of its benefits. Bayside capering with the boys here was just another means to keep second-guessing over Judy down. That palm-trees-meet sand lushness, the denim-and teal-colored waters, the rpm thrills: it was its own machismo club.

Gordon wasn't subtle, either, about monopolizing *The Take One* as his floating man cave and ocean hot rod. Joe often had to battle to reserve an open date to get his family time for a pleasure cruise. Every weekend, it seemed, Gordon's guests arrived at the docks in motley bunches bearing towels and ice chests. Soft-spoken CPA Jack could be a spectacle unto himself when he brought his children. If they pushed his buttons by misbehaving, everybody else stopped what they were doing to watch him trundle angrily after them on stumpy half-legs, his prosthetics being too unsteady aboard. Comparisons to a white gorilla in a Hawaiian shirt were not that far off. Nathan Jones, a swarthy, bearish real estate man who talked almost as fast as he drank, was a maritime rascal, too. After he'd gotten a little sauce in him, Jones loved nothing more than taking the wheel and launching *The Take One* at top speed off the incline of a big swell or another boat's wake. Propeller spinning midair, they could fly a football-length first down before a juddering water landing that made Gordon yowl, "Wahoo!" (The repair bill from the cracked hull caused by Jones' antics produced a different type of squeal. As in, "You're paying for it.") Missourian native Walter Greene, fast on his way to becoming Gordon's in-house composer, was every bit Jones' match in the annals of intoxicated boating. According to Jimmy, he "drove the boat like a bat out of hell."

Stephen's Landing, *The Take One*'s dock, was a favorite of Southern California's moneyed set, along with the better-known Balboa Bay Club. Most boat owners leasing slips were the puttering-around, sun tanning sorts. Not Gordon, Joe, or their pals. Joe, given a chance, was a speed demon, opening her up on thirty-three-mile trips to Santa Catalina Island. Inside the jetty was no safety zone for him. Pearly whites agleam, he'd spin the boat in "water doughnuts" while the Harbor Patrol debated whether to ticket him, either. When the local bayside restaurants drew big, holiday crowds, he and Gordon sometimes gunned the boat straight toward them, cranking a sharp turn at the last second. The resulting rooster-tail spray doused the complimentary bread and enraged the waiters. What can you say? Arrested development put the starch in their sea legs.

After one outing, Gordon informed Joe that their floating toy still wasn't synched right. He hadn't coughed up this type of dough to continue reclining in a locked wheelchair. Joe grit his teeth hearing where his co-owner intended to sit from now on, and the following weekend a handyman spent half a day bolting it in place. Gordon's "boat chair" was less handicapped-adapted furniture than padded cathedra. The castoff TWA jetliner seat was donated by an airline-industry buddy, and then mounted atop engine casing, a boxy, protective structure behind the dashboard. The jetliner chair was aerodynamically unsound, but what was sacrificed in knots-per-hour Gordon more than offset. Secured into it, he became the tallest person around, unlike dry land. After he'd acclimated to it, he was in full command, bellowing speed and coordinates with a peppery sureness that rung of fingernails on a chalkboard. "Port, port, port, port, now starboard. Swing it, but watch the buoy. It's coming up hard. Starboard." Joe later waved Jimmy over to discuss surviving their Captain Bligh. "Think he'll buy that we can't hear him?" he asked.

Los Angeles, the "paradise" tilled from desert, had lumped these men together, with not a diploma among them. Jimmy had crocheted a good life, despite the wrong skin color and lack of education. If there was anything he could affirm, it's that you had to suffer to get what was due you. Endurance was Jimmy's secret sauce. He hadn't volunteered to drop out of fifth grade. His father just needed manpower. He had forty acres to hoe and required the extra arms, especially after his wife and mother of ten children died of tuberculosis. Toby Gillard donned as many hats as he had young-ones: agriculture, child-rearing, preaching, and defusing Jim Crow-era racial hate. All things not being equal, the Gillards had it better than most, though not as good as the white kids free to sit on school buses and at lunch counters. The fields were the Gillards' liberation, their bounty, but they extracted flesh, too. Many of Jimmy's siblings were working the cotton fields when a bolt of lightning from a wicked-gray sky killed his ten-year-old sister. She was electrocuted with such violence that it broke almost every bone in her body.

Jimmy's restlessness to shake bayou country grew with every tear shed. Wanderlust fueled it, and the disadvantages of being an African American multiplied it. A teenage run-in with a white cracker was his periscope into how things would be if he stayed. Livid that Jimmy had spoken with a black girl he had a crush on, he'd shoved a loaded gun into Jimmy's snout. "Nigger, don't ever try that again or else" was his warning. World War II supplied Jimmy with an excuse to leave. Mid-war, he and a cousin enlisted in the Marines, believing no woman would be able to resist them in uniform. Jimmy's Marines, though, were different than Joe's. He was assigned to a segregated unit at Camp Lejeune, North Carolina, an eleven thousand-acre proving ground whose beaches were used to train for amphibious landings. The Marines intended to remake the farm boy into a "yes-sir/no-sir" killing machine. Jimmy immediately knew he'd erred. Nobody at the recruiting office had disclosed that ten-mile runs, 5:00 a.m. wake-ups, and saltpeter-spiced grub were the price of glory.

Camp Lejeune was now the second place where he didn't belong. How to concoct a way out—without going AWOL—was Jimmy's dilemma. Illness, it had to be a chronic illness with untestable symptoms. First, he pretended to suffer debilitating headaches, but the drill sergeants had heard that one before. Back to your unit, they ordered. Jimmy went lower with his next pretend ailment. He started nocturnal bedwetting as evidence of a malfunctioning bladder. Nice try, his supervisor said. But Jimmy kept up his unregulated whizzing for three soggy months. Adding an extra layer to his ruse, he hung yellow-soiled sheets off a railing close to where sergeants took their smoke break. They sent him to camp infirmary to get to the bottom of it, and Jimmy peed on the bunks there, too. Tired of the whole thing, the Marines granted him a general discharge. *Tada*. Jimmy had urinated his way out of the leathernecks.

Back home in Shreveport, it was the same withering, second-class citizenry, the same humid despair, so before long he was on the road west. Jimmy and his first wife, Lovella, tried raising their five kids harmoniously in Los Angeles. Tried. The marriage proved less stable than even his California employment. They split up, without a formal divorce, and it was then Jimmy's fertile libido cha-cha-cha-ed. Many nights, he headed straight to the dance clubs and bars of blue-collar South Central from Gordon's side. They were his happy hunting grounds, though getting through the next workday on a few hours of shut-eye took practice. Humble Jimmy wasn't much for bragging about his conquests and in a way he didn't have to. After Lovella, or maybe during the tail end of Lovella, had come Florence, with whom Jimmy produced six children over a decade. "Wild things, uncontrollable events" drove them apart, Jimmy would stutter later. Her successor was Peaches, who Jimmy had picked up on at a bus stop. Other pretty women would get horizontal with him, too, and there'd be more offspring out of wedlock. Jimmy swore to own up to his responsibilities, every cute one of them, never mind their habit of always outgrowing their sneakers.

*   *   *

SNIPPETS OF THIS JIMMY confided, usually in CliffsNotes depth, during smoke breaks at General Music or weekend boating at Balboa.

Ebullient Joe was more forthcoming about his past. The history of the talkative underachiever who'd introduced them was the spottiest accounting of the three. Neither heard Gordon bellyache that he didn't deserve the stinker hand that the Marshall gym had dealt. What he might blurt in an offhand moment over a drink was that paralysis was his hall pass for an extended life span. "Without it, I'm telling you, I'd be dead or in jail."

After more time on *The Take One*, the vision of an incarcerated Gordon in jail-grays had an attraction to it for Joe and Jimmy. Nobody, however, could doubt his radar for opportunity. While Joe hosed down the boat one Saturday, Gordon noticed a distinguished, balding gentleman with a thirty-five-foot yacht roughly a half-dozen slips from his. He'd seen the man's face dozens of times on TV and in print, just never in person. *Woooooh!* Gordon whistled for Joe to get a look-see for himself. "You know who that is, right?" Gordon said, talking a hundred mph. "You know what's he's worth?"

"Yeah, so?" Joe answered.

"So push me up to the marina office. I want to see about moving the boat next to his."

A month later, Gordon was dockside at Stephen's Landing, yanking friends' chains from his relocated slip. It was spring 1962 in a nation agog over quiz show cheaters, Camelot in the White House, and Wilt Chamberlain's one-hundred-point game. Vietnam? Still back-page filler. Between gulps of Budweiser, Joe and Jimmy had no shortage of fat-chewing topics as they painted *The Take One's* cabin. But with Gordon masterminding a plot, who had time?

"Joe," he said, observing him through a porthole, "you've got the imagination of a house fern. If we can launch a man into orbit, anything's possible. That's it. With the grain, back and forth."

"First off, I don't see what rockets and you waterskiing have to do with the other. Second thing, quit the nitpicking, goose stepper. I've done a lot more painting than you have."

"Sure doesn't look that way from what I'm seeing. If you're so good, why are bubbles forming under the paint? You sure you know what the grain is?"

"Jesus, for once in your life, can't you sit there and enjoy the air?"

"Me? Never. Now back to strapping skis on my chair."

"You're insane. You really are. You have about as much chance of waterskiing as I do getting rich off you."

"Just do me a favor and paint with a little pride, okay? We can't be half-assed after we took the time to prime the interior and lay down the tarps?

"*We?* You have a pronoun problem, Gordon. It's half my boat, too, remember?"

"Jimmy," Gordon said devilishly. "Talk some sense into our son of Hollywood. Maybe he can call Humphrey Bogart for help."

"Leave me out of it. You boys sound like my brothers bickering over chores."

"Come on, be a sport," Gordon teased.

"Naw." Jimmy took a long, malty swig from his red and white can. "I like being the silent one. Keeps me out of trouble."

"Benedict Arnold," Gordon laughed.

The banter would've ceased there had Gordon not been plying an agenda. "You know what I think, you two? Jimmy should've been a diplomat and Joe should stick to editing. He couldn't paint a flower box."

That last crack hovered in the salty vapor. A buoy clanged and Joe's eyes narrowed into felonious slits. "Couldn't paint a flower box?" He dropped the paintbrush in the can and jammed his head through the porthole. "That's it," he said. "I warned you. I fucking warned you." Joe shot out of the cabin, jumping off the bow to within inches of Gordon's tanned face. "You listen. I gave up Saturday for your precious paint job. 'Has to be shipshape.' Does that ring a bell in that memory of yours?"

"Easy man, you're gonna pop a blood vessel."

"Good."

"Maybe you should take a walk to cool off."

"I got a better idea. Maybe instead I should push your chair off the dock. Then you can tell the fish about going with the grain."

"They'd get it faster than you. Joke, Joe. What's with the wild hair?"

"Just keep it up." Joe's words trailed with a Doppler effect. Purple-cheeked, he stormed off the dock toward the smoked-glass marina building.

Before he'd disappeared, Gordon yelled with nasally melodrama: "You're not going to strand little me here, are you, Joey?" Joe shook a balled fist from behind.

Gordon remained parked where he'd been cursed; Jimmy stayed in the galley, humming something Elvis. Barely two minutes had lapsed when a sixty-three-year-old man in khakis and a blue plaid shirt stuck his head out of the cabin of his adjacent yacht—a yacht that reduced *The Take One* to a dinghy. "Excuse me," the stranger said, "but I couldn't help but overhearing your tiff. I was wondering if you needed a hand."

"Very considerate of you to offer," Gordon answered, "but I have someone else here. And I'm going to apologize to my friend when he comes back. If he comes back."

"Here's hoping he does," the good Samaritan with kind eyes and liver spots said.

They talked cross-ship for a bit before he insisted, as in wouldn't-take-no-for-all-the-sand-in-the-Sahara-insisted, that Gordon and Jimmy stroll over for martinis and his wife's fresh-grilled crab cakes.

Twenty minutes later, Joe and his easygoing disposition were back. His problem now was returning to a deserted boat. "Hey!" Gordon shouted. "To your right. Head over." Joe nodded okay, and then his chin bobbed harder and harder. Gordon's infuriating sarcasm, Joe recognized, was a trump card. On the back of the yacht was a stencil of a cartoon bird with a spiky red mane, a machine-gun laugh, and acerbic wit. Woody Woodpecker had earned tens of millions for Universal Pictures, plus a load for its creator. Joe climbed up the ramp, where Jimmy shrugged toothily at him.

"Joe von Stroheim," Gordon said brightly, "I'd like you to meet Walter Lantz."

"Nice to meet you," Joe said. "Of course, I already know Woody."

"As long as you have earplugs," Lantz chortled. "May I offer you a drink?" Soon he'd met Lantz's wife, Gracie, who'd placed a Tiffany martini glass in his lacquer-smelling palm.

"Gordon here was reminding me about your dad. I'm sure I spoke to him at Universal a few times. Incredibly talented man really put through the ringer. I was sorry to hear he passed. I don't think I missed one of his movies."

"Nice of you to say."

"Joe," Gordon interrupted, veering the civilities to an off-ramp. A smirk dimpled his right cheek. "I have some incredible news. Mr. Lantz…"

"You mean Walter," Lantz said.

"Sorry. Walter wants us to do the postproduction on the new Woody cartoons he's planning. Music and effects!"

"Tell him what else," Walter said.

"You betcha. Got ahead of myself. We're going to organize a music company for him so he can collect the royalties instead of it all going to Universal. Should be quite a take."

"I meant to ask you before, Gordon," Lantz said. "Do you think Universal's lawyers will stonewall us?"

"Let 'em. As long as you didn't sign the original music rights away, they're your property. If they own 'em, we just record new material that you'll own outright. Whatever you do, you'll be making money."

"You can do that? Arrange new music?"

"Absolutely. I know about five composers who'd do a tremendous job."

"Excellent. But I like choices. Will it be possible for me to hear samples of their work before we go forword?"

"Of course. I wouldn't have it any other way." Gordon said, taking a sip. "Hey, Joe, aren't you going to add anything?"

"Yeah," he said chomping a martini olive. "Does your deal mean we're done painting?"

"Inside joke," Gordon told his new partner.

CHAPTER SEVENTEEN: LADIES CRAVE EXCITEMENT

J UMPING INTO BUSINESS AS Walter Lantz's music man instilled confidence in him where cockiness had preened before. His lawyer and other advisers witnessed the subatomic transformation vibrating around his chair. Now that Gordon was hanging with an authentic Hollywood legend, waiting for his "one great thing" struck him as too passive. He didn't need to run around town anymore as a scrappy cripple flouting those doubtful he could get in a network door. Creating a stable lifestyle for himself and his mother had been the goal, and his tenacity had pulled it off. Having spent ten years on the editing lines, he was no longer content sidling up to his next stage. He wanted to grab it before his next birthday.

He burrowed into his new mindset dictating grandiose memos about financing packages and "four picture deals with Desilu." In flying to Germany and Austria to record fresh catalog music, he stayed at the finer hotels, regardless of cost, because you had to act prosperous to be it! Occasionally, he pitied the browbeaten production assistants scurrying around, knowing they'd rebuffed saner professions in the hopes, per chance, of becoming an industry somebody. That, however, didn't cut it for him anymore. Ask Joe. There had been that time at Stephen's Landing when they'd spotted a prominent, married producer engaged in lusty revelry on his eighty-foot yacht. Giggling and clinking champagne glasses, he'd crawled out from underneath a tarp with a voluptuous blond adjusting her black panties. "Keep your fucking mouth closed," Gordon warned Joe. "You didn't see that." Yet, for months afterward, Gordon saw it in his ambitions. He didn't aspire to be an exhibitionist adulterer—just a showbiz triumph ankle-high in his own party favors.

Lantz's bootstrapping past was the actualization of this dream. The son of an immigrant grocer had gotten his start as an office boy at *The New York American* owned by William Randolph Hearst. At sixteen, he was already at Hearst's animation studio. Carl Laemmle, as he would with Sonny Ross, saw limitless upside. Lantz was soon running Universal's cartoon studio, making *Oswald the Lucky Rabbit* cartoons and employing animators who would later make their own splashes. Lantz, thinking more business-like, convinced Universal to allow him to both produce and own all his cartoons. The successful *Andy Panda* series illustrated his touch. But honeymoon coitus interruptus at a lakeside cottage would blast him into another stratosphere. "We kept hearing this knock, knock, knock on the roof. And I said to Gracie, 'What the hell is that?' So I went out and looked, and here's this woodpecker drilling holes in the shingles." She recommended that instead of wanting to strangle the bird, her groom usurp it as a character.

Lantz's team got busy developing the cartoon that would enshrine his legacy. Voice-over actor Mel Blanc was the bird's first voice until Blanc signed on with rival Warner Brothers; he later sued Lantz in a beef over it. In 1950, Lantz held blind auditions for a permanent replacement. The golden throat he selected was Gracie, which left him queasy about the public reaction. "I thought, *Oh God, no! What are people going to think...?*" Nobody cared. She'd be Woody's hyper-pitched alter ego and laugh—*ha-ha-ha-ha-ha*—for hundreds of cartoons that would air in seventy countries. Each cartoon took about five thousand drawings and four months, and that suited Lantz fine, despite the comparisons to Walt Disney, who'd left Universal after it had rejected his sketching for an animated mouse. Lantz's caustic bird gave him everything, from wealth and Oscar nominations to trademarks and perspective. "It's hard to think of Woody in terms of paper and pencil," he explained in 1958. "He's quite real...a likable, mischievous little character." Maybe that's why one of America's most celebrated animators agreed to go into business with Gordon. He was Woody incarnate.

Filmmaker Sam Fuller, a cigar-gnashing fireplug known for his corrosive depictions of the American psyche, further ratcheted Gordon's ascension into the higher ranks. Leonine and blunt, Fuller had culled his experiences as a pugnacious New York crime reporter and World War II rifleman into a no-punch-pulled directorial style. As was the case in his masterpiece, 1980's *Big Red One*, he never sugarcoated darkness. Soldiers were shot in the head in his scripts, not their shoulders, and the good guys were never all that good. Fuller hired Gordon to strip the music and sound effects for one of his iconoclastic showcases. *Shock Corridor* was hands down the best film Gordon had contributed toward so far. A Pulitzer-hungry reporter (the saucy Peter Breck) in it goes undercover at an insane asylum to ferret out a killer. A labyrinth of mayhem, racism, gender tumult, and other sub-themes society kept muffled from polite company explodes. Fuller populated his scripts with a Tarantino-Kubrick aesthetic, and *Shock Corridor*, menacingly lit and jarringly told, was a gamma ray on society. It was *One Flew Over the Cuckoo's Nest* before its time. A southern black student deluded he's a KKK Grand Dragon implied an America losing itself to hatred. "My nature has always been to tell people the truth, even if they feel insulted," Fuller once elaborated. "I care too much about people to bullshit them."

Gordon knew that critics who disdained *Shock Corridor* as an over-baked descent into lunacy missed the point. Besides, he empathized with the film's lead, a man required to fraternize with crazies to wrest his own greatness.

* * *

AT SIXTY-ONE, ROSE WAS in the same, fossilizing generation as Lantz. After that the comparison fell apart as Gordon shunted her to the margins. Her caretaking wasn't required much on the weekends, thanks to Gordon's boating trips with Joe or nights out with buddies like Nathan Jones. Travel-wise, Gordon bounced around Europe and Manhattan perfectly with Jimmy tending him. She was fading, fading from relevance. When Gordon listed directors for Sunset Music, a second company he'd founded exclusively for music publishing, her name was missing. Rose, as always, tolerated the snubs, going about her tasks in a flower apron that shouted Cézanne on Quaaludes. Being Gordon's mother this late in life was tricky, and often un-maternal, even for someone as duty-bound as her. Sometimes she was his punching bag, other times a dissenting voice roping him off from adult desires she worried would crash in disappointment. She'd agreed with his breakup with Judy, telling friends how uneasy she was about him being ground up in an untenable marriage or exploited as a sugar daddy. But talking to him about it or trying to console him was bumpy. The occasions she tried, he'd either clammed up or acted ornery. Could he really be in love with the Bullocks Wilshire girl? Or, Rose questioned, was he thinking past her?

Truth was, mother and son had wedged each other into toxic positions. Having thwarted poverty together, their equilibrium as a tandem now slanted decidedly toward youth. Gordon hustled. Rose cooked. He envied Lantz's millions. The hunt didn't thrill her. He adored gadgets. She pestered him about his catheter. He trusted salesmanship. She harped on him to "Put his trust with the Lord." She tried feathering him with the trappings of an otherwise ordinary lifestyle—pork chops fried crispy, slacks fastidiously ironed—but her miscalculation was overvaluing those accouterments now that he'd tasted the planet. Hence, she won and she failed. By submerging her own needs so he could be "normal," she aimed a bulldozer at herself.

Gordon was stuffed inside his quandary, as well, imagining Rose fussing over him into oblivion. Paralysis had such staying power in what it demanded of others. His mother, by now, should've been in the arc of leisure, feeding her grandkids baloney sandwiches in the park. Opportunities missed, caring for him was all she'd mastered. She was indifferent about the apartment he volunteered to rent her as a pension. The status quo was her security blanket. Until this living arrangement changed, Gordon knew the breakout life he yearned for would be like trying to nail Jell-O to the wall. No wonder he vented at the mother that so many people wished were theirs over the silliest issues. Every day he resided with her cast Rose more as a martyr and him as the heel.

∗   ∗   ∗

JUDY, THOUGH, REMAINED LODGED in a brain deft at compartmentalization. *Judy-Judy-Judy-Judy.* Aware of this, Jimmy was petrified to let on he'd seen her running errands off Sunset. Rose, of all people, conceded to Abe's wife that Gordon was more unbearable the longer the separation lasted. The verdict was in. Gordon's name might have been all over low-budget sci-fi films and cartoons, but he was miserable as only earthling love can make you.

At dinner at his sister's house, thirty years before fire almost leveled it, he slouched in his wheelchair, dwelling on what he'd blown. "I must've been brain-dead running away from her, Mur. The prize was right there, the woman I'd been waiting for, and I told her to go off with another man." Muriel mistrusted her ears hearing a brother allergic to wallowing beat himself up. "Want me to try to talk to her girl to girl, see if there's any chance you could patch it up?" Gordon dipped his head up and down yes at bobble head speed. His forced, yearlong sabbatical to test Judy's sincerity had lasted eight and a half months.

Judy was nibbling a tuna fish sandwich in Bullock's paneled tearoom when Gordon's intermediary approached. The vibe she gave out was arctic. Muriel quizzed her about Fred, Judy's uninteresting boyfriend, and Judy curtly said he was, "Fine, just fine." (In reality, Fred's mother resented Judy, whom she considered too strong-willed and conspicuously non-Catholic.) "I suppose you expect me to ask about Gordon, now," she said sharply.

"Maybe not. I just had him over to dinner last week, and he's a wreck without you. A mess. I've never seen him like that, honest."

"Well, he deserves the suffering. The way he dropped me was one of the worst things I've gone through. And I've gone through more than *you* know."

"Give him a second chance. One look and you'll know he's crazy about you."

Judy took another bite of her sandwich and made sure her supervisor wasn't watching. Light in her face that hadn't been there before had a halo sheen. "Have him call me in a few days. I'll judge for myself how sorry he acts."

Lee and Gordan Zahler, 1930s

Gordon "recuperating" with his friends in Sierra Madre, early 1940s

Gordon with Nat King Cole and friends at the Trocadero nightclub in Hollywood, mid 1940s

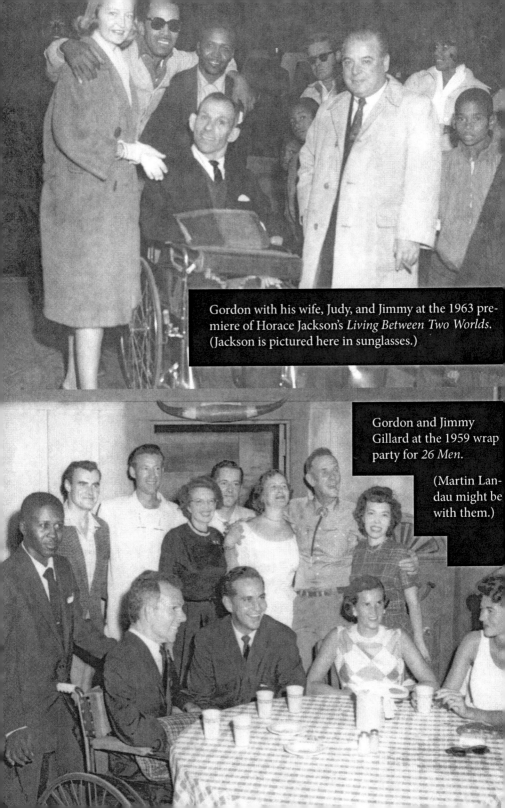

Gordon with his wife, Judy, and Jimmy at the 1963 premiere of Horace Jackson's *Living Between Two Worlds*. (Jackson is pictured here in sunglasses.)

Gordon and Jimmy Gillard at the 1959 wrap party for *26 Men*.

(Martin Landau might be with them.)

Gordon on the set of the nationally broadcast sewing program he developed in the mid 1950s

Lee Zahler (second from left in tie) on the set of Universal Pictures' *Crooked Alley*, 1923

Nat "Sonny" Ross, Gordon's uncle, as a young filmmaker

Lee Zahler with his trusty portable organ on unknown set

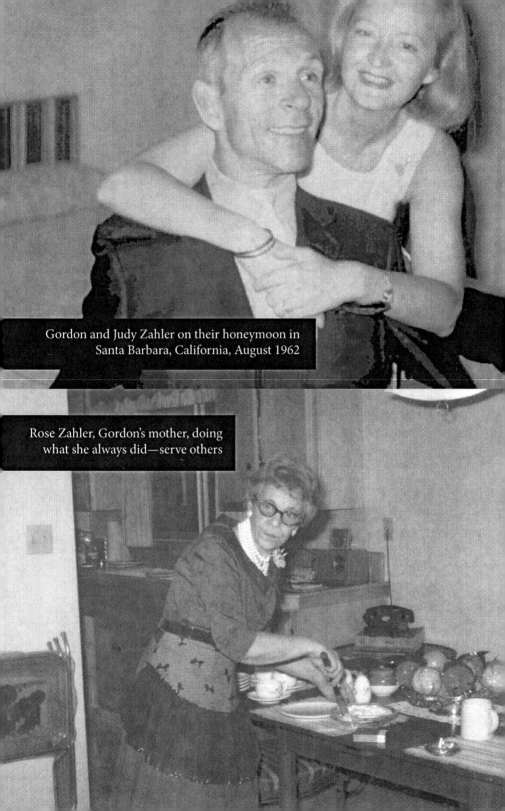

Gordon and Judy Zahler on their honeymoon in Santa Barbara, California, August 1962

Rose Zahler, Gordon's mother, doing what she always did—serve others

Jimmy Gillard and Gordon on a business trip through Europe, 1960s

Famed cartoonist and business partner to Gordon, Walter Lantz, with Gordon at a marina, early 1960s

Legendary African American architect Paul Williams overseeing construction of Gordon's Sunset Strip home, mid 1960s

Gordon and the monkeys of Nazima Springs, Kenya, likely in the early 1970s

CHAPTER EIGHTEEN: PASADENA'S ROSE PARADE

THE CEREMONY WAS A location shoot privy only to invitees. Fault Cupid. On a Thursday afternoon in August 1962, hours after Marilyn Monroe's suicide, Gordon and Judy sat in the backseat of Gordon's Cad with the roof down and the wind in their goofy smiles. Jimmy was hotfooting them up the Ventura Freeway, past the earth-tone hillsides and farmland, until the whitecaps of the Pacific Ocean marked their spot. They were traveling north to Santa Barbara, a sleepy, coastal town dotted with eucalyptus groves and bohemians one hundred miles northwest of Los Angeles. A small wedding set against that picturesque coast would inaugurate events, and the caravan trailing them would ensure there would be liquor-fueled celebration the rest of the weekend. Joe and his wife occupied one car, Walter Greene and his spouse another. Behind them were Hugo Grimaldi and Dorothy Chester (one of Gordon's secretaries), and editor Axel Hubert. Technically, this was a road-trip nuptial and not an elopement. The obvious ones missing had been blatantly excluded: Judy's mother, Billie, and Rose Zahler.

The reverend at Santa Barbara's First Methodist Episcopalian Church performed a no-nonsense ceremony finished in a Vegas-like ten minutes. The mid-thirty newlyweds commemorated it with a short, deep kiss. Gordon wore a dark jacket with a white shirt and matching tie, mobster-suave. Judy was in a cream-colored wool outfit with red and blue trim on the button line and her hair pageboy-style.

On her wrist looped the Rolex watch that Gordon had presented her as an engagement signing-bonus. On her finger was the modest diamond ring she received for going through with it. In just-tied-the-knot photos, Gordon looked enraptured, Judy supremely relieved.

Afterward, they all retreated to the local inn where they were staying to guzzle Dom Perignon out on the balcony as the afternoon sun painted the Pacific orange. That night, after their initial buzzes wore off, Gordon treated his guests to a first-rate dinner at Victor Hugo's restaurant in nearby Montecito. He ordered tender veal medallions, baked Alaska all around, though he only ate about a fifth of his meal. It wasn't nerves. A "kiddy" portion could stuff him.

Joe, meantime, was never so bittersweet about love as he was that first night. On the two-hour drive to Santa Barbara, he'd turned to his wife, Phyllis, and told her what he had been longing for months to say: he wanted a divorce. Phyllis, a plump, bull-necked woman, reacted calmly, knowing her drinking had flung their marriage past fail-safe. At a party at Gordon's six months earlier, she'd gotten so wasted that she'd spilled a plate-full of potato salad onto her lap. "I think you ought to take her home," Gordon whispered to Joe. Not long after, when Phyllis had departed for an extended stay in Hawaii with the kids, Joe had fallen for a cute interior decorator with a '57 T-bird and a minor prison record. Certain that he and Phyllis were through, he brought her around to the soirees, positive that she wouldn't embarrass him.

Back in Santa Barbara, Joe grappled with emotional vertigo. Outside on his balcony next to the bride and groom's, he smoked a cigarette and pondered the black heavens. (Phyllis had just arranged her own hotel room to weep in private.) It was then Joe's curiosity got hold of a carnal stumper. How would Gordon, he of the broccoli anatomy, spend a honeymoon night typically dedicated to bump and grind? Specifically, that is? Joe guessed that their socially approved sex probably entailed kissing with the TV on. Yeah, that had to be it. During the next few minutes, Joe chided himself from voyeuristic urges. Willpower, he told himself, the golden rule, common decency. But he smoked a second one, remembered his looming divorce, and vilified all the good willpower had done him.

Quietly, he snuffed out his cigarette and tiptoed up to the sliding glass window of the adjacent room. He studied the action for a minute, trying to block out the glare. He had to rub his eyes a couple times, because what they were telling him wasn't possible. "Oh?" he said, "Ohhhhh." Gordon hadn't short-armed his sexual mode of attack. He was lying as flat on the bed as his V-shaped body allowed. But a moving object obscured his face. It was a disrobed Judy straddling and bucking her cunnilingus-savvy husband. Joe crept back to his room shaking his head. *Gordon, you dog.* You had to give it to him and his tongue. He'd snagged his blonde.

* * *

AND ROSE TOOK ANOTHER spear to the flank. How could he be this petty, acting so big for his hemmed-in britches that he'd betray her like this? Without the sum tonnage of what she'd given him over the last twenty-one years, he never could have gotten within miles of an altar. Gordon had told her about the elopement a few weeks before it. Even that was mean. He was making the domestic preparations, and this required her cooperation. Obviously, she'd have to vacate their house. He couldn't have Judy brushing up against her mother-in-law at the bathroom sink, or worry about the bedroom noises she might hear, in the opening innings of their marriage. How unfair that would be. "You can understand, can't ya?"

Never had she felt so backstabbed by circumstance—not after the murders, not after Lee's affair, not after Columbia Pictures thumped her in court. What would Lantz or Fuller think of their golden boy now? She'd never expected her son to remain a bachelor forever. She just assumed he would treat her with more dignity than evicting her on two weeks' notice from the residence on Shoreham they'd slaved to acquire. A house that had punctuated the end of zigzagging family misfortune. Did Gordon think he was fooling her with this smokescreen about claustrophobic living conditions when this was about *his* new order? Splashing cold water on her face didn't do much to calm her down. "God help you," she said acidly, "if you're capable of doing this." When he maintained his position, Rose defended herself with fangs you wouldn't know she'd been born with.

While Gordon had been at the office before the elopement, Rose committed herself to digging out of Hollywood. Three days later she was staying in Pasadena with Muriel, who was ready to tar and feather him, too. Rose a few weeks later had signed a lease on a one-bedroom, ground-floor apartment in Sierra Madre not far from her old Mountain Trail place. There she put pencil to paper, working with her mathematical son-in-law to assess her finances. Told she owed him, Gordon repeated he wanted her in comfortable exile. Since she wasn't speaking to him, he instructed Jack to communicate his offer. He'd pay her two hundred and sixty dollars per month, minus what Social Security gave her, and forty percent of the Shoreham house when sold on one condition: she waived her interest in the company. Should he die before her, which seemed both impossible and imminent, Rose would inherit half of his music royalties, or approximately one hundred thousand dollars a year. Next thing anyone knew she dolefully signed some papers and Gordon got himself hitched.

The wedding present Rose put in an envelope for him was not fit for display. In cold parlance written by a lawyer, it accused him of business coercion, as no statute existed criminalizing dickhead hubris. "Gordon Zahler did extract from me my signature on several documents that I herewith repudiate and renounce. These signatures were obtained as a result of a series of threats and extracted from me under extreme emotional duress. (He) did not explain to me the nature of the documents he demanded that I sign and I did not understand their content... I now believe that the purpose...was to obtain my release of any claim to interest in the stock of the General Music Corporation—an act that is exactly contrary to my wishes and desires. I was paid nothing for my signing the stock release (if that is what it was) nor did I receive a copy of what I signed. I hereby put you on notice I do not consider these signatures binding on or of any affect whatsoever." Another way of expressing this: Rose had lost her raison d'être when Gordon told Judy "I do."

Rudderless. Summary retirement had consigned her to a rudderless, lonely end. At first, she tried filling the void with trivial acts. She mailed dresses and tie tacks to distant relatives and dropped by her daughter's for regular suppers. She revived her interest in politics, this time as a Goldwater Republican, and cleaned stains real and imagined in her new flat. Terrible isolation of an empty calendar stalked her anyway. Never much at holding grudges, she in due course forgave Gordon for sweeping her aside and freezing her out of the wedding. Reflecting back, she'd done what she could, and had gotten him past the thirty-six years of life that had tripped up others. She accepted Judy, too, as a companion for him there out of love, though she tended to accept everyone's best premise.

Some months later, she sat Muriel down on the couch in Muriel's high-ceilinged living room. There was a mutually beneficial proposition that she needed her daughter to weigh. It was out there, so be open-minded. She wanted Muriel's middle son, Peter, brought back from the live-in school for the mentally retarded that he'd recently been shipped to so *she* could raise him. On her own. In her new apartment. Doing this, Rose said, would accomplish two goals: it would supply her motivation to get out of bed every morning and remove Peter from the care of strangers. If she could handle someone as alternately helpless and obnoxious as Gordon, dealing with a twelve-year-old boy with a misfiring brain wouldn't overwhelm her. (Rose's own mother, Sonya, no longer required attention. She'd spent her last years in downtown's West Adams district feeding pigeons and converting to Christianity before succumbing to a heart problem.) Rose's panacea, however, wasn't Muriel's. Not even close. She couldn't have Peter— the boy prone to running away, kicking holes in the walls, and going on food strikes—ping-ponged into yet another new environment. He'd already bounced back and forth between Pasadena and Devereux School in Goleta for years.

Spurned again, Rose probably stared into the white shag carpet, gut burning.

CHAPTER NINETEEN: CODE OF THE FEARLESS

MARRIAGE AGREED WITH GORDON, the fracas with his mom notwithstanding, and Jimmy as a result had a tighter schedule to maintain. By taking insider shortcuts, he was to deliver Gordon home to Shoreham before 7:00 p.m. to begin the second half of his day. Judy, vying to be the model wife, wanted him there to make the space theirs. When he rolled in off the elevator, frazzled by deadlines and prickly composers, she was ready with her rouge freshly applied and his scotch rocks premixed. "Meet anybody interesting today?" she'd ask smiling, pampering him with a warm face towel. "Anything new on that foreign deal?" she'd inquire from the kitchen while basting the rosemary lamb chops. Those evenings when affections flickered, she'd scoot under the sheets with him in his orthopedic bed, tugging a pillow over her head later if her husband's compact metabolism awoke him before sunrise.

He was happy, dopy happy, and by that first year hitched, he'd kind of reprogrammed his inner compass for two, primary coordinates: grooving a married rhythm with Judy while slaking his impulses for adventure and money away from her. Together, they hosted regular dinner parties, where Judy's cooking and hospitality won raves, and socialized regularly at the Lantz's Beverly Hills home. *Fondue, anyone?* Gordon next took Judy to Acapulco, and chartered a fishing boat to "teach" her how to catch marlin. This was how: Jimmy held the pole, Gordon said when to reel. On certain Friday afternoons, if his work was done, he'd wink at Jimmy and they'd sneak away to throw down fifty dollars at Santa Anita Park racetrack or make a Dodger game to watch Sandy Koufax hurl missiles. Unshackled, Gordon was making up for lost time.

Judy was liberated herself, what with spending money in her designer purse (assuming she stayed on Sunset, not Rodeo Drive) and status as a Hollywood spouse. She quit her Bullocks Wilshire job to concentrate on wifehood, though she'd later bug Gordon to let her tinker with song lyrics for a passel of *Woody Woodpecker* cartoons. What Judy sought most—to be indulged on a trip to Europe—Gordon aimed to give her in spades. For goodwill, he even parceled out an allowance to his mother-in-law, Billie, who half-joked she'd have wed Gordon if Judy had bowed out.

Pockets jingling with disposable income from multiple directions, hence, might have been his most welcomed sound effect. They made the whims possible. They bankrolled the trips and paid Paul Williams. Only a meathead put all their eggs in one Hollywood basket. Gordon wasn't just scraping by on *Craig Kennedy: Criminologist* and a few industrial films, anymore. Cartoons, outer-space movies, features, music licensing, and such watered bank accounts that were gulch dry in his isolated, early years.

But with money also came tension. Editors miffed that Gordon underpaid them co-opted the company's rising balance sheet as an excuse to rebroadcast their grievances. Where was their cut, their cost-of-living adjustment? *Where?* Packed into running the lean operation his CPA insisted he uphold, he'd retort in quiet talks or at bullhorn levels, depending on the situation.

Jack, whose firm handled General Music's accounting and payroll minutiae, was his fiscal overlord. The only sustainable budget, Jack harped, was a disciplined one. When Gordon veered from it, Jack called him on the carpet to remind him to guard every dollar. Use him, Mr. Green Eyeshades, Jack said, as a scapegoat to blunt the malcontents. So Gordon did. A so-so editor cornering him about a raise would often hear this phrase: "Sorry, I just can't swing it— Jack's orders. See me in six months." Some grew to doubt this was anything but a filibuster, and a few droned on about exploitation in salty language. The noisiest of them were usually brought back into Gordon's office, where they were reminded about Jack's law and openings at other postproduction shops.

Showbiz's capricious tendencies rewarded those thinking steps ahead; a hit-show here today could be eighty-sixed tomorrow. If Gordon was the piker his reputation suggested, he was a piker who had network contracts cancelled over weak ratings and advertising. General Music also was owed big, maybe as much as twenty-five thousand dollars or more (in excess of two hundred thousand dollars today) by B-movie outfits like Crown International Pictures and San-S Productions. Hang tough, their lawyers would try pacifying him; one of the producers absconded with the cash, so we'll have to pay you in installments. Claptrap begging patience was another ready-serve excuse. His debt would be repaid, the movie's representatives said— after enough theater owners were inveigled into airing the putrid thing. Gordon's response to the stiff-arming: think again! Either you made good on your tab or you were a rat. Lowballing a contract or neglecting to fully license every song he used was not moral equivalency. A bill was a bill. Abe's legal meter spun continually on his behalf.

Gordon and his deadbeats became a long-running saga often more colorful than the movies in dispute. Ed Wood, into General Music for thousands, was more cagey than repentant about what he owed him for *Night of the Ghouls,* his trashy story about a duplicitous psychic buried by his own karma. Here's what Wood wrote Abe: "When it looked like we would sell the picture some months ago I contacted Gordon and got what the full price was… Atomic Productions (was) a Corporation (that's now) extinct, but (was) well in force during production of the film, (so) I am not personally responsible." On his hand-edited note listing his Glendale home address, Wood closed saying that his own attorney, Art Toll, was in charge of whatever he owned Gordon. Bottom line: don't hold your breath.

Charles Shows was another debtor fleeing Gordon's legal dogs, albeit with more pathos than Wood. In his don't-sue-me note, Shows choked up that he'd rather be in hock to his mother than to one of his "best friends." Hollywood, where Shows had been a triple-threat writer, director, and producer, had dumped him so quickly he'd had to work as a part-time mailman to subsist. The six hundred fifty dollars that he owed for music, sound effects, and other services on *Boothill McGill*, a cartoon produced by Larry Harmon, was dough he just didn't have. Give him time: he was embarrassed enough. "As you know, [Gordon], the television business is about as secure as playing the races."

Where Wood blew legal smoke and Shows petitioned for mercy, a man who'd come to the planet's TV mecca after a previous life as an African mercenary and wild-animal trafficker was no softy about his IOU to General Music. This roughneck that we'll dub Arty Jamieson was a brilliant, if scary, thirty-something who'd killed natives in the Congo, sat in pits swarming with rattlesnakes, and exported African animals in B-25 bombers that he'd piloted himself. Accustomed as he'd become to writing checks—to six wives, among others—he was loath to make one out for his wildlife TV show. In Jamieson's eyes, weak species, whether in Hollywood or the bush, didn't dictate terms.

"Arty, you owe me," Gordon told him in his office one day. "My accountant is busting my chops about it."

"You're gonna get your money, Zahler. Just edit these last couple shows and I'll tell you what. I'll throw in a hundred dollar bonus."

"Gee whiz. A whole hundred! Now I can retire. The answer's no."

"Listen, if I were you, I'd be grateful I had any business," Jamieson said, lighting a cigarette from the butt of a previous one.

"If you were me?"

"Don't play dumb. Doesn't suit you, my friend. Let's be honest. We both know that if the bleeding hearts around town didn't feel so sorry for you, you'd be out on the boulevard, hand—or whatever you call that thing at the end of your arm—with a tin cup."

"Ok, I see. Must've been hard for you to have to stoop coming to us at all. What, NBC wouldn't cut you a discount?"

"I'll ignore that snide comment. Edit these shows and you'll get your money. All your money."

"Sorry, Arty. Your credit's no good here. Especially after today. My lawyer will do my talking from now on."

The veins in Jamieson's wind-burned neck dilated. "If that's the way you want to play it, I'll get you your money next week. But a gimp thinking he's going to intimidate me with an attorney." Sam grabbed his valise. "What a joke you are."

Later in the day someone asked Gordon what to do if the former soldier of fortune returned, assuming he wasn't armed? "Give him the bum's rush," he laughed.

By 1963, Gordon's rangy set of business interests allowed him to sever ties with fishy sorts like Arty, knowing he had backup. His push into music sales alone made the metallic clack of the office mail-slot a heavenly noise. Checks were in there, checks to him from a platinum, moneymaking institution. The American Society of Composers, Authors and Publishers, or ASCAP, was the juggernaut performing-rights licenser and clearinghouse responsible for doling out tens of millions of dollars to artists and others yearly. After ASCAP conferred on him full membership (once he'd jumped through its bureaucratic hoops), Gordon toted up his share of catalog royalties like he was on a religious high. He was now part of an economic priesthood that most of the Hollywood cognoscenti poorly understood. But that was their oversight. As Abe and Jack drilled into him for years, copyrighted music was global cash flow. It didn't matter if a song he licensed aired prime time in the states or was broadcast with subtitles at 2:00 a.m. in Brazil. If it played, Gordon got paid under ASCAP.

Songs, in other words, were different than people. They were capable of immortality. Original, recorded music could be reborn in syndication, reruns of old movies, or sliced and diced into new efforts. Gordon's recycling of his father's music, by itself, echoed this in *Underdog* cartoons, MGM's *Tunnel of Love*, Wood's *Night of the Ghouls*, and dozens of other projects. Simpler, still, was packaging material in bulk to competitors of background-music titan Muzak, which piped homogenized versions of just about anything—Beatles' toe-tappers, soulless champagne music, Golden Oldies —into offices, elevators, supermarkets, and stores. Atmospheric ditties were everywhere in America's consumer Valhalla of the early sixties. Sociologists who theorized it was subliminal mind control knew their stuff. Up-tempo, gum-snapping rhythms, for example, were designed to stimulate workers' sleepy brains or to prod diners to eat faster to make way for the next party. Moving "product," Gordon spouted, was easy cash if you knew a copyright from a mechanical right and had an ear for what sold.

Agreement by agreement, he cultivated a shrewd side business feeding the mood-music stampede. He'd hired Walter Greene partly for that reason and retained several other composers (Tim Spencer and Earle Hagen) to pen material he could record with foreign orchestras. From his partnership with Lantz, he fashioned deals with sub-publishers across Europe to ensure airplay that would insert liras, pounds, deutsche marks, and francs into everyone's pocket. Formalizing a bond with the once-legendary Hans Salter might have been Gordon's niftiest maneuver. Over forty years of composing and conducting at Universal Pictures, years that had earned him multiple Oscar nominations, the Austrian-born, Vienna-trained musician wrote music for *Dracula, Frankenstein, Sherlock Holmes,* and *Abbot and Costello,* among other popular films. Impressive career and all, Salter's résumé hadn't funded him a plush retirement. He was just another forgotten, émigré composer trying to pay his bills. Introduced through Abe, Gordon had to debunk the old man's skepticism that his beloved creations could live another day in sitcoms and foreign radio. "You sure I'll make money from this?" he asked. "You betcha," Gordon assured him. From ingenuity, SALZA Music (a hybrid of Salter and Zahler) was born. Royalty checks soon rained.

*   *   *

GENERAL MUSIC'S BUNGALOW FELT more like an overstuffed storage room than a regulation office with every deal Gordon inked. Success was too much for the confined locale with the connect-the-dot decor. Word leaked that the postproduction house needed digs matching its workload, and an industry source told Gordon about something available at Samuel Goldwyn Studio a few miles to the southwest. Though victim to the wrecking ball today, the site on Santa Monica Boulevard near Formosa Avenue had been a sort of Hollywood Mesopotamia. It was there in 1928 that a knot of filmdom's dominant personalities—Mary Pickford, Douglas Fairbanks, Charlie Chaplin, and D. W. Griffith—christened United Artists. Goldwyn, a former glove salesman and the "G" in MGM's original studio configuration, bought it in the fifties to produce his own movies and rent space. Marlon Brando, Jack Lemmon, and Eddie Cantor acted on its grounds, as would Marilyn Monroe, Clark Gable, and Frank Sinatra. Howard Hughes' RKO Pictures was there; the reclusive magnate even kept a secret garage onsite. Playboy Errol Flynn had his own clandestine spot—a tunnel connecting a Goldwyn soundstage with a watering hole across the street—so he could drink between takes. Should Gordon finalize a lease at the studio, he knew ghosts of the silver screen would be swirling above him.

It was a tantalizing idea—swapping the fixer-upper that General Music's editors couldn't wait to leave for a maize-colored, corrugated-metal structure formerly utilized as a prop warehouse. Goldwyn's "Barn" had it all, starting with elbowroom from a bank of large offices, many of them with cubicles inside. In the far back was a scene dock perfect for rebooting into a Foley stage for recording sound effects. The parking here was good. So was its location only a few blocks from the labs and dubbing houses that were the firm's homes away from home. Boasting an address on a teeming movie studio wouldn't hurt the company reputation either. The cooing, crap-happy pigeons that periodically roosted under the twenty-five-foot-high eaves just gave the place color, assuming they didn't guano-bomb you.

Strapping leading man Burt Lancaster was more than bewitched with it, too. No matter General Music's interest, he wanted to snag the Barn at the last minute for his own production company. Modular, adaptable, roomy, even historic: what wasn't there to like? He must have gauged the space was his to lose for: 1) *he* was freakin' Burt Lancaster, and; 2) his outfit, Hecht-Hill-Lancaster, was already housed on the Goldwyn lot. Alerted to Lancaster's poaching, Gordon rushed onto the phone with his advisors to strategize. Good luck there. Gordon was up against a seven-hundred-fifty-thousand-dollar-per-film superstar who'd just collected an Oscar as the lascivious swindler in *Elmer Gantry*. "Who the hell does he think he is?" Gordon vented. "The guy's a great talent and everything, but he's got some big ones trying to muscle in ahead of me. I'd heard he was such a gentleman." Brainstorming and fulminations ensued. Afterward, Abe may have phoned Lancaster's representatives. Their client—the one who made ladies weak in the knees onscreen while taking gutsy, liberal stands offstage—might appear a tad hypocritical gainsaying someone "like Gordon." Given the scoop, *Daily Variety* would have a field day. Whether veiled threats were issued remains muddy. General Music's eventual leasing of the space that Lancaster tried weaseling no one can dispute.

But relocation day sloshed with foreshadowing drama. Pulling up to the Goldwyn entrance in a rented truck and two cars one Saturday morning, a ruddy-faced Teamster held up his arms for them to stop. Not so fast, said the human traffic cone. In a New York accent, he asked who was leading "this circus." Index fingers pointed through car windows at the gnarl-bodied fellow in front.

"Me," Gordon stuttered. "My company's moving here. You can call the property manager if you like. Nothing sneaky is going on."

"And you are?"

"Zahler. Gordon Zahler. Head of General Music. We have a signed agreement."

"Congratulations, Mr. Zahler. But have you read the rules about physical labor around here?

"Rules?"

"Yeah, you should get a copy of them cuz you ain't coming in here like this."

No one had ever seen Gordon so flustered—tongue-tied, unsure of the Svengali words to talk his way out. Evidently, he'd breached the studio's collective bargaining agreement before he'd registered Day One at Goldwyn. Only union members were permitted to lift stuff over a certain weight. For fifteen minutes, he got an earful about it before the gates swung open. "I'm being generous. Don't let it happen again," the cheesed-off Teamster said.

"You betcha," Gordon fibbed.

* * *

Outfoxing Lancaster and the Teamsters added to Gordon's own peculiar legend, but his head drifted elsewhere. The married man in him ached to show off the European continent to Judy on a business-pleasure junket. Consequently, as John, Paul, George, and Ringo invaded the states with their moptops and snappy lyrics, he, Judy, and Jimmy hurtled themselves toward the lads' home country at thirty thousand feet.

Danny O'Brien, Gordon's forty-ish man in London, greeted the jetlagged trio at Heathrow Airport, *hip-hip-cheerio.* O'Brien was quintessential English, jowly and loyal, devoted to God, country, and a decent commission. An affable entrepreneur, he'd met Gordon in New York in the mid fifties, as Gordon pitched his sewing program and O'Brien represented the Josef Weinberger music catalog. They'd already recorded material together in Germany, where Gordon impressed the jaded musicians that he wasn't just some profiteering dilettante from Lotusville. Danny since then had added film to his management repertoire, and hoped now to bridge Gordon's moviemaking prospects with the foreign connections brimming in his Rolodex. Wait, Danny thought, until they get a load of him.

After a few days in England holding meetings and drinking strong tea, the four boarded an outbound plane, probably to Stuttgart. There, they sandwiched themselves, their luggage, and Gordon's collapsible chair into a rented Opel sedan. Jimmy drove the loaded-down vehicle without incident, probably to Vienna, on what was now his third European trip with Gordon. After some meetings, they planned to load the Opel onto a special, car-carrying train for overnight passage from Austria into neighboring Switzerland. But they arrived behind schedule, and the car-train had rudely left without them. Everyone moped except Gordon and his dangerous smile. "Hey," he said. "I have an idea. Let's cross the Alps ourselves. We can do it."

Danny shook his meaty face no way. "You're daft, Gordon. We're not familiar with the roads, and if there's one place you don't want to get stuck it's high up there. Better we call an airline to be safe than sorry."

"Oh, don't be such a pantywaist, Danny. It'll be an adventure. Jim has faced worst conditions on Sunset Boulevard."

It was 9:30 p.m., dark and nippy, when they acquiesced to Gordon's thirst for escapade. Jimmy wound the Opel along a sloping mountain road that soared seven thousand feet above sea level at its peaks. Vast sheets of snow laid on one side, lethal plunges on the other. The road was so treacherous at its narrow bends that when another car's headlights splashed them, Jimmy had to go in reverse a clammy eighth of a mile to allow the other vehicle to pass. In the pitch black, their elevation was, in Jimmy's words, like "looking down on the stars." The Opel remained in second gear, grinding ice and pavement much of the way. Everybody was furious at Gordon for imperiling them on this de facto ice rink while he sat in the front wishing it would never end. By 5:00 a.m. they'd descended the Alps, eardrums popping and stomachs growling. The manager at the Swiss hotel where they'd booked rooms ridiculed them for attempting that drive, much less at night. Next he informed them they were too early to check in. Gordon shot him his pitiful-cripple look, and the manager not only showed them mercy, he arranged their breakfast.

The trip's final leg was a commercial flight to Rome, and Gordon swore it would be all recreation and no ice-driving. The Italian music publisher keen to see him would have to wait for another visit. Being Judy's docent was his mission now. He'd shepherd her to museums, the Colosseum, the Vestal Virgins' cave, the Spanish Steps, Gucci, Prada, whatever made her heart skip.

An excursion to St. Peter's Square to hear a papal Mass conducted by Pope John XXIII was penciled in for the end of their stay. Again, their timing reeked. This being the summer tourist season, they were squeezed like sardines in the plaza outside the baroque Vatican with ten thousand other Christians and assorted believers fanning themselves silly in the heat. "Ah, bloody hell," Danny said gruffly. "Maybe we should call it a day and settle for a Coke." Again, Gordon rebelled against Danny's common sense. He asked Jimmy to wheel him over to a Swiss Guard, a beefeater-sort in tunic and helmet. Gordon made himself look runt-ish as he spoke.

But what he needed instead was a skillful translator. He wanted to guilt the sentinel to rope off four good seats for them to observe the Mass. The Swiss Guard, though, misinterpreted Gordon's words. He thought the cripple was bemoaning being tardy for the contingent of the diseased and dying that popes personally bless before conducting their outdoor ceremonies. Suddenly, he decided to act on his hunch, and signaled Gordon and the three others to follow him through a basilica side door. Down a ramp they went into the musty darkness, unsure what was happening. They passed cubbyhole rooms and ducked underneath an arch. They trudged through moist hallways and, eventually, by a lit, brick wall where bodies of dead popes laid for centuries in the grotto. Each was preserved in his own sarcophagus with a thick, crystal-like bubble over him not unlike Vladimir Lenin in Moscow's Red Square. Our travelers were in the storm cellar of the Holy Ghost.

After a few minutes, the Swiss Guard pointed to a subterranean ramp leading to a stage centered by a crushed-velvet throne. Not far away, the pope worked his way down a line of sick kids, disfigured adults, and other misfortunate beings. Danny began a flop-sweat. Gordon swiveled his head. It was too late to confess a misunderstanding, way too late. One of the pontiff's black-clad lieutenants gestured for them, and they tottered over with rubbery smiles. The pope made signs of the cross for the walkers in the bunch: Judy, Jimmy, and Danny. The high-hatted one took on Gordon last, spending extra seconds with him before uttering something in Latin about the sufferings of Jesus.

Back at their Rome hotel that night, Judy did some talking to Him. Jimmy was snoring in his hotel room when his phone rang at 3:00 a.m. with a frantic pitch.

"Come over right now," she said in near-hysterics. "Something's wrong with Gordon."

"What?" he asked.

"I don't know," she said. "I think it was those awful clams we had at dinner. Hurry!"

The hotel doctor rapped on the door moments after Jimmy arrived. Gordon admitted the last time he'd felt this lousy he'd been hospitalized with a life-threatening bladder infection. Judy noted that he'd been vomiting since midnight. The doctor took Gordon's temperature, and the mercury displayed one hundred and four degrees. The physician said in clipped English that he too, suspected food poisoning. An outbreak of salmonella-tainted shellfish had been picking off tourists left and right. It could be deadly for someone with Gordon's metabolism, he volunteered in so many words. "We must take precaution."

Wary of his patient's unusual torso, the doctor rolled Gordon onto his left flank to listen to his heart and lungs. Mistake! In doing so, Gordon's eyes spun up like white gyros into their sockets. In chain reaction, his head slumped forward and his lungs no longer moved.

The cheeks of the formerly placid hotel doctor went pasty as Gordon fell unconscious and Judy cried, "What's happened? Why aren't his eyes open anymore?" The doctor fiddled nervously with his stethoscope. He'd never witnessed this reaction in all his years of practice, and he'd seen some things, too. "Stand back," he said. He moved closer to the un-breathing lump, preparing to start mouth-to-mouth resuscitation, until Jimmy told him to stop.

"Put him flat."

"What?" the physician asked condescendingly.

"Flat!" Jimmy repeated. "All the way flat. On his back."

The doctor went along, lying Gordon as he found him, but he had his doubts. In ten seconds he'd contact the hotel operator for an ambulance. What could this Negro pacing in front of the bed smoking know about respiratory shock? More, apparently, than he did. Gordon's chest shuddered on its own almost instantaneously. Judy rushed toward him, rejoicing, "Oh, thank God. Thank God!" Gordon hacked a few times, took a deep breath, and coughed some more. In five minutes he was conversant, albeit dizzy. "I'm better, honey, really." Judy didn't believe him, so the physician measured his pulse and listened to his heartbeat through his chest. Surprise number-two: his vital signs were normal.

After the mystified clinician departed, Jimmy gave Judy his homespun explanation. "If you twist him hard on his left side, his breathing stops. It's like the on-off switch on the Moviola. Guess lying down all those year pinched how he gets his air." (Point of fact: some quadriplegics rotated too sharply to one side can develop a circulatory condition called autonomic dsyreflexia, which is known to trigger dangerously high blood pressure and suppressed respiration. Jimmy didn't know the lingo, only the result.) Gordon's on-off switch, he said, had been tripped a couple of times with him. "Don't worry about it," he told Judy. "He always gets over it."

In a few days, with some antibiotics to handle the clams and tranquilizing wine for his travel mates, Rome was theirs again.

CHAPTER TWENTY: THE WHISPERING SHADOW

THE WOMAN IN THE chiffon dress, white gloves, and trademark pillbox hat imagined something violent with every squeak. Gertrude DuCrest, alone with a mysterious noise emanating from the rear of the Barn, might have been a girly-girl, but she was conversant with showbiz's history for random bloodshed. She'd been the first one in that Monday, there at 8:30 a.m. sharp, and now she wished she'd phoned in sick. The former RKO studio librarian, who maintained Gordon's files and protocol with stringent care, felt the goose bumps pimple her arm. Editing equipment or whatever that racket was hadn't supernaturally flicked itself on.

She pushed away from her neatly arranged desk and began tiptoeing toward the din. "Who's there?" she yelled into the darkness. Nothing, only the persistence of that same sound: *thwip, thwip, thwip, thwip.* "I'll have security here in thirty seconds if you don't identity yourself." The gussied-up secretary crept deeper into the Barn, peering into offices and craning over her shoulder. When Gertrude reached the cavernous scene dock where Joe von Stroheim and others cut sound effects, she heard human grunting layered over the squeak. Black dread—was it rape, murder, burglary, arson—arced inside her. Whatever exactly she was interrupting might claim her, too.

Not until Gertrude was debating trotting out the side door and shrieking about an intruder inside did she notice an illuminated lamp on in the back. A few strides closer to it confirmed the police would be unnecessary, as well. Her gut was right. Someone had broken in. And now she was the luckiest woman in the solar system.

Whipping around a gymnast's high bar was Burt Lancaster. The only stitch of clothing he had on was a pair of skivvies. *Thwip, thwip, thwip, thwip.* Gertrude, who'd been around movie stars by the dozen in her career, flushed like a schoolgirl. She cleared her throat to get his attention, and the onetime circus acrobat noticed her between revolutions. He slowed them, stuck a sure-footed dismount, and swiped the perspiration from his brow. Gertrude tried steadying herself, but by then he'd strutted over, all six feet one of him. Within feet of her was that beefcake chest bared in *From Here to Eternity.*

"I hope I didn't give you a fright," he half-giggled, wiping his arms with a towel. "Apologies if I did. Gordon said it was okay to set my equipment up over the weekend and use it when no one was around. Obviously, I lost track of time."

Gertrude, beet-red where she'd just been pale, tried reconstructing how to speak. "Uh, yeah, I know. How it goes, I mean. Let me start over. I'm Gordon's secretary, Gertrude DuCrest."

"Well, looking the way you do, I didn't think you were his mechanic."

"You're too sweet, Mr. Lancaster."

Lancaster, who regularly exercised on his own gym equipment to keep in shape, canvassed her with his eyes. Then "The Grin," who'd depicted boozers and pirates and a mean Wyatt Earp, reached up. With the back of a dried-off hand, he brushed the shoulder of her tapered dress. "You're so beautiful in that outfit. Like a perfect milk bottle," he said in his mellifluous way. "I hope you don't mind me being that forward after you could've had me arrested for breaking and entering."

"Mind?" she said. "I'm expecting you to make this our routine."

Gertrude spread her Lancaster encounter around the office in woozy delight, and Gordon, hours later, corroborated Lancaster's account as true. But there was more to it. The box office stud wasn't just working out in the Barn. He was kicking the tires on *his* production company's new office. His ardor for the space remained undiminished, as if it were shelter from the professional jealousies, money crises, and marital infidelities encircling him then. Goldwyn Studios was obviously aligned. Some weeks earlier, unbeknownst to most, it delivered an official letter notifying Gordon that the studio wasn't renewing his lease. Typically, he would have swung back, perceiving it insulting to an enterprise moving in brisk strides. General Music had just completed work on two sci-fi flicks in which Hugo owned a directing credit: *The Human Duplicators*, about ETs fabricating a race of ceramic-esque people, and *Mutiny in Outer Space*, an *Andromeda Strain*-ish yarn about a space station contaminated by pathogens in lunar ice. Neither tore it up commercially and still the company was thriving. A recent deal to furnish music for *The New Three Stooges* further ingrained it in cartoons, and better projects were lined up behind. Gertrude, the eccentric who ate her lunch in the front seat of her Corvair, was among the first to learn why Gordon could graciously *yuk-yuk-yuk* losing the Barn after only a few years there. Walter Lantz was his new landlord.

The cartoonist/businessman owned a beige, two-story Hollywood office building at 6410 Willoughby Avenue, between Santa Monica Boulevard and Hancock Park. Its vacant space seemed practically tailor-made for postproduction. For eight hundred and seventy dollars per month, plus utilities, General Music had the run of three thousand square feet in a property built originally by...Walt Disney. Once unpacked there in summer 1965, Gordon split the largest room with his new general manager, Bob Glenn. His days of employees complaining about flatulent pigeons and drafts were over. Down the hall was a series of ample rooms; no longer would the tape library and film transfer operation have to be shoehorned into places as an afterthought. Gordon's mind spun over another rectangular space there. He'd convert it into a moneymaking, mini-recording studio, 'cause why pay for what you can do yourself?

This was more like it, being in the thick of things. Above General Music and it's now six subsidiaries, Lantz's animators sketched *Woody Woodpecker* cartoons for the bird's global audience. How sweet it was renting from a first-class Hollywoodite, one grateful that the Lantz Music was raking in thousands of dollars for him in ASCAP royalties.

All in all, Gordon had acquired a premiere office, though he didn't realize yet it would be the last business address he'd ever have.

* * *

HIS HOT STREAK WAS not everyone else's, as the feel-good zeitgeist of the early sixties metamorphosed into something decidedly un-*Leave It To Beaver*. Once jaw-dropping spacewalks were getting to be blasé. Ever since President John F. Kennedy's assassination, a youth movement of discontent over American escalation in Vietnam and Establishment hubris was bubbling; in a few years there'd be a paisley counterculture of free love, antiwar marches, and dinner-table arguments. Closer to Jimmy's home in Watts, race riots that first convulsed the South had migrated west, strewing the land of milk and honey with ill will and despair captured regularly on the national evening news. Gordon, heretofore an nonpolitical cat, stayed out of it. He had land to conquer.

Jack, his CPA, and Abe, his lawyer, recommended he wait. The economy was mushy, and all that social unrest—Southern bullwhips, fiery campus demonstrations, emerging feminism—was bound to roil Hollywood programming that was his cornerstone. Don't be rash, they warned him. Judy was all thrills and chills listening to the scene he painted, and said he had her vote. So, they hired a real estate agent to comb the steep hills north of Sunset for a new place. They hit open houses and took tours, one fading into the other. They saw dated mansions and overpriced teardowns. After a while, Gordon said he was disillusioned by the slim pickings, and that maybe they should be hunting for land instead of a for-sale sign. Why not build from scratch, he said? He could mentally sketch the design and leave it to an architect and contractor to interpret the theme; it could be their affordable dream house for some phenomenal years.

"You're kidding," Judy said during a weekend chat about it. "You're already swamped at work. You won't be able to take a breath"

"Don't worry. I'm not planning on doing the blueprints. Just some thoughts about how the floor plan might go. We want this to be our chateau."

"But a chateau might be out of our range. I hadn't realized Jack was so against this before you let me in on his reservations? Postponing it for a year might make sense."

"Jesus H. Christ," he said perfectly calm. "As the world's leading authority on waiting, I can assure you it usually leads to nothing."

They chose a spit of hillside on a half-developed street about five minutes north of Shoreham, in a rustic canyon between Coldwater Canyon Drive and Laurel Canyon Boulevard. The Beverly Glen community, like Sierra Madre, had once been water-rich Indian territory prior to settlers grabbing hold of it. "The Glen," technically eastern Bel-Air, was minutes from the Westside, San Fernando Valley, and the beaches when traffic was accommodating. 1634 Blue Jay Way had a decadent convenience itself. It was due west of Mel's Drive-In and the old Marlboro Man sign, where the Sunset Strip bent into a cradle of snooty boutiques and trendy cafes you could airdrop onto Paris. Entertainment types, not surprisingly, populated the undulating, private community known for pitch-black nights and howling coyotes. Getting there from Sunset was a car ride along winding, snaking roads like Thrasher Way, toward hills later speckled with vain, postmodern architecture. But if you didn't need a barf bag from the drive up and your lungs were resistant to the smog, there was majesty in this hillside crevice. Besides, the spyglass perch above Los Angeles' floor-bed was an affirmation of making it.

Gordon, stubborn about what he desired and flexible in how he'd get it, parlayed a time-tested strategy to stake his claim here. As he had with Walter Lantz and Hans Salter, he approached an aging legend and flattered him into a partnership. Paul Revere Williams, America's most esteemed black architect, was Gordon's Johnny on the spot. On windblown days in The Glen, Williams' legacy shimmered below—the redesigned Cocoanut Grove nightclub and Beverly Hills Hotel, the three-legged restaurant at Los Angeles International Airport, downtown's Shrine Auditorium, Saks Fifth Avenue-Beverly Hills. Williams, orphaned at four and educated at USC, also had designed scads of churches and some two thousand private homes across Southern California. Hollywood celebrities—Tyrone Powers, Danny Thomas, Lucille Ball, and Sinatra, among others—vied for his drawings. The subdued elegance in his Tudor-revivals and French Chateaus, his genius permeating them with clients' tastes were unparalleled. Even so, bigotry haunted Williams. Some of his projects violated antiquated segregation laws, meaning it was illegal for him to stay overnight in edifices his own imagination had spawned; in earlier days, he'd learned to draw upside down so white clients wouldn't have to get too near him. "Dreams," he wrote, "couldn't alter facts."

Williams, white-haired and dignified, was in his mid sixties and walking with a cane by the time Gordon phoned. He had an unconventional proposition for an icon he'd never met before; an unabashed dare. Erect him the first house *ever* designed for a quadriplegic. Make it another lasting feat. Williams said yes, whether for the novelty or because of Gordon's irritating persistence. During an initial meeting, Gordon asked another favor for him. "Reach in my breast pocket," he said. "I have a few ideas to brainstorm about how we should do things."

He and Judy relocated into Williams' design in 1966, shifting from lunch-pail Shoreham to upper crust Blue Jay Way after Gordon closed the postproduction deal of a lifetime. From the curb, the house was Exhibit A that underdogs can occupy penthouses. The suspense was how long he could maintain the artifice before it cracked.

The façade of the one-thousand-six-hundred-square-foot residence was paneled in earthy, shelf stone and wood. The overall design was that of a sleek fortress carved effortlessly into the sheer terrain. Rolling in from the short, curvy driveway, visitors were greeted by an immense, gray roof, a high French door, and an attached, two-vehicle carport. Just inside the front door was an entryway that spilled into a hallway floored in neat, parquet squares. A left took you to a small, back bedroom where Judy typically slept and a pair of very different toilets. To the right was a smallish living room with a couple of beige, muslin couches that hardly got any action. Keeping them company were a telescope, a fern, and Lee's pump-action, portable organ. Gordon had recovered the instrument in some studio-executive's garage, and had it lovingly sanded and re-laminated to help remind him of the fallen people—his father, Sonny Ross—who made his arrival possible.

All the same, his king-size, contour bed was the estate's center of gravity. Of that, there was no dispute. Situated fearlessly in the middle of the house, it functioned as the hangout room, conference center, captain's bridge, love-nest, dining room, and party grounds. Elevated on it, Gordon was the reposing baron of Blue Jay Way. He could watch the twenty-five-inch color television recessed above the stone fireplace, or entertain guests in a semi-circle around him. He could follow Wall Street on the stock ticker below the set, or daydream out the bay window whose sight lines he'd refined with Paul Williams. Out that window, incidentally, were scruffy highlands that you wouldn't want to hike through, but running beneath it was a uber-varnished bench that was Gordon's pride and joy. Rub your hands over it, he lured friends; examine the craftsmanship. There was nothing comparable around. Twenty types of wood, including teak and birch that he'd personally handpicked on a trip to Mexico, lathed it together.

The rest of the floor plan was a tribute to tidy efficiency and warm elegance. The kitchen, though condensed, was outfitted with brushed-steel appliances and olive-green, Formica cabinets dotted with gold sprinkles. The bathrooms were a paradox. One was regulation porcelain toilet and sink. The other was a vision from a future disability manual. Williams made sure that Gordon's shower stall was wide enough for him to be seated in and cleaned. A bidet, which puzzled guests who mistakenly went in there, was his undercarriage sprayer. Williams' conception overall was so seamless in accommodating a socially minded quadriplegic and so fluid in its adoption of hillside and light that no one thought to publicize the understated marvel that he'd delivered. Gordon may not have been able to stride a foot here, but he glowed when others did.

Realistically, too, if the activity didn't twirl around his bed at first, it wouldn't have twirled at all. They'd so overspent on designs, construction, and the small, kidney-shaped swimming pool they added late to their wish list that there was only leftover money for essentials. Spare furnishings, knickknacks, assorted housewares, and landscaping had to be teased in over time. Judy laughed it off to her girlfriends as the chic, minimalist look.

Overlapping with the move to Blue Jay Way was Gordon's concluding foray into sci-fi. This one had the potential to pass the eyeball test. The story pivoted off a provocative book, *The Earth's End*. Roger Corman, the so-called "King of the Bs," lauded for his film adaptations of Edgar Allan Poe stories, was an executive producer. Mamie Van Doren, the top-heavy, dyed blonde who worked with Gordon on *Women of the Prehistoric Planet,* was the project's designated babe, and one of Orson Welles' cameraman was on the job, as well. None of that mattered. A time-transported Ridley Scott, as the box-office gate and reviews drove home, wouldn't have mattered. The movie, shot in ten days for less than two hundred thousand dollars, mainly at Raleigh Studios across Melrose Avenue from Paramount, was a joke intended as serious drama. The action opens in Antarctica, where scientists on "Operation Deep Freeze" discover mysterious trees have been inadvertently shipped to an isolated US military base in the South Seas. Low and behold: Mother Nature has gone supernatural, and the missing island penguins are just the first victims. The transplanted vegetation are actually acid-secreting man-eaters and they were hungry.

Before audiences panned it, the crew beat them to it. Van Doren, who only agreed to her part because she owed Corman another picture, was disgusted. She and her colleagues threatened a mutiny after producer Jack Broder sensationalized the title, changing it from *Night Crawlers* to *The Navy Vs. the Night Monsters*. Despite the meddling, director Michael Hoey hoped for a suspenseful, original thriller of which everyone could be proud. Broder, a shameless corner-cutter, wrecked that. "He'd say, 'The budget is too high. Why do we need these Quonset Huts?'" Hoey recalled. "I asked him how do we shoot interior and exterior shots? He said, 'Project (actors) onto stock footage'... I was very unhappy...but Broder said it was his movie." Gordon, Hoey added, seemed like an angry Prussian general, none too pleased with the result. Indeed, he was done with the genre he began with Ed Wood, the Transylvanian from outer space.

* * *

THEY FIRST DIAGNOSED ROSE'S cancer while the walls were drying on Gordon's dream house. She'd been grappling with stomach pain alone in her apartment, and when the distress grew unbearable, she visited her doctor. In his office, he asked her if she'd felt listless, experienced any weight loss? Bloating, heartburn, nausea—what about them? Tests were scheduled, X-rays taken. Once the results were in, a local oncologist became her mortician. The tumor in her belly, he said, was both malignant and inoperable. So how did she react? Granny glasses removed, Rose massaged the bridge of her nose and formed a knowing smile. As in not a frown. The doctor who just dropped the bombshell on her misread her expression as classic shock. It wasn't. Rose Zahler refrained from blubbering because now she knew her timeline. At sixty-six, with Gordon bound to outlive her, there was no point to resist going skyward.

I was a mischievous, five-year-old boy with a gnat's attention span and the best Hot Wheels collection on the block when the woman I knew as "Mama Rose" took ill. Gordon's eviction of her after he'd wed Judy had given me an unwitting present: a grandmother two miles away with the propensity to say yes to all the things to which I customarily heard no; yes to more Bazooka bubble gum and Cracker Jack, yes to an extra hour at the park. Being a child was never more rewarding than bouncing on her apartment's daybed like a circus trampoline. "Be careful," she'd quietly say as I tried touching the cottage-cheese ceiling. But she was different by fall 1966, and apologized about being too winded to walk a few blocks down Sierra Madre Boulevard to buy me candy. "Oh, come on, Mama Rose, *pleeeeeeeease?*"

"I just can't today, darling," she answered. "Forgive me. How about a cookie?"

My cancer-riddled grandmother made amends on my birthday in October, handing me a red-and-white-striped package that could've only come from Macabobs, Pasadena preeminent toy store. I tattered the wrapping paper like a raccoon. Inside was a plastic-molded, kiddy pool table matted in imitation green felt. To my extra wonderment, two boxes of Cracker Jack were taped on top. I bounded into Mama Rose's arms talking hyper-speed. "Oh, thank you, thank you! Can we open the Cracker Jacks right now?" She'd been in and out of the hospital, half-numbed with morphine, until recently. No one told me she was on her last rebound, or that she was even sick. All I wanted was to bask in her warmth—elbows on the floor—playing pool on that pee wee, die-cast table. Death for me then was an abstraction, something that befell villainous Nazis on TV programs or a friend's ancient pet hamster and not the sweetest person in my life.

Rose Zahler died on Election Day 1966, hours before Californians officially voted her law-and-order hero, a B-movie actor and corporate pitchman, into the gubernatorial mansion. Had she not been terminally ill, Mama Rose certainly would've stumped for Ronald Reagan at every precinct she could.

The daughter who herself idolized Reagan also had a passable excuse for not knocking on doors on his behalf. Muriel Jacobs needed be somewhere else. On that Tuesday evening, she stood in the parking lot of Huntington Hospital screaming at her little brother over cause-and-effect that she'd bottled up for years. Her fist-shaking, cigarette-breathed tirade was delivered into the passenger side window of his Cad. Diners inside Monty's Steakhouse across the street probably heard it. Gordon, while never one to take crap, reacted uncharacteristically, in a sense imitating his deceased mother. He sat there taking every stabbing insult without so much as a cocked eyebrow.

"Don't you have anything to say for yourself? Don't you?" Muriel yelled. "You put her through hell and back, then you kicked her out."

"Mur, I'm not going to fight with you about this. Definitely not here." Judy was in the rear, Bob Glenn behind the wheel. They'd been there to say farewell, which Mama Rose would've corrected as a celestial see-you-later.

"That's too damned bad," she continued. "You're not getting off that easy."

"Easy? That's what you think I feel? You..."

"She'd be here right now if you hadn't beaten her down," she interrupted. "I hope you go to sleep tonight knowing that. Knowing that *you* killed her as much as the cancer!"

Muriel heeled out her cigarette, tugged her scarf low on her neck, and was ushered home by my father, presumably toward some Valium.

The collective soothing commenced once the rant was over. Bob guided the Cad out of the parking lot while Judy massaged Gordon's shoulders in tender circles.

"I'm sure your sister didn't mean that," Bob said. "She's distraught like anyone would be."

"I guess." Gordon said.

No one spoke for a few blocks while the car floated by the one-story shops and properties whose lights were coming on in the gray dusk. Why would Gordon ever want to return here to Pasadena, bastion of science, John Birchers, and Marshall Junior High?

"Muriel will be better in a few days," Judy whispered. "Give her time to grieve."

"I will. But what she said was still right."

"C'mon," Bob interjected. "You're being too hard on yourself. She got sick. End of story."

Gordon stared blankly from the window. "Even before Muriel tore my head off," he said, "I've been realizing that it's people who give each other diseases." Judy lit him a cigarette. "And if you want to know the truth," he said, blowing out a lungful of smoke, "I did the same thing to my dad."

Hearing that, Bob veered the car over to the side of Fair Oaks Avenue on the bunny-slope-long stretch toward the 110 Freeway onramp. "Now wait a second. I distinctly remember you telling me your father died of heart disease. Probably ran in the family."

"Sure. But anybody with the real scoop knew it wasn't clogged arteries that did him in. It was yours truly."

"That was, what, almost twenty years ago?"

"Nineteen."

CHAPTER TWENTY-ONE: LAW OF THE RANGER

THE GUESTS PALMED COCKTAILS in a horseshoe around Gordon's bed, spellbound by his tale of misadventure at sea. Comical, reckless, deadly—the mishap could have been a screenplay. The late-summer sun was punching the clock for the day, transitioning to a night at Blue Jay Way rent with trilling laughter and sardonic repartee. "Man, you're bullshitting again," someone in the crowd laughed early in his narration. "I'm going to need to hear from eyewitnesses." Brassy trumpet music, Herb Albert perhaps, jangled out of the hi-fi, a few guests tapping their loafers to the rhythm. The Flower Power generation could have Jimi Hendrix or the Jefferson Airplane. This crowd, the one swilling Gordon's liquor and drinking his Kool-Aid, swung to snazzy instrumentals or Tom Jones. White steam from flaky hors d'oeuvres and cigarette smoke fused into a party inversion layer over heads that didn't notice it. Just up the street, a dozen or so vacant-eyed groupies loitered outside the house they mistakenly believed a rock god was leasing.

Gordon spoke with infectious energy that he embroidered with crescendos and inflections and the occasional windmilling arm. His house in the Glen had been planked for uproarious gatherings like these. Whether groovy existence or believable mirage, what Gordon had acquired was striking. In the carport was a Ford Mustang convertible for Judy to putter about wherever she pleased. At Gordon's side laid a spoiled, milk-white poodle named Chicken that he allowed to lick food off his lips. Off to the right was that one-hundred-and-eighty degree view refracting ten thousand city lights.

Nobody here needed to be reminded, either, that Gordon could out-jaw anyone naive enough to try. Where his legs failed, his electrifying tongue rarely did. He was living the kick-ass adventure his Humpty-Dumpty neck was supposed to deny him, and he was eager for you to know he'd been in Italy's Blue Grotto at high tide and had broken bread with *I Dream of Jeannie*'s Sidney Sheldon. Clients chewing the fat with him at General Music heard his litany of antics; sometimes he'd even retell his employees' funniest anecdotes as if they'd happened to him. He was an avid storyteller about his own past as well, especially the boyhood shit-kicking. Yarns about Hugo were another gift that kept giving—slapstick ones about how Monaco secret service agents tailed Hugo when Prince Rainier was in town just in case Hugo made any ruckus about who should be king. "You ought to see how Hugo and I ditched them off Mulholland," Gordon snickered in that echoing voice, which some compared to Harvey Keitel with a head cold. "Hilarious." Overload him with caffeine and he'd nearly short-circuit the phone system initiating calls on his headset. "Morning, Sweetie Pie" he'd say to the phone company operators he knew by name.

This latest story he prefaced by explaining its innocent roots. He'd wanted to relocate his boat from its original Orange County slip where he'd "met" Lantz to a more convenient dock near Los Angeles International Airport. (The decision was Gordon's alone, Joe having sold his share after the divorce.) A relaxing Saturday cruise aboard *The Take One* with Joe and Bob Glenn, his new office lieutenant, was how he spun it. They'd chugged out of Stephen's Landing in the early-morning mist, hoping to reach Marina del Rey not long after lunch. It was only a matter of hugging the coast. Their three wives would be waiting for them in anticipation of a fresh seafood meal together in a picture-postcard California moment. Every detail was planned—a full gas tank, maps, a stocked ice chest, paperwork for the new slip—except the weather check. All of them missed the news reports about how large swells from a bruising Hawaiian Island storm would soon be pounding the Southern California coast. Nice information if you knew it.

They'd scarcely passed the Balboa jetty when whitecaps frothing two hundred yards from shore made everyone gape at each other. By the time they reached the oil derricks near Huntington Beach, roughly one-third of the way to their destination, the gapes had become gasps. Set after thumping set, *The Take One* was being shellacked. Making it to this leg already consumed two hours. South of Long Beach, Bob and Joe were green around the gills and huddling. Maybe they should take refuge behind the upcoming breakwater to reconsider whether pushing on? Gordon, mounted in his airplane chair, enjoying the rough surf like a mechanical bull ride, asked what all the whispering was about. "Nothing," Bob said; Gordon didn't buy it. Fine, Bob admitted. They needed to get out of the open sea unless Gordon wanted their breakfasts all over his deck. The diversion gave them about forty minutes of peace.

In the heaving ocean afterward, the waves slapped harder and the wind yowled psychotically. All Joe and Bob could think was whether to circle back to Long Beach. Gordon, though, was thinking, too. Thinking about a snack. "I'm starving," he announced. "Salt air and the stomach, you know." Reluctantly, Joe took the wheel so Bob could remove the dimpled lid from the Coleman ice cooler. Sitting on top of the Fresca was the ham-and-Swiss sandwich that Judy prepared with Gordon's favorite spicy mustard. With each bite Gordon took from his elevated seat, Bob had to stretch his arm out thirty degrees. After half a dozen repetitions, Bob's concentration moseyed from Gordon's caloric intake to a terrifying scenario. What if a honking wave capsized the boat? Gordon would be flipped upside down into the cold, green waters, buckled into his chair, while he and Joe either dogpaddled for their lives or ducked under the murky current to try to rescue him. A couple of them would die, at least.

This bleak image snatched Bob at an inopportune time. A swell that none of them saw coming rammed the port side, thrusting the boat sideways. Bob just then was feeding Gordon the last quarter of the ham sandwich, but the jostling caused it to bypass his waiting mouth en route to Gordon's ear. Mustard now yellowed his sideburn.

"You know what I said?" His guests tilted forward, ready to erupt. "Please get lunch out of my head." While they laughed, he sipped scotch rocks from a straw and took drags from a cigarette that Judy merrily held out.

*   *   *

BOB, A SHARP BUCK with a slight resemblance to the tormented priest in *The Exorcist*, was comfortable around boats. A military wet suit, after all, circuitously sent him to General Music. After a stint with the Navy's underwater demolition team during the Korean War, Bob had attended electronics school to expand upon what he'd learned in the service. Soon, he opened a TV/radio repair shop in Studio City next to Republic Studios. John Wayne was his first customer; Clint Eastwood, Peter Lorre, and the like would follow. Replacing fried transistors and vacuum tubes for the famous (or whomever) was a living, but it wasn't stimulating next to celluloid attractions across the street. He enrolled in acting courses and earned a running part on a detective show set in Miami. Moviemaking fascinated him too, and he produced a small film that Gordon worked on the cheap. My uncle knew Bob was a revelation from their first get-together. Brains and composure don't just fall from the sky. Join us, Gordon pitched him. We'll complete each other.

Norm Pringle was another new recruit, though he joined the gang more out of necessity than recruitment. Norm went into radio after a stint in the Royal Canadian Air Force during World War II. His media highlights: meeting Elvis and discovering Leslie Nielsen. Friends in the Great White North urged the gap-toothed family man to move south to California, sure he'd make an impressive splash in Los Angeles radio. They were wrong. None of the stations bit on Norm's deejay routine. Jittery his work visa would expire, Norm cinched up his trademark suspenders and got his paychecks from a Sunset Boulevard recording company. The irony taunted him. As a sound engineer, he taped big names—Jack Benny, Eddie Cantor— without anyone asking about his ideas, of which he had a million. Norm was just about to pack up the family car and retreat to Canada with his excuses rehearsed when a chatterbox cripple he met at the studio said *whoa*. General Music could use a versatile, part-timer doing film transfers. "Interested?" Not only was he, he'd never leave Gordon's side until Gordon left his.

Horace Jackson was a different kind of stray—a strident, Black Philadelphian who didn't want to be tamed. Heeding Horace Greely, he'd traveled west with an artistic goal. He needed financing for the autobiographical film he'd written about a young man torn between the pulpit and jazz. Horace was a helluva good pianist, and he was nearly as gifted at charming people more sympathetic to Davids than Goliaths, specifically people like Gordon, who'd once lent five hundred dollars to an acquaintance with a movie idea. Horace bleated that the studios that received copies of his treatment disrespected him by refusing to even give him the time of day. Gordon told him not to waver. The brash, devout kid, who wore sunglasses at night, would be *his* protégé. "I'll help you make your movie," Gordon said. He did too, low budget all the way. When *Living Between Two Worlds* premiered under the klieg lights at South Central's Balboa Theater, Gordon, Judy, and Joe were the only Anglos invited, "token whites" in Horace's words. The movie attracted hundreds, and the association continued. Horace, who disciplined himself to say, "motorcycling" instead of motherfucker when irked, repeated it constantly after Gordon assigned him film transfer work next to Norm.

Igo (pronounced "ego") Kantor entered General Music with the best pedigree among Gordon's new group. The wide-faced son of a Portuguese diplomat had grown up mesmerized by American cinema. In California to study foreign affairs, he found his passion for editing overwhelmed his interest in academia. Columbia Pictures hired Igo, and away he went, cutting music into network staples such as *Hazel* and *Father Knows Best*. At twenty-three, he was anointed head of its music-editorial department. Igo, aware of his value, billed himself as the "fastest editor in the West." Give him scraps and he'd make them sing in half the usual time. Hopping between Columbia and Universal, he edited for A-releases such as *Bye Bye Birdie* and *Pal Joey*. After his mentor, Johnny Green, quit Columbia, Igo phoned Gordon, who said, "You're hired, my boy."

His growing company now consisted of people with radically different backstories and a potpourri of temperaments—calm sorts, flamboyant dressers, attention-lovers, wannabe producers, and sharp minds with middling self-esteem. About their only overlap was faith in Gordon's business model. While the studios paid well and offered union protections, they could also be soulless institutions run by cultish personalities and nepotism. General Music, now one of the larger independent shops around, was a solid alternative to corporate enmeshment for those able to wait for their big moment a few turnpikes ahead. Until then, they spliced sound and music. Until then, they edited cartoons a league below *Bugs Bunny*, spruced up B-grade sci-fi, and toiled on commercials plugging meat, aluminum, aspirin, kitchen cleanser, and Frisbees. None of it was profound, though the "mouths" in the office made the workdays entertaining.

Out of all these fresh enlistees, only Bob, the Navy vet, was regularly invited onto *The Take One*. After some voyages, Bob must have been tempted to seek combat pay.

*   *   *

THE BOAT, GORDON EXPLAINED, continued plodding through the angry Pacific, making it to within three miles or so of Marina del Rey. Getting this close took forever, and the afternoon seas felt nastier than the morning chop. They swooshed sideways then forward, hammered by "five, no, six-foot waves," lifted up onto a swell's crest before a rollercoaster down into the sudsy trough. At the peaks, Gordon said he could make out the house lights on the Palos Verdes Peninsula. Up the coast a bit, he searched for the beacons near LAX to gain orientation. That's when the Chrysler engine decided to be the drama queen. First it coughed, then it sputtered, and, finally it conked out, dead. "Damn it," Joe cried. "Not now."

Not one of the three was panicking, but their lizard-survival neurons were getting there. Within a few moments, the current from the Hawaiian storm that should have kept them on dry land was heaving them shoreward like a wine cork. Hulking, taupe-colored cliffs three hundred yards away loomed scarier each time they glanced over. Bob knew they had to restart the engine, and fast, and there was no time to unlatch Gordon from his perch to do it. Bob just grabbed him from behind and tipped him backward, which retracted the engine casing and exposed the metal cylinder block. Gordon quipped that with the chair parallel to the deck, toes pointed skyward, he "probably looked like a dummy astronaut the NASA boys use as a test subject." His audience roared. Ice cubes clinked.

Seawater backwashing into the engine faster than it could be bilged out was why the propellers had stopped gurgling. Bob tried countering it with arm power, cranking the manual pump to siphon off as much as water he could. Oily, black fumes clouded from the engine as he did. Already supine, Gordon said the vapors nearly knocked him out. How Bob managed it, neither he nor Joe were sure, but he pumped another gallon out with his head engulfed in dark smoke. "Try the engine, Joe. Nice and easy." Joe took a breath and complied. *RRRRRhhhhhh-na-na-na-na.* Success! Engine bubbles; lathery foam. The propeller was back from the dead. Joe gave her some gas, and they put distance between them and the rocky peninsula. Crisis averted.

Just about everything onboard—the cushions, the food, Gordon—was now waterlogged. Bob and Joe's next job was cleanup patrol. First, they righted Gordon's chair and toweled off his damp neck. They wicked away deck puddles with a beach towel. On soggy shoes, they snapped a blue canvas canopy over the bow. *Anything else?* Bob fished his Marlboros out and passed them around. *Ooo, awww.* Nicotine sedation never tasted so divine.

But smooth sailing? Not on this day. Not with these Magellan's. Faster than Joe could curse it, the propeller ceased again. The pleasure craft within a few minutes lost any semblance of forward propulsion, what with the current sucking it ever closer to the cliffs of Playa del Rey. It was palpitating seeing the craggy, dagger-shaped rocks like this, knowing the ocean had slowly ground it away. If the surf could dissolve that hard-pack, imagine how fast it would reduce *The Take One* to toothpicks? The cruelest part, Gordon noted, was that they were almost within shouting distance of their destination.

Bob, the least ironic in the group, could hardly contain his feelings. What else was there to do against an ocean bent on drowning them? From his recesses arose a belly laugh that doubled him over. Gordon, remembering similar lunacy from his mother after Lee's funeral, frowned at him to stop. This only made Bob laugh harder. In all probability, these were everybody's last moments dry and maybe alive. Pious beliefs and all, an irreverent shriek to his maker seemed cosmically apropos.

Joe was caught in his own delirium, Gordon said, basically French-kissing the ship-to-shore radio. "Mayday! Mayday!" he speed-talked. "Can you hear me, Coast Guard? This is an emergency. MAYDAY!" Gordon, unable to contribute anything except commentary, said he hoped they had a better escape plan than this. "Coast Guard, Coast Guard," Joe continued. "This is The Take One and we have an emergency. Our engine's dead and we're near the rocks. We have a quadriplegic onboard. Repeat, a quadriplegic. MAYDAY!"

"Any time now, Bob," Gordon said. Again, he'd been tilted into his astronaut position so Bob could pump seawater out.

"*Ha-ha-ha-ha,*" Bob chuckled, hands around the manual bilge. "Can you imagine what the papers will say?"

"Tell you what, let's think about that later. I'm dizzy."

"It's just so silly," Bob said. "Listen to Joe...*He-He*...thinking they're going to rescue us just...*He-He*...because of you. YOU."

"Coast Guard, Coast Guard," Joe begged. "Our position is..."

Their position was fifty yards from the cliffs.

Last-resort-time arrived as Bob let the pump go. He reached into the ship toolbox, shoving away screwdrivers, barnacle-scrapers, an empty bottle of suntan lotion. Even free of seawater, the engine remained unresponsive. The tall can of ether that Bob now clasped was their only chance to resuscitate the motor. The plastic cap came off, and Bob sprayed the liquid stuff made from petroleum and stabilizing agents onto the carburetor. Applied judiciously, the formula prods fuel and oxygen to combust safely. Inject too much and brace for an explosion. Bob's Hail Mary to get the boat to limp into the marina could go either way. One spray, a second, and a third: the misted catalyst that smelled like nail polish wasn't working. Some magic. Bob checked the engine-oil mix before a fourth try. "Forget it," Gordon scolded him. "Use the whole damn can!" So Bob did, shot-gunning it dry. "All right, Joe," Bob said. "Cross your fingers." He and Gordon shut their eyes while Joe turned the key. The Chrysler motor stammered initially, like an old man trying to clear his voice in the morning. After a few more attempts, that changed. The ignition turned over and the propeller churned. Carefully, Joe throttled her up and once more the cliffs receded.

A harbor master tugboat was in sight afterward. The Coast Guard must have heard Joe after all, and dispatched the closest authorities. The tugboat slowly brought *The Take One* into the marina, depositing her into its new slip. Once they'd stored everything, the three men dragged themselves up the boat ramp, bedraggled, sunburned, and roughly three hours late. Waiting for them were their incensed wives, who'd earlier been scared out of their wits overhearing dockside conversations about the brutal conditions. Nobody was in a mood for the shrimp, calamari, and highballs they'd planned to cap a victorious day.

Hold on, Gordon told his listeners. Wait to top off your drink for the finale. At 7:30 the next morning, he received an urgent call from the Coast Guard. *The Take One* had leaked gasoline overnight. For everyone's safety, it had been towed out to a jetty buoy, where the remaining fuel was dumped. Bob had the honor of driving Gordon back to Marina del Rey. After monotonous hours watching the boat lugged back to the harbor and inspected in a dry dock, Bob conferred with the repairman. When he walked over to Gordon to explain it, he was ashen.

"What gives?" Gordon asked. "How bad?"

"Not nearly as bad as it could've been. Your boat has a clogged air intake. That's why she kept stalling. But there's a more serious problem. You have a punctured fuel tank; don't ask me how. Gas was all over the place."

"And?" Gordon said.

"And remember how we pulled the canopy over us and smoked our brains out after we got the engine restarted that first time?

"Yeah."

"Lighting a match in all those fumes should've gotten us blown to kingdom come. The mechanic said there wouldn't have been pieces of us big enough to float."

"You know what I said?" Gordon dragged out the punch line. "I said, 'Don't crap yourself, Bob. Next time we'll bring oars.'"

Peals of laughter sent shock waves from the bed, followed by knee slapping and a fluttering of eyes. Somebody derisively hummed taps. What a raconteur! What a trip. "Oh, Gordon, you missed your calling. You should've been a comedian," a movie friend hee-hawed. "You really should've."

*   *   *

DURING THAT SAME SUMMER of sixty-seven, the manager representing an English guitarist rented him a small cottage at 1567 Blue Jay Way. The property, owned by a vacationing entertainment lawyer, was a few doors down the street from the Zahler's. As real estate happenstance would have it, George Harrison and his wife, Pattie, were on the cul-de-sac north of the Whisky a Go Go, both unfamiliar with the area. Derek Taylor, The Beatles' press agent, understood that, and made arrangements to visit them. But, like so many, he got all turned around in the misty canyons that can make houses seem closer than they appear. Harrison was bored waiting for him, so he ambled over to the homeowner's small Hammond organ, one probably similar to Lee's. There, he tinkered with a chord, which he then connected to his state of mind. The Indian-influenced "Blue Jay Way" on the group's *Magical Mystery Tour* album was his travelogue lament. "There's a fog upon LA. And my friends have lost their way. We'll be over soon they said." Critics interpreted the lyrics as a commentary on toxic society. Harrison probably laughed that they were overthinking it.

Gordon eventually capitalized on the buzz in his neighborhood. Girls—attractive, longhaired girls in psychedelic dresses with stoned, kaleidoscope eyes—routinely rang his doorbell, mistaking his address for Harrison's. "Is he here?" they'd say in their sandals and sunglasses. "We're his biggest fans and wanted to say hello." Some carried brownies. Judy got sick of it, so Gordon had her let one pack in. "Well done," he effused. "Nobody was supposed to know he was staying here with us writing new material. But you Sherlock Holmes solved it. He just went down the hill to try to find some tea. You're free to stay, too, though I do have a small request. Our pool man is out and I was hoping you being young and all, might clear out the leaves?"

For a chance to lounge with George, they went along. They even blew up a deflated raft. After forty-five minutes passed with no sight of him, they realized they'd been hoodwinked and let themselves out the side gate.

CHAPTER TWENTY-TWO: KING OF THE WILD

HAD THERE BEEN A smartphone around to capture the scene that day in the MGM commissary, even the crustiest skeptics of Loch Ness Monster sightings and Bermuda Triangle disappearances might've begun carrying a talisman or a crucifix. One doesn't see a quadriplegic levitating off his chair without revisiting the existential. Gordon's liftoff, whether myth or exaggerated, was not wasted on the trivial. It was his equivalent of a backflip to celebrate a new partnership with a show-runner unlike any he'd ever associated. A juicy, Kansas City steak sandwich or spaghetti Neapolitan, Tuesday's daily special, was in order. The commissary's "Elizabeth Taylor Salad" he'd leave for less fortunate sacks.

Moments earlier, Ivan Tors had congratulated him for beating out the competition. Drumroll, please: General Music would supply the music and sound effects for three of the prime-time network shows Tors had going concurrently: *Gentle Ben, Cowboy in Africa,* and *Daktari.* Other projects from the executive breathing down Walt Disney's neck as proprietor of wholesome family entertainment would fall into Gordon's lap, too. Only Jimmy and Tors' brother, Erwin, a chubby, bright accountant who worked for him, were with them at the studio's Culver City headquarters. Erwin Tors, however, was still rubbing his eyes. Had a cripple really just hovered in front of him?

"Ivan, Ivan that's terrific," Gordon effused. "We're going to do some great things together, and not just with your programs."

Tors, bearded and ruffled as a middle age Harvard anthropology professor, smiled thinly. Then he held up his hand in a tempering gesture. He'd seen this rodeo before. "I appreciate your enthusiasm, Gordon, but you need to be realistic. All seems right with civilization, I know, but mark my words. We'll be out of business in five years. It's Hollywood."

"Five years?" Gordon laughed. "Who cares after that?"

While the Tors' brothers noshed their Monte Cristo sandwiches that day in sixty-seven, Gordon floated on his mathematical cloud. They'd pay him three thousand, nine hundred and fifty-eight dollars per *Gentle Ben* episode, six thousand, two hundred and eighty-six per *Daktari*, and, best of all, eight thousand, two hundred and ninety-eight per *Cowboy in Africa*. Multiplied by the projected number of episodes per season, his firm would be on the receiving end of four hundred and ninety thousand dollars in gross income annually (or about three and a half million dollars today). This was the economic tamale that he'd been praying for, the cash flow that could lubricate everything: fresh business ventures, his lifestyle at Blue Jay Way, better globetrotting. He'd taken a giant stride toward his "one great thing." Nat Winecoff may have been his first mentor, Lantz a father figure who'd trusted him with his golden goose, *Woody Woodpecker*. No disrespect to them, but Tors, forty-nine, was a species way higher on the food chain.

* * *

THE FREETHINKING PRODUCER GOT as good as he gave. By outsourcing postproduction to a stickler like Gordon, he'd spend less time managing tasks as rousing to him as watching paint dry and more time broadcasting shows telegraphing his passions: animal-rights, zoology, ecology, rotting Western society. Inside General Music's cutting bays, Gordon's editors applauded his deal making but were less ecstatic over how he flyspecked them at first on Ivan's shows. In perfectionist-manager mode, he could be as endearing as an infected toe. Joe was fond of telling strangers that whatever sensation his boss had lost below his collarbone had redoubled in his vocal chords. "Where the hell you going?" Gordon would grill workers swinging their car keys at day's end if they hadn't crossed all the "T"s on an assignment. "We gotta redo this." His brain micro-processed every frame. Should he zero in on something slipshod, he jerked his shoulder to indicate where to revise it. When a complete overhaul was needed, he studied the rough cut like a doctor would an MRI, juxtaposing cues slugged with letters. "Switch G with I, D with B, put A here. Toss out E. You don't need it, believe me." Played over, his suggestions usually worked fluidly, and the editors' frustration and admiration for him gurgled up simultaneously. If he could dream it, *you* did it.

Second guessing Gordon's ability here was to second-guess someone whose mastery of the art nearly embroiled him in scandal. Seemed a Hollywood awards group had nominated him and Walter Greene for best original score on a documentary. Humbling tribute, right? Time to dust off the tuxedo? Nope. The two had grafted the entire program from the catalog and waited too long to inform the nomination committee there was nothing original about their effort. By the time of the awards ceremony, Gordon's gray-haired, broad-shouldered composer was trembling. Better pray we lose, he said, or they'd be mocked as frauds, or maybe even driven out of the industry. Thankfully, someone else won the award, Gordon woofing at the gala, "Yeah, yeah, yeah. You guys deserve it!" Walter, the veteran drinker, probably ordered a double in relief. The sole editor anyone can remember outwardly questioning Gordon's melodic judgment was the testy Ted Roberts. "You can't tell your ass from third base," he once ribbed his employer. Privately, Gordon might've concurred. Ask him to identify a Brahms concerto and he might say it was Beethoven. If he spoke into a songwriter's ear, it might be to suggest he try reversing the notes to an existing ditty to sell as elevator music. Lee had been the musician. He was the businessman.

Able as he was to afford Blue Jay Way, let alone a luxury sedan and new subsidiaries, Gordon also remained headstrong about salaries in this golden era of his. Base pay continued to sag at the tightwad end of the scale. Industry guidelines recommending time-and-a-half for overtime and other employee perks were often ignored. Labor reps alerted to his take-it-or-leave-it practice by malcontents warned him to comply or they'd cite him. Gordon, however, flouted the threat or slicked his way out of it, that being *his* practice. If he had to, he'd hire a journeyman scab for smaller jobs or promise a unionized editor a future raise. This was who he was: a child of the Depression scarred by tragedy. He might spring for lunch or offer someone a second chance if they bungled an assignment. But staffers displeased by their paychecks could howl at the moon.

*   *   *

TORS, MEANWHILE, WAS BORN to be a man of the future. When he and Erwin immigrated to the US from their native Hungary in 1939, the twenty-three-year-old was already a published playwright and journalist. He joined the Air Force, which granted him citizenship, and went into military intelligence training that, some believe, led to espionage roles with the CIA's predecessor agency. An injury ended the cloak and dagger, and Tors was reassigned to write for Glenn Miller's wartime swing-band squadron. After the war, the studios hired him, and Tors didn't disappoint, penning scripts about gangsters, composers, historical melodrama, and love. Before thirty, he'd illustrated he could craft popular story lines for the likes of Katharine Hepburn and Judy Garland. But the former honor student was only warming up.

As a science fiction screenwriter and producer, Tors pioneered like no other for America's baby boomers. They watched *Magnetic Monster* and *Gog* in theaters and next tuned into his TV shows, including the first-ever underwater series. The three networks that passed on Tors' *Sea Hunt*, the Lloyd Bridges-led series about a Navy-diver now making his living as frogman, regretted it. Tors didn't. He leveraged its popularity as a fulcrum to promote other ideas clanging off his typewriter. In 1961, however, his integrity nearly gored everything. Called before a Senate subcommittee investigating TV's influence on juvenile delinquency, he did the unthinkable. He told the truth. He testified that NBC arm-twisted him to knit sex and violence into his G-rated *The Man and the Challenge*. The network eventually terminated the show.

Tors got his payback through serendipity, and he had a sea mammal to thank. While filming *Sea Hunt* in Florida, he'd co-chartered a production company in the Bahamas specializing in underwater cinematography. His partner there, Ricou Browning, was no dummy, either. He suggested they develop a series around a dolphin with a *Lassie*-like lovability. As it turned out, a Florida Key's "porpoise school" kept a highly trainable one (Mitzi) to get things rolling. The result was the sensation called *Flipper*. Two successful movies turned the rubbery-skinned, bottlenecked creature into the world's most recognizable marine animal. Riding high, Tors in 1964 chartered his own studio in North Miami; the so-called "House That Flipper Built" would grow to employ one hundred and fifty as the largest production complex east of Los Angeles. Tors, in demand as animal-entertainment became the rage, received thumbs-ups for his next series. One was about a behaviorist-minded veterinarian in Africa, *Daktari*; the other, *Gentle Ben*, about the adventures of an Everglades-romping bear and the boy he loved (Clint Howard, Ron's brother). Tors had trial-ballooned both concepts in movies first.

Privately, Tors was as eclectic and quirky as he was professionally versatile and opinionated. Some regarded him pompous, others brilliant. Trendy Holmby Hills in West Los Angeles, not far from the Playboy Mansion, was his neighborhood, though he probably would've swapped it for Africa or the Outback. Jetting off to Bangkok or other exotic locales on ridiculously short notice relaxed him. So did punching up a script with a boa constrictor at his feet. Summoned to a network meeting, Tors had about two suits to choose from, and would rather topple from an airplane—which he almost did once accidentally over Africa—than don a tuxedo for a self-congratulatory awards banquet. His wife, Constance Dowling, a Cate Blanchett-esque, onetime actress, had given him three sons, but Tors was determined not to allow California's Gomorrah of narcotics, cults, loose sex, and abundant deception pollute them. "I was born a mammal, and now in a big city I have to live like an insect," he fulminated to *TV Guide*. "In a car I feel like a bug. Even on a freeway I'm just an ant in a long line of other ants... We live a phony existence. We don't understand life and death. We fell out of rhythm with nature. We pretend we don't kill, but let others kill for us."

Except for chutzpah and Hungarian ancestry, Gordon had little in common with his prolific associate, so he went in guns blazing to win the contracts. In memos and meetings, he vowed to pair quality and competence. Onerous deadlines that lesser sorts would've fled he welcomed; heck, he'd been cutting tape for network shows while Tors was still writing his early scripts for MGM. General Music, Gordon noted, bristled with all the equipment, manpower, and protocols any heavy-hitting producer needed for a sound night's sleep. He was exaggerating, of course, and doing so was crafty. For all of Tors' mastery pitching shows and packaging them, wags knew he wasn't exactly a fastidious CEO. Rather, he was a first-impression, non-confrontational fellow reluctant to say "no" to babied stars or crews, including the bunch that'd gorged on thousands of dollars of French pastries on the *Gentle Ben* set. Perhaps his inattention to detail was brain chemistry essential to creativity, but it drove his brother and studio bean counters batty. Tors' fierce loyalty and refusal to fire anyone for anything short of animal cruelty further made him susceptible to my uncle's salesmanship.

Where Tors shone best were the themes linking his shows— feel-good narratives about Americans living morally in unforgiving lands. Lantern-jawed outdoorsmen in khakis played his leads (Chuck Connors, Dennis Weaver) alongside anthropomorphized monkeys, lions, and such. His villains tended to be ham-fisted criminals out to poach the animals or virgin land for the sake of short-term profit. Which Tors regarded not all that differently from his network superiors.

Quarterbacking multiple programs while preparing feature films and managing hundreds of employees at three locations would've have fatigued anyone. Yet Tors did it unflappably, without losing his soul or deprioritizing his family. Occasional absentmindedness and a fondness to hear his own voice came with the territory of being him. As Gordon learned early on, driving with someone who preferred a jeep on the veldt could be life-endangering in Los Angeles. Tors was once so immersed recounting a wild animal experience that he steered his Mercedes-Benz the wrong way over a set of metal parking lot spikes at the Lantz Building, blowing out all four tires in staccato pops. What could you do? Tors' bottomless well of research anecdotes—how, for instance, two lions had stalked him on the Serengeti plain until they started humping—meant that once he got humming, listeners were wise to locate a comfy chair.

Gordon, who'd seen a lot over his forty-one years, hadn't seen anything yet. Tors took care of that when he chaperoned his new, postproduction man to the epicenter of his zoological franchise. "Africa USA." In Soledad Canyon fifty miles northeast of Los Angeles, three hundred to six hundred lions, bears, snakes, cheetahs, jaguars, elephants, hippos, zebras, anteaters, yaks, alligators, leopards, and his other Hollywood varmints resided in arguably the planet's largest private zoo. Animal trainer Ralph Helfer had launched it, and Tors' success had enriched it. By mid-decade, nearly every challenging wild-animal scene in movies and TV were shot at this simulated "jungleland."

Gordon, as would other visitors, rarely spied a gun, whip, or similar weapons to control the denizens. Instead, the animals learned by "affection training," a cousin of psychological positive reinforcement. Africa USA was a Petri Dish that'd proven itself. Animals living unconfined there with benign human contact performed on camera at levels that traditionally treated animal "stars" couldn't. (They were also less apt to kill or maul someone after years of corporal punishment and imprisonment). Clarence the Cross-Eyed Lion, the headliner in the eponymous, 1965 movie, lived well in this commune-type environment. So did Bruno, the seven-hundred-pound black bear known as *Gentle Ben*, and Patricia, a Bengal tiger from a recent Disney move. Gordon's jaw was about down at his knees. Around the soundstages here on an ordinary day you'd see a cheetah attack a hyena, a chimpanzee escort a baby lion atop a crocodile, a rhinoceros charge a car, and a tiger leap into a station wagon. Amazingly, everyone stopped fighting and began playing as soon as the cameras turned off. No split-screen photography, glass walls, or people dressed up as gorillas—techniques that Old Hollywood employed—were needed with affection training. Rarely was anyone hurt, for the animals were more like colleagues than subjugated servants. When one turned ornery, a trainer shot a fire extinguisher at it or dappled whipped cream on its nose.

Tors, boned up on the subject like a PhD candidate, preached his unconventional philosophy to Gordon, as vulnerable an organism as Africa USA ever hosted. (Even the tamest of the lot must have licked their chops fantasizing how he'd taste.) To Tors, fish were psychic and dogs candidates for tranquilizers. (Tors years earlier had volunteered to be an LSD test subject for the government, so he had familiarity with pharmaceuticals). Coming from a mother who wouldn't allow him to have pets, he was the world's most unexpected advocate of the tailed, winged, and furred. After shoots, animals received time off and ones too old to act won a pleasant retirement. Tors' conviction that some predators had bad raps was not just words for him. During the filming of *Thunderball* in the Bahamas, a scene called for 007 to swim with tiger sharks. Sean Connery worried about being their lunch. Tors knew otherwise, and bounded into the water uninitiated, splashing around the dorsal fins. Connery followed.

Tors' influence on Gordon, not to mention the money he was paying him, was profound. Since boyhood, he'd yearned to see Africa, where man began. He kept his nose in *National Geographic* reading about the Dark Continent, probably when he should've had it in his textbooks, and promised himself footsteps there one day. Time at Africa USA reinvigorated that whim. Six months after joining forces with Tors, Gordon phoned his travel agent about seeing the great escarpments. Fantastically, he could write off much of the trip by meeting with Laetrec Music in Johannesburg, South Africa.

Meetings finished, he and Bob would charter a plane from the sub-Sahara's most cosmopolitan expanse into wildlife and history. They'd land in Nairobi, Kenya, and drive southwest into the Great Rift Valley. Their destination: the Safariland Club. Bob had a connection, some high roller named Dirk Brink, who'd helped them book hard-to-get reservations. The trip would've been an unadulterated dream had it not been for the hard knuckle realities of segregation in the nation at the intersection of the Atlantic and Indian oceans.

South Africa, where untamed savannahs segued into rising skylines, was not for everybody. The white minority Afrikaners imposed police-state command and control over the native blacks outnumbering them roughly five to one. Apartheid was official law of the land. Blacks were so disenfranchised that it was illegal for them to own property that traced to their forebears, centuries before colonialism and the Boer Wars. After seventy protestors were killed in 1960 at Sharpeville, the Afrikaners banned the dissident African National Congress (ANC) as a terrorist organization. It was their Al Qaeda. An articulate, ANC lawyer named Nelson Mandela paid for his belief; in 1964 his white masters slapped him with a lifetime sentence breaking rocks at Robben Island prison, a former leper colony off Cape Town. The country's polarized racial atmosphere wasn't exactly calmed in 1966 when a mixed-blood assassin stabbed right wing Prime Minister Hendrik Verwoerd to death.

Jimmy assumed he'd see the blanket injustice firsthand, and why not? Over the years, he had logged thousands of miles tending Gordon from Manhattan to Havana, London to Geneva. Once, he used Gordon's head to push their gondola out of a low-hanging Venetian grotto after a premature high tide rolled in. With the chintzy wage Jimmy brought home, globe-trotting represented a thick slab of his compensation. Bob, though, was the first to suggest he stay home. "They might not let you stay in our hotel. We don't even know about the restaurants. Don't subject yourself." Jimmy tried playing it stoically, but Gordon read the disappointment in his body language. "Edit to your heart's delight while I'm gone. Come in at eleven if you want. You've earned it." Jimmy said fine, and faked something to do in the other room.

*   *   *

MOBILE DEVICES FILLED WITH your associates' phone numbers and addresses; talking gas-station pumps; stadium music; community-access TV; a doll whose face changed colors when you pressed it; a pocket docent. As the campuses burned and the longhairs loafed around Sunset, Gordon, mostly, divested himself from the social tumult and reengaged the creative side of his neocortex. His finances, better than they ever were, inspired him to think humongous.

Altogether, he oversaw thirty-five postproduction editors on site—so many, in fact, that he encouraged some to work for an associate. Six music-licensing sub-units, including Ivan Tors Music, oozed extra money. Now was his time to dabble in electronics, and he occupied his imagination for gadgets without fretting about outstanding bills. The ideas split into two camps: get-rich-quick schemes and more visionary propositions as a digital-thinker in an analog era. Although not specifically about touch-screen technology and wireless communications, Gordon tickled the edges. Sometimes, his torrent of futuristic concepts came so quickly that his secretary could barely get the dictation down accurately on her steno pad.

His tenth-grade-educated mind believed the American consumer was being stupidly targeted. An upwardly mobile population with more disposable cash than any prior generation should have advertising shadowing their routines. When Ralph Sixpack filled up his car at the pump, Gordon pictured a friendly cartoon-type voice automatically clicking on from a mounted speaker. What about adding a lube job or tire rotation since you're here, it would ask? No, maybe a soda or pack of Wrigley's would lift your day? When Ralph's missis was having her hair tinted at the beauty parlor, a song—bookended by ads and tailored for her socioeconomics—might caress her eardrums inside her cone-shaped blow dryer. To him, delivering content in slick, new ways was feasible so long as it was General Music's exclusively licensed tapes supplying it. Morticians could lease solemn background music for funeral services. Hotel lobbies might play ditties to steer couples into the lounge for cocktails, or into their rooms for a carnal break. Sports arenas and fields, with captive crowds of fifty thousand or more, were particularly luscious possibilities for canned music and ads. He'd leave bothersome kinks, legal and otherwise, to specialists to unknot.

His would-be blockbuster often began with a holler. In those days, Gordon rallied Bob and Harriet, his newest secretary and Joe's second wife, to powwow in his office, thinking caps donned. Sometimes he had the bead on patent-quality concepts; others were pie-in-the-sky concoctions that made the collective eye rolls sound like slot machines.

"What if," Gordon posed, "we sold our tapes to every gas station in the United States? Multiply fifty thousand by our per-unit cost, and you have what, ten million bucks to divide up among three partners. Not bad."

"Right," Bob answered with a skeptical brow. "And we better assume every one of the oil companies will go along. That's a pretty tall assumption. You have an in with Shell?"

"Okay, maybe shooting for one hundred percent is overly ambitious. Let's revise our expectations down to, what, eighty percent. So, it's forty thousand times two hundred. Eight million works for me. Bob, stop making funny faces at Harriet."

"Eighty percent?" Bob said. "That's your idea of a more realistic projection? Earth to Gordon—no way."

"All right, you wet blankets. Suppose we drop it down to forty-five percent of the stations? Now you happy? Type that up in a memo, Harriet, and let's go through the Rolodex this afternoon to see who might finance it."

"Do I have to?"

"Only if you want to get paid."

"That's it," Bob said, half-smiling. "I'm going to lunch. And I won't be listening to the background music, either."

"Before you go, let me ask you this. Try to be analytical for thirty seconds, okay? How much time do you think people spend in Laundromats? I keep thinking it's like the sewing show that got me going—an audience everybody has ignored. Nobody's invented self-cleaning clothes yet. That's a lot of empty ears to target."

Spitball, adjust, present, and ditch: that was the sequence his notions about piped-in music and pop-up services had traveled, all to nowhere. The miniaturized wrist-record player foreshadowing the iPod segued to his "microphonograph," a pocket-sized tape recorder for tourists eager to learn about foreign landmarks at their own leisure. Neither sniffed mass production. Every time Gordon tried branching into fields outside his wheelhouse, either by himself or on somebody's coattails, the limb snapped. Either no investors would bankroll him or there'd be migraines running down licenses and potential factories. Unlike Hollywood, where he'd demonstrated that mettle resides above the neck, he possessed neither the retail history nor the right blend of hucksterism and hard data to convince deep pockets. To outsiders, furthermore, he appeared more like a gnarled Ron Popeil than a get-it-done Thomas Edison.

None of this would have been necessary if he'd been quicker on his heels. He'd partnered years earlier with a New York company that contended it had the inside track on an auditory sensation sure to be worth tens of millions. It was. The cassette-tape player would revolutionize everything, from miniaturization to car stereos. Yet, Gordon & friends never stood a chance. By the time his group tested an assembly-line-ready prototype, the record companies were already miles ahead of them, monopolizing the plastic rectangle. Americans' love affair with push-button technology wasn't just for dishwashers and transistor radios anymore. Bashing around, Gordon did sell a canned-music system to a San Fernando Valley company peddling continuous-loop tape players to restaurants and such. The pittance it netted him still felt like a game show consolation prize. History had repeated. His instincts to give consumers what they craved—even if they didn't know it—were regularly eclipsed by shoddy follow-through. What he needed was a millionaire champion who focused more on the invention than the inventor.

*   *   *

GORDON'S PERSONAL LIFE MOVED at a more predictable clip than his technological aspirations. Saturday mornings—if he wasn't overseas, on the boat, or inside the office double-checking the music and sound effects rushed to Tors each Monday—he spent at Blue Jay Way kibitzing with clients over the phone. On afternoons "he" might run through the punch-list of house fix-it projects that Judy compiled—a leaky faucet, a bent screen door a drunken partygoer knocked off its metal track. If leaves obstructed the rain gutter, Jimmy was the one up on the ladder scooping them out while Gordon chipped in his two cents. Later, he'd be on his bed watching USC football or the baseball game of the week on TV. On scorchers, he'd have Jimmy lay him on a raft and push him into the deep end of his pool to further decompress.

Flipping over and drowning completely unconcerned him. It was a hesitation to live that spooked him.

He recognized, of course, there'd be no growing old, no retirement to mothballs and mushy meat in a nursing home like his contemporaries. Making fifty was unlikely, so why embrace caution? Occasionally, he clucked gallows humors, telling friends readying for a trip: "Before you leave, touch my head for luck. You can't end up any worse than me." For Judy's benefit, he usually kept this to himself, sticking to maximizing what woeful physicality he had. Others with devastated, shut-in conditions could weep onto their bibs all day. To him, limitations were not disabilities. They were hurdles he'd trounce by ingenuity, science, and balls. Him, a role model? You're kidding. Acquaintances curious how he felt about *Ironside*, the TV show about a paralyzed former cop, misunderstood his bearing.

After he'd adjusted to working with Tors, Gordon began investigating ways to gain more freedom. Judy thought it sounded ghastly, he pragmatic. The question was whether to have his left hand surgically amputated at the wrist. With it gone, a stainless steel, pirate-like hook would replace it. Once medicine advanced, it could be upgraded to a lifelike, prosthetic hand. For now, a hook affording him a small radius of functionality was enough. In an archetype, a sleeve fit over a working shoulder muscle connected to a metal pincer by guide wires and hinges. This, in theory anyway, would enable him to grasp, maneuver, and release all sorts of reachable objects. Consider what this might mean, he told Judy, who remained staunchly opposed to any body-parts removal. He could hold his own cigarette, turn a page, or press the remote control. "You should be jumping for joy. I wouldn't be on you all the time." But she wasn't jumping. She fretted that somebody's eye could be gouged out.

Gordon brought home a model that an inventor fabricated for him. Had it performed as advertised, it would've been cause for delirium. The tryout, however, underscored it wasn't ready. Everything he pinched with the claw slipped from it within seconds. "Mechanical bug," he pooh-poohed. "They'll fix it in production." Despite questions about its viability and Judy's opposition, Gordon was ready to embark. The X-factor was mustering a winning argument to convince his insurance company to pay for the ten-thousand-dollar operation. The first time he asked, it said no.

Gordon about this time also chased another supercharged desire related to his disability: a method to have sex with Judy. So far, kissing and cunnilingus constituted their marital relations, and this, to him, wasn't lovemaking. Judy disagreed, proclaiming herself sated. He asked for how long? Then an automobile-dealer bud with a screenplay mentioned a class of experimental drugs for just the problem. Supposedly, men waylaid by spinal injuries could receive a chemical injection along their shaft and, with any luck, up sprang a woody where there'd been flaccid hydraulics before. Interest whetted, he researched the issue, as was his way. Adrift from sensation for so long, he asked what harm a needle plunge between the legs could do? Chastity was infuriating.

The West Los Angeles urologists who examined him confirmed that erections could be in his future, if he accepted the risks. The feds had approved the injections, but they were known to cause seizures, penile malfunction, and other side effects that made today's Viagra and Cialis seem as dangerous as Tic Tac mints. Alternatives the disabled and performance-challenged tried, including noisy suction pumps, induced less engorgement. Outside of them or continued abstinence, there was only that needle. So that's what he chose. How many times Judy loaded up the syringe and waited to mount him is a secret gone to the ages. What matters here is that Gordon and Judy, behind shut curtains, against all neurological likelihood, consummated their bond the same as any heavy-breathing "normal" couple.

It's just that neither ever imagined Gordon's boys were capable of impregnation.

CHAPTER TWENTY-THREE: MILLION DOLLAR BABY

THEY MIGHT HAVE BEEN sitting on the secret inside Judy when Gordon toasted associates and worker-bees with unbridled munificence. As rich as he'd get, he splurged for a holiday party unlike any he'd thrown. The hoity-toity Beverly Hilton Hotel was the site. The date: Christmastime 1967, the best professional year of his life. Open bar; three-course dinner; music; elaborate floral arrangements: no expense was spared. Every contributor to his improbable success was in his rented ballroom, dressed to the nines: Tors, Lantz, Hugo, Nat, Jack, Abe, Nathan, and sundry movie people. Williams, who'd redesigned the hotel in the forties, was practically the only dark face around not carrying bags. Bob, Joe, Jimmy, Norm, and other employees were in attendance too, for how often did Gordon un-padlock his wallet for them?

Drinks flowed and personal stories unfurled. Gregarious Joe regaled his table about his college-age daughter Lori, an apprentice animal trainer at Africa USA Evidently, the occupational hazards there were nothing to sneeze at, whatever its culture of animals hugs, not cages. Joe, making sure Tors was out of earshot, said Lori had recently come home to the Valley with a disconcerting bandage taped over her chest. "'Hon,' I asked her, 'What happened?' She said, 'Dad, you won't believe this. I was working with a monkey and the goddamn thing bit me on my ti…I mean my breast. But don't worry. I'm fine.

No infection or anything. And I got even. I took it behind a tree and kicked the living shit out of it.'"

Across the table, Norm was probably stupefied there was any festivity at all. Six months ago, he'd requested permission to skip out a few hours early to attend his son's high school graduation in the Valley. A stressed-out Gordon said no, "A deadline's a deadline." Norm was stunned that the employer he so admired—and was so devoted to—could be such a Mr. Scrooge. "Gordon, come on!" he fired back. "Gary will be crushed if I'm not there. This isn't a picnic I'm asking to go to, for crying out loud." Norm bailed from the transfer room before he screamed his way out of a job. Another editor who'd overheard the exchange, perhaps Ted Roberts, softly berated Gordon for being such a hard-ass. Gordon waited until he left to call Norm back to say, "I'm sorry, man. Of course you can go." Lady Karma must've taken note, Norm told his seatmates, masking his laugh with a painstakingly starched napkin. Gordon, he said, was so chockablock juggling Tors' shows, music acquisitions, and side interests that he had to delegate this night's preparations to his secretary, Dorothy Garner, a perky woman adroit at spending other people's money. Gordon only got around to inquiring about the tab this morning, and when he heard she'd racked up an astronomical five-thousand-dollar bill, he reacted as if he was straining to pinch a badly overdue loaf.

But that was hours ago, and come 9:00 p.m., as he made the rounds, one of the Hilton's expensive candles couldn't have melted his smile. A man at his height shouldn't sweat a runaway bill. Nor should he lose discretion, and that's why Gordon parceled out his secrets—how he was crippled, the atomic bomb it dropped on his family, the living being Judy was carrying—on a need-to-know basis. Only Igo, his quick-gun, Portuguese editor, was made aware. Gordon said it'd been a spectacular combination of science and kismet, this conception. Imagine him, father of a miracle baby? He might just have to buy a crate of cigars. The legacy, the possibilities were almost beyond words—and the whole subject had to stay between them, anyway. "Understood, Igo?" Gordon needed that firewall separating his life at Blue Jay Way and his one on Willoughby Avenue preserved. History with long shots fizzling out had seasoned him. Jazzed as he was to call everybody in, he resisted. When Judy showed, then they'd uncork the champagne and maybe some baby names. Gordon knew his loins' accomplishment would ignite a thousand private discussions. *How, how, how?* He understood the curiosity. Most quadriplegics couldn't translate libido into anything seminal, because their blood-controlling brains and peckers were out of communication. Nor could they feel anything much down there. Assuming there was arousal, only a measly five percent of paralyzed men in that era could manufacture worthwhile sperm. Gordon's were the outliers.

The company water cooler, accordingly, never hurt for conversation, provided voices were kept low. An employer that a satirist might lampoon as a pussycat and monocle shy of being a Bond villain was its perennial topic.

"I heard he busted his neck on a trampoline," one editor said. "Guess he tried some daredevil flip."

"Wrong," another answered. "He took a swan dive off Santa Monica Pier, and it didn't go as planned. Either that or the monkey bars."

"Well," the first editor said. "Did you know about his photographic memory? Supposedly memorized every cue in the library. Crazy, huh?"

"I don't care about his recall," the second editor replied. "I know a client, that same guy who did that pro football promotion, who calls Gordon the biggest music hustler around."

"I can beat that," the first editor said. "One of the girls said they overheard him talking to a doctor. Get this. He takes injections so he can get it up for Judy. Makes me want to cross my legs thinking about a needle down there. *Eww.*"

"Easy for you to say," interjected Norm. "What would you do if your dick was a wet noodle? Chant at it?"

"Okay, Normy, since you're defending him out of the chute, doesn't he get under your skin with his 'do-that-over, it's not right?'" the first editor asked.

"I'd be lying if I said no. My wife says she thinks Gordon's first name must be 'damn' cuz on deadline days I come home swearing about that damn Zahler."

Jimmy, Joe, and Bob typically weren't part of these discussions. Bob didn't gossip, Jimmy rarely divulged secrets, and Joe wasn't sure who'd believe him anyway.

Gordon had been smart to impose an information blackout on the pregnancy. Inescapably, there was disappointment of a sizable magnitude. The child was not meant to be. Judy miscarried, when and how it's not exactly clear, though the telltale hemorrhage probably occurred at home. Scrub any announcement. "Gordon was devastated for a month," Igo recalled. "Just devastated." He shed his gloom as time went by, but the little piece of him that broke off wasn't coming back.

News-wise, Judy acknowledged her miscarriage to only a few, including my mother. Glossing over her heartbreak, she argued that she was relieved. "Sounds funny, I know." But how, pray tell, could she take care of an infant when caring for Gordon in the hours she did could knock her off her feet? A baby created another downside, she added. The lifestyle they adored—the star-studded parties up on their hill, their extended trips deep into Europe and, now, Africa—would be effectively torpedoed. "Muriel, I don't have to tell you how much attention kids need." Really, she said, this was a blessing in disguise, no bereavement necessary. Judy, a natural with kids and a Hollywood wife, could act when need be.

*   *   *

Jimmy's paycheck-by-paycheck existence, much of it behind Gordon's chair, was getting old. He'd been at General Music since it was little more than hustle and bailing wire. He'd helped Gordon bulk up from a fast-talking wheeler-dealer to a whirling entrepreneur running the most successful indie postproduction shop in town. Jimmy remembered it all—the dumpster diving for scripts, those partying nights when he held Gordon by the scruff of his soldered neck so he could projectile-vomit his liquor out the car window. He could reminisce about escaping Castro's Cuba, the boss' semi-death in Rome, and that time he nearly jumped off *The Take One* into a swarm of blue sharks. Just recently, he was with Gordon inventorying the Hollywood apartment of Gordon's deceased cousin when cops tipped off to intruders materialized. "LAPD. Stay where you are!" one said. For ninety minutes the officers detained them, Gordon occasionally piping up, "Excuse me officer, but do I look like a burglar?" Jimmy's storehouse of memories was the gift of a lifetime. A durable bank account should've accompanied it.

Being Gordon's everything man had hurt Jimmy as a family guy. Ten- to twelve-hour days were so customary that he usually said goodnight to his young ones by phone. The next morning he'd be back at Blue Jay Way, taking orders anew, sublimating himself on a new shift. "I'm getting to it as fast as I can," Jimmy repeated throughout the day. Everywhere they ventured, he was Gordon's secret service agent, shielding him from hazards, assessing needs, dealing with the biological nitty-gritty, without complaint. He didn't blanch at full urine bags or food-streaked mouths. To his credit, Gordon kept his word to let Jimmy sound-edit once he'd learned the fundamentals, but that took a backseat to his schlepping-around chores. Most galling of all was his take-home pay. It should've been triple its disrespectful amount. No doubt about it: Jimmy's job was surrendering its sparkle.

Often, too, he inhabited a less friendly Hollywood than his lighter-skinned cohorts. Most blacks not in front of the camera then were still mainly errand boys for executives and their cronies. Tors, for all his progressive views about endangered species and predatory man, could've been nicer. When Gordon asked Jimmy to hand-deliver papers or edited tapes to him at his MGM office on Washington Boulevard, the producer was frequently more preoccupied with the tamed critter near his desk than welcoming his partner's aide de camp. This to Jimmy wasn't racism; it was narcissism. On a few occasions, Jimmy traveled to Tors' Holmby Hills home, discovering him frolicking in the pool with his four-hundred-pound, defanged lion, Clarence. Jimmy's instinct told him to throw down the document and sprint, but he knew lions smelled fear.

Nothing, though, stays the same, and after early 1969, it was Tors who probably wanted to run. Jimmy actually felt sorry for him. A once-in-a-century rainstorm clobbered Southern California with a biblical wallop, dropping fourteen inches of moisture in twenty-four hours. A swollen dam just above Africa USA overflowed, channeling torrents of water and suburban debris into the preserve. The result was at once madcap and frightening, a Dr. Doolittle nightmare. Soledad Canyon homeowners locked their doors, anxious about wild animals on the loose. You could almost hear a bath-robed wife exclaim, "Honey, is that a rhino behind the hedge?" The deluge capsized tractor-trailers, and two trainers almost drowned. Many of the soaked, terrified animals needed rescuing; one staffer waded across a river lofting a python that outweighed him. Out of the hundreds of animals there, only a lion, a Pakistani eagle, and two wolves perished. Clarence and Judy, the chimp from *Daktari*, were unhurt. But Bruno (aka Gentle Ben) was gone. Tors and his partner jumped on radio and TV, asking for assistance bringing him home. Two days later Bruno padded back unassisted, putting himself into his enclosure. Quizzed where he'd been, Tors laughed it off. "My guess is that he decided it was time for a personal appearance tour." The damage assessment later wasn't so humorous. Gordon might've had Jimmy whisk him there to glimpse the million-dollar flood damage, for his own fortunes were enmeshed there.

While everyone focused on what to do at Africa USA, Jimmy gnashed his teeth over what's now called "driving while black." Jimmy used to be so thankful Gordon let him take the Cad to go home and wherever after work. Not many on his minimum-wage block had access to such chromium wheels. It was around the Sunset Strip, near the liberal WASPs of Beverly Glen, where accusatory red-and blue strobe lights continually flashed a hateful message in the rearview mirror: Jimmy must be guilty of something. The area had become his pullover zone. "Get out of the car and tell us where you stole this thing," the LAPD officers sneered. "Bo-oy, you realize this ain't Watts? Wha-cha doing up here? A little grand theft?" They'd rummage around the interior sometimes for guns or drugs. This, if nothing else, gave them an excuse to slap the cuffs on him for a few minutes. "You can go now, Mr. Gillard, but we'll be keeping a lookout for you." On a couple of occasions the cops—whose department was being glorified for its just-the-facts-ma'am professionalism on *Adam-12*—manhandled him. They shunted him toward the curb, and the beautiful people of Laurel Canyon slowed down to gawk.

He'd tried shrugging off the harassment as tolerable indignity. Compared to the rabid bigotry in Louisiana, this rousting was dime-store stuff. (His brother Spencer could attest to that. A few years earlier traveling through Alabama—as a member of the US *Olympic* pistol team—he'd nearly provoked a race riot for daring to sit in the front of a Greyhound bus.) But even mellow Jimmy had his cracking point, and after one bullying pullover he spilled to Gordon. He was flabbergasted—flabbergasted it was occurring and disconcerted that Jimmy sat on it for so long. Immediately, he got the desk sergeant at the LAPD's Wilshire division on the line for a royal ass chewing. "Guess that saying about being there to protect and serve, the one on the sides of your cars, isn't worth the paint it's written on," he said. "Next time I'm calling my lawyer and filing a citizen lawsuit." After a loop of mollifying phrases from the sergeant—"I understand, Mr. Zahler," "I'll check into it, Mr. Zahler"—he vowed to take this up the chain to ensure Jimmy wasn't targeted anymore. But he would be.

Even that humiliation Jimmy could have abided if his salary wasn't at a janitor's level. When he wasn't chauffeuring or caretaking, he edited and spliced truck backfires and monkey squeals into network programming as well as most. Big deal that he misspelled show titles on tape canisters, or was unable to conjugate his verbs. Fair was fair. In his previous life, he'd been a trash man whose rig collected Jerry Lewis' stinky detritus. (Every time Gordon and Jerry, light friends, got together for drinks or talk, Jimmy cringed that the high-voiced, funny man would recognize him.) He shouldn't have been that same exploited breadwinner anymore, not after his years of duty here. Frankly, the two hundred a week Gordon paid him battered his pride more than the LAPD had.

Then again, alley catting around South Central as Jimmy did would've strained anybody's bank account. By the time his zipper slowed down in the late sixties, he'd fathered, depending on whom you asked, nineteen to twenty-seven offspring with a gaggle of wives and girlfriends. Just as Gordon refused to allow a trifling condition like quadriplegia to ground him, Jimmy's expertise separating foxy women from their panties was unstoppable, even pathological. Every hot, domestic mess where pregnancy followed equaled another bite out of his net worth, and still the lady's man couldn't help himself.

Jimmy's romantic tricky wickets came to involve my parents' own house. This was after he split with Florence and before he hooked up with Peaches. One evening, maybe around 1968, Jimmy ferried Gordon and Judy to Pasadena for dinner. Gordon was in the dining room and with Muriel feeding him Jimmy could lounge in the kitchen. Score! Standing between the oven and the yellow Formica counter was a Costa Rican lovely the Jacobs' employed as a live-in housekeeper-cook-nanny. Clara was sultry and high-spirited, and maybe bipolar. The smooth operator from Shreveport was infatuated before dessert time. Clara reciprocated, and the kitchen acquaintances fogged up some windows when they had an opening. Clara believed she met her Prince Charming, and damsels don't clean windows. So, she alerted her bosses that she'd have to resign. A lady needs to prepare herself for matrimony. The dress; the church; the honeymoon; living arrangements: all that happily-ever-after detail requires time. Interestingly, all this would be news to her purported fiancé, who'd only invited her to move in with him as a shacking-up arrangement. Nonetheless, after some pell-mell packing and hasty goodbyes, lovestruck Clara left us on a Friday.

The next Monday, as Jimmy was setting out for Blue Jay Way, Clara complained about a "sour stomach" that'd probably keep her in bed all day. Feel better, he told her. Eat some dry toast. Little did Clara realize what else would be curdling her. Hours later came a knock on the front door. On the other side of it was one of Jimmy's former (or soon-to-be) wives, three of their children with them. Jimmy's ex judged Clara a revolting tramp, and unloaded on her. "Since you took my husband," she said, "I'm giving you his children." Go inside, she ordered them. Clara stood speechless as they awkwardly tromped in behind her.

Around 9:00 p.m. that evening, Jimmy slipped the key into the door. This was supposed to be a fireworks occasion, just him and the Costa Rican. Instead he was screwed over. His modest, well-lived-in house was cleaned out. "Daddy," one of his children asked with infuriating innocence. "Are we moving?" Jimmy answered no, but he was less positive about Clara. As he pieced it together, she'd called a friend after her confrontation on the doorstep. Together, they rented a Beacon's van and hauled away a good portion of his earthly belongings. They'd swiped his refrigerator, his pots and pans, and the two thousand dollar furniture set he'd bought on credit from Sears. Big items in the cargo-hold, the thieves even went back to snatch his drapes and cuff links.

"What the hell did you do that for?" he bellowed over the phone. "I thought you liked me?" She did, she said. She just got cold feet about their future after her surprise introduction to his rug rats. Jimmy growled he wanted his stuff back—tomorrow. Clara said no-can-do: she needed to liquidate his stuff to finance her return to Costa Rica. Over my dead body, Jimmy warned her. Don't even think about a plane ticket! (Before he died, Jimmy disputed this chronology, though he acknowledged the pound of flesh it exacted.) Clara turned vindictive. Make one move, she warned, and she'd drench his things in gasoline and stoke a bonfire. Neither of them cooled down for face-saving reversals. Jimmy, on principle, stopped making payments on furniture stolen from his own house. The Mexican standoff dragged into a statutory fiasco. Sears filed charges against him for defaulting on his installments and next garnished his wages. Gordon finally intervened, hiring Abe's law firm to settle the case for six hundred dollars. Sears was indifferent. The company repossessed Jimmy's furniture once Clara un-stashed it. She dodged jail only because my parents paid the fine she was levied. Afterward, she split for Central America. Back in Jimmy's spartan living room, meantime, the soap opera was over, but he felt poorer than ever.

* * *

JOE VON STROHEIM BY then was done bitching about his salary, and pretty much everything else. When he burst into Gordon's office that Tuesday, his attitude led the way.

"Okay," Gordon said, "I'm betting you're not here to talk about the Rams."

"Cut the crap," Joe said. "I just got done talking to Ted, and he told me something very interesting. He said you're paying him three hundred a week. Three hundred? Shit-all-mighty, Gordon. That's fifty bucks more than me!"

"Oh, come on, Joe. That's Ted's business, not yours."

"Bullshit it's not my business. Bullshit! It's a competitive industry, in case you haven't noticed. Aren't you the one who always says he values talent so much?"

"I do. You're my best editor."

"So pay me like it then!"

"I'm really buried right now. Do we have to get into this today?"

"Yeah."

"All right. You've heard me say this before, but I'll repeat myself. I have a budget to stick to. I just can't rip it up when somebody decides they deserve more money. Do you have any idea what I go through to keep your paychecks coming when the shows go dark for the season? It's not simple."

"Don't turn this around on me. What I'm asking isn't going to break you.

"Understand where I'm coming from. We'll have to keep you where you're at until next season. After that, if things keep panning out, I'll give you a bump."

"No deal. Maybe you've forgotten I was here way before Ted, when all you had was Bozo the Clown and a few other chicken-shit projects? Pay me what Ted's making and I'll get out of your hair."

"Why do I sense an ultimatum?"

"Only because you're being an unreasonable tight ass. I know you're making good coin off of Ivan."

"Back at you, Joe. Don't be so ungrateful. Think of the peace of mind you've had with me. You wouldn't have gotten that at another shop."

Joe's cheeks were crimson as he drummed his fingers on top of a filing cabinet. *Ba-de-da, ba-de-da.* "I really hoped it wouldn't get to this but it obviously has. If you don't raise me up to what Ted is making I'm gone. Like now! I won't have any trouble getting three hundred at Desilu. In fact, they've already offered me a job—a damn good one, too. Harriet and I are trying to buy a house. You know that."

Gordon's bemused expression hardened into a poker face seen by adversaries during negotiations. It took him some time to speak. "Well, since you've applied elsewhere, and they're wagging a big salary under your nose, I can't stand in your way. So to speak."

"And you're not even going to counter?"

"Why should I? You just said you'd be happier someplace else."

"Clean out your ears. What I said was that I'd be making a lot more."

Gordon went quiet again listening to his office phones jangle and editing equipment drone. "Then go. No sore feelings. It's not like we won't we see each other."

"And that's it?" Joe asked. "After everything we've been through you're going to play the tough guy?"

"Sorry. I've got seven companies to manage and an accountant always breathing down my neck about overspending."

Joe marched to the side of the bed near the phone lever. "Overspend, huh? Consider this my two-week notice."

"Done! Heard loud and clear."

He and Joe stared each other down like a pair of mountaintop rams when Harriet popped her head into the transom. Pardon the interruption, she said timidly, but Gordon had an urgent phone call from an overseas music supplier.

"Not now, Harriet. Please." Gordon said. "We're in the middle of something."

"Actually," Joe corrected, "we're at the end of something." A scowl reminiscent of his father, Erich, creased his face. "See ya, Gordon."

Being a man of his word, Joe made good on his threat. His last official credit with Gordon was Tors' *Daring Game* about Navy SEAL-like skydiver-commandos. At Desilu, he cut sound effects for TV's *Mission: Impossible* and *Mannix*. He'd be nominated for four Primetime Emmys, winning twice for his small-screen work. Seventies' moviemaking kept his hot streak going, putting him on the sets of *Jeremiah Johnson*, *Three Days of the Condor*, *A Star Is Born*, and *Every Which Way But Loose*. Before that acclaim, his snap departure from General Music as the senior guy, the funniest, most irreverent of the bunch, was a wind tunnel that sucked esprit de corps from the place. The secretaries, Joe's wife, Harriet, among them, shot Gordon *how-could-you* looks for weeks.

Chalk another one up to oppressive pay. Igo, by then, had already tendered his resignation. But it wasn't for a studio. Igo decided to be his own shot-caller at the new postproduction house he was launched. Gordon was gracious about the surprise, expressing no resentment and earnestly wishing him well. Besides, Tors was *his* bread and butter.

Of all these changes, Jimmy's declaration that they "needed to speak" a month after Joe walked was the most blindsiding. They were in the Cad—Gordon's third model by now—heading toward Tors' MGM office for a meeting. His minions wanted Gordon's input on a half-million-dollar "Daktari Junction" attraction they were pitching Universal Pictures as it geared up to construct a theme park on its studio grounds. Jimmy had another imperative as they crept at ten mph through midday traffic blurry in dark exhaust. Without asking, he steered the car to the curb a few blocks from Tors' building. He'd been subdued since he picked Gordon up that morning.

"Something wrong?" Gordon asked. "We're already late."

"I know, boss. I know."

"Jimmy, look at me," Gordon said. "You're talking into your shirt."

Jimmy brought his eyes up. "This is hard to say so I'll just say it. I have to leave. Got myself a job at Desilu. On Mannix. Going to be an assistant editor under Joe."

"You are?" Gordon asked. Inside he was rabbit punched.

"Hope you understand. Between Lovella and Florence, I got eleven children to support. This money you've been paying me ain't nearly enough. Not unless you can get me to two-twenty-five a week right away."

"Two-twenty-five? Out of the question, Jimmy. That's way too much. For Crissakes! You guys are killing me."

"Thought that's what you'd say."

"Haven't you been saving anything? Like we talked about before?"

"I tried. But my family has already spent my money before I earned it."

Neither man said anything over the purring white noise punctuated by an ambulance scream on Pico.

"I hope you and Joe will be happy out there." Gordon's tone was flat and grim. "Drop me a line so I can let Judy know how you're doing. I'm sure she'll miss you."

"I knew you'd get hot. But you gotta know this ain't personal. You're…" Jimmy cleared his throat. "A brother to me. A real broth…"

"As in, 'Brother can you spare a dime?'" he said bitingly. "Some idea of family you have."

"Gordon, you couldn't be expecting me to stay with you forever making what I'm making. Been ten years. It's embarrassing how little I bring home. Not right."

"Don't be so naïve, Jimmy. If I start throwing out raises, everyone's gonna start asking. Then I'll be worried about my own bills. You on welfare when you first moved out here? I've been on it. You wanna talk fucking humiliation. The answer is no. I can't make exceptions, even for you."

Jimmy drew in his lips so his mouth disappeared. He then leaned in tight and said at a volume rarely heard from him. "Then you can have your job. I'm done with ya."

The meeting over bringing *Daktari* to the Cahuenga Pass was pointless in the end. Money-conscious Universal was, in one insider's words, "too rigid." Imagine that?

PART III—REDEEM

CHAPTER TWENTY-FOUR: THE VANISHING LEGION

WITH JIMMY GONE AND Joe history, a new personality dawned over Gordon's grand adventure: Bob. Action now ran through him. Classic good looks—Brylcreem-styled hair, that solemn smile—made him look the part, and as everyone learned it came standard with backbone. Well-rounded Bob had the gravitas to tell the boss he was on the wrong side of an issue or needed to double back on his own logic. Gordon's comfort level with him could be summarized as if he were currency. "In Bob I trust." He never had an executive lieutenant of this caliber. Then again, never did he ever have so much to lose. During Pepto-Bismol weeks at the Lantz building, they'd split the managerial workload, sometimes rendezvousing on weekends to distill the chaos.

A yin latched onto its yang. Where Gordon could be overly bulldog-ish in negotiations or swift to offer concessions to a heavyweight name, Bob brought a more levelheaded composure that impressed their progressively global clientele. In him, Gordon had someone able to sniff out a mediocre deal cloaked to look better than it was. If Bob's born-again Christian pieties occasionally ruffled his co-workers, Gordon nodded understanding, hearing echoes of his mother in him. They first got to know each other in the editing bay, where they disclosed bite-size parts of themselves between tape rotations. Weekday mornings Bob wheeled Gordon down the linoleum, where the lion roars and chimpanzee squeals being spliced was the gratifying sound of company *cha-ching*. "You know, Bob," he'd smirk, "it's getting interesting." When their editors did well, the two eased off the reins. Gag reels the office comedians assembled by dubbing curse words into the maws of Gentle Ben, Clarence, and Tors' other show animals, they admitted, were hysterical.

Bob's diplomacy complemented Gordon's take-charge absolutism. His Number Two massaged blown deadlines incensing producers, and goaded know-it-all employees to sharpen their game. Folks resentful of Bob's status, or quick to peg him crassly as Gordon's "hay boy," had yet to comprehend that his follow-up and taming of Gordon benefited them if he helped slingshot the company forward. But since Gordon had never deputized a real chief of operations before and Bob wasn't much for self-aggrandizement, some questioned his value. Hence, a tangle with the six-foot-three-inch, two-hundred-thirty-pound former-athlete that Gordon hired to replace Jimmy became his unscripted audition.

"The next time he bugs me, no matter where we are, I'm going to grab him out of his chair and slam him into the ground," the attendant said one day after Gordon riled him. "Right there."

"Oh yeah?" under-weighed Bob replied. "Then you'll have to do it through me."

"Don't tempt me," the attendant said. "I could put you in the hospital with my left hand if I wanted to."

"If someone told you this is how to endear yourself at a new job, you might reconsider their opinion. In fact, you've just lost yours in record time."

"Lost what?" The man was no longer so pugnacious.

"Your job. Lost your job. Now please leave while we cut you your final check."

The office of chatty, smoking secretaries, short-sleeve editors, and fussy composers wanted to clap. Sam Fuller could've filmed this drama. Until a new Jimmy was secured, Bob took over the role, and with newfound confidence and cunning. When Gordon wilted at 7:00 p.m. complaining, "Take me home, I'm beat—we'll have to finish in the morning," Bob intermittently refused. He might haul out a syringe loaded with vitamin B-12, or threaten to; the stimulant could produce a cocaine-like high that would keep Gordon up half the night, leaving him a zombie the next day. Likewise, it was Bob giving him a sip of tea as a reward for sorting out hopelessly tangled cues. It was him there doing everything on wearying, transcontinental flights from Los Angeles to Johannesburg. Should Gordon plead with the maître d at a crowded restaurant for a table in his best Tiny Tim falsetto, who do you think was beside him?

Bob was dedicated—dedicated even when he could have been busy on a major film —for he was having a blast here when it wasn't a slog. Living in Gordon's contrails was a killer seat at Cape Canaveral watching a rocket either roar skyward or detonate on the launch pad. The magnetic spectacle was unlikely to recur. There Gordon was every morning, in a pricy suit Judy had deliberated over, with a *let's-get-after-this-sucker* expression as minty as his aftershave. That's why he relished the contract haggling, or insisted on driving with the top down, sniffing like a sheepdog. The sanctity of being in the thick of it registered more than any check a producer could write him. Watching the priceless reactions Gordon evoked from newcomers was entertainment on its own. Many didn't know to react around somebody with such conflicting exuberance and motionlessness. Some developed nervous ticks, others the urge to invite him to dinner to have him explain how he did it.

The bandwidth of jobs Gordon had his mitts on in the late sixties made Bob's days zesty, as well. Over a few months, assignments oscillated between supervising their network nature programs, including a live-action *Tarzan* series (this one starring Ron Ely, not Marshall Jr. High) and a slew of new cartoons. On the peripheries were side projects, music catalogs, and Gordon's unflagging beguilement with over-the-horizon technologies: videocassette recorders, talking gas station pumps, speaking books. Bob might've judged it scattershot, but he rarely judged it dull.

A few months before NBC formally canceled *Flipper* from the Saturday-night lineup, Gordon was already compensating. At Blue Jay Way, he met with Lou Scheimer and Norm Prescott, a pair of forty-ish cartoonists who'd broken in drawing for Larry *Bozo* Harmon. They had their own shop now, Filmation. From it, they intended to challenge

Hanna-Barbera, the General Motors of animation companies, for the lucrative, kiddy-TV audience. (Hanna-Barbera then was producing *The Flintstones, The Jetsons,* and other top cartoons.) Their upstart rivals from the Valley hadn't gotten this far flying blind. They'd gotten this far flying acrobatically. Years earlier, they'd asked DC Comics to license them a few of its action-hero characters. Knowing little about them, executives insisted on visiting Filmation's Los Angeles headquarters. With few employees, this could've been deal kryptonite, but Scheimer and associates were resourceful. They called their friends and positioned them with "fake drawings" for the inspection. DC Comics bought the ruse and awarded Filmation the rights to animate the man of steel in *The New Adventures of Superman*. Gordon, after supervising the music for six episodes of it and doing the same for Filmation's *Journey to the Center of the Earth*, liked their style. They possessed the kind of derring-do others ascribed to him.

Why not, he proposed, allow him to open a music company for them? Just as he had for Walter Lantz and Ivan Tors? Don't throw royalties down the drain, not with the surging youth/teenybopper market. Yes, they said, yes. Gordon, high octane as ever, framed what the corporate superstructure would be. They talked future series. The only remaining issue was the company's moniker. After bogging down on something original, their inspiration was the nickname for Gordon's poodle. Chipper Music was another way of saying pop-music jackpot. Bob heard it, too.

And with Gordon, there was always a "next." Soon, the two of them were in New York City, where Gordon had finagled a sit-down with one of the more phenomenal guys in his field. Promoter Don Kirshner, later known for his deadpan, leisure-suited introduction of hard-rocks acts on his late-night concert show, was a trend reader for the ages. Observing Beatlemania, Kirshner had capitalized by Americanizing it on TV. *The Monkees* was his brainchild, and when the hot selling group bristled about creative freedom, Kirshner ruthlessly put his muscle behind *The Archies*. Gordon believed he was just the big-fish they needed to turn Ivan Tors Music into a thriving brand. The former music publisher with a Fifth Avenue office could market sand if he tried.

Bob sat back as Gordon jutted his head forward in sales-attack mode. Millions could be on the table. To make an opening splash, Team Gordon proposed arena extravaganzas highlighting the recognizable animals with Hollywood-type pageantry. "Don, imagine this. Gentle Ben, Clarence the Cross Eyed Lion, and the bunch are led out on stage while a live orchestra strikes up those theme songs. *Da, da, da daaaah.* Every paw step is choreographed. Dramatic lights. Poses. The whole magilla. You wouldn't believe the stunts they can do. Lions and lambs playing ball, chimps piggybacking alligators. What do we call it? Prepare yourself! We call it…an African Rodeo! Gives me the chills just saying it. Ringling Brothers will be crapping their pants, they'll be so jealous."

Returning home, Gordon found Kirshner insisting on a king's ransom to lend his name. He wanted half the profits, which Abe lambasted as "unconscionable." Gordon, yearning to work alongside Mr. K, didn't care about the percentages as time went on. And went on it would. For months, Kirshner gave Gordon the long-distance brush off. A dozen calls and a stack of fawning letters failed to elicit so much as a courtesy callback. Tors' personal appeals were equally futile. Kirshner, discoverer of the two Neils (Diamond and Sedaka), the preternaturally tanned New Yorker, had lost interest. With it, Gordon's bid to take Ivan Tors Music global petered out.

A more resounding whiff was necessary before Gordon's winning streak could be certified as over. Before finalizing the deal to incorporate Chipper Music, Gordon tried asserting his leverage to get Filmation to honor an outstanding debt. The company had promised to send Judy and him on a trip worth two thousand, seven hundred and fifty dollars as repayment for postproduction on Filmation's first cartoons. In the broad scheme of what they were devising, this minor irritant should have been papered over. (Why Gordon wanted an invoice settled this way was anybody's guess, but tax reasons probably influenced it). Prescott, a no-nonsense Bostonian, snooped into the matter to reeducate himself. After looking over the accounts-payable, he told Gordon he was overstating how much he was due. Gordon, surlier this time, said Prescott was wrong. In the spirit of compromise, Filmation offered to pay for a Hawaiian vacation. Gordon answered that a European trip with return passage through Tokyo was more like it.

The disagreement over the old tab persisted, taking on a venomous dimension. Gordon and Prescott fragged each other in letters about phony integrity. Lawyers for each side earned billable hours nitpicking contract details. It became a pissing contest, General Music versus Filmation, and Gordon's advisors privately beseeched him to split the difference. Chipper Music's future returns were worth some loss of face. Sacrifice pride for incoming revenue, they said. Go back and read *Billboard* to see what *The Archies* had made. Gordon plugged his ears.

On the surface, this was about broken promises, about being professionally wronged. That unpaid invoice could have gone to payroll, or song licensing, or a rainy day fund. But pricking beneath, Gordon's insecurity was showing. Abjectly. Relent on a debt like this, and who knew if other clients might begin perceiving him as a handicapped cream puff they could flatten next time? He blew up the dispute as if it were law of the jungle; yielding to Filmation was to asking to be eaten. His pride, his survival instinct that'd allowed Joe and Jimmy to walk over a few hundred a month, had been overreacting since the miscarriage. On top of that, he was already nervous after Filmation brought in-house some of the work it previously farmed out to General Music. Industry trend or company snub, Gordon took it personally.

After going round and round over the bill, Filmation's prior enthusiasm to partner with him simmered into a hot resolve to dissolve ties completely. The company wrote Gordon a two thousand three hundred dollar check, put the kibosh on their nearly activated deal for Chipper Music, and incorporated on their own. Norm Prescott, Lou Scheimer, and associates were about to hit the mother lode. The very next year, the bubblegum hit "Sugar Sugar" from *The Archie Show* cartoon went double platinum, selling two million records. Filmation's "next" was the lucrative *Fat Albert and the Cosby Kids*. Gordon, had he listened to saner voices like Bob's, could have had vacation houses in places out of Hugo's price range.

* * *

IN DEFEAT, THE TIRELESS optimist recommitted himself to friendlier climes. Who needed Kirshner or Filmation when he had Tors? His people were all over him for cross-merchandising savvy for what everybody reckoned would be a sure-fire hit: a *Gentle Ben* album. The cast would sing, and the wandering bear (Bruno) would pose pretty on the cover. Gordon, album executive producer, enlisted English composer Joe Lubin to write the songs while he ironed out the contractual kinks. An ill-timed kidney infection that added to his medical dossier kept him away from the recording sessions for days, but he recovered fast enough. A General Music editor used his absence to smoke pot and strum Bob Dylan songs in his cubicle, but Gordon filed it under the these-things-happen category. Ditto for the bouffant-haired actress who played Dennis Weaver's wife on *Gentle Ben*. Beth Brickell couldn't carry a tune to save her life, and others were tone deaf, too. The *Bear Facts* album was sinking fast. Approached in the summer of sixty-eight to distribute it under their labels, neither Capitol nor Columbia Records wanted anything to do with it. They didn't believe songs like "Don't Cry Little Gator" would catch on. A tiny label in Century City was the only one willing to sell the vinyl.

Something was happening that hadn't after other missteps. A faint exhaustion with Hollywood game playing and a grass-is-always-greener view of South Africa began tapping at him. Having traveled there a few times, he began wondering about a life split between Africa and Los Angeles. Say what you would about the sub-Sahara, but cretins and brown-nosers happy to stab you in the back for better ratings didn't run it.

Dirk Brink, Gordon's sandy-haired chum, deduced this in him. And Dirk was a fellow who knew things. Before *The New York Times* printed it, his sources had whispered to him that the stodgy Afrikaners had decided to join the twentieth century. After years of political jousting (and angst they might be slitting their own throats), the conservatives had finally bowed to grass-roots demand: they'd introduce TV to the populace. Vilifying it as "the destroyer of once-mighty empires" was no longer a tenable red herring, not when South Africa was the last industrialized nation to join the club. Whites, who'd long rented 16-mm movies for home entertainment, were restless for programming, especially after smaller countries around South Africa welcomed it. The rollout, all the same, had to be nuanced. As liberals and native activists knew, the central government in Pretoria wielded and withheld information to perpetuate its regime, and banning TV had helped maintain it. The fear had always been constant: a flick of the dial allowing the subjugated to measure themselves against the enfranchised whites could not only imperil their grip. It could ignite a race war.

Brink, trim and sandy-haired, a financier who reminded you a little of The Crocodile Hunter, thought like an insider here. He realized South African TV could enrich whoever got in on it early. Someone, too, had leaked Brink confidential information. The government planned to ease TV in between 1969 and 1970s, if the radio-oriented South African Broadcasting Corporation was up to the task. First, bureaucrats needed to conjure up the nonexistent infrastructure—studios, postproduction facilities, cameras, transmitters, offices, original content, and whatnot. Until now, the Luddites who spoke in that Dutch-British accent had been all thumbs.

At Brink's urging, Gordon and Bob winged across the Atlantic in mid 1969 to see for themselves. They first met up in Kenya, three countries north of South Africa, because Gordon jonesed to get back to the Great Rift Valley after his previous visit to the Safariland Club. Staying at the nearby Mount Kenya Safari Club, they toured the lands, ogled Mount Longonot (a semi-dormant volcano), and got close-ups of deep-water lakes and marshes pulsing with wildlife. This expanse was a birdwatcher's paradise and a zoologist's Candyland. Pawing about were wildebeest, gazelles, vervet monkeys, waterbucks. Teddy Roosevelt once trekked here for big-game hunting, and one could understand why.

During his own exploration of Mount Kenya, Gordon struck up a conversation with a genial, moon-faced politician a lot more relaxed around the ceremonial dances than him. Gordon had seen his face before in photographs with JFK, and even on the cover of *Time* magazine. Tom Mboya, thirty eight, was Kenya's great hope to transcend its bloody, colonial past. A former trade unionist, he'd condemned secret trials, detention camps, and other dregs of British rule. Now that Kenya was independent and Mboya its economics/development minister, pundits handicapped him as the odds-on future president, a people's champion. But he needed to take a load off, and he and the American vulnerable to a tsetse fly gabbed as if they'd known each other for years.

A few days later, a small charter plane lifted Gordon, Bob, and Dirk over the treetops and buildings of Nairobi, Kenya's dusty capital, to Johannesburg, South Africa's Manhattan. Over drinks in their hotel lobby, Dirk outlined his magnetic scheme. "Gordon, with your years of know-how, you could be—how can I put this?—the wizard of TV here. The South Africans, they're oblivious to all this technical stuff. Make a deal with them. If not you, it's gonna be somebody else." Gordon asked Dirk how he knew so much, and Dirk said he had his birdies. They discussed it more, brainstorming and playing devil's advocate, when the papers stunned them with a reminder how tribal much of the continent remained. It was news heard round the world: a killer linked to a rival party had gunned down Tom Mboya on some road. Kenya's dream of a fresh start died at the speed of a bullet. Gordon's *Forrest Gump* moments knew no end, either.

Dirk, still, could regain anyone's attention—with his past, where he was going. He and Gordon shared much in common. Both in their early forties, they shared the same zeal to try new things, to live unconventionally, and forget their darker moments. Dirk, born abroad to parents of American and Dutch descent, had been a Japanese prisoner of war during World War II, some of which he spent imprisoned in Malaysia. Today he was a ranking executive out of Hong Kong for foreign-currency-exchange giant Deak-Perera, doing quite well, thank you. Some of his wealth he invested in Safariland as a minority owner. He also owned land in rural South Africa, which he saluted as "the greatest country around despite what the bleeding hearts said." Any doubt that Dirk ran in different circles than the insular Hollywood types Gordon and Bob were accustomed to was evident on the front page of Kenya's main newspaper a week earlier. An article, alongside his photograph, declared he was wanted for alleged currency violations. No worries, Dirk assured his most unassured travel-mates. Don't sweat a thing. The short chat he planned with his accusers would resolve this misunderstanding. Dirk was correct. Just like that, the charges dissolved.

* * *

GORDON WAS ABOUT THIRTY seconds squished inside that revolving cup on the Mad Tea Party ride when the hot dog and fries he ate an hour earlier near Tomorrowland threatened to come back up the way they went down. "Bob, I think I'm going to get sick." Next to him on the circular bench, Bob leaned in. "If you do," he said, "just try not to aim for our guests." He was referring to their delirious South African seatmates, eyes wide as they spun around on a giant platter that wasn't exactly quadriplegic friendly; Gordon's odd constitution was much better shock-absorbing rough ocean chop than a few dozen rotations on the vomitus carousel inspired by *Alice in Wonderland*. By the time he made it through and was back in his wheelchair, he had a notion to call his friend Nat Winecoff to ask him to tear the contraption out. "That thing should be against the Geneva Convention."

He wasn't too giddy, either, about soaked pants from the Matterhorn or the grating redundancy of the "It's A Small World" theme song. But this—the theme park experience—was what his South Africans wanted, so he and Bob gave it to them with their usual mock enthusiasm. Whether from Johannesburg or Tokyo, visitors frequently made the Happiest Place on Earth their must-see destination, and who better to chaperone them, they asked, than a couple of locals? After multiple trips handholding clients there, they so tired of the Magic Kingdom that they rechristened it "their mutual suffering." Navigating the obnoxious crowds; staying awake through the Main Street Electrical Parade, the punch-able figures in Mr. Toad's Wild Ride: the mutual suffering could be a twelve-hour marathon of "fun." Disdain aside, they conceded, it was superb for business. Newcomers usually returned with mouse ears for their kids and a pliable attitude toward deals.

Dirk was pushing hard on South African TV, for reasons that included his own cut; so hard, in fact, that he flew from Hong Kong with his insider man for a more discreet conversation on the subject. Zachariah Swaenopoel, "Swanee" for short, worked in South Africa's Hong Kong trade office, fully confident about the information he bore. With him, it was a family thing. His boss was his uncle, and that uncle happened at the time to be South Africa's trade minister. Gordon forced himself to blink hearing that. Swanee, too, was pumped to tell what he'd learned from his channels. He'd just be in a chattier frame of mind doing it, he said, after he sampled as many rides as possible at world-famous Disneyland with, of course, the Californians. "We'd be honored," Gordon said, lips pursed. "Bob and I have been looking for an excuse to go back."

After Swanee got his day there, he gave them the lowdown the media hadn't published so far. The government, he said, was earmarking seventy million dollars (roughly 450 million today) in start-up funds, with part of that allocated to hiring contractors. A spanking new transmission-production complex would be constructed on the edges of Johannesburg. Here, Swanee said, is where Gordon fit in. As fast as possible, he should submit a formal bid to supervise postproduction there—every cue, every frame. Swanee said he could arrange the introductory meetings with the instrumental suits in power. Gordon's heart started beating in this throat.

But there was another opening to leap on, as well, an opening Dirk mentioned before about how South Africa was a polyglot nation where you could hear twenty-seven dialects being spoken. Even if the state-run broadcasting corporation alternated programming on the same channel in the two, white-man languages (Afrikan and English), it would eventually need to transmit the same show in tongues spoken by the black majority—isiZulu, IsiNdebele, Sesotho, and half a dozen more. None of this came as a surprise to Gordon, who'd already gotten a jump on the problem after he'd returned from abroad. John Hall, a lanky, local engineer who developed prototypes for the experimental gadgetry Gordon was hyper-charged about at the time, had been on the brunt end of Gordon's redundant question. "It has to be possible, right? With some ingenuity it just has to be. What's your gut tell you?" John sketched it out. He burned through pencils and ignored the ringing phone. Finally, he knew: yes, he answered Gordon. It was doable, and he whittled down the alternatives to the most feasible option: parallel frequencies.

Complementary audio feeds, distant relations of today's digital streaming, could be re-synched into whatever dialect was needed, John reported. So long as the transmission signal was potent and TV receivers were engineered for them, the concept worked. Whatever companies sold South Africa TVs could custom-manufacture them with a switch enabling the viewer to dial in the frequency for the language they understood. The postproduction effort to continually translate, redub, and broadcast so many versions of the same show would be gargantuan, Sisyphean, at least initially. Linguists, editors, technicians, and others would be crammed into rooms, grappling with complexities beyond anything that ABC, NBC, and CBS ever worried about in English-only America. John's innovation really was space age. Indeed, it had its own verb. "You multiplex it," he said. Pretending he'd known all along, Gordon hyped it to Swanee, and Dirk insisted it was drinks on him. All they had to do was bag an investor.

Gordon, fresh off the Chipper Music-Filmation disaster, might have just pinpointed his "one great thing." Handled right, he'd be a millionaire with the resources to pursue his hand surgery, private-pilot lessons, and whatever in the wide-open spaces. Though a year or more away, Swanee's proposition was his chance to be truly extraordinary rather than a periodic genius. Every time Gordon tantalized his inner circle about what he had cooking, Dirk's words about being a "TV wizard" did half gainers off his tongue. So, when Bob felt tempted to leave, Gordon's panoramic ambitions tended to dissuade him.

South Africa might just become their foreign branch. Gordon's name already was being bandied about, and one producer courted his association. Boet Troskie was stout and take charge, self-made and a chick magnet. His company, Mimosa Films, was seated in Bloemfontein, a borough halfway between Pretoria and Cape Town and notable for its roses, cheetahs and grasslands. Troskie's most valuable possession was his connection to director Jamie Uys, then South Africa's most acclaimed director. It was the oddest of matches, but sensitive, obsessive Jamie was somehow able to work with Troskie's alpha male persona. Under a handshake agreement, they had already collaborated on two successful movies, one of them distributed internationally by Columbia Pictures.

Troskie invited Gordon and Bob to his place on a get-acquainted stay. Out on his patio they bantered and drank, and then turned to politics. Gordon predicted South Africa was facing a gory uprising if the whites refused to loosen their chokehold on the black majority. "Let's see about that," the conservative Troskie said in his he-man voice. He called over his longtime Bantu servant and presented him with a hypothetical scenario. If revolution broke out, Troskie asked on this blue-sky day, would his loyal man slaughter his family? "Oh no," the Bantu replied with a loving expression. "I'd never do that." He thought for a minute, though, and his face tightened. He pointed to other Bantus servicing a farmhouse down the road and admitted, "But they might."

Before returning home, the Americans had a final stop to make. Sanlam Limited, an insurance colossus with all sorts of business interests, wanted to hear about Gordon's multiplexer, too. Inside Sanlam's Cape Town office, a heavyset executive and his underling listened intently to the dog-and-pony show. Two million dollars in seed money: that's what Gordon said he needed. Whoever furnished it would automatically be in on the government-blessed action. The apparatchiks of the actuarial table looked at each other afterwards. Thoughts, Gordon asked? Yes, they had one in particular. They were taking his request to the company's board of directors for *immediate* consideration.

Gordon barely needed a plane to fly home to Blue Jay Way.

CHAPTER TWENTY-FIVE: CAVALCADE OF THE WEST

C HUCK CONNORS, THE GRAVEL-VOICED prima donna, had
Ivan Tors right where he wanted him. Cornered! Before ABC
green-lit the *Cowboy in Africa* series, the network had insisted
that Connors be anchored in the spotlight role or it would walk. The
first *Flipper* movie in which Connors starred churned good box office,
so ABC was confident TV advertisers would throw money at it for
commercials likely to produce a solid return. Tors, a non-argumen-
tative sort anyway, went along, knowing full well that the face of the
program had a reputation for sometimes being a serial pain-in-the-
ass. But a higher calling was at stake here. The program's subthemes—
wildlife preservation, mankind's trashing of the planet—mattered
deeply to Tors. They mattered so much, in fact, they influenced his
continuing willingness to remain under the thumb of profit-obsessed
suits. Nobody who'd worked with Connors since *The Rifleman* series
was astounded that he took advantage.

The former minor-league baseball player—six foot five inches
tall with bright blue eyes and a New York accent—wanted everything
and then some. Each episode paid him twenty-five thousand dollars,
an eye-popping amount for the era. To go with it, Connors' agent
negotiated a buffet of perks for him: control over show merchandising,
a limousine that chauffeured from him home to the lot (or Palm
Springs on weekends), a stocked personal trailer, and the right to
fire guest stars whenever *he* chose, among other benefits. Whatever

his earlier reputation for politeness, Connors' demeaning, stuck-up attitude toward the crew proved he knew who was running things.

By the end of the first season, Tors' accountant brother, Erwin, itched for an exit strategy. Not only could Connors be a selfish jackass, his salary was so high and Tors' deal so lopsided in the network's favor that the operation was hemorrhaging thousands every month. *Cowboy in Africa* was unsustainable, and Erwin lobbied his brother that there had to be something better for them to pursue. They still had *Daktari* on the air and a knot of brand reinforcing, feature films in development. Tors, the hungry intellect and distracted administrator, was wishy-washy about ousting such a bankable lead. Erwin, however, wouldn't back down. They were deluding themselves they could survive him financially or psychologically. During a recent shoot, Connors had sideswiped a crewmember with a dune buggy that he was fooling around in—an accident the union targeted by forcing him into a settlement. Still throwing his weight around, Connors later billed Tors' production company for a hundred and forty four pairs of underwear. Yes, he expected to be comped for that many following an episode where he had to do repeated takes jumping into a lake fully clothed. Erwin agreed to only pay for a dozen pairs and Connor was displeased. "I take care of bastards like you," he told Erwin during a threatening, cursing phone call.

Erwin said he couldn't take it anymore, and his brother, painfully so, concurred. He arranged a meeting with ABC to tell them what he'd never imagined: the show could not go on. Just one season in, it was a financial sinkhole made worse each week by the Chuck-ster. The network, probably baffled and infuriated, heeded Tors' unusual request. When the September 1968 *TV Guide* appeared, the show was scrubbed from its pages. But just about everything else in Tors' heretofore-sizzling run seemed to unravel afterward. Blame it on it what you will: the looming corporatization of the entertainment-industrial complex, the hex of Chuck Connors, anemic management, insulted TV gods, the capricious elevator of fame. The next year the ax didn't just fall lightly on Tors or Gordon by extension. It guillotined their franchise. CBS in January canceled *Daktari*. Months later, it abruptly ended *Gentle Ben* after three seasons of good ratings.

"Outdoor-adventure programs," executives said, were a trend come and gone. Advertisers coveted hipper, edgier material—*The Mod Squad, The Dating Game*—to rope in younger demographics. Losing *Gentle Ben* to shifting viewership of the baby boomer generation hurt. More galling, if not bias confirming, for folks already jaded about Hollywood was the rumor that wended to Tors camp. The opinionated wife of a CBS official had seemingly nagged him to chop the "cutesy" program from its prime-time slot. A misfit like it worked better with the Saturday morning cartoons or nowhere. Tors' people never dug up her identity. They did, however, live with her result—staff left jobless, trust ruined.

In October 1969, Tors took another existential kick in the nuts. Constance, his wife of fourteen years, dropped dead from a heart attack at forty-nine with no warning, and Tors' already shaky attachment to residence in Los Angeles went with her. Though he'd successfully pitch another series (*Primus*), he wanted off the Hollywood grid. As quickly as he could, he tried moving to Palm Springs. Soon, with his sons, he pulled up his California tent poles for a reset in Germany and Africa. Even his skeptical prediction about the insect-like life cycles of his programs had been rightly overstated. They didn't last five years.

Gordon, who'd weathered up-and-down cycles before, could talk about bright spots or the unicorns of South Africa all he wanted and it still wouldn't backfill the crater left on his balance sheet. Losing *Cowboy in Africa, Daktari,* and *Gentle Ben* in such a truncated way obliterated ninety percent of his postproduction cash flow. The nearly twenty thousand dollars General Music was grossing monthly for three years was now gone. Partnering with Tors, Gordon had been greater than the sum of his parts. Now he felt the opposite. Some mornings in the aftermath, Judy discovered his pajamas moist with sweat. The morning newspapers were certainly no pick-me-ups. They sounded the claxon about recession ahead, with Hollywood due for the worst of it.

At their regular Monday morning appointment sometime later, Gordon's CPA skipped the playful routine in which he teasingly censured Gordon for overspending on extravagances—a gadget prototype, a top-of-the-line Nikon. Instead, Jack used his prosthetic legs to scoot closer to the client whose financial muck was lapping around his wheelchair tires. Gordon, he said, had to either embark on some Draconian moves now or start cushioning himself for a bankruptcy filing later. During the next year, he needed to fire most of his thirty or so editors to slash overhead. Aligning so heavily with Tors had been a grave miscalculation. It set him up to fail. Take the warehouse storing two thousand *Bear Facts* records that expected to be paid. Besides collectors, who'd want an album riffed from a canceled show? "I'm sorry, Gordon," Jack said. "I know you'd hoped for better news." Gordon's face drooped right there; Jack would never see light bouncing off it again. From deep inside him, a windy sigh emerged, followed by the single word he keened. "Shiiiiiiit!" Meeting adjourned.

Events negative and absurd dog-piled thereafter. Arriving at the Lantz building one Monday, he rolled into a panicking staff. The sound effects editor that he'd hired for *The Pink Panther Show* cartoon was passed out drunk on the cutting room floor without having done a lick of work on NBC's pilot. The studio hadn't even wanted to farm the job off the lot, but Gordon was persuasive. In a Chinese fire drill, an untested staffer and Bob cobbled together a finished tapes and raced them off to the waiting producers: Mirisch Films and DePatie-Freleng Enterprises. Once he woke up, the sauced editor was fired and General Music kept the contract. Still, Gordon's losing streak had traction. A con man posing as a dealmaker fooled him into getting dropped off, sans attendant, for a Sunset Strip-area meeting. Before Gordon realized he'd been flimflammed, the man pickpocketed his Carte Blanche credit card and deserted him on the street. The police had to drive him back to Blue Jay Way. Arriving there later would be an eight-hundred-thirty-nine-dollar bill in fraudulent charges rung up on his account. Hard to outrun anarchy like this when you can't feel your feet.

* * *

JUDY, TOO, WAS RIDING the turmoil as every dark day Gordon encountered in his post-Tors epoch gave her a crankier, more judgmental spouse. Her own stamina to cope with it, on top of part-time caretaking, was being tested. At weekend get-togethers, while the men huddled around Gordon's bed engrossed in a game, girlfriends like Hank and Frieda noticed the shuffle in her gait. "Don't you ever get worn down, honey," they asked in hushed voices, "taking care of him and the house?" Judy, her Benson & Hedges smoldering close by, usually denied the obvious. "No dear," she'd answer. Unless she'd picked up a flu-bug from a trip, she was as healthy as they were. "Well," the women pried, Aquarius-age, women's-libbers at heart, "how do you stand it when he rides you for not doing every little thing the exact second *he* wants it?" Judy's standard answer had become rueful: "If there's one thing I've learned, it's that Gordon has his good days and his bad days and on his bad days I tend to be a little deaf."

For the time being, the overarching benefits of the sequined lifestyle Gordon labored to create for her still eclipsed her grievances with him. She just couldn't enunciate that. Mrs. Gordon Zahler remained the antithesis of the working girl she once was. On regular shopping trips to Saks, Neiman-Marcus, Bullocks, and I. Magnin, she needn't bother calling out her dress and shoe sizes because the salesgirls had already memorized them. The Sunset Boulevard boutiques with the classy names, the ones west of the bawdy rock clubs Judy never dared to step into, considered her a regular. Treating a friend to chardonnay and sandwiches at Le Dome once a month was magnifique. There was always scads to cover—a novel she finished, the protestors handing out antiwar pamphlets on Sunset, upcoming travel, her mother's Southern eccentricities.

The wizardry of Gordon, the Gordon she still mythologized seven years into their union, merited a half-hour exposition alone. She cackled about his "dynamite" prowess at bridge, able as he was to mentally Xerox the deck, or how "he" repaired the living room TV the previous weekend; the repairman had unscrewed the back and Gordon specified which shorted vacuum tube needed replacement. Sure, she might pout that he wounded her with an unkind potshot or two, but her voice regained its cheerleader pitch describing his bountiful collection of ideas. His latest one (the multiplexer) she'd been sworn to secrecy over, she'd say. "How he thinks them up all is beyond me," she'd giggle. "Did I ever tell you about him and the tape cassette? Or Bibleland? He just has the most marvelous imagination."

After lunch, maybe two-ish, Judy would be back in the second car Gordon bought her (a brown Mercedes-Benz) crossing off the errands. She was off, blond locks bouncing, collecting his dry-cleaned suit or popping by General Music for any number of reasons. Then it was home to take Chicken for his rabies shot, capped by a run into the grocery store for the freshest ingredients needed for another gourmet meal. Preparations for a looming trip were a more thread-the-needle activity. Not only did Judy have to button up the house, board Chicken, and square her elderly mother away. She needed to organize Gordon's diapers, catheters, pills, rubs, and injections into the same suitcase as his spiffy wardrobes.

They were worldwide citizens, Gordon and she, landing in cities off the tourist circuit: Ensenada, Bloemfontein, Rio de Janeiro, Buenos Aires, Lisbon, Beirut, Hamburg, Bangkok, Nairobi. Often, they explored the areas and sampled their exotic cuisine through the grace of Gordon's business partners. These were enchanting men, Judy would write—accomplished, welcoming, and all floored by her hubby's kinetic drive. Customs cleared, it was one spectacle after another hanging out with them or going out on their own. In Hong Kong, they stayed at a hotel with a breathtaking view of Victoria Harbor. In Thailand, they lowered Gordon's chair into a boat to visit a floating market, and a native boy on the riverbank flashed his genitals for Judy's enjoyment. No place was too remote for them. Gordon pined to see every continent besides Antarctica, and maybe there, too. So, Judy went where he said. For her, breakfasting on a Kenyan game reserve yards from milling elephants was "God's Country," and nothing she could've imagined years ago when she'd had to embellish her past.

Hobnobbing with industry luminaries was another advantage in her marital-benefit package. How magically rewarding her Blue Jay Way cocktail parties were when Sidney Sheldon, Jerry Lewis, Sam Fuller, and others turned up. Paired off around the room might be George Putnam, the fire-breathing conservative newscaster, and Larry Hagman, the male lead from *I Dream of Jeannie*. Behind them could be Mel Blanc, the cartoon voice of Bugs Bunny and Barney

Rubble, with John Banner, the roly-poly nincompoop Sgt. Schultz from *Hogan's Heroes*, and others. Nat King Cole, who Gordon met at the Trocadero in the forties, sometimes made an appearance, too. Having their personal numbers in her phone book, reliving how they'd praised her salmon mousse and chocolate cherries was an ego-stroke. Chatting up any of them on the lot—Burt Lancaster, Lucille Ball, Red Skelton—confirmed her induction into their club. Judy knew they were very different away from their craft than in it. As for insider peeks cordoned off from outsiders, she had that, as well, sitting in her husband's recording studio listening to her professed "gal pal," Gracie Lantz, dubbing *Woody Woodpecker*.

Judy took seriously her showbiz responsibility, most notably projecting Gordon as a suave operator whose road-kill-looking body she was expert at underplaying. Tapping her sartorial training from her Bullocks years, she attired him in suits that gave his underdeveloped shoulders respectable width and safari outfits that made him look fairly normal. Her meticulousness in dispensing gifts wrapped with the utmost care, right down to the curly-cued ribbons, showed her artistry. Those men who pigeonholed her as a ditzy blond with a serving tray and a soft life were ignorant of the day-to-day reality of being her. How many of them could have withstood Gordon's zingers and impatience as a man with worlds to conquer and not much time to plant his flag? Let's see them survive a few weeks of doing that.

Judy tried ignoring the mockery that she was a vapid trophy wife, just as she tried ignoring Gordon's digs after Tors' precipitous implosion. Letting hurtful words float into the rafters at Blue Jay Way was one of her methods to defuse him. When Gordon became more caustic than she could handle at the moment, she'd stroll into the kitchen for a cigarette. Inside, she recognized he didn't mean it. Coexistence with him required a thick, carbon-fiber skin and a philosophy. None of her contemporaries—not Hank nor Frieda— attended to such a vulnerable, multifaceted man unable to lift a pencil for their own cause. None. If her regular tactics failed to temper him on a bad day, Judy could always resort to what Jimmy had taught her to shut him up. She'd feed him a few sifters of Benedictine brandy and he'd be asleep within the hour.

CHAPTER TWENTY-SIX: KID 'N' AFRICA

THE PAN AM 747 was on its final approach to Pretoria, the de facto capital of South Africa, and inside the cabin things were vibrating—improperly stowed tray tables, overhead luggage, Judy. Below the lumbering aircraft carrying her, Bob, Gordon, and his go-to engineer spread a fertile basin of jacarandas trees, veld, government offices, and museums. This was Gordon's future, in a northern province off the Indian Ocean, coordinates 25°44′46″S 28°11′17″E. But his tomorrow wasn't Judy's preferred one. The only reason she was aboard was because South Africa was the middle stop of a broader trip that started in Europe. It definitely wasn't because she was gaga about relocating here, to a tense, Second World country, as an expatriated American. Given truth serum, she'd confess to shaking over the prospect.

So, after she smoked through half her pack and made Gordon presentable for landing, she applied her lipstick alarmed by the rapidity of events. Judy was so bothered by the situation that she raised a stink over it, a rarity for her. During a testy weekend before this trip, she questioned him whether he'd really thought this through. Yeah, he answered, he had; the economics compelled him. He was only hanging on doing *Woody Woodpecker* and *Pink Panther* cartoons. Under Jack's orders, he disassembled his editorial workforce, shrinking it from thirty-five people to seven, and relied on temps for large jobs. She remembered, right, that he'd just sold one of his subsidiaries to breathe life into the others. And that was after they sold their old house on Shoreham instead of continuing to rent it. "Please don't rehash that," she'd snapped. "But you'll soldier through. You always have before." For Pete's sake, didn't their safety worry him? It wasn't as if they were transitioning to Montreal. Boet's Bantu servant made that clear with his admission about payback against the white man. "I hope that registered with you, because it sure frightened me. Besides, you know as well as anyone I'm not an outdoors type of girl."

Gordon attributed Judy's pickled disquiet to nerves of the unknown. Someday, after she'd given the place a chance and tasted the fruits of what his ingenuity had reaped, she'd appreciate they'd traded up. People didn't lock doors in South Africa. Charles Manson-type demagogues weren't ordering the slaughter of pregnant women and other innocents, let alone a few miles from where they lived. Gordon, though disgusted by apartheid, admired the country's law-and-order, frontier society. Judy, he believed, would grow to feel the same.

*   *   *

Maybe by then, too, she'd appreciate just what he'd gone through these last months to make a reboot even possible. Lantz was a sweetheart of a guy and by the early seventies a Hollywood dinosaur. Nat Winecoff, beloved chum, lacked big-tent money. Tors, globally connected and faithful, had flown the Hollywood coop. All this rendered Nicholas Deak a different breed of champion. Beyond all those zeroes his company was worth, the "chairman" was endowed with qualities that Gordon's other benefactors lacked. He had the brains, f, and discipline to lend a visionary a few million dollars and trust he'd make history.

Deak, sixty-five, was a New Age Rockefeller as well as Dirk Brink's New York-based boss. He was silver-haired and urbane, a devout vegetarian, and a workout nut able to jog eight miles with no hitch. His résumé was something: the Hungarian émigré had served in the Office of Strategic Services during World War II and when the espionage ended, he'd gradually built up what *Forbes* magazine estimated was now a 400-million-dollar business. Deak-Perera foreign-currency exchange offices were staples across the US and around the world. Just like traveler's checks, they could be indispensable. Deak himself was a rare combination of Old World charm, diplomacy, and wiles. He and associates trafficked in commodities more traditional firms eschewed. They imported precious metals from behind the Iron Curtain, dealt with the Yugoslav dinar, and cultivated niches in gold bullion and coins, South Africa's Kruggerand included. Everything about Deak told Gordon that he'd tripped into the one rich dude able to convert pipe dreams into done deals. Nothing, either, signaled he was bound for a mysterious, tabloid-esque murder; or that his company worked hand-in-glove with the CIA for decades, feeding the agency tips in return for who knows what.

Naturally, Bob accompanied Gordon to Deak's art-deco-themed office tower at 29 Broadway just off Wall Street. Inside, hundreds were on the phones moving money across datelines. For all their differences, Gordon and Deak, the so-called "James Bond of Money," were two peas in a pod. Deak was so captivated by Gordon's shtick that he invited the Angelenos for an afternoon at the Westchester Country Club outside Manhattan. Social talk over club sandwiches then turned to business, which drifted to South Africa, a land Deak intoned he knew well. Gordon sketched his intentions while trying not to seem too gung-ho. He'd knew he'd probably struck out with Don Kirshner coming off too eager (or desperate).

Deak was all ears listening to Gordon's explain his TV initiative. Next, his pupils must've dilated surveying the blueprint Bob held up. Gordon said he wasn't waiting for the South African Broadcasting Corporation to fly him back for technical consultations. In the gap, he'd commissioned someone to rough out a horseshoe-shaped, postproduction complex ringed with theaters and a performing arts center in Johannesburg. It was immense, a sub-equatorial version of Universal Pictures. Gordon told his ultra-rich acquaintance that several South African film companies had already expressed interest in using it for their projects. They'd cut him checks once the government presented him a long-term contract. Gordon saved the best for last: the trailblazing multiplexer. With the proper coordination, melting-pot cultures would possess the power to broadcast the same TV show in countless languages. Consider the demand this could elicit not just in Africa, but across the sectarian Third World, Gordon said. Shouldn't Deak-Perera be in on it as a financier and consultant?

The foreign-currency magnate lobbed a few questions while Gordon caught his breath. He rubbed his distinguished chin and said he would have to talk with a few experts. When Deak phoned Gordon in Los Angeles a couple weeks later, he didn't pussyfoot around: his company would have to pass. The projects were too far afield its core business. On the upside, Deak said he and an aide would invest some personal money in the multiplexer and dole out advice. But that was the extent of it—thousands, not millions. Gordon kicked himself about whiffing with one of the planet's wealthiest men until he realized he shouldn't. Deak's illustrious name might prompt others to crank open their vaults.

Sometime between hearing from Deak and the trip he was now on, Gordon dictated letters to Danny O'Brien in London confiding to him in what few else knew. It was a bombshell. Gordon said he was shuttering General Music, within the year if he could tie up loose ends. For two years it'd been bleeding money in the Hollywood production slowdown. Studios had scaled back everything—films, movies, projects under development—while the economy languished. All you had to do was scan *Daily Variety* or drive along Santa Monica Boulevard to tally the Closed signs hung crookedly in windows. Rest assured, he added, this wasn't retirement. Just because he was quitting music and sound effects editing was different from hanging it up. Background music that he moonlighted in as a side business for years would be where he'd partly reposition himself. In two words, its future was "truly astronomical." Together with new distribution partners, he'd organize a coast-to-coast sales effort promoting a three-thousand-song library spanning the genres, Rogers and Hammerstein to the Rolling Stones. All companies would have to do was purchase, for three hundred forty five dollars, the eight-track tape playback system that he helped design. They'd wow some of America's nameplate corporations with his Globemaster machine: Bank of America, JCPenney, Shakey's Pizza Parlors, and "Community Access TV," soon to be called cable. All this he'd half manage from Johannesburg. Keep that to yourself, Danny.

*   *   *

As THE 747'S WHEELS screeched on the tarmac in early 1971, the defeats and unrealized dreams screeched away, too, like burnt rubber. They were in his past. This was South Africa.

By milking Swanee's contacts and demonstrating uncharacteristic patience, Gordon had scored an audience with the nation's ultimate decision-maker. None other than Prime Minister John Vorster was making time for him. A meeting with him was why they'd sandwiched Pretoria into the itinerary. Vorster's seal of approval on the multiplexer would knock the dominos in his favor. It would prod Sanlam to hand over two million dollars to replicate and develop the gadget, and the film companies and others next would throw resources at him to take his Johannesburg postproduction complex from sketch to shovel-ready. *And people claim I'm immobile.*

On his day to strut his stuff, a driver picked up, Bob, engineer John Hall and him from the Rand International Hotel, taking them to a nondescript government building. For weeks in Los Angeles, the three had rehearsed with the multiplexer. Their mission: demonstrate technology that the South Africans had to believe they couldn't live without. An assistant escorted them to a standard screening room. Most of the chairs were vacant except for a few, choice ones the VIPs occupied. The tension was chewable. Wall-mounted speakers hissed the crackle of equipment on standby. Cigar smoke from the fat cats curled in the hot beam from the projection room. Plopped down in a chair up front was their real target—a pudgy, bald man with bushy eyebrows and a natural scowl.

John Vorster, a man in endless meetings, knew better than most about pressure. Fellow Afrikaners expected him to preserve their God-sanctified way despite United Nation's condemnations, trade sanctions, and the country's exclusion from the 1964 Summer Olympics. Vorster's response since coming to power in 1966 was mainly smoke and mirrors, telling the West that he was slowly liberalizing relations with the natives when he continued to marginalize them into shantytowns and artificial homelands. This he did to honor the sacrifice of the ancestral Boers, he said. This he did to disarm the terrorists at the ANC. Detractors ridiculed him as "Jolly John"—a man almost incapable of smiling. But the former justice minister, who'd once said he wanted his country to emulate the Nazi government, didn't listen. He championed the "Sabotage Act" allowing the government to detain subversives for half a year. According to *The New York Times*, Vorster was "a granite symbol of apartheid," and we all know granite frowns.

For Gordon, the imminent question was whether the barrel-chested leader could be sold. Up near the projection room, where John Hall set up the multiplexer, Gordon perspired sweat-moons into his Oxford shirt. They'd been allotted ten minutes for a crisp presentation. The prime minister, an aide said, would have no time for banalities afterward; too many other matters for him to attend to. *Okeydokey.* They'd broadcast a short clip from a recent South African movie, running it consecutively in three languages—Afrikan, English, and isiZulu—to illustrate how their device harmonized the same visuals with different dialects. If it worked for film, it'd work for TV.

If, that is, it worked at all. John's sheetrock-pale face was better left unseen in the semi-darkness. The engineer glowered at the black, shoebox-size control box powering their multiplexer as if eye contact would scare the thing. Here Vorster was in place and the doohickey supposed to excite him was unresponsive. When Gordon whistled Hall to begin, Hall stammered what no one wanted to hear. "Uh, give me a sec, okay?" A routing glitch or another electronic goblin had cut the signal output. None of this had occurred in California, so maybe it was the electrical-current converter. Seconds dragged into a minute. Gordon tasted bile. *Jesus, John will die a painful death if this flops. I'll do it myself.*

Whap, Whap. The sound of John's palm slamming the metal casing caused Vorster and his cronies to twitch in their padded seats. Gordon wondered how long before he marched out, upbraiding his toadies on the way? Deliverance (or more accurately, John's machine punch), forestalled such a calamity. "Okay, ready to go," he told Gordon quietly. "My screw-up." John nodded to the projection room to roll and the floor lights were cut. Onscreen almost two years of labor made its case. The first clip was in Afrikan to please the homers. Delivering TV to South Africa's "mixed-race" population, the Americans knew, was what Vorster's regime desired least but had apparently accepted. Why else would they be interested in the multiplexer?

The lights winked on as the screen went dim, and Vorster rose from his chair like a dynastic emperor. He adjusted his jacket and one of his minions pointed him toward Gordon. He was larger in person than he was scowling in photos. Something was peculiar on this point, too. Happy—Jolly John looked happy. *Stay calm, Zahler.* "Anything we can answer for you, mister prime minister?" Gordon asked decorously. Vorster, known for knifing gestures, acted as though he didn't hear the question. He cupped a burly hand on Gordon's shoulder, towering over him for the edict. "Listen, my good fellow. When we have TV, *this* system is the one we'll use. You have my congratulations. My people will coordinate the next moves. Now if you'll excuse me."

The return flight across the Pacific was a tale of two people. Gordon basked in a near-heroin-buzz while Judy out-smoked a crematorium, dreading that the multiplexer had brought her and Gordon closer to a fateful confrontation. It had, too. In April 1971, two months after the demo, Vorster publicly announced that South African TV would go live in 1974 as part of his "outward policies" to remake his minority-majority country. Sanlam Limited reacted favorably, if still not wholeheartedly, giving a preliminary yes to fund Gordon's machine with two million dollars. After he flushed the champagne from his system, Gordon was a man renewed. 1971, he wrote Tors, "is going to be our turnaround year. I can feel it."

Who needed Nick Deak now? Or Chuck Connors?

CHAPTER TWENTY-SEVEN: TARS AND STRIPES

LET THERE BE NO doubt: South Africa marked the X for his "one great thing." It was the timeline for his *bon voyage* that was fuzzy, but he'd occupy himself. Up at Blue Jay Way, guests sat through his travel slideshow without feeling drowsy. Frames clicked through alligator-filled lakes, sapphire horizons, Johannesburg high-rises, and the pièce de résistance: a photo of the monkeys of Nazima Springs, Kenya crouching on Gordon's shoulders, inches from his jugular. "You gotta make it over there," he'd say from his pool deck, vapor-locked in Los Angeles' aerial crud. "We'll bop up to Safariland. You won't look at America the same way again." He was rarely as Gordon-esque than after Vorster's assurance, flashy in his plaid trousers, twitching his shoulder, swaggering and cigarette smoking, selling Africa as his personal antidote to the showbiz hamster wheel.

The rough idea was for him to spend half the year in Johannesburg supervising postproduction for South African TV while co-producing programs for it with Tors; Sanlam and Nick Deak, it seemed, had cut deals with Tors for that. The rest of the year he'd travel, much of that in California on music business. No hand wringing for Judy's dislocation, either. Kruggerands would pour out of her Gucci purse and everything she hated about the Westside—traffic, pollution, rude hippies, haphazard murder—would afflict her no more. Her mother, Billie, would be flown over and coddled there, too. The days of him shallowly hanging around for his Hollywood blue ribbon were finished. In a quarter century in the industry, he'd watched too many bright minds have their talent compromised because they confused notoriety for achievement. Better late than never, he'd devote his talents elsewhere, and maybe even decode the riddle of why he'd outlasted the Marshall gym. Until then, he'd exist between two continents.

In his absence would be a congregation of familiar faces who'd become less familiar. There was his sister, Muriel, Hugo Grimaldi, and Nathan Jones, none of whom he'd be leaving in a monetary lurch. But faithful employees like Norm Pringle and Harriet von Stroheim had no such luxury. They'd have to pound the pavement in the throes of a dismal job market the Arab oil embargo hadn't helped. Harriet, thankfully, had Joe's studio salary behind her. Gordon would keep doing what he could for Norm. He'd continue paying him a part-time salary, though there was often little for him to do, and applying that same creative bookkeeping so he received state benefits. (At the Hollywood unemployment office where Norm filed his paperwork, some applicants completed their forms in cowboy chaps or cancan outfits to prove they were hunting for work. A few arrived in limos.)

It was Jimmy who most pressed Gordon's South African guilt meter. Desilu, where Jimmy had been one of the first black members in the editor's guild, had laid him off during a summer hiatus a few years after he quit General Music. (Gordon had waited about five seconds after that before offering him his old job back with a substantial raise. The first act of Jimmy's second stint with him was, of course, bizarre. The attendant Jimmy was replacing had basically stolen Gordon's latest Cad. He'd dared Gordon for days to snatch it back, so Jimmy did it for him.) Now the best Gordon could do to express his eternal gratitude was to offer to sell Jimmy the car at a major discount. Assuming, that is, Jimmy would even want it.

One way or another, Gordon had to bail. Robert Evans, Steven Spielberg, Martin Scorsese, and George Lucas represented the new Hollywood, not the studio bosses and executives who'd once taken his call. He felt like something Mesozoic. Lantz, who Gordon wished would have thrown him more business, was weighing outsourcing some animation to Japan. Tors, meanwhile, was just as cynical living in West Germany as he'd been in Los Angeles. Fare such as *Midnight*

Cowboy, he sermonized in a letter, was film committing "moral treason" against the planet. Definitely an upended world, all right. Richard Nixon toasting Mao Tse-tung in Beijing, Gordon deserting the town his ancestors once lit up.

Entrenching in the day-to-day was how he'd distract himself before he could triumphantly purchase his one-way plane ticket. The months that'd crept by since he met Vorster crystallized the glacial pace of complex initiatives like this. It was the government's way or nothing, and their Johannesburg lawyer reminded him and his partners to hold their water. At worst, the TV start date could be delayed until 1976. Afrikaner paranoia about the medium smearing their cultural purity was a topic long over. Free-market hustle—what firm would manufacture the sets, how to divvy up what had grown to 333 million dollars in start-up funds—were the attention-getters. So, stay on your toes, Gordon's sources urged him. The day for General Motivations Corporation, the name they'd given their South Africa venture, was about to pop.

Never doubting it would, Gordon accepted ad hoc editing jobs. He managed postproduction for *Mister Kingstreet's War*, a grisly, South African-made film about Kenyan poachers starring John Saxon and Tippi Hedron. He committed to two other South African movies next. About this same point, he also held auditions to cast English voices for the US dub of *Pippi Longstocking*, a *Willy Wonka*-esque, European feature about a precocious orphan who moves to Sweden with her horse, monkey, and bag of coins. Beloved by kids, adults forced to watch the movie endlessly must have fantasized about stringing Pippi up by her rebellious ponytails. Adults like Gordon. Hundreds of children and their parents, many of them practicing squeaky voices, jammed the parking lot of the Lantz Building for the *Pippi* cattle call. He and Jimmy laughed about it on the drive home, just like old times. General Music followed it up with a Sunsweet Prune commercial and more *Bozo* cartoons.

Gordon practically said yes to anyone or anything. In 1972, he was in Munich, perhaps visiting Tors or a music publisher, when the world got its first glimpse of prime-time terrorism. Palestinian extremists calling themselves "Black September" kidnapped members of the Israeli Olympic team, killing two. Munich's airport rushed into emergency shutdown, and the twentieth Games came to a halt. Gordon did as well in another *Forrest Gump*-ian incident, blocked for a few days from leaving as scheduled. Why did this keep happening?

Jack had no answer, scientific or cosmic, to Gordon's mysteries. He only had more bad tidings to discuss with a client in receipt of a certified letter from the state's taxing authority. In it, the California Board of Equalization accused him of neglecting taxes on two hundred fifty thousand dollars worth of payroll from his days with Ivan Tors Productions. Translation: he was on the hook for seventy thousand dollars he did not hav––e. Gordon, with one foot in South Africa, urged his glum CPA not to fret. He'd seen worse. Hours after the meeting, Jimmy drove him to Nickodell, where he downed a steak sandwich in an ode to compartmentalization. Next time this year, the debt would be a hiccup. In a few days, South African consular officials were flying down from San Francisco for a firsthand briefing on the multiplexer and Johannesburg production complex. Boet Troskie and Jamie Uys (pronounced ace) from Mimosa Films would be in town the following week. They'd expect sparkling times with him, not directions to a bus for a tour of movie stars' homes.

Gordon determined this is where his head should be, and if the Board of Equalization didn't like it, too bad. From the open air of his Cad, he soon introduced his guests to a Southern California they'd portray as hypnotizing and immoral. Freeways; Hells Angels; hot pants, pot smoke; airport Hare Krishnas; Rodeo Drive: the sensory overload glazed their faces. Equally discombobulating was a host they speculated about over brandies at the hotel bar. They puzzled how a gent whose head rose to their beltlines had the influence to get them onto the Paramount lot to watch an expensive movie being filmed. They marveled at his ability to pay every dinner tab. Ultimately, they reasoned that a cripple could do anything in America—an America that condoned interracial couples holding hands in public. Their society never would have cottoned to such gene-pool blasphemy. Otherwise lovely people, the South Africans grimaced at integrated California (such as it was). They fidgeted when left alone in the same room with Jimmy. Asked about apartheid, one of them lectured that the main difference between their two nations was that "they hadn't killed their Indians."

Gordon parroted their lines once they'd flown home, including their advocacy of gradual racial integration that didn't leave bodies in the streets. His few full-timers clucked their tongues hearing the spin, turning back to their machines unconvinced. This being sensitive turf, Gordon left it at that. It was all just opinion, anyway. In fact, *he'd* already predicted to his Afrikaner chums that their police state wouldn't last into the new millennium. "Just remember I told you if I'm not around."

*   *   *

EARLY 1973 FOUND ME wishing that Gordon were already living in South Africa. Had he done so, this kid from there probably would not have been staying with us during the worst month of my life. Judy had driven Waynand Uys, the son of Gordon's director-friend, Jamie, to Pasadena, talking up how much fun we'd all have over the next three days. Neither my mother nor I believed it but we tried faking a welcome for the sake of Gordon's big dreams. *Yippee.*

Weeks earlier, my distant father had moved out, announcing he wanted a divorce. My mom, though miserable in the union, had invested her entire identity around being "Mrs. Millard Jacobs." As a result, she was now a bad hair day from a nervous breakdown. Adding to the casualties, my best friend—my pet beagle—and our cat had gone missing a few days before Waynand's arrival. (We'd find them a week later nearly starved to death, right where my emotionly whiplashed mother had accidentally trapped them—the cat in the bomb shelter, my dog in the boathouse that would burn to the ground twenty years later.)

Waynand was probably fourteen, which put him about three years older and a couple of inches taller than me. He was an intelligent, sunny kid, dressed in navy-blue knee pants, with an exotic accent and a harsh bowl haircut. The fact that he starred in one of his dad's movies (*Lost in the Desert*) about a young plane-crash survivor blinded by a spitting cobra carried no truck with me. I just wanted my dog back and to be left alone. If memory serves, we took him on a drive around the Rose Bowl, wasted time at a Disney movie, and spent an afternoon at Knott's Berry Farm. In me, Waynand found a sullen boy indifferent to anything he said or the driveway soccer he suggested. When Judy picked him up, it was bye, door slammed. I could pity myself fulsomely now.

In our upcoming visits to Blue Jay Way, where Gordon exhorted my mom that she was stronger than her separation, I faked interest in his telescope to avoid self-expression. Fate had shown me who was boss. And, truth be known, my previous terror of Gordon as a diabolical spider whose bed I didn't want to get near had transitioned into an outright dislike of him. With a little more courage, I could've learned so much—how he'd picked himself up after every wicked blow, laughing, how he was an inflatable clown that could bounce up after a hurricane. These things I'd have to learn tracing the back roads of his life as an adult.

Any grumpiness he dished out at me then, too, was nothing compared with the verbal beating he was progressively heaping on his wife. "JU-DEE," he'd erupt. Whether it was missed phone calls, over-tipping, unwise auto repairs, or other inconsequential issues, he was on her case. Unlike their earlier era, when his charm mellowed the growls, this Gordon had a brutish dimension. Though he loved Judy madly, doleful she had to scurry for his basic needs, he also seemed to have licensed himself to persecute her. It was as if beneath the bluster, he gauged his life fuel was low, and assumed she'd forgive his barrages once he was gone. People noticed. Bob, among others, chided him for his sulfuric meltdowns. Gordon, rather defensively, said he had to raise his voice occasionally because when Judy bumbled something, he paid for it.

Girlfriends who witnessed the browbeating in person encouraged Judy to retaliate. But Judy, passive-aggressively, was more interested in classifying it. Orneriness enflamed by a bout of poor health or office stresses she could handle. It was Gordon's resistance to ease off his gratuitous demeaning of her around company that spoiled her cheery view of their life together. "Hurry it up with that drink, will ya?" The idea she was his doormat, after all the daily nursemaiding his body required, was incomprehensible. Sometimes it soothed her hearing he was churlish around the office. Even so, she had to live with it.

Until 1973, America's Watergate year, Judy limited herself to cold shoulders or intentionally scorching a roast when he acted up. A Christmas party at the home of one of Gordon's editors turned out to be her Maginot Line. She got lost trying to find the address, and Gordon ripped into her in front of their passengers. Judy, normally ever smiling, got visibly angry. Inside the home, she shoved him into the corner as Perry Como blared from the hi-fi and everybody else drank holiday spirits. For fifteen minutes or so, he was in isolation like a defiant child in a timeout. Wheeled out of exile, he apologized sheep-faced for being a prick. Judy dared do no more than that. She loved him too much to consider a formal ultimatum. The uncertainty was whether his cruelty would activate her sense of self-preservation. Divorce was legal for a reason.

Being a quadriplegic means being an astute observer, and Gordon knew to repair the previous damage inflicted by his mouth with contrition and, periodically, jewelry. By 1974, a gold tennis bracelet wasn't what it used to be. Travel would have to be his peacemaker. On a business swing through Europe, he veered off to the French Riviera. They saw Cannes and strolled along the Promenade des Anglais in Nice as any continent-hopping sophisticates might. Next, he hired a driver to tour Pablo Picasso's village. That night they dined at a legendary restaurant a table away from Natalie Wood and Robert Wagner, draining a two-hundred-dollar bottle of wine. Later on the trip in Florence, after a glorious day of sightseeing, Judy listened to him wax forth about a foreign music deal. As she'd confess to friends, it was there she fell in love all over again with her tempestuous hero.

And he'd need it. The good luck that aligned with him from his post-Ed Wood days forward felt like a century ago. His stumbles were now tragic-comic. A scumbag editor stole roughly thirty thousand dollars in editing gear after everyone went home for the evening. Contact with two brothers from the mega-wealthy J. Paul Getty oil family interested in producing a movie might've been heaven-sent, except they had no money, because they were quarantined from the patriarch's millions. Even worse than false hopes, his half-baked ideas to bring quick money in diluted potential world-changers that could have saved him. *Dr. Doolittle* cartoons; surveillance cameras; how-to-play Roulette albums: he was throwing concepts at the wall to see what stuck, and none did. Trying to incite something, he, Hugo, and one of Tors' executives approached Sonny Bono to star in a film about a peasant and a Texas oilman. The bantam entertainer said no to the part in *Antonio*. Trini Lopez, who'd crooned "If I Had a Hammer," said yes.

*   *   *

THE BROOKLYN COMEDIENNE INSIDE his recording studio begin her bit with a commentary about the state of American education. "Nobody," she said, "should be surprised that little Johnny can't read. He's dropping his chalk all day to look up his teacher's dress. Why? Because she was not wearing any panties."

"I love it," Gordon buzzed in from the recording booth. "Why don't you try it again, except this time accentuate the word any. It'll give the line some kick."

"Don't you have a meeting?" the woman asked.

Thirty years before she became a one-woman conglomerate— red carpet fashion goddess, QVC superstar, girl-power inspiration— Joan Rivers was a hump-busting stand-up working at nightclubs from Greenwich Village to the Catskill's Borscht Belt. Routines wisecracking her own horsey face, yenta family, and life's small idiocies had, by the early seventies, scored her regular gigs in a male-dominated industry. Late-night TV king Johnny dug her so much he named her his fill-in. The light bulb that went off over Gordon's head involved broadcasting Rivers' sendups over the car radio dial. He'd sell her observations in five-minute segments so commuters struck in the red, brake-lit hell of standstill traffic would have a reason to laugh. Advertisers searching for new, cool trends would flock to him. It was a can't miss! *You're welcome.*

For about a month, Rivers and her stolid husband/manager, Edgar Rosenberg, came to the Lantz Building to tape samples inside Gordon's no-frills studio. They were here on spec, getting nothing up front in expectation of lump sums later. Each bit was done in a

"Dear Abby" format. Before tape rolled, Gordon pumped everybody up about the killing they'd make at an upcoming radio convention at the Beverly Hills Hilton (the same Hilton where, six years earlier, he'd hosted that exorbitant party.) He was so certain he'd found his winner that he planned to rent a room upstairs where station syndicators could pitch him. Tens of millions of drivers in gridlock could be worth tens of millions in ad revenues and sponsorships. Radio comedy, in fact, could be bigger than the Pet Rock.

Gordon's assessment might have been sterling, his vision true, but the big mouth he kept closed around Vorster had lost its discipline. He couldn't stop giving Rivers pointers delivering punch lines she could have done in her sleep.

"I don't understand today's feminists," Rivers said during one session. "They're out there burning their bras. Since I'm a centrist, I just burned one cup."

"Another dynamite joke, Joan," Gordon said. "May I suggest, though, that you pause between sentences?"

"No, you may not," Rivers lashed back.

"I'm trying to help you."

"You can. You can have Jimmy wheel you someplace else so I can work with Norm. I don't need your help. So get the hell out or I will."

Gordon left, but it wouldn't matter. What'd appeared so promising at the outset face-planted during the execution stage. The syndicators he met with at the hotel required two hundred prerecorded segments, plus other provisions, before they would pay him a dime. As they learned, he was nowhere close to completing a finished product, and when he was unable to answer other questions, they left. Told there was no deal, Rivers stomped out of the recording bay, infuriated that Gordon had wasted her time with his poorly thought-out scheme. If he said, "Oh well, her loss" it was to mask his dejection in front of others.

Shotgun approaches to projects like these tripped him in other ways, too. They sidetracked him from nurturing his most original creation yet, an application so ahead of its time that it probably came across as wacko novelty to the orthodox corporations of the seventies.

A visit to a boringly quiet bookstore was his muse for it. The place could've been a graveyard, for all the anemic energy it had.

Enlisting a stable of classically trained actors who spoke with robust, crisp voices would be the first step. Next, he'd select a few bestselling books and contact their New York publishers about their willingness to collaborate. Should they be interested, Gordon would bring the thespians into his Lantz building studio, rehearse them until their throats rasped, and, when ready, record their dramatic narrations of the juiciest passages. Swooping in for sales would be a cinch. The major retail bookstores could broadcast the excerpts, provided they used General's Music's Globemaster tape player, as three-and-a-half-minute, in-store promotions. *Ta-da*: customers would get the flavor of a novel without turning a page! Different clips could be sold as thirty-second radio ads. Airlines in search of in-flight entertainment, other than fuzzy movies projected onto plastic bulkheads, could contract for longer versions. Passengers could hear Ernest Hemingway or James Michener through their headsets. Sooner or later entire books would go audible. Harlen Carraher, an actor-pal from *The Ghost and Mrs. Muir*, volunteered for a beta test of Gordon's Book Mark enterprise.

What Gordon stumbled upon then is the backbone of the mammoth audiobook industry today. Known early on as books-on-tape and now digitally streamed for millions of eardrums, the two-billion-dollar market lists tens of thousands of titles. Before the Internet, though, Dayton Hudson Booksellers, Pan Am, American Airlines, and a couple of publishing houses all expressed beguilement with Gordon's vision. Bristol Myers and US Steel flirted with subsidizing it. They wanted to know more. So where did this all lead, this aggressive sell of a new medium? It led to animated promises by many of the corporations that they would evaluate it in-depth. They'd never considered cross-pollinating the literary and the aural.

Regrettably, they needed time to poke around that he didn't have. Judy finally realized how parched Gordon was for money after Jimmy wheeled him in one evening, tie unknotted, shoulders U-shaped. She asked what'd happened? Gordon asked her first to mix him a scotch rocks before he emceed his latest capitulation. Jack said there'd be days like this, what with a quarterly profit-and-loss statement more red than black. The "horrible meeting" he just left felt like blood loss, too. His Book Mark endeavor needed money to pay the narrating actors and other initial expenses if it had any chance of taking off. But Hollywood's slump and what he'd invested in South Africa had butchered his cash flow, so he couldn't dip into that. And he was reluctant to sell his valuable Lantz Music Company stock with the state's tax hounds nipping at his heels.

So, he'd surrendered *half* the future profits on one of his few moneymakers in exchange for a two-hundred-thousand-dollar loan and an employment contract for himself. Project-7 Inc., a New York closed-circuit-TV outfit, recognized the untapped potential of Globe Music Corporation. Besides the income it would pocket, the company negotiated the option to purchase Globe Music outright if it saw fit. A domineering codger was Project-7's chief and a "competent sharpie," in Gordon's words, was its president. Globe Music's five-thousand-five-hundred-song catalog had been in their gun sights for years as the background music business grew. Holding sway over that big a portfolio would jack up Project-7's stock price, among other benefits, should it ever go public. In essence, Gordon was corporate prey.

"Want to hear the insult to injury?"

"The way you've described it, I can't imagine there is one," Judy said.

"There is. At the end of the meeting their president, this kid, came around the conference table and kissed me smack on the forehead. It was right in front of the lawyers and everything."

"He kissed you? That's strange."

"No, it was humiliating. It was his way of saying, 'I feel for ya, buddy.'"

Woebegone incidents like this whispered to Judy that she could never leave.

CHAPTER TWENTY-EIGHT: THE LOST JUNGLE

WAIT, A FRIEND ASKED, you were at the Coliseum last Sunday watching the Rams play when you're up to your eyeballs in debt? Shouldn't you have been meeting with your advisors? Holding a lawn sale? Oh, please, Gordon answered. He didn't waste sunshine. He sweet-talked a buddy with sideline passes to slip him a couple so he and Jimmy could be on the floor of the stadium seeing, hearing, and feeling twenty-two large men slamming into each other with violent intent. Mostly, he wanted to watch the San Francisco Forty-Niner's quarterback slobber-knocked up close. So what if he owed thirty-five thousand dollars (and potentially ten times that)? Weekends were for kicks.

Mondays, Lord knows, were for reality. From San Francisco to Stuttgart, partners he fostered witty camaraderie with over the years insisted he repay them, to hell with any more excuses. The California tax board toed the same line. Every week, its barbed letters came, and every week Gordon dreamed of Johannesburg and Safariland. He'd finesse his way out, and if that weren't possible, he'd work emergency back channels. He was a lot of things—future-minded, the occasional asshole—but he was no deadbeat and definitely no quitter.

Denial, still, only worked for so long. Jack beat down the state to reduce his seventy-thousand-dollar bill for delinquent taxes to fourteen thousand. Fantastic news, except he lacked the fourteen large to be done with it. No more friends in high places, either.

Representatives for Ivan Tors Music, the company he set up, declined his offer to waive interest in the company if they paid off his balance with the state. Nice loyalty. Foreign income was just as hard to come by. His editors cut music and effects for Uys latest film, an offbeat documentary entitled *Animals Are Beautiful People* (or *Beautiful People*) that critics worldwide raved about. Uys's victory, though, only conferred more pain on him. South African currency restrictions tying up money due him from Mimosa Films meant checks that he wrote could bounce. Shaky cash reserves also prevented him from repaying the loan to Project-7, and their executives were vultures. They implicated him for "defaulting" on the agreement, legalese for "we're planning on suing your ass." Even tight friends like Leo de gar Kulka, his Northern California music supplier, lost faith. "Over a year has passed and we have not received a single statement and not one red cent!!!... The time for nice promises is past, Gordon, and we have to put up or shut up."

Dog paddling for time, with no raft around, was all he could do. He tried placating debtors by noting how he'd already sold chunks of his catalog to 3M, a conglomerate that'd brought the world Scotch Tape. But getting its bureaucracy in St. Paul, Minnesota, to send out his royalties was a hair-pulling exercise. Likewise, he mailed an apology to a Tokyo customer who'd received badly scratched tapes from him— defects that he pinned on a crooked manufacturer in Haiti. Tors was one of the few who heard it forthright: if this continued, he might have to sell everything and beg Nick Deak for a job.

Meantime, office dramas that would've been forgotten before were metaphors for his shambles now. One Friday, the lazy, pothead editor who managed to keep his job through the downsizing dared Norm with a five-dollar bet. The caper? Norm had to make a copy of his butt cheeks on Gordon's new, Xerox copier. Norm, with little transfer work to complete, proclaimed they should up the ante. He wagered his associate he was too chicken to photocopy his wiener. "I'll take that bet," the editor crowed. Pants were unbuckled and the Start button pressed. But instead of one copy, dozens were reproduced off a machine neither of them knew had to operate. They snatched as many copies as they could and flushed some of them down the toilet. A secretary aware of the Xerox's Off switch had to be called to discontinue the paper-penises. Knowing it was best to get out in front of it, Norm confessed. In another time, Gordon would've applauded the stunt. In this one, he was apoplectic, threatening long-timer Norm with "grounds for dismissal."

With prospects bleak at home, Gordon flew with Judy and Bob to Europe, where he scavenged for any deals he could find, and then on to Johannesburg, where he scratched for answers. Jimmy stayed back at General Music answering phones, wishing he could go and wondering if he ever would. Probably not with heavily armed riot police patrolling townships there and an incipient "liberation movement" flickering. At the UN, some recommended expelling South Africa for human rights violations. Gordon digested the news, hoping the multiplexer and postproduction plans would eventually oil the way for a just society—after it enriched him with "fuck you money" to move there. Whether the ideas he was banking on remained viable had become a flashpoint. Both propositions were now four years old and looming more speculative by the minute. Swanee and Deak's aide moaned about nothing happening. All they'd achieved in the tail chasing, they said, were debts, including a hefty one to their lawyer. Gordon cloaked his temper, needing this team. Everybody, he believed, should stay positive. The South African Broadcasting Corporation still intended to farm out work to contractors like them, whatever the bubbling cauldron breaking down along skin tones. Patience, fellas, patience.

From Johannesburg, they drove via jeep for eleven hours to Dirk's spread in White River, a banana and avocado farm town in the boonies of northwestern South Africa. Here, Dirk opined, life sparkled again after a morbid stretch—the former wife who died in a horse-riding spill, his own compromised health. There was also that lion, the lion at the Hong Kong city zoo that'd nearly ripped his son's arm out of its socket when the boy stuck it in the cage. Dirk sued the zoo, claiming negligence, and retreated to White River for sanity. Gordon, Judy, and Bob, who now only paired with Gordon on a project basis as he spread his interests, spent Easter weekend with Dirk. Gordon yakked about how he yearned to be Dirk's neighbor while Judy prayed to the saints not to let it happen.

Being in the vicinity, they traveled north to Kenya for a safari, for outdoor pleasure, but it was just another emblematic concession. Deep down, where bravado was shushed, Gordon knew he'd never visit Africa again. The law of averages he'd head-faked for so long was gaining on him. The bush confirmed that.

Out in it, he overhead a game ranger crabby about a rogue leopard slaughtering the livestock of nearby cattle farmers. Before he metabolized everyone's livelihood, the baited traps with bloody chicken carcasses and hung them from low tree branches. The game ranger's quip about going to check on the traps provoked something in Gordon. He flailed an arm, blurting: "Mind if we join you? I'd love to see that cat." (The only leopard Gordon had been around was a tame one that lived at Africa USA; Tors contended it had a thing for blondes.) "Oh, I don't think that's wise, Mr. Zahler," the ranger said. "It's right risky out in the open." Leopards, he explained, are not only fast, their bites can be poisonous from consuming rancid prey. "And your chair will be hell to push in the terrain. *Hell.* It'll bog like mud." "That's okay," Gordon chirped. "Bob can do it, can't you, Bob?" He was always saying that.

Knowing he'd never dissuade him, Bob said he'd go under one condition: if they saw the spotted predator loose, they'd ditch Gordon's treasured Everest and Jennings chair and haul ass for the jeep. The only reason Bob agreed to go at all was the pistol swinging from the ranger's hip. Out they went, trudging along the banks of a riverbed with the tawny countryside fanning out before them and misty-green mountains in the background. Stands of unevenly spaced papyrus trees rooted into one side of the ravine exposed the primordial marsh to the west. With every step the African sky grew more infinite and them more connected to it. Gordon was in such rapture that he made himself ignore the breaking spokes of his sand-dipping chair. *Ping, roll, ping, ping.* At the tree where the four-legged criminal was supposed to be apprehended, snapping its jaw upside down, all Gordon felt was empty. Dead chickens, their intestines swaying in the breeze, were the only animals he saw.

Jimmy resigned not long after Gordon returned from his Kenyan disappointment. His father, Toby Gillard, had heart disease and probably progressing Alzheimer's, too. After raising that family solo, Mr. Gillard deserved more tenderness than a filthy nursing home could supply. Without telling Gordon first, Jimmy volunteered to take care of his incapacitated parent after his brothers squabbled about it to no end. Jimmy, secretly, was glad for the excuse to leave. Southern California's pricey, hectic, vice-enabling lifestyle wasn't for him anymore. This time Gordon offered zero resistance to Jimmy's exit. "This time," he said, "follow your intuition." They said their goodbyes unsentimentally and never saw each other again.

If their sendoff was ordinary, maybe it was because the relationship behind it was so profound. Gordon and Jimmy had been a partnership defying sassy descriptions about a white, alpha male and his deferential black attendant. They wheeled the continents together. They navigated the underbelly of early TV. They guarded and tolerated and rooted for each other. What love they couldn't vocalize because male pride hogtied it they displayed in winks and small favors only two people who smelled each other's breath daily could appreciate. Neither was as good apart as they were together. Gordon employed other attendants before and after Jimmy—professional chauffeur-types and the college-age sons of friends. None of them were ever as dexterous as the man from Bossier Parish, Louisiana.

Weeks after he left, Gordon hired a new attendant, a handsome, aspiring black actor named Lloyd. One afternoon, Gordon was late for a meeting and instructed Lloyd to take a shortcut through the Hollywood Forever Cemetery on Santa Monica Boulevard near Paramount Pictures. The graveyard half owned by a convicted felon, held the bones that helped make the town—the DeMille's, the Fairbank's, the Lasky's, the Cohn's. (Mickey Rooney and two members of the Ramones had future reservations.) Anyway, the Cad spun around a bend in the road at about twenty mph when it clipped a speed bump neither anticipated. *Clank.* It was Palm Springs all over again. Sorta. Gordon was thrown from the front seat, but the ejection didn't produce any compound fractures or anecdotal gold this time.

Lifting his face to check his whereabouts, he noticed he was feet from the headstone of a silent-picture star his father once knew.

He enjoyed better summers. Old mates like Hugo and Nat were hardly seen. Nathan Jones, who shared Gordon's weakness for Nikons and dangerous boating, spent drunken weekends holed up in hotel rooms. Jack and Abe were knee-deep in their own business troubles. With too much space and too little business, Gordon asked Lantz if he could reduce some of the space he rented. In phone calls, a subtle urgency crept into his tone about "really needing" this or that.

Back home, he delayed informing Judy about the house a month longer than he should have. Mustering the nerve was tough, for Blue Jay Way was her bulwark as much as his. Jack then scolded him that he couldn't wait: she needed to hear they had to sell it and soon. Gordon waited for the right moment after a nice Sunday dinner. He tried assuaging her that it was only temporary, that they'd replace it with a Johannesburg mansion once the government got off the schneid. Judy, to his surprise, accepted the jolt impassively. By then, however, she was such a pro at disguising her confusion about their general descent that saying, "We'll manage, dear," had a robotic tone.

In what would be his last hours abroad, there appeared a kernel of hope, an unforeseen genie. On a jumbo jet from Monaco to London, as he tried selling off his music catalog at ridiculously low prices, Gordon fell into an animated conversation with the stranger seated next to him. He impressed him—probably by name-dropping moneyed associates such as Deak—and the passenger requested Gordon's card. In a series of transatlantic phone calls in the weeks that followed, this man, a Monte Carlo resident whose first name was Roman, acknowledged one of his jobs. Roman said, in cryptic language, that he represented "tremendous sums of money in Kuwait," a small, oil-rich Islamic country on the shores of the Persian Gulf (which Saddam Hussein's Iraq would invade in 1989). He explained that his Kuwaiti clients were shopping to buy a controlling interest in an established European food or beverage manufacturer—a seventy-five million to one hundred million dollar controlling interest. If Gordon could match them up with a buyer from his contacts, he'd pocket a half a million-dollar commission. Rope this, Gordon pumped himself up, and a new day would break.

Even so, it was an iffy gamble sheathed in half information. Roman cautioned Gordon not to tell anyone except his most trusted associates, lest he stop communicating with him. Uneasy, Gordon went along, phoning an English music executive. Could any of the London accountants he knew sniff out prospective companies for sale? The Kuwaitis were only interested in an operation that grew, packaged, and distributed their own food, why Roman hadn't divulged. There could be no production middleman, either. The Kuwaitis would decide, based on the candidates that Gordon selected, if there would be a face-to-face meeting with the principals.

*   *   *

THE GOLDEN GLOBE FOR best picture that year went to another Roman—Roman Polanski's *Chinatown*. Newspaper columnists covering the awards show rubbed elbows with Jack Nicholson and leered at Raquel Welch's clingy red dress. Everyone there gave the aging Fred Astaire an ovation. Whether starstruck or inattentive, none of them devoted a solitary word to the perspiring quadriplegic in a rented tuxedo accepting a statuette for someone else. Jamie Uys was in Africa when *Beautiful People*, his heartwarming portrait of the animals of the Namib Desert, won 1974's best documentary. (Uys, the cinephile, had suffered a heart attack during his painstaking work, and later camped out at General Music for months obsessing over the postproduction.) For the first time in eons, Gordon had a reason to gloat. As if anyone heard him.

By January 1975 his one great thing had atrophied into nothings. The bonanza he envisioned in the multiplexer was but optical illusion. It unraveled in blown government deadlines, unreturned phone calls, and mealy-mouthed excuses from Pretoria, and his partners at General Motivations recommended ditching it. Swanee condemned it as "dead and useless." He and Deak's lieutenant wanted Gordon to assume financial responsibility or they'd "put it to sleep." Given the culture he was trying to penetrate, it already was.

The Nationalist Party that controlled South Africa for thirty years was never serious about disseminating television to the masses. It was the public relations capital from leg-teasing the possibility that made Gordon their expedient patsy. TV, after all, was now in black-run Uganda and the Congo, and it had facilitated a military coup in Nigeria. The last white regime left standing on the Africa subcontinent was anything but suicidal. The Afrikaners worried how average blacks would react switching on their set after a day sweating in the gold mines or the factories. With TV magnifying the consequences of being born the wrong genome, what new demands would boil up in them—due process, decent sanitation, representation, reparations? Gordon's language transmitter from this lens was especially menacing technology. Vorster's agenda, thus, was obvious. Stall the wizened American marketing it with false promises. Not surprisingly, when "regular" TV service debuted in January 1976 there was one channel—for the whites.

The film companies and others interested in bankrolling Gordon's postproduction complex dropped their interest about the same time the multiplexer was euthanized. One year Sanlam was enthused, the next year restless. Executives there no doubt understood the minefield better than someone subscribing to fairytales. Gordon's pals differed over how he reacted to this withering away. Bob argued it was just another flier that he could use as a stepping-stone to something else. Others asserted it nicked his last vein of optimism. Beneath his capitalist veneer, Gordon's debunked notions about TV as a race equalizer left him with a sour aftertaste. They "gave him a lot of promises, a lot of horseshit," Danny O'Brien recalled. "He was furious... Sanlam and the South Africans (just) wanted (his) ideas." That's why "they buttered him up... He kept using the phrase, 'Danny, I was robbed.'"

CHAPTER TWENTY-NINE: THE LOST JUNGLE

MANIPULATED YES, VICTIMIZED NEVER! He persisted in that belief even after the Kuwaitis' front man phoned to inform him that his services were no longer required. They'd pin down a food company by other means. "Good day, Mr. Zahler." He tried marching forward, carrying on about this idea or that. For once, however, the person he was pitching the sales job to was himself. He stared into space a lot more now. His shoulders bent inward like the handicapped kids you saw on Jerry Lewis' telethons. His face was skinnier near the cheekbones too, which gave his head a light-bulb-like form instead of its prior, aerodynamic shape. Increasingly, he requested his secretary to shut his door for long durations so he could have private conversations on his headset. Sometimes in the middle of unrelated topics he piped up about how much he wanted to water ski.

The one arena where he could still make money was down the hall in his recording studio; the one Joan Rivers had been in years ago. So when he first started feeling ill, intractably ill in early 1975, he cleared his light schedule to record a slew of new tracks. Bob Gillies, his voiceover man, knew some excellent musicians, among them Page Cavanaugh, the jaunty pianist who'd started out with Sinatra, and studio musician Bob Jung, who just recorded with *Earth, Wind & Fire*. They hired four other musicians who sat for thirty sessions when everybody was free.

Among them were a guitarist, a trombonist, a bassist, a drummer, a pianist, and a combination violin/clarinet/flute player.

Over some months, they laid down hundreds of songs, mostly two-minute instrumentals, in Gordon's four-track studio on Willoughby Avenue. Before each session, Gordon outlined "the product" he needed from his group: so many hours of Dixieland, this many of jazz, and so forth for cocktail and Mexican mariachi. "By the way, can you guys do country-western?" Absolutely not, they said. They deplored that slop. Jazz was their bag. Gordon said he'd sell their creations as mood-music to Shakey's Pizza, Farrell's Ice Cream Parlours, and other franchises. (Years later, Page heard one of their tunes in a Toronto mall.) He was shooting for familiar-sounding melodies just different enough from the originals not to get anyone in dutch with copyright lawyers. Done right, Gordon estimated they could be dividing ten thousand dollars monthly. In actuality, the largest check they ever split was for a thousand.

Gordon usually sat in the recording booth, swinging his noggin to the backbeat. The musicians with a leering contempt for producers were pleasantly stunned when, over the intercom, he offered mild opinions on key changes and such. Damn if he wasn't right that a certain chord progression was awkward. "Go out and jam," he said, "I'll worry about the everything else." Bob, Page, and the fellas worked up a lather recording up-tempo, anonymous material. On breaks, out of his range, the session men expressed what, in his prime, was the conventional wisdom about Gordon: his spirit obscured the hoax for a body entombing it. Their primary beef was about the shabby studio piano that Cavanaugh joked was around since "Christ was a corporal." To achieve the fashionably out-of-tune sound he favored, they lifted it up and let it slam to the floor. It must've echoed like the windup chord in the Beatles' "A Day in the Life." *Daaaaaaaaaaa.*

One late morning, the gang burst into General Music, all frisky. They were headed for a wet lunch at the Tower Bar at Sunset and Vine, and hoped to drag Gordon along to get hammered. "Sorry guys," he said. "Too much paperwork." Four hours later, plastered to the gills and barely able to stand, they returned. Gordon just smiled. "On second thought, I'm sorry I didn't tag along." Weeks then passed with nothing from him about scheduling the next session. They called Norm, who wasn't sure what to tell them. Gordon, he finally admitted, was in the hospital.

*   *   *

WHY HAD HE WAITED so long for this one after rolling over every woulda-coulda this side of Tangiers? Cost to the wind, he should've coughed up whatever it took for a carpenter to custom-build him a hydroplane with a plastic chair molded on top so Joe could've slung him at velodrome speed. A crowded Fourth of July at Balboa, when the bay restaurants decorate their patios with cheap, miniature flags, is when he should've let her rip. Buckled into his seat, ski rope attached, he would've shouted what he always imagined: "Hit it." In his dreams, he'd skimmed along at twenty-five mph, women and children thunderstruck at the site, Evel Knievel himself, too. *Hit it!*

Instead, he committed a wildly responsible act by contacting his life insurance agent to ask a question. What was his coverage in case of a "recreational accident"? The agent said waterskiing or similar activities were an "uncovered risk" for a quadriplegic. Read the fine print; should he die behind a boat, the claims department wouldn't honor his policy and Judy would be out a one-hundred-thousand-dollar payout. He couldn't do that. Just chancing it for a minute outweighed the hell-raising excitation it would confer. It was sort of late for hydroplaning anyway. He sold *The Take One* months earlier to retire a debt, and now he had a more urgent problem. Cancer. The doctor said it was definitively cancer, and an aggressive one at that. *Man, I should've waterskied when Joe was around.*

There was dark humor in what was progressing—how someone who led with his head was being taken down by his butt—and a crusty inevitability to it, as well. Like most paralyzed folks, Gordon had developed a hundred bedsores. Unless they'd become infected, none of the deep-tissue fissured caused him much suffering, since you can't hurt from what you don't feel. But this one on his right buttock was a hostile bugger, severely inflamed, leaking pus, and still not satisfied. Antibiotics did zilch to blunt it, and Judy was terrified. The doctor who examined him at St. John's Hospital in Santa Monica said he'd have to remove dead tissue around the sore and patch it via skin graft. Gordon agreed only if it were done fast, as he still hoped to make it to Australia on business before year's end. Director Claudio Guzman, from I *Dream of Jeannie,* was eager to get him down to South America for a film, too. And there was always that crook in Haiti to confront.

Judy was with him in the recovery room in May 1975 when Dr. Wagner, a white-haired, seen-it-all-type, entered grimly. "It's not good, Mr. Zahler" was his hello. While scalloping tissue, Wagner said he found Gordon's colon infiltrated with sinister, granulated masses. "No bullshit, doc?" Gordon asked. "What are we talking about?" An immediate biopsy was what he was talking about. This sample told the larger story. The cancer had originated on the surface and metastasized without him being any the wiser. Black nodules now colonized his lower intestine. The third surgery in seventeen days was arranged for June. This time they'd be removing much bigger swaths of him.

His hospital room in St. John's oncology ward contained parallel universes. He lay there sensationally detached, acting as if he was facing an appendectomy. Judy, though, couldn't keep her freckled hands from shaking as she gave him water. Out in the hallway, she smoked neurotically. Inside his room she set up house. She'd never considered being widowed this abruptly. Gordon's weird anatomy, it seemed, could've survived a sixteen-wheeler running over it. As a kid, he'd outlasted every dire prognosis. As an adult, he never shied away from activities prohibited in the life-with-paralysis handbook. She just wasn't prepared.

A few days before his operation, Gordon beckoned my father and Jack to his hospital room. Pull up a chair, he said. This will take a while. Assets mentally inventoried, he wanted them to avoid auctioning off valuable stuff in a rash estate sale if he died on the table. He covered everything on the burner, from his Book Marks project to the devolving situation with Project-7. Luckily, music publishing was protected from his creditors. Judy, as such, would probably receive forty thousand dollars a year in royalties that he'd hustled to broaden with Page and the others. "Watch out for her" just the same, he said.

He fretted his adversaries would try making a meal out of her in perverse revenge against him.

Gordon was semi-doped up, with a vague, visual sense of people in lime green-masks, as he went back under the operating-table lights. The surgeon directed his people to administer the anesthesia and prop him onto his left side to operate. His woozy brain caught on the word "left." *Is that what they said? They can't. My on-off switch. Use the right side. I'm toast.* He tried yelling at them to stop, that an Italian hotel doctor nearly killed him over it, but sedated up, he slurred his syllables like the neighborhood lush. He hadn't been scared until now, until he grasped how powerless he was to dictate his end.

He woke up, stoned sideways on painkillers, so the surgeon must've reviewed his chart. Removed from him during the cancer cleanout were his rectum and other parts with which he'd been born. Gordon from now on would crap into a bag attached at his flank. All the black rot able to be expunged, was. Actually, for a dude with terminal cancer and a colostomy bag, he was sanguine a week after the operation. "Look at this wonderful thing they gave me," he told Norm on a visit. "I hear Fred Astaire dances with one."

By July, having spent weeks in bed "living" on pills and soup, Gordon recuperated enough to be sent home and allowed to return to work. It's exactly what he wanted, or figured he did. Waiting for him at the office were tottering files and unopened mail a foot high. He missed Jimmy. His four or five remaining employees did happy dances seeing him, but his gaunt appearance froze that. "Not you too," he said. "Just bring me up to speed on what's been happening around here."

Damn, he really should have skipped the letters. Creditors conveyed sympathy for his disease in one paragraph and waved ultimatums in the next. The indignities of desperation were upon him, so he let the word "illness" trickle into his correspondence for the first time in twenty-five-odd years. An English licensee suggested he "come up with one of his normally brilliant ideas." Sure, he must've thought. *I'll just rifle through the secret save-my-bacon file.* He was so parched for cash that he had Norm duplicate his entire sound-effects library to try to sell retail. According to the packaging, this fifty-five-tape collection, "selected from the master vault of 25,000 effects created by top Hollywood technicians," garnered almost no sales. The Free University of Tehran was one of the few customers, and it botched sending its six-thousand-dollar money wire.

Optioned out, he phoned Boet Troskie in South Africa to ask for help, even though he'd already received a loan from him. My dad gave him an additional three thousand. But a month later, all that turned to peanuts. The Project-7 people sued him for nearly four hundred and thirty thousand dollars for breaching their deal. Gordon must've wanted to scream, "Bite me" from the roof of the Lantz building. That or jump off of it.

*　　*　　*

HE REATTEMPTED HIS OLD, ten-to-six routine when, honestly, Saint John's never should have discharged him. Woozy, he dictated letters about frontloading music tapes to 3M that rambled nonsensically. He phoned Danny O'Brien in London, but instead of percolating with ideas he forgot why he called. "Gordon," Danny inquired over the transatlantic static. "Are you okay?"

"Yeah," Gordon exhaled, "I'm...I'm still here." One of the few tasks he managed to complete was donating eight hundred and ninety three *Gentle Ben* albums to the only place willing to accept them: The Crippled Children's Society of Los Angeles.

By September the cancer reappeared in his belly, and so had the hooded figure that Gordon first noticed floating in the corner of his room at County General. Dr. Wagner ran him through a battery of tests to determine what to do. The "last course," meaning the last chance, was radiation treatment. For nine weeks, if he approved, Gordon would be zapped with low-dose radiation beams from a three-headed machine that could have been dragged from the prop house of a Roger Corman movie. The objective was to cripple the cancer-cell DNA and hope. Gordon said he'd mull it over. And he would—unemotionally, analytically. "I haven't quite figured out what I'm going to do about this cancer," he told someone. "On one hand..."

He decided to give radiation a try. There was no heat from the radiation gun, just whirling noise and waiting around. The first two weeks the side effects were so mild that Judy was unsure if the machine was plugged in. The next four weeks they tortured him. Food juiced through him. He had no energy, some mornings just laboring to open his mouth to swallow water. The oncologist adjusted the X-rays to his shrunken, seventy-three-pound body, and that quelled his nausea. But when his one good kidney acted up, his mood spiraled into blackness unseen before.

The Gordon of fall 1975 was an ogre who verbally pummeled his wife. More than that, the spunky grit that engrossed movie stars, tycoons, songwriters, and classmates, the spirit that proved feet were supplemental, had vanished. It was old-fashioned cripple's rage now. He was mad. Mad about dying and madder still about *how* he was dying. Wasting away in the hopes of a miracle to bring him back until the cancer returned was the bête noire of the death he'd wanted. Didn't logging thirty-five years in a wheelchair buy him an ending sexier than cancer? Give him a leopard mauling in Kenya. A malfunctioning jetpack in Buenos Aires. If nothing else, persuade him that his circumstance was less pathetic than it seemed. Otherwise, he'd wilt into the mattress coils.

At Blue Jay Way early one day, Judy asked him if he could handle some breakfast. She sat on a chair next to his contour bed.

"I already told you I'm not hungry. Get that through your thick skull."

"Gordon, I know you're feeling lousy but there's no reason to be mean."

"Do me a favor and shut up. See, I asked nicely?"

"Take your medicine with a little orange juice and toast before Lloyd comes and I won't say another word. I promise."

"You take the damn pills."

"But we're going to be late for your treatment. I thought it'd be easier if you…"

"Leave me alone!"

"Lloyd's going to be here any minute."

"Bitch, you're not hearing me."

Sniffing, Gordon turned his head toward her. A thick, yellow loogie shot towards her; most of it missed. Judy didn't speak for a minute, undecided whether to slap him or retreat to the kitchen.

"You can be a monster, you know that?"

Judy had Lloyd take him to St. John's alone that day. Then she remembered the music and wished she had gone.

CHAPTER THIRTY: GORDON OF GHOST CITY

THE REALITY THAT UNKILLABLE Gordon was going down for the count lit up phone lines and letters as if he were trending on Twitter. Bob, now living in Florida to work for the curmudgeon who'd invented the Nautilus fitness machine, heard. Out in Los Angeles on business, he offered to drive his old friend to Saint John's for a radiation treatment. After the machine sprayed its nuclear beams at him, Bob got him dressed and steered him into the antiseptic hospital corridor.

"Take care. See you next week, Mr. Zahler," a peppy young nurse said waving.

Gordon grinned at her twenty feet away. Under his breath, Bob then heard him say: "Oh no you won't, sweetie. You won't see me because I ain't coming back."

And he wasn't. Disease had the bead on him, and there was no use prolonging the agony. Hostile attorneys and creditors could pulverize each other all they wanted without endangering Judy's protected share. What mattered was a choice—his and only his. In deciding to call it a life, Gordon was abdicating on his own terms. He was done with radiation and everything it represented. This was the golden statuette he could accept himself. This was a great thing unto itself. While too enfeebled to sit up much, Gordon's old twinkle returned. Bob noticed that before he flew home to Florida.

Gordon was in a private room at Saint John's receiving hospice-type care for kidney failure and end-stage cancer soon afterward. This was when my mom dragged me in there as the me-me teenager who wanted nothing to do with him.

On December twenty-first, following a night she didn't think he'd survive, Judy conferred with Dr. Wagner. "To be honest, Mrs. Zahler," he said, "we're all astonished he's made it this long." Judy got busy.

By prime time that evening room 203 rollicked in guests and action. Someone brought a tape player and blasted Glenn Miller songs like a modern disco king. Cigarette smoke wafted around the "No Smoking" sign. A procession of familiar faces made their way in. Lantz and Tors strode in together; Abe Marcus and Jack Perry arrived in dour business suits with their wives in tow not long after. A secretary came, and so did Hank and George Gale, who Gordon befriended through Tors. They loitered around his bed, as did Nathan Jones and a few other stragglers. Joe, Jimmy, and Bob weren't there, maybe expecting Gordon could still outfox the black nodules. Altogether, there might have been a dozen people there. The guest of honor wanted refreshments to thank them.

"Judy," Gordon said midpoint, "Run down to the gift shop and grab everyone some ice cream." Abe, ever the gentleman, proposed to go in her stead, but Gordon was adamant. "Nah, Judy will do it."

A girlfriend went with her, remarking in the elevator, "I see he still pushes you around."

"Well," Judy said, "I understand it better now."

The elevator stopped on another floor while a couple of orderlies galumphed in. In front of them, she lowered her cracking voice and sniffed her runny nose. Her friend listened as she described how Gordon had ramped up his background music catalog so she would have a nest egg to live on in his absence. (How he forswore the waterskiing was too intimate to reveal.) "It was the most romantic thing anyone has ever done for me," she murmured before weeping again. "And the last."

Around 9:30 p.m., the head nurse with the cleanup hitter's forearms sauntered in and announced visiting hours over. Final words were said, moist eyes wiped. Judy, maybe half an hour later, left the room to sign some papers. When she returned, she went directly to Gordon's ear. "You know what they said? They said that you must be somebody really important to get all this attention. They have famous actors and directors in here all the time, but nobody who had a party like this." Gordon smiled, doubting her a little, and for once let it rest.

*   *   *

JUDY, AS SHE FREQUENTLY did, slept that night in his room on a folding cot a foot too short for her. Gordon woke up around eleven, mumbling he felt exhausted. "Mind if I go back to sleep?" No, she said, nod off. The eyes he cracked open at 3:00 p.m. were jaundiced slits.

"Judy," he said faintly.

"Yes, sweetheart?"

"Thanks."

"Oh, for last night? Wild horses couldn't keep them away."

Gordon shook his head.

"Then for what?"

"For that beach ball." A minute later he let out a beastly grunt. "God, it hurts. Like somebody's got pliers on my neck."

"Hey!" she said. "You want me to call for a pain shot? I'll buzz the nurse."

"No," he wheezed, "I want you to call Muriel."

My mom, normally as put-put a driver as Judy, reached Santa Monica from Pasadena in thirty minutes, record time. Gordon was breathing erratically as she reached his bed.

"He's been waiting," Judy said. Her face was in teary deconstruction, features touching. It was 4:09 in the afternoon.

"Gordy, I'm here. I'm here." My mom held his hand, which he hadn't felt since he was fourteen, midair at Marshall Junior High. "Is there anything I can do?"

"I...I..."

"What?" she said. "I couldn't hear you."

A wink, teeth-gnashed, was his way of saying see you around. Then he groaned again, as much a Tarzan yell as death rattle, gallivanting into the ether on fresh legs.

* * *

A HOLLOW, SIX-PARAGRAPH OBITUARY full of gaffes and omissions ran in *Daily Variety* a few days later. It misidentified him as a paraplegic. It applauded him for *Woody Woodpecker* and early TV's *Private Secretary* but completely neglected his work with Russell Hayden, Loren Ryder, Sam Fuller, Ivan Tors, Jamie Uys, et al. Five days later, his funeral was held at Forest Lawn Mortuary in Glendale, where his parents' bones resided on a piney hill not far from the dream-makers at Walt Disney and Warner Brothers. John Richards, a mild-mannered protégé of Mr. Burnell, performed the service inside the Little Church of the Flowers. But Nathan Jones was the scene-stealer, skillfully emceeing an hour-long, impromptu recounting of Gordon's life that had the two hundred and fifty or so mourners rolling in the aisles and clutching their tissues. At the conclusion, Nathan told everybody that his old boating cohort had handpicked the closing song to his own eulogy. People who knew him well snickered when the organist pressed the introductory chords to "The Battle Hymn of the Republic," for Gordon had about as much use for weepy anthems as he did jogging shoes. Even in death—and here was the medical wonder boy who lived 12,820 eventful days with an obliterated spine he wasn't expected to outlast more than two weeks—Gordon adored tweaking convention.

The single memory I have was acting as a pallbearer next to my father, Norm, and four other men in joyless suits. Other than having an available set of limbs, I had no clue why I was chosen. Our job was macabre transportation. It was to heft his maple-wood coffin from the hearse to the grave trenched into the steep, grassy mound. Moisture from the previous night's rain left the site deceptively slick, and that dampness nearly precipitated a commotion we should've expected burying someone of this caliber. Sodden footing on that basil-green hill caused the man in front of me to stumble as we stepped sideways toward the hole. In attempting to regain his balance, he momentarily released his grip on the casket. The chain reaction made us all lurch forward, and we bobbled and struggled not to lose our cargo. Only mourners whose heads weren't bowed in sniffling tribute witnessed our jostle against gravity and weight. For a very real second, Gordon's final joyride was nearly tobogganing down that knoll with pallbearers in black loafers giving chase. From my vantage today, I'm sorry it didn't happen.

*   *   *

JUDY IN THE ENSURING year tried keeping General Music afloat as an educated amateur. After a while, she realized it was a charade. Gordon was human duct tape that bound the motley pieces together, be it Hollywood postproduction, elevator music, or an invention. Judy, though, wasn't doing this for food money. Royalty income coupled with Gordon's cashed-out investments gave her the means to stay in West Los Angeles. Liquidating his stake in Lantz Music Company alone put two hundred and fifty thousand dollars into the bank. Altogether, including the appreciated value Judy received from the sale of Blue Jay Way, her husband's estate was valued at close to half a million dollars (or about 1.4 million in 2016).

She began dating a few years later, eventually meeting a widowed businessman with no physical limitations or Gordon's joie de vivre. They fell in love and she moved in with him. Wedding planning was well underway when the man slumped over dead in his car one day from a massive coronary. Judy's interest in "conventional" romance, where she'd never enjoyed much luck, disappeared with it. No loner, she drew close to her niece Karen and my mom, threw herself into charity work, relocated to Pasadena, and even became a late devotee to The Instruction. In 1990, those thousands of long, filtered cigarettes she puffed around the world repaid her with her incurable lung cancer. She passed away that March at the same place her mother-in-law had: Huntington Memorial.

Many of Gordon's associates weren't far behind him drifting into the blue. Ivan Tors died of a heart attack in 1983 on location in Brazil preparing a new wild animal show; he was sixty-six. Some believe his ghost still hangs out at his old Florida office. In March 1994, Walter Lantz succumbed to coronary disease at ninety-three; Gracie, whom he had trouble living without, died almost exactly two years earlier.

Those endings were storybook compared with Nick Deak's bloody dénouement. A gray-haired woman carrying a backpack in November 1985 entered his Broadway office, insisting to speak with the silver-fox financier. Told by the receptionist he wasn't in, Lois Lang got angry and plunked herself down at a coffee shop to watch the lobby. After a limo dropped Deak off, she returned to the twenty-first floor. With icy precision, Lang shot the receptionist dead with a bullet between the eyes from her 38-caliber revolver. "What was that?" Deak, then eighty, shouted. Seconds later, he and Lang were wrestling for the gun, but she shoved him backward and clipped him above the heart. "Now you got yours," she gloated (not unlike Maurice Briggs after butchering Nat Ross in 1941). She then dragged his corpse into his office and reportedly snapped his picture. Lang was convicted and institutionalized afterward. Yet the mystery was just starting about whether she was psychotic, or something else: a loon brainwashed to be an assassin to take out Deak for his CIA or other off-the-book activities. Whatever the case, Deak died with his renowned company shamed. A federal crime commission accused Deak-Perera of laundering more than a hundred million dollars for South America's cocaine cartels. The company denied the charges even as it was implicated for tax evasion and funneling bribes to Japanese officials through Lockheed Corporation. Customers spooked by the notoriety withdrew their money, and the business eventually filed for bankruptcy. Good thing Gordon didn't partner with it.

Jamie Uys, the liberal Afrikaner, had the brightest future of Gordon's gang. In 1980 he released *The Gods Must Be Crazy*, the endearing story of an African bushman traveling to world's end to destroy a Coca-Cola bottle that disrupted his tribe. The movie shattered South African box office records, grossing more than half a billion in today's dollars. Just before, John Vorster became a newsmaker of a different sort. He resigned in disgrace from the presidency after a government inquiry fingered him for directing slush-fund-type money to promote South Africa's tattered image. A seventy-million-dollar-interest in a Sacramento newspaper and, tellingly, international TV news-film services were among the illicit payouts. The scowling Afrikaner died in 1983 from a pulmonary blood clot.

Two years earlier, what Vorster tried filibustering went live: a channel for people speaking in isiZulu, Xhosa, Sotho, and Tswana. History next came full circle in 1994. Nelson Mandela, former accused subversive, was elected South Africa's first black chief executive.

Our roster of the dead wouldn't be complete without Ed Wood. Unable to ever become a legendary sci-fi director, he turned to writing sex, pulp, and horror stories. Alcohol and money by the seventies were his real-life demons, though, and his wife made him leave. Staying at a friend's place in North Hollywood, Wood in 1978 penned the liner notes for the album release of *Plan 9*'s "original" soundtrack. Wood was alternately contrite and proud of the kitschy classic, and especially grateful to one collaborator. "I would be lax if I did not mention the wonderful music by Gordon Zahler. I think it is his finest work, surpassing even his superb scores for *Mutiny in Outer Space* and *Women of the Prehistoric Planet*." He died a few weeks later.

Whatever you think of Gordon's legacy, you have to admit his circle made the *Star Wars* bar scene look tame.

CHAPTER THIRTY-ONE: SECRETS OF HOLLYWOOD

JIMMY'S PLACE WAS FIFTEEN minutes outside Shreveport, where the church steeples outnumber the mini-marts and the rolling, leprechaun-colored hills remind you that not all of America is asphalted over. Lining the country road to his house were forests, bayous, emu farms, creepy coves, and explained shacks all new to a city boy like me. So was summer humidity that bathed me in my own juices. I'd flown here from Los Angeles to interview Gordon's longtime attendant expecting a muggy-greeting. What I didn't expect was the shape of Jimmy's residence, which my mother had described as a small, manicured estate. So much for truth in real estate! Jimmy's palace was actually a mobile home propped up on blocks. Rust stains slithered down the lip of a corrugated metal roof, and a weather-beaten statue of Jesus sat to the side of the rickety steps leading to his front door. All this rested on maybe a half-acre dirt square bookended by a dilapidated sedan at one end and a garbage pile on the other. Jimmy's retirement crib was a bulldozer job.

I should've known I'd flung myself into misadventure as soon as I opened my rental car door. A red, jiggle-necked rooster jumped in, pecking my shins as if I were trespassing. I swatted him away with my laptop, which made him caw disapproval, and wondered about how Jimmy would react seeing me after a twenty-five-year absence? Ten minutes of knocking and pounding on his door elicited no answer. Suspecting he forgot our meeting time, I walked around the mossy side of his mobile home searching for him. But he wasn't there, either. I trudged deeper into his property to no avail. Near a grove of thin dank trees is where I finally heard noises. "Jimmy," I called out, and trotted that way. There was something living, just not him. A dozen Louisiana hogs grazed and grunted in a makeshift pen. *Wok, wok, wok, wok.* Each was the size of a large, overstuffed duffel bag and covered in bristly, pale gray skin that offered no suggestion of bacon. These were hardly the cute, cuddly swine one pets at a country fair. Jimmy's were ominous, if not unhappy with a stranger like me hollering for their owner.

A half hour passed with no hint of him. I padded back to his shanty-ish house, widening my search. "JIMMY!" I yelled into the trees. Annoyed he'd left me hanging, I kicked a dirt clod toward the rooster. I un-crumpled some trash for clues. I was preparing to return to my hotel, where I planned to leave him an angry voicemail, when I noticed a twenty-something man repairing a wire fence across the road. After I introduced myself and explained what I was doing out here, he opened up. He said that he was one of Jimmy's nephews and that he knew exactly where his uncle was at that second. If I wanted to see him, all I needed to do was get into my car and drive. Where, I asked? To the community hospital, the nephew answered. Jimmy was recovering from a stroke. I felt like I'd been heaved from a plane.

Jack Perry had been the first person outside the family that I interviewed. Snug in his home kitchen, the accountant who once prepared Dinah Shore's taxes and pooh-poohed Gordon's crackpot schemes was fully alert. But the years had been callous in piling on him. His own stroke confined him to a wheelchair and, effectively, stole his speech. A few of the decipherable recollections he stuttered were instructive. Mostly, it was watching him trying to provoke his mouth into action while his limpid, blue eyes whimpered, "I'm sorry."

This silence would become a familiar refrain. Before I learned about Jimmy, I discovered that lawyer/confidant Abe Marcus was dead, as were composers Walter Greene and Hans Salter. Hugo Grimaldi told me in a feeble voice that he was in the process of dying and in no shape to talk. Nathan Jones? MIA in Northern California. Twenty others were unreachable, too. A few of Gordon's celebrity friends—Joan Rivers, Sidney Sheldon—couldn't be bothered. Larry Harmon was more open-minded. According to his aides, I just had to pay him for an interview. *Bozo's* attempted shakedown had been my low point, until I'd gone to Louisiana.

Everything had flipped after the blazing start I'd gotten off to one rainy evening in the Valley. Norm Pringle and Joe von Stroheim, white-hairs themselves by now, were itching to help me reconstruct Gordon. Inside Norm's sunken family room, they hauled out photos and yellowing business documents. They scribbled numbers of other old-timers for me and poured alcohol down my gullet during four hours of laughter and disbelief recounting stories about my gonzo, fragile uncle. Their wives, Elsie and Harriet, treated me like their adopted son, plying me with tasty food and encouragement. By night's end, I was walking on the misty air. Best hangover I ever had.

Over the next years, I interviewed all of them repeatedly and bird-dogged news archives. Joe, who'd tear up speaking about his father, was my jewelry-wearing, rip-snorting guardian angel. On my first trip to his house, he showed off the full-sized Nazi flag that he smuggled out of Germany and got uncomfortable talking about his Emmys. Norm, by then running his own website and thinking just as imaginatively as he had in the sixties, never lost patience with my pesky questions. He'd pull up his suspenders, scratch his Elvis-long sideburns, and say: "Let's see if I can find something for you."

But that's as good as it would get, which wasn't terrific since Gordon lived so many existences away from them. Nobody documented his Sierra Madre years, or his early ones in two-bit sci-fi, or even the undulations of his South African aspiration. Judy had bequeathed no diaries or personal records, either.

Jimmy, small and bald, said not to worry. He bucked up immediately when he spotted me from his hospital bed. "Chipper, my goodness." He clasped my hand with a rock-crushing grip that he attributed to tending his disgusting hogs. "Ask whatever you want," he said. When I told him I should come back, he told me to sit down and fire up my computer. "Just had me a little decline," as he called his stroke. "That's all." In short order, Jimmy recalled some incredible antics—Cuba, Rome, boating-escapades, star meetings. But when I sought more details about their foreign travels, Jimmy vacillated. I apologized for cramming too much into one conversation. "Let's take it slower, all right?" I said. "How old are you? Jimmy?" He didn't know.

Inside my rooster-pecked rental car later, I slumped in the seat, as rain from a thunderstorm clinked on the windshield. The reviews were in. I'd committed the biggest mistake of my adult life walking away from daily journalism to chase the uncle I once detested. Everything about him was gone or hurtling there.

*   *   *

VEXED AT MYSELF, I returned to Los Angeles in an epic snit. Who was going to help me now? Gordon's sister—that's who! The one who'd coaxed, wheedled, and pestered me that her brother's journey merited a biography. To her, Gordon had conquered more and suffered greater than Christopher Reeve. To her, a saccharine *Lifetime* movie would follow. "The best story around," she huffed, "is right under your nose." Meaning all the ones I'd written about for newspapers—state slumlords, corrupt subway projects, suspicious military deaths—were insignificant next to a portrait of "Gordy," kid pluck. In her campaign, she acted more like my career advisor than the woman forever hounding me that my wardrobe was too dark for my olive skin or that my stereo was too loud. Why all this mattered so desperately to her I wasn't sure, but she helped get me to leave a job I loved at the *Los Angeles Daily News* for this plunge into the unknown.

Back from Louisiana, I confronted her one afternoon as she lay reading on her ocher-color chaise lounge. She'd spent half her life on it, napping, reading right-wing magazines, and smoking. "Tell me everything," I said. "The sugarcoating ends today. No more fluff." The Gordon she'd described so far in interviews was an undersized immortal who razzle-dazzled the globe from his chrome-wheeled chariot. Lantz this. Tors that. And here sat his sister still making excuses with her revisionist history. In the preceding months, she'd glossed over her parents' marital discord and her father's affair. She downplayed the murders of her grandfather and uncle, and said nothing about the skinflint, despotic side to Gordon's persona.

Or even the fact he was negotiating with a notoriously repressive government. She wanted a canonization of everyone because the raw truth elemental to me was too messy.

"Sensationalist!" Her finger stabbed the air. "That's what you're being. Exactly what kind of story are you planning to write?"

"The real one. The one you've stomped down my whole life."

"I'm not stomping anything. You're just focusing on things that don't matter."

"Like your dad with that Goldwyn dancer?"

"I don't want you to include that," she said, her face splotchy and pinched. "Understand?" She lit a cigarette at the wrong end. She junked it in the ashtray and relit a new one. "I thought this was Gordon's story."

"It is—him and everyone connected to him."

"I'm starting to wish I hadn't got you started on any of this. I want you leaving people's private lives out. That goes especially for Judy's pregnancy. Don't make me sorry I told you."

"Listen to yourself. You've read thousands of books and you're telling me to censor the drama? Why don't I just draw stick figures?"

"You know what I mean. And I don't appreciate the sarcasm."

"If you won't tell me about the underbelly stuff, I'll go to Uncle Harold (Rose and Nat's younger brother and my mom's uncle). "He promised me on the phone he'd set me straight."

"You're going down a dangerous path if you take his word. He's senile. All he talks about are conspiracies."

"I know. That's why I want to hear to judge for myself."

"I'm warning you…I won't tell you another word. I don't want my friends reading this trash."

"Fine," I said. "I don't need you."

She wasn't looking at me by then, going back to her *National Review* as if I weren't there. The entire story was falling apart. *"Oh, sport,"* I could hear Gordon say into my ears, *"you're royally blowing it. Here's a newsflash, Mr. Hotshot Writer: put yourself in my shoes. Good luck there."*

* * *

THE ONLY PERSON CAPABLE of giving me what my mother refused—the truth—lumbered around the room in his old-folks home. Ninety-two-year-old Harold Ross scratched a wispy, white hair at the base of his nearly hairless skull. Things, he babbled, were easily misplaced here, and now he lost some papers. Harold, six foot one and still in command of that booming, honeyed voice reminiscent of *his* uncle (Broadway's Alexander Carr), was a gamer about his dotage, though. He wrote a lot about his pantheistic religion (Theosophy) and visited his wife, Dorothy, then in a nearby convalescent hospital dying of brain disease. Everybody knew she was the grounding to Harold's quixotic search to understand why treachery had stolen his father and brother.

He and I sat on a lumpy sofa staring at each uncomfortably. We'd seen each other on maybe ten occasions, if that. Why had I come, again, he asked with geriatric discomfiture? "I'm Muriel's boy," I said. "Remember? The writer? The one interested in the family." "Oh yes, oh yes," he said. He flicked eye crud out beneath his thick glasses. "Tell me where you want me to start." I said from the beginning, and with a minimum of direction, out cascaded unfettered history bottled for half a century. They were gothic tales about lost people and murdered dreamers that he retold impassively, with none of the victim's rage my mom said poisoned his spirit.

When we were done I thanked him for his courage retelling his stories and hopped a plane home. Inside I knew I'd achieved little. Even with the background he'd revealed, my descent into Gordon's tracks had barely broken earth. I needed my mom and she'd dummied up.

EPILOGUE: THE SPEED REPORTER

WE WERE AT AN Italian café on one of those smoggy, August days when everything moves torpidly and nothing, seemingly, gets done. Not me: I was here with an urgent agenda. Our checkerboard tablecloth was cluttered with plates, focaccia bread, a photo album I'd cobbled together, and assorted papers damp with my iced tea drippings. I was interviewing my mother yet again, this time hiding my panic. If she continued stonewalling me about Gordon's post-accident years, the curtain would drop. I'd have to ditch the book and skulk back to my old newspaper job, provided it would have me. None of the libraries I tore through, none of the people I met over coffee, alcohol, cigars, and heart monitors knew what she did. She was my bridge to the past, and so far it was a conduit to the superficial.

After a round of blame and counter-blame, the same dynamic we'd been in for years, I handed her a photograph of Gordon taken a few months before he died. He was in front of his Amega tape deck with a lizard-gray complexion. He looked aged beyond his years, defeated. My mom's posture stiffened examining it. "Shocking," she said. "It's not how I remember him." Her insinuation was that I shouldn't, either.

But I looped things back to her, asking what I'd been afraid to so far. Had *she* ever pondered how different her life might have been if Gordon cleared the pommel horse that day in October 1940? Whether she might have given acting a second try or joined a traveling singing group? Perhaps there would have been other options to marrying the brainy engineer that her parents disliked? "Of course I thought about it," she replied sharply, taking a bite of food. Not exactly the amplification I needed.

I tacked another new direction. "Don't you think, then, what the coach did after Gordon got hurt meant this was fate?"

"What nonsense are you talking about now?"

"About Harold Turner—about how he dealt with the fall. You're not going to deny that too, are you?"

"No, because I still have no idea what this is about."

"C'mon. The family must've known at same point. Joe (von Stroheim) can't be the only one Gordon told. Think."

"I said I don't remember. Why are you pushing me?"

"Because it's important."

"To you it is."

"Do you want to hear it or not? Maybe it'll jog a memory."

She waited so long to answer I feared she might get up to leave.

"Since this is going nowhere," I said, "I'll give you the short version. Gordon *still* had feeling below his neck after he landed on the gym pads." My mother shook her head no as I said this. "Yep, he did," I continued. "He was dazed from whacking his head, but he had tingly sensations in his hands and feet. I guess he was trying to explain that to Turner when Turner decided to lift him up on his feet. He probably wanted to get Gordon's blood circulating. But he shouldn't have laid a hand on him. Not with a spinal injury. Guess they didn't know that in 1940."

From her dazed eyes, I could tell this was coming as a bombshell. Not a word of this was in the Zahler lawsuit against the Pasadena school district. And Gordon, evidently, had kept it a secret from the family. "Go on," she said curtly.

"When Turner stood him up, Gordon heard a snap. After that, everything below his shoulders went numb. Years later he supposedly asked Dr. Risser about it, and Risser said that might've been what made his paralysis permanent. Something about crushing the nerve instead of bruising it. Who knows? Risser said Gordon might've walked."

"And you are sure about this?" she asked. "It's not from Harold, right?"

I said I was sure. Just then our waitress, an LA Valley-girl-type with pink, oversized gums, approached to see if we needed anything. "No," my mother said authoritatively. "We don't need anything. Okay?"

But she wasn't *okay*. She was better than okay. Something deep in her broke free of an ancient grip. She sipped her iced coffee, thinking. In the silence between us her body language relaxed. Her brow lines smoothed out. Her jaw un-jutted. Studying her angled cheekbones, beneath the pleated skin, I understood why an old boyfriend labeled her "the belle of Sierra Madre." She asked to see the photo album, and nagged me to finish my coleslaw. You could tell she wanted a cigarette.

"Ask whatever you need. Let's get on with it."

I couldn't believe the transformation. It was as if my mother, the woman convinced Charles Darwin was a fraud, had started believing in predetermination. "All of what you have been raising is so painful, to be honest, I made myself forget. The accident cut me off from…" She concentrated on selecting the right verb. "From developing. I couldn't go to college. I didn't press it because I knew there was no money. But that changed my life." As in not for the better!

There it was. I had focused so hard on breaking her silence for my own selfish ambitions that I'd missed what mattered more. Gordon's reckless jump had been voodoo powder that rendered her invisible, shrunk her future, and choked off who she could have been. Somebody a long time ago needed to comfort her better that it wasn't fair. This, to me, was the key that unlocked her. It explained why she clung to social airs (salad forks and first impressions) and slept half her life away. Not doing more with her own talents, in the blue cornfield of possibility, was her self-paralysis. This was who she was, and why she lived vicariously through Gordon's Hollywood.

✳   ✳   ✳

SAY THIS FOR MURIEL Jacobs: she was loyal. Even after she'd had surgery to remove part of a cancerous lung, she continued her relationship with two of her favorite male names: Benson & Hedges.

She smoked during her recuperation and through multiple hip-replacement operations. She lit up back home after signing hospital papers affirming she had less than a year to live, and in bed next to her flammable oxygen canister.

Before I knew it, she was headed downhill with a deep, crackling cough that made me want to hide in my old childhood spots. Morphine came next, vials of it. She said her goodbyes and I love you's to those she could and drifted in and out of consciousness. We never had that mother-son closure moment, and truth is, we didn't need it. After our revelatory lunch, we went back to the closeness I once believed we'd never recreate. Yes, she could still be erratic and stubborn, but so could I. The mother I'd continually squabbled with all those years faded to black. Replacing her was the woman who believed in me more than anyone else on earth, the one who walked on jagged beach rocks to show me tide pools at high surf, quizzed me on my English, and perfectly cooked my favorite macaroni and cheese as the worst cook you'd ever meet. This was Gordon's personal gift to me. His ghost, or whatever form he took the day of the fire, made it possible. He saved my life so I could resuscitate his colorful existence and acknowledge our accomplished, suffering kin. This I know as well as my name. But his true purpose was altruistic. He drew me backward to show me a beautiful creature named Muriel.

A few days before her death, she was too incoherent to speak. I knelt down at her side, teary and gulping hard, and whispered, "Mom." She opened eyes that hit me like high beams, and I showed her the cover of an earlier version of this book. She rewarded me with a smile that crossed the generations.

*　　*　　*

SOMETIMES THERE'S A DREAM. Not every night, but periodically. Mostly after a spicy meal or a phenomenal day. Here I am a kid again at Blue Jay Way in the middle of a raucous party sloshing with adults, some of them famous and all of them jubilant. In this rendition, things are different from 1967. I'm no longer cowering under the kitchen counter with the Friar Tuck cookie jar praying for Gordon's thunderous storytelling to end. No, I'm running—running like he used to after a Sierra Madre prank—to catch good air for a daredevil leap onto his bed. His face is electric tracing my arc, and upon landing he turns to say: "We've been waiting for you, kiddo." In that second, that magic interval, all I want to be is like the little man with the witchy arms.

ACKNOWLEDGEMENTS

EXHUMING THE PAST TO bring this book to life meant plenty of heavy lifting. Fortunately, I never had to shoulder the burden alone.

My own mother, who sometimes dreaded what she'd unleashed in goading me to chronicle this story, bravely cut through her own dark memories when it counted to reveal her family's inner-truths. My dad and brother Paul never wavered, either, in providing me with their recollections, even when they weren't sure what all this digging would produce. Safe to say, too, that my wife, Kate, and our children, Samantha and Lauren, were my trustiest pillars. They not only put up with my obsession in separating a million shards of fact from myth but also made room in our house for a spirit named Gordon for the many years he lived with us. To all of them, I say thank you for believing the switchbacks I was traversing were a worthwhile journey.

Beyond my own kin, I owe *everything* to Gordon's former entourage. Bob Glenn, Jimmy Gillard, Igo Kantor, Norm and Elsie Pringle, and Joe and Harriet von Stroheim were his Hollywood family and my inside sources. Without their cooperation and grace, this effort would've been scuttled on the launch pad. My heart sags knowing this rendition follows the passing of so many deserving a public bow. Somewhere in the great beyond, I hope, a lollapalooza is roaring.

Such a large cast deserves my gratitude. In alphabetical order, they include: Don Berg, Herb Bernard, Rob Roy Bowman, Danny

O'Brien, Jeff and John Bushelman, Karen Conway, Stan Frazen, Hank and George Gale, Spencer Gillard, Mauro Giordani, Ben Gouin, Gino Grimaldi, Bob Gustafson, Michael Hoey, Horace Jackson, Keith Jamison, Bob Jung, Karen Leaf, George Mahana, Mike and Hazel Marcus, Carl Marshall, Murray Neidorf, Jack and John Perry, Teddy Phillips, Norm Prescott, Mitchell Reinis, Veronica Rosenblatt, Lou Scheimer, Marion Seeman, Don Slack, Erwin Tors, Boet Troskie, Normalouise Walker, Betty Woods, and Bob Wright.

To friends, mentors, and others curious why I'd left daily journalism without openly questioning my sanity, your robust support meant more than I can express. Among this group are: Mark Arax, David Bloom, Jeff Charlebois, Mike Consol, John Corrigan, David Ferris, John Frook, Mike Hamilburg, A.J. Langguth, Jodie Levine, Peggy Luddington, Jaxon Van Derbeken, Tristine Rainer, Ray Richmond, and G.R. Walper. Of course, none of this would've been possible without the superhuman talents and hustle of the people at Rare Bird Books. I'm talking to you, Tyson Cornell, Seth Fischer, Steve Eames, Alice Marsh-Elmer, and Julia Callahan. We may be the storytellers, but you guys are the story believers.

INDEX

H

I

J

CHIP JACOBS IS THE author of five other books: *The People's Republic of Chemicals; Smogtown: the Lung-Burning History of Pollution in Los Angeles* (both with William J. Kelly); *The Vicodin Thieves: Biopysing L.A.'s Grifters, Gloryhounds and Goliaths; The Ascension of Jerry: Murder, Hitmen and the Making of L.A. Muckraker Jerry Schneiderman*; and the privately issued *Black Wednesday Boys*. Jacobs' reporting has appeared in the *Los Angeles Times, The New York Times*, CNN, Bloomberg View, the *Daily News of Los Angeles, LA Weekly*, among other outlets. Jacobs, the recipient of numerous writing commendations, lives in Southern California.

CPSIA information can be obtained
at www.ICGtesting.com
Printed in the USA
FSOW01n0001160116
15721FS